MW01194658

Shantyboats

~~~~~~~~~~~~ AND ~~~~~~~~~~~~

Roustabouts

Shantyboats

AND

Roustabouts

THE RIVER POOR OF ST. LOUIS
1875–1930

Gregg Andrews

LOUISIANA STATE UNIVERSITY PRESS

BATON ROUGE

Published by Louisiana State University Press
lsupress.org

DESIGNER: Michelle A. Neustrom
TYPEFACE: Whitman, text; Moccha, display

COVER PHOTOGRAPH: Flooded shanties by the railroad tracks in St. Louis during the
flood of 1903. Courtesy Grossman Flood Album, Missouri Historical Society.

LIBRARY OF CONGRESS CATALOGING-IN-PUBLICATION DATA

Names: Andrews, Gregg, author.
Title: Shantyboats and roustabouts : the river poor of St. Louis, 1875–1930 / Gregg
    Andrews.
Description: Baton Rouge : Louisiana State University Press, [2023] | Includes bibli-
    ographical references and index.
Identifiers: LCCN 2022017755 (print) | LCCN 2022017756 (ebook) | ISBN 978-0-
    8071-7847-8 (cloth) | ISBN 978-0-8071-7907-9 (pdf) | ISBN 978-0-8071-7906-2
    (epub)
Subjects: LCSH: Shantyboaters—Missouri—Saint Louis | Steamboat workers—
    Missouri—Saint Louis | Poor—Missouri—Saint Louis | Waterfronts—Missouri—
    Saint Louis | Mississippi River Valley—History—1865– | Saint Louis (Mo.)—History
Classification: LCC F474.S257 A57 2023 (print) | LCC F474.S257 (ebook) | DDC
    977.8/660086942—dc23/eng/20221003
LC record available at https://lccn.loc.gov/2022017755
LC ebook record available at https://lccn.loc.gov/2022017756

Contents

7
The American Fondness for Humbug

8
In the High Waters of Sin

9
Neither Pumpkin nor Paw-paw

10
The Ruthless Advance of Civilization

11
Gone Are the Old River Days

Epilogue

~~~

Preface

My grandmother came from a shantyboat family in Mark Twain's boyhood home of Hannibal, Missouri, where I grew up south of town in the Mississippi River bottoms. Until a census discovery in 1992, I was unaware of her early childhood on the riverfront with her mother and grandmother's hard-luck, hard-living, and hard-drinking band of hardy river folks. Fishermen, day laborers, and washerwomen adrift in the Depression of 1893, they were among those harassed and evicted from Hannibal's south-side levee by Burlington Railroad agents and vigilantes in the dead of winter 1900–1901. Downstream about three miles, my ancestors tied up their three shantyboats on the river's west bank in the northeast corner of Ralls County, near the Atlas Portland Cement company's plant construction site. They soon settled in the new company town of Ilasco, where tar paper shacks and jobs enticed them from their boats. My mother's jaw dropped at our discovery of a new piece to the family puzzle. In a family known for storytelling and gossiping, she somehow missed an important secret buried in the past.

In *My Daddy's Blues: A Childhood Memoir from the Land of Huck and Jim* (2019), I explored my perilous childhood in a cluster of modest river houses along the railroad tracks dubbed "Monkey Run," a section of Ilasco on bottom land that once was a slaveholding tobacco farm. Some might call the houses "shacks," but we didn't. Monkey Run held about thirty-five families of cement plant workers and fishermen. Marble Creek ran past the bottom corner of our property and emptied into the Mississippi a rifle shot away. My earliest memory is of being rushed in my mother's arms down a dirt alley and up the tracks to "Red Bridge" to stare at the scene of a drowning at the mouth of the river. I was two and a half years old. My father, a blaster ("powder monkey") in the Atlas quarries, was fishing nearby when Walter "Tudie" Smith drowned in 1953. The river meant everything to me as a child. I learned to fear, respect, and treasure it as a close, if at times terrifying, friend. To fish and daydream under the tall cottonwoods was a favorite pastime from age six to my middle teens. The riverbank was the place for a furtive cigarette, an escape from the blues and battles of my parents to make ends meet.

In my early life, I knew nothing about shantyboats or roustabouts, but a so-called "river trash" childhood in a stigmatized, crumbling company town of Eastern and Southern European immigrants instilled a consciousness as an "outsider." My lookout perch on the American dream was the rickety, mouse-colored porch of a tiny house that lacked indoor plumbing. I was out of step with most "boomers," especially those with whom I later shared space in the corridors of higher education. To mention packing water from a well, bathing in a galvanized tin tub or the river, hitching rides, coon hunting at night with a carbide lamp, and squirrel hunting by day sometimes elicited nervous smiles and awkward glances. Beginning at age eight with my Mossberg bolt-action .410 shotgun, I coon hunted with uncles in the hills and "hollers" of the high lonesome bluffs that towered above the Mississippi's west bank. In the dark, isolated hollows were a few old-timers with stories about the river and its islands. Sometimes fishermen took me with them to run trot lines, bank lines, jug lines, and baskets filled with buffalo, carp, and catfish. We camped and coon hunted on the islands, including Gilbert Island, near today's Ted Shanks Conservation Area in Ashburn.

The spiritual connection I felt to Huck Finn and the river as a child never left me. It's why I've written this book. At the time I stumbled onto my ancestors' shantyboat past, I was in the early stages of a new book project on the rise and fall of Ilasco as a company town of immigrants recruited by Atlas agents. Three generations of my grandmother's family left the river shortly after they were kicked off the Hannibal levee, but other shantyboaters tied up near Ilasco and Saverton, a river village about three miles to the south. A popular mooring place in Ilasco was near a favorite childhood fishing spot I knew as "The Island." As I researched the area, a fragmented childhood memory surfaced of two dilapidated boats on the bank where the river cut around a tiny island near shore and created an inlet north of the mouth of Marble Creek. I fished in the inlet waters in the 1950s and 1960s. Try as I might, I can't recall what the boats looked like, but I seem to remember torn screens on them. The old weather-beaten relics on the shoreline of my flickering memory bore no resemblance to boats I saw on the river.

In 2011, I published a biography of Thyra J. Edwards, a Black civil rights and labor activist whose grandparents used the Mississippi River, a birch canoe, and the Underground Railroad to flee slavery in the Hannibal area. Retired and relocated in Hannibal at the time I finished the book, I was ready for a slower pace of life with time to fish and play music on the river that provided the props for my songwriting and recordings as Dr. G and the Mudcats. My swampy blues songs and writings as a historian have mutually reinforced each other in a creative dialectic of storytelling that did not end when I retired. I released two more CDs of original songs, most of which were river themed. I wrote "Evil in the Delta" to dramatize the Elaine Massacre of 1919 and the ongoing struggle of Black sharecroppers for labor and civil rights in the Arkansas delta. "Gonna Be Free" was inspired by the daring escape from slavery by Edwards's grandparents, who paddled across the river to freedom on the eve of the Civil War.

The retirement years in Hannibal rekindled interest in my family's history on the river and the mysterious dilapidated boats abandoned on the water's edge of my faded memory. In a quest to put my ancestral river heritage into a broader cultural context, I searched for a deeper understanding of the harassment and waterfront evictions of shantyboat levee dwellers. Research led me to St. Louis, where police in 1895 used a gang of hoodlums to terrorize and destroy part of a squatter settlement known as "Little Oklahoma." In 1905, longtime residents of "Sandy Hook," a shantyboat community in East St. Louis, threatened armed resistance against evictions by the Wiggins Ferry Company and sheriff's deputies who came to tear down their workshops, chicken sheds, and any boat that didn't float. As a lifetime Cardinals baseball fan, former resident of St. Louis, and labor historian, I was hooked. I chose the city's waterfront as the focal point of this book, which I call a "history from the river bottom up." The city, less than a hundred miles downstream from Hannibal, seemed a panoramic window into the world that shaped river folks like my ancestors. After all, St. Louis was the largest city on the Mississippi River in 1900 and the home of dozens of riverfront settlements and a few thousand shantyboat wayfarers. Besides, it was where Mark Twain's duties began as a cub steamboat pilot for Captain Horace Bixby in 1857.

The deeper I dug into St. Louis waterfront settlements in the late nineteenth century, the more racially diverse and complex they became. At first, I intended to write only of shantyboat colonies, but as an outgrowth of my biography of Edwards and earlier article on Galveston's Black dockworkers in the *Journal of Southern History,* I decided to include river roustabouts, most of whom were Black. St. Louis's waterfront was a major headquarters for Black roustabouts, who worked the steamboat packets between terminals. A cultural symbol of the steamboat era and the nation's long obsession with romanticized, racist nostalgia, roustabouts were indispensable to the packets. Brutalized by a waterways labor system that resembled slavery, they were routinely kicked, cussed, beaten, and abused by white steamboat mates and other officers. Like shantyboaters, roustabouts either were scorned and feared as river riffraff, or they were regarded as childlike figures who sang and danced on the freight deck of steamboats to entertain white passengers for pennies from above. Most roustabouts in St. Louis were young single men who lodged in Italian and Black waterfront district saloons, but some, especially elderly ex-roustabouts, lived in shantyboat settlements. Although in most cases distinctly separate groups racially and culturally, they and shantyboat "gypsies," regarded as dregs of the Mississippi basin, shared a class-based levee culture in more ways than is traditionally thought.

It has been a pleasure to work with Rand Dotson, editor in chief, and the entire staff of LSU Press. I appreciate Derik Shelor's superb editing, and I want to thank an anonymous reader for a thorough reading and publication endorsement of my manuscript. Thanks to journal editors Lauren Mitchell, Kristie Lein, and John Brenner, earlier portions of this book appeared in *Gateway* and the *Missouri Historical Review.* I owe a special debt of gratitude to Sara Hodge, curator of the Herman T. Pott National Inland Waterways Library Collection of the St. Louis Mercantile Library, for her research assistance at a time of Covid-19 restrictions. I dedicate this book to Vikki Bynum, my wife, fellow historian, and artist, who in 1992 was the first to discover my ancestral roots in a shantyboat settlement at the foot of Jefferson Street, near the mouth of Bear Creek in Hannibal. Based on an 1895 photograph in *Leslie's Weekly,* she drew the stunning sketch of Rose Mosenthein that appears in the book.

Shantyboats

~~~~~ AND ~~~~~

Roustabouts

Introduction

The river is the highway of the poor.

—W. A. CURTIS, "On the Upper Mississippi," 1915

The steamboat age perfectly expressed America," wrote Bernard De-Voto in *Mark Twain's America* in 1932. The Pulitzer Prize-winning historian, novelist, and editor of Mark Twain's papers pointed to a cast of picaresque characters in the Mississippi River valley who helped fuel Twain's literary creativity. The river attracted its share of hucksters, shysters, and roguish drifters who, like tangled driftwood, formed the cultural landscape from which Twain drew his fictional portraits. Steamboats died a slow death between 1875 and the Great Depression, but the river continued as a home for outsiders—the levee poor, miscreants, moonshiners, misfits, and cultural refugees from an industrializing society on the make. "Even the debris through which it passed," DeVoto observed, "was vital and eloquent—the dens at Helena and Natchez and all the waterside slums; the shanty boats with their drifting loafers; the boats of medicine shows, daguerreotypers, minstrel troupes, doctors, thugs, prophets, saloon keepers, whoremasters. The squatters on the banks and the unbelievable folk of the bayous. It was a cosmos."[1]

St. Louis's riverfront was a magnet for the "debris." In 1875, the *St. Louis Republican* painted a vivid picture of the levee as a place to avoid at night. Prowlers, prostitutes, and pickpockets along with thieves, scoundrels, and hustlers of every sort roamed the wharf. If you were looking for "forty-horse-power whiskey at ten cents a drink" and a night of carousing and debauchery, the levee was your place. But unwary visitors, beware! Front Street was "an unsurpassed place for a confiding Granger to get his eye blacked, his pocket picked, and his body chucked into a cold, wet sewer."[2] A booklet that further warned readers in

1885 to avoid the city's opium dens, alley dives on Morgan Street, Clabber Alley, Kerry Patch, Biddle Street, and other slum areas described the waterfront as a place where "two bits is sufficient incentive to murder":

> The respectably-dressed person who visits the Levee after dark without police escort takes his own risks. After nightfall a motley gang throng the streets along the shore of the Mississippi. Half-drunken roustabouts shove pedestrians into the gutter. Wrecks of Womanhood hold out invitations couched in language most obscene in one hand and vile curses in the other. Bummers are there to bum and river thieves and cracksmen hurry along to keep appointments with "pals" in the low dives which line the Levee. . . . The man who goes on the Levee in a new hat comes off hatless, and the wearer of a new coat returns to civilization in his shirtsleeves.[3]

As steamboat traffic declined after the Civil War, the levee of the nation's fourth largest city in 1900 attracted shantyboats from the "Father of Waters" and its tributaries. Within a forty-three-mile stretch to the north, "water gypsies" on the Illinois and Missouri rivers joined a stream of wayfarers from St. Paul and other towns on the Upper Mississippi. Approximately 175 miles below St. Louis, shantyboats from Ohio River valley towns floated out into the Mississippi at Cairo, Illinois. The destination of many was New Orleans for the winter. "The river is the highway of the poor," wrote W. A. Curtis aboard a steamboat from St. Louis to St. Paul in 1914. "Rafts with families on them floated by us. On island after island queer looking sloops were hauled up among the trees and people camped beside them. How sailing vessels manage, with the changing channel, I could not imagine and could not learn."[4]

Seasonal migrations of shantyboats were iconic features of the Mississippi River valley. According to an 1896 estimate, twenty thousand "river gypsies" made up these restless migrations, lured by the river's deep mysteries, rhythms, moody cycles, and promises of freedom and adventure. Ben Lucien Burman, a prolific fiction and nonfiction writer, musician, and song collector who revived literary interest in the Mississippi River in the late 1920s and 1930s, put the number at thirty thousand. On a canoeing voyage to New Orleans in the late 1870s, Nathaniel H. Bishop observed that the annual ritual showcased "a peculiar phase of American character . . . a curious set of educated and illiterate nomads, as restless and unprofitable a class of inhabitants as can be found in all the great West."[5] The wanderers risked countless tragedies and dangers to enjoy cheap river living. Their favorite pastime was the art of storytelling. Dubbed "water sprites," "river nomads," "water gypsies," "American Arabs," "river trash," "river rats," "wharf rats," "swamp trash," or worse, they played an important role in the cultural preservation and transmission of legends, music, and river lore on the Mississippi and its tributaries. The rivers furnished fish for their food, water for their coffee, and driftwood for fuel. As waterborne migrants in the Mississippi valley's ecosystem, shantyboaters bowed to the river's wildness, basked in its calm, and with remarkable stoicism accepted as a matter of fate its often destructive fury. Together with year-round squatters in tents, huts, and shanties, they formed lively waterfront communities wherever they clustered in comfortable coves or on bayous, islands, land accretions, and unimproved parts of a city wharf. Whether fortunetellers and fishermen, deckhands and day laborers, roustabouts and river pirates, or preachers, professors, pearl hunters, and patent medicine peddlers, the settlements attracted an eclectic population that shaped the river valleys of America.[6]

In 1903, an estimated three thousand shantyboat squatters occupied waterfront settlements between the Chain of Rocks and Jefferson Barracks in St. Louis. Although settlements in Brooklyn, Venice, Alton, and East St. Louis were under the jurisdiction of Illinois authorities, they were part of a greater St. Louis riverfront and a common feature of river towns. Not all inhabitants were seasonal nomads. For many in crude shanties, wigwams, discarded streetcars, dugouts, and dilapidated shantyboats, the settlements were a year-round home. In some cases, the levee was a temporary way station for those down on their luck until they could bounce back from a job loss or personal misfortune. In others, alcoholism, a job injury, or illness might send them to a shantyboat. The levee was their only safety net in an age of Social Darwinism that despised and feared its "debris." More prosperous shantyboat owners and long-term residents in waterfront communities improved their dwellings, developed a sense of governance, and chose "mayors" or "kings" who adjudicated disputes and presided over informal councils.[7]

On a chilly late October day in 1895, a *St. Louis Post-Dispatch* reporter and staff artist boarded the *Austria*, a yacht commissioned to transport them on a story assignment about the annual fall migration of shantyboats south for the winter. With much difficulty due to low water and marked changes in the Mississippi River channel, William Zink and his pilot steered north to the hazardous Chain of Rocks. From there, they turned and worked their way back down the Missouri shore to south St. Louis, docking in waterfront settlements to interview "nomads." Near the city's new waterworks plant at the Chain of Rocks, the crew found a lone family of five. "We've just pulled in here from St. Paul," Jack Berry greeted them. "Gettin' too chilly up there and we're going down de stream." Berry, a "swarthy complexioned" father, and his four children, ages two through seven, were on their annual journey south. Despite chilly temperatures, the oldest child ran around barefooted with fishing tackle. "Them's my children," he nodded. "We're kind o' keeping this old shanty together." The family's cobbled-together home was more akin to a raft with a tent or wigwam on it, "a collection of old rags, etc., patched together and stretched over a limb of a tree which formed the pole, with a short cross piece on top in the shape of a figure 'T.'" While Berry stood in awe of the yacht, the reporter stared in bewilderment at the shantyboat. "Ain't you afraid the wind will sweep you away?" The reporter asked. "Not a bit of danger," Berry replied as he pointed to the layer of four boards in the boat's hull. "We got de rags tied down good and hard. T'aint no show of this outfit going under. . . . You can't sink it."[8]

The reporter listened as Berry reflected on family trials and tribulations, most notably the death of his wife, Maria, on the previous autumn migration when their shantyboat "spun around like a top" and capsized when a ferry boat struck it north of Cairo. They clutched the children around them in the water and held on for dear life until the ferry operator pulled the family safely aboard. "We all goes in for a ducking," Berry recalled. "Mighty narrow escape for us." Dumped later by the ferry at river's edge in Cairo, the family was soaking wet without matches to get dry and keep warm. "The best we could do," Berry shrugged, "was to jump out of the wet rags, ring them as dry as we could, and let the wind do the rest." Soon afterward, Maria "just kicked up and got sick and then she died." With mourning children around him in the fall of 1894, Berry dug her grave in the side of a cliff near a tree. Around the grave he scattered pieces of their boat's wreckage. "We buried her right thar and staid around for three weeks fixing a new 'squat,'" he reminisced. Then he and the children resumed their float south. "All of us were mighty nigh dead when we got down to the warm country," he explained. "Now me and the children are all alone.

Maggie, she's 7, does the cooking. The others help fish and we manage to get along. I miss the old woman. She was a good worker."

Berry, who planned to visit his wife's grave on the journey, took to the river as a child. He didn't remember his mother or father. At one time he toiled in a Cape Girardeau mill, where he and Maria met, but the river life lured them. Berry once owned a nicer boat that caught fire and burned in the early 1890s. Hard luck was his traveling companion, he sighed, but he hoped to scrape together enough money for a new boat, preferably one with a steam engine. His dream, shared by many who grew up on the Mississippi, was to get a steamboat captain's license and haul freight on the river.[9]

On the way back from the Chain of Rocks, the *Post-Dispatch* reporter found three shantyboat families tied up near the Merchants' Bridge, where today's Mary Meachum Freedom Crossing commemorates the role of Mary and John Berry Meachum in leading the enslaved across the river to freedom via the Underground Railroad. The shantyboaters were birds of passage on the southern migration. The men were seated around an open fire on the riverbank when the yacht crew docked. Aged storyteller Joseph Shannon, "a thriving fellow," held court as a black kettle supported by a strong forked twig over the fire sizzled with a catfish tail sticking out at the top. A smokestack painter who serviced patrons from St. Paul to New Orleans, he regaled the reporter and crew with story after story, pausing at times to show them a tattoo or a place where he once was shot. Lace curtains adorned the windows of Shannon's houseboat, and the interior featured an organ. His adult son and daughter were aboard with him. They and the other two families traveled together in "fairly well-kept" houseboats. When asked if they planned to spend the winter in St. Louis, Shannon replied, "Wall, we're late, but we ain't gwan to pitch up here all winter. None of us shanty house folks stay around cold places. I should say not. In the early spring and in the late fall we're on the move."[10]

The river was alive with southbound flatboats, at times called "squats" in New Orleans or "flatties" in the Ohio River valley. Several shantyboat settlements were virtually deserted due to the annual migration. Many houseboat owners in "Little Oklahoma" (or "Oklahoma" or "New Oklahoma"), "Chickentown," "Sandy Hook," "Buzzard's Bay," "Squatters' Town," and other colorfully named settlements on both sides of the river already had gone south. The *Austria* docked at the foot of Buchanan Street to find that it was wash day. The men were gone, and the women gave the crew a cold shoulder. In Buzzard's Bay, south of the Mill Creek sewer, residents in about twenty-five flatboats greeted the *Austria*. Among them were a watchmaker, a feather dealer, and a tailor. A medical student who recently received his license to practice had lived there until two weeks earlier. All the remaining residents planned to join thousands of others floating south in search of a warmer place for the winter. When spring flowers bloomed and cottonwoods blew white kisses into the air to seed, shantyboat travelers searched for a north-bound tugboat operator to tow them upriver for a fee. Sometimes they teamed up to split the fee or worked as deckhands in exchange for a tow. Often, they returned to the same waterfront settlement and tied up to the same stake as the spring before. "They travel in bunches," observed the reporter. "It is a sight—one worth seeing—to watch these strange curiosity shops floating along—stranger still to talk with the occupants."[11]

Shantyboat communities in the St. Louis area drew increased attention by the late 1880s. In April 1889, a newspaper reporter called attention to them from East Carondolet north to Alton on the Illinois riverfront. Accompanied by a staff artist, he traveled by boat for a story on the settlements. Near Cahokia, he met "Old Tom," a fisherman who boasted about how much money he made by pulling "floaters" from the river and taking them to the coroner's office, which paid $5 per river corpse. Mr. Newport, an elderly ex-steamboat pilot who lived nearby with his wife, was a fisherman who supplied a stall in St. Louis's French Market. At one time he piloted a large steamboat, but a run of bad luck plagued him when the steamboat burned and he was thrown out of work. Finally, he recovered enough to buy a houseboat, which he crowned with the surviving pilothouse of his former steamer.[12]

North of Alton, the reporter's boat turned up the mouth of a slough on the Missouri side. Thick willow trees and brush that covered the banks of the narrow passageway impeded access a bit at first, but then the channel widened as cottonwoods and elms replaced willow trees. The boat entered an enchanting lagoon and followed it for nearly a mile. The waters were perfectly calm. An occasional drift log, or bob sawyer, from previous floods peeked above the water's surface as if to listen to the songs of little yellow finches in the trees. Suddenly, the channel narrowed, and in the bend a docked flatboat came into view. The writer described the bucolic scene: "Right in the middle of the slough stood one of the greatest little flatboats I ever saw. Simple in its form, in neatness it was perfect. White as snow, with little red curtains at the windows and actually a vine growing over one corner, being planted in a large box on the deck. All around was a little railing, and a railed bridge joined the boat to a little grass plot on shore. On the grass plot stood a tent quite as white as the boat."[13]

At the sound of oars, an old man stepped from the tent to greet the visitors. Nearby was a cleared garden spot. Upon learning that the artist was doing sketches for a story, he called to the flatboat. His sixteen-year-old daughter, Mamie, darted out with a pitcher of water to offer the visitors. She sat on a wooden bench near them. She and her father didn't have a well, so when he went to town once a week he brought home water. "Mamie's got to have nice water," he told the newspaper crew. Mamie quickly interjected, "Pa says t'aint healthy for me to drink river water same 's him and Nero drinks." The old man, when asked about nomadic life on the river, opened up: "I used to float down the river a good deal but my gal didn't like it cause she all'ys got skiert." Mamie interjected again, "The boat creaked awful in the night." Her father continued, "So four years ago I and Mamie and my wife, she's not here anymore, we came in here in the high water and here we ayre . . . my wife is buried over there just beyond that crooked cottonwood. That was three years ago and since then Mamie and me have kept house, and Nero, too, Nero's our big dog as [he] takes care o' Mamie when I'm gone."[14]

Most waterways birds of passage in the St. Louis area were white, but squatter settlements overall were racially diverse. In an era of hardening segregation, some of the settlements were entirely white. Others were racially integrated with whites in the clear majority. In other instances, the city's wharf settlements were overwhelmingly Black. In reporting on flooding in north St. Louis in the spring of 1897, a newspaper called attention to a section of Little Oklahoma north of Dock Street: "A row of picturesque shanties occupied by a mixed population of negroes and whites have been invaded by the flood and its occupants driven out."[15]

Most stevedores and roustabouts who shaped the city's levee culture were Black. Stevedores, or longshoremen, loaded and unloaded steamboats when they docked at the wharf, but roustabouts—river nomads of sorts—traveled on the boats roundtrip, loading and unloading heavy freight and passengers on the packets between terminals. Many were formerly enslaved, once owned by or leased to steamboat captains for backbreaking labor on the cotton boats. Highly knowledgeable of river matters, they established friendship, romantic, and economic networks on the waterways, and a highly masculine identity tied to the Mississippi and its tributaries. At age seventeen, Langston Hughes put the river experiences of Black roustabouts, firemen, stevedores, and cabin crews into a broader poetic, historical context that linked their identity to rivers. In reflections that inspired one of his most widely circulated poems, "The Negro Speaks of Rivers," the young Black poet, novelist, and playwright gazed upon the Mississippi from a train in 1920 as it slowly crossed the river in St. Louis at sunset. As he peered out the window, he thought deeply about the river's meaning to Black Americans. He reflected that the river conjured up competing images born of the nation's history and the African diaspora:

> I looked out the window of the Pullman at the great muddy river flowing down toward the heart of the South, and I began to think what that river, the old Mississippi, had meant to Negroes in the past—how to be sold down the river was the worst fate that could overtake a slave in times of bondage. Then I remembered reading how Abraham Lincoln had made a trip down the Mississippi on a raft to New Orleans, and how he had seen slavery at its worst, and had decided within himself that it should be removed from American life. Then I began to think about other rivers in our past—the Congo, and the Niger, and the Nile in Africa—and the thought came to me: "I've known rivers," and I put it down on the back of an envelope I had in my pocket, and within the space of ten or fifteen minutes, as the train gathered speed in the dusk, I had written this poem . . .

> I've known rivers:
> I've known rivers ancient as the world and older than the flow of human
>   blood in human veins.

> My soul has grown deep like the rivers.

> I bathed in the Euphrates when dawns were young.
> I built my hut near the Congo and it lulled me to sleep.
> I looked upon the Nile and raised the pyramids above it.

I heard the singing of the Mississippi when Abe Lincoln went down to
New Orleans, and I've seen its muddy bosom turn all golden in the
sunset.

I've known rivers:
Ancient, dusky rivers.

My soul has grown deep like the rivers.[16]

For Black squatters in St. Louis shantyboats, there were compelling reasons
why migrations south in the fall held little appeal. Even if they scraped together
funds to buy or build a modest seaworthy shantyboat, a float south in search of
a cozy, warm place to tie up for the winter held frightening implications and
conjured up past fears of being sold down the river as slaves. Eddy L. Harris, a
Black travel writer and adventurer who grew up in St. Louis and canoed to New
Orleans more than sixty-five years after Hughes's poem, observed that "the Mississippi River is laden with the burdens of a nation . . . I have watched this river
since I was small, too young to realize that the burdens the Mississippi carries
are more than barges loaded with grain and coal, that the river carries as well
sins and salvation, dreams and adventure and destiny."[17] The river resurrected
dark images as an artery of enslavement and brutal exploitation, but life on a
steamboat also stirred a longing for freedom among the "hired out" enslaved
and offered new possibilities for escape. For example, William Wells Brown, of
St. Louis, escaped to freedom and became a noted abolitionist and author. Life
and labor as a roustabout on steamboat packets after the abolition of slavery
presented new opportunities to freedmen. In spite of harsh working conditions
akin to slavery aboard the packets, the river offered a more promising option
to many, one preferable to debt peonage in southern plantation agriculture.[18]

As roustabouts loaded and unloaded crushing freight, stubborn livestock,
and passengers at steamboat landings between packet terminals, white mates
routinely cussed, beat, and demeaned them. Served food on tin plates, roustabouts sometimes had to eat with their fingers if they didn't bring their own
spoon. They grabbed a few minutes of fitful sleep whenever and wherever possible on the lower deck of the steamboats. When not at work on the river, some
lived in shantyboat settlements, but most stayed in saloon lodging houses in the

waterfront district of St. Louis. The hardest-working and most abused laborers, steamboat roustabouts left a cultural imprint on the riverfront and its music. As a writer noted in 1903, they were "as much part and parcel of the river as is the water, and quite as necessary."[19]

Roustabouts and shantyboat migrants arguably were the most despised elements in the Mississippi River valley. Under constant scrutiny and harassment from authorities, they were profiled, feared, condemned, and caricatured as murderous river riffraff. The longstanding, mistaken claim in Hannibal that Mark Twain's villainous literary character of "Injun Joe" in *The Adventures of Tom Sawyer* (1876) was based on the life of Joe Douglas says more about racism and public contempt for roustabouts than about Douglas. Of African American and Osage ancestry, Douglas saved his earnings as a hard-working, thrifty roustabout and drayman on the town's levee, bought real estate, and made Black home ownership affordable to freedmen in the neighborhood of Douglasville, the heart of Hannibal's Black community named in his honor. Thanks to Mark Twain scholar Shelley Fisher Fishkin and decades of efforts by Rhonda Hall, Faye Dant, Dixie Forte, and other Black activists in Hannibal, a historical marker dedicated in 2016 now pays tribute to Douglas.[20]

A set of parallel images cast roustabouts and shantyboat migrants as objects of amusement and entertainment. In such depictions, they were relics to be laughed at, minstrelsy reminders of slavery and a preindustrial frontier world that was fast giving way to railroads, robber barons, and Jim Crow. Left behind in the nation's rush to industrial riches, the river poor were a cultural symbol of the hardnosed waterfront as the long steamboat era yielded to smokestack America. The regimentation and bureaucratization of industrial society held no appeal to them. In a noisy world attuned to factory whistles, clocks, and industrial discipline, the river clung to its own cycles and sounds, rhythms and rhymes. So did the cast-offs who squatted on its banks, sought fresh-air cures, caroused in its nearby saloons, and endured public scorn and condemnation.

Houseboat birds of passage cherished river life more than acquisition of material possessions in a grasping, dog-eat-dog society. Many remained outside the market economy, preferring to barter and exchange labor and services. They often traded fish, driftwood, or pieces of coal they picked up along railroad tracks in exchange for coffee, tobacco, flour, or other necessities. Someone's misfortune upriver often became someone's good luck downriver. Shantyboaters plucked floating items from the river and sold them to secondhand shops that lined the levee. "While the river is mean in taking things from us," observed Wilson Crist, a fisherman in Aurora, Indiana, "she is good in bringing to us that which she steals from others. All the furniture that I have, I caught floating. . . . A lot of funny things come down the river. . . . In all the years I have lived on the river, I never bought a nickel's worth of fuel. I always use the wood that floats by my home. Sometimes a barge sinks and the current washes out lumps of coal for us."[21]

The river shaped every aspect of shantyboat life. A clock was of no practical use to many water gypsies. The overhead honking sounds of geese in the fall and the fragrance of spring flowers reminded them when it was time to untie from their moorings and migrate. From an ecological perspective, the river lifestyle did far less damage to the environment and natural resources of the Mississippi basin. Certainly, itinerants on the waterways lived in more balanced, sustainable harmony with the environment than did the forces of industrialization that polluted and tried to tame the river, or the steamboats that chewed up beautiful forests on its banks for fuel. Shantyboaters appreciated the river's life-sustaining force and beauty in spite of its dangers and often violent cycles. Not only were they respectful of the ecosystem that provided their basic needs, but in some ways they were an organic outgrowth of it.[22]

Waterfront culture softened in the late nineteenth century but still retained its antebellum coarseness and roughness in masculine frontier traditions of brawling, heavy drinking, chewing tobacco, gambling, and frequenting levee brothels. A crew member or steamboat officer who didn't carry a revolver or knife was rare indeed. Even captains of the packets didn't hesitate to get involved in fistfights and altercations, including those involving unruly passengers. Life on the levee for many was like shooting craps. It was a game of chance. Live hard, drink hard, and roll the dice! Maybe pay a visit to the shantyboat with a "fortune-teller" sign, or to a voodoo practitioner for a magical Egyptian amulet. For casual Sunday sightseers and strollers, the wharf provided a shocking reminder of the underside of waterfront life: grafters, grifters, gamblers, and staggering drifters sleeping it off wherever they happened to fall the night before. Hard-edged, hard-nosed, foul-mouthed, pistol-packing women on the levee bore no resemblance to the bourgeois images of Victorian womanhood so celebrated at the time. Loud admonitions of street preachers met with steeled resistance from wayward waterfront souls for whom religion was a mere tool of the well-dressed. Gospel hymns and river preachers in mission boats lost out to ribald banjo songs in competition for listeners. In a harsh 1896 portrayal of the St. Louis levee's "river rats" between the Eads Bridge and Poplar Street, a reporter wrote: "Many of the denizens of the Levee district are little higher in their mode of life or thoughts than the lower animals. They have the gift of speech, truly, but it is used chiefly in profanity, obscenity, indecency, a mere vehicle for the expression of the base thoughts their brains are alone capable of conceiving. For the rest they are housed worse, and fed worse than the horse or dog, and are less cleanly than most animals in their wild state."[23]

According to precepts of the age of social Darwinism, primitive levee inhabitants were among the unfit of the species. The reporter, as indicated by the subheading of his article, called attention to important racial and class features of levee life regarded as objectionable at the time: "Here Social Inequality Is Unknown and Color Proves No Bar." Inhabitants, whether white or Black, were of the same primitive state. "There is no moral code on the Levee," he complained, "and as to the legal code, it is observed to the extent of not being caught violating it by the policeman on the beat. For the rest the principles of life consist principally in living with as little manual labor as possible, and surrounding as much liquid poison as they can by any means acquire." Black and white wharf dwellers seated alongside each other at the same crude bench in a levee restaurant caught the reporter's eye as he toured the waterfront. So did their utter disregard for conventional morality and sermons of levee preachers. Lack of money did not bar access to cheap food and drink in saloons, where a nickel bought a beer and free lunch of crackers, bologna, and more. If you didn't have a nickel, there was always a generous fellow patron willing to set up a round. "There is a certain communism existing among these men," the reporter observed. "All of them when they acquire money by labor, gambling, or theft, spend it freely, and when they are broke they are treated with like courtesy."[24]

The river poor, many of whom were part of the Mississippi valley's itinerant working class, showed resilience on the margins of a heavily industrializing society that piled up phenomenal wealth and produced a large middle class and cheap consumer goods. The years between 1875 and 1930, on the other hand, gave birth to Jim Crow laws, two incarnations of the Ku Klux Klan, lynching, harsh cyclical depressions, labor upheavals, and social unrest. Industrialization likewise produced bitter poverty and squalid living conditions for those at the bottom. The restless migrations of river nomads perhaps signaled the last hurrah of the American frontier and its squatter traditions, but waterfront settlements also reflected the failure of industrial St. Louis to provide adequate housing for its poor. Novelist Theodore Dreiser, a reporter for the *St. Louis Globe-Democrat* and later the *St. Louis Republic* in the early 1890s, recalled that "along the waterfront was a mill area backed up by wretched tenements, as poor and grimy and dingy as any I have ever seen."[25]

Homelessness and hard times drove a growing number of city residents to the waterfront, but despite what appeared to onlookers as a rootless, shiftless lifestyle, a number of squatters formed a core of settled residents and brought a measure of stability, continuity, and informal governance to wharf communities as St. Louis transformed into an industrial city. Many called the same settlement "home" for fifteen or twenty years. They weathered countless floods, tornadoes, and ice gorges, and they withstood endless police evictions and threats of eviction. In 1897, the *Alton Evening Telegraph* condemned the "shanty boat evil" that attracted nothing but "ignorant and criminal persons, who are anything but desirable citizens."[26]

St. Louis provides a panoramic window into the world of America's rogues and river poor—DeVoto's "debris" and "cosmos" of the Mississippi basin. The city's waterfront settlements and roustabouts' hangouts were eyesores to many, nuisances to city officials and waterfront developers, and criminal dens to police. They attracted high-rolling riverboat gamblers, circus entertainers, medicine boat shows, "floating palaces," Gospel steamers, and pirates and counterfeiters who sought to hide among the honest dwellers. The levee poor came under fire from child rescue societies, preachers, social welfare agencies, state legislatures, and moral reformers of all stripes. For a corrupt child trafficker like Georgia Tann, head of the Tennessee Children's Home Society in Memphis, waterfront settlements were a place to pluck away children to sell to desperate adoptive parents with money to throw around. For authors of dime novels and adult popular fiction, songwriters, and early filmmakers, the levee provided subjects of artistic inspiration to romanticize, poke fun at, and wrap into the nation's Jim Crow nostalgia. In the face of relentless condemnation, shantyboat wayfarers and roustabouts did the best they could against great odds to carve out a meaningful life at the water's edge. The levee shaped them, and they in turn left a mark on American culture for decades to come as St. Louis transformed from a river town into an industrial city.[27]

I

A Tranquil and Unhurried Life

THE RIVER PEOPLE

Maybe you never happened to see a house from the back window
of which you could go fishing, or where the bucket had only to be dropped
down from the porch and water hauled up to wash or scrub with, and
where the front yard never needed sweeping, and no expense was
necessary for a cellar-wall, or yard-palings, or gate-hinges.

—JOHN FRANKLIN COWAN, *The Jo-Boat Boys*, 1891

Not being strong enough to make circumstances serve them,
they become creatures of their environment, stagnant pools
of life's highways or like static snags in life's river.

—EMMA KOEN MEACHAM, "Sketch No. 10"

Picturesque flotillas of shantyboats adorned the cultural landscape of American rivers in the late nineteenth century. Chicken coops and cages of pet pigeons often rode atop the boats' flat roofs with trammel nets stretched across the tops to dry. Atop some of the boats was a sail. Kids, coon dogs, and cats scurried about on the sides of the boats amid ropes and barrels. A low railing with small slots around the deck kept them in most of the time. A few larger boats had aboard a cow, a tame duck or two, hog, pet coon, or goat trained to walk a gangplank. Some of the older models had a steering rudder. The rest relied on poles and oars for steering and included an attached skiff. More likely than not, a rifle or double-barreled shotgun and an American flag hung on an interior wall. In addition to steel traps, there was plenty of ammunition, tobacco, and "squirrel whiskey" aboard.[1]

Calked with oakum and rags and its seams made watertight with pitch or tar, a houseboat built of pine boards or odds and ends of driftwood and runaway rafting logs or sawmill logs plucked from the river cost about $20. The most humble versions resembled a raft with a "dog house" or wigwam built onto it, similar to the one used by Mark Twain to send Huck and Jim floating down the river. A more typical boat, six or seven feet high, ten feet long, and eight feet wide with a couple of doors, featured walls covered with battened tar paper, and windows covered with mosquito netting and an oil cloth or tarpaulin in bad weather. Inside even the humblest houseboats were a few cooking utensils, an old trunk and primitive bunks of some kind, sticks of driftwood, and an iron stove for cooking and heating. A crude, bent pipe ran from the stove through the roof to serve as a chimney. Hot and loosely constructed for circulation of air in summertime, the boats were brutally cold in winter, but dogs and cats added sleeping warmth on cold nights. The size and decor of houseboats depended on the income of occupants, a few of whom were actors, artists, preachers, teachers, musicians, or circus performers. More pretentious boats with three or four papered rooms might cost $200–$300, if not more. Most took a beating on the trip south. A boat that cost $100 might be good for nothing but kindling by the time it reached New Orleans, if it made it that far. On a steamboat down the Ohio, American writer William Dean Howells described a line of boat homes along the shore:

> The houses had in common the form of a freight-car set in a flat-bottomed boat; the car would be shorter or longer, with one, or two, or three windows in its sides, and a section of stovepipe softly smoking from its roof. The windows might be curtained or they might be bare, but apparently there was no other distinction among the houseboat dwellers, whose sluggish craft lay moored among the willows, or tied to an elm or a maple, or even made fast to a stake on shore. There were cases in which they had not followed the fall of the river promptly enough, and lay slanted on the beach, or propped up to a more habitable level on its slope; in a sole, sad instance, the house had gone down with the boat and lay wallowing in the wash of the flood.[2]

Steamboat pilots, who often tried to bully shantyboaters off the river, complained that they created nighttime hazards because they were drunk and asleep in unlighted boats. As a former cub pilot, Twain sympathized with those who steered the steamboats and had to dodge shantyboats as well as upended loads of runaway logs, coal boats, and other debris. Those in the steamboat trade regarded shantyboat traffic as a nuisance at best. "Pilots bore a mortal hatred to these craft," he wrote in *Life on the Mississippi*, "and it was returned with usury." By law, shantyboats were required to display a light, but they often failed to comply, as Twain noted with characteristic wit and satire:

> Once, at night, in one of those forest-bordered crevices (behind an island) which steamboatmen intensely describe with the phrase "as dark as the inside of a cow," we should have eaten up a Posey County [Indiana] family, fruit, furniture, and all, but that they happened to be fiddling down below and we just caught the sound of the music in time to sheer off, doing no serious damage, unfortunately, but coming so near it that we had good hopes for a moment. These people brought their lantern, then, of course, and as we backed and filled to get away, the precious family stood in the light of it—both sexes and various ages—and cursed us till everything turned blue. Once a coal-boatman sent a bullet through our pilot-house, when we borrowed a steering-oar of him in a very narrow place.[3]

Dexter Marshall pointed out in 1900 that houseboat inhabitants resented the contemptuous term "shanty-boat people," used by reporters and others to disparage them. They preferred "the river people," a reference that set them apart from steamboat deckhands and roustabouts, oarsmen, and river "pigs" who steered rafts of white pine logs from St. Paul. "To be considered truly of the river people," wrote Marshall, "you must be lulled to sleep at night, in your own floating home, by the gentle lapping of water, all the year round. You must be capable of living mainly on fish which you have taken from the river's tawny depths. You must cook your food over driftwood fire. You must bear with fortitude the malaria and the rheumatism which curse all who steadily breathe the river vapors."[4] Older river people called their homes "cabin-boats," but younger ones preferred "houseboats." A rule of the river, according to Marshall, was that the two terms not be used interchangeably. River etiquette among houseboat dwellers required use of one term or another but never both in conversation.

Burman observed that most shantyboat folks he met in the early twentieth century were of English-Irish ethnicity. Many came from poor areas of Appalachian Kentucky and West Virginia. According to William Alexander Percy, an aristocrat writing of the Mississippi delta, they made "ideal bootleggers." Mistakenly asserting that "no Negro is ever a river-rat," he described shantyboat wayfarers as "illiterate, suspicious, intensely clannish, blond, and usually ugly." His unflattering portrayal cast the typical "'river rat'" as "white, Anglo-Saxon, with twists of speech and grammatical forms current in Queen Anne's day or earlier, and a harsh 'r' strange to all Southerners except mountaineers." Percy added:

> Where he comes from no one knows or cares. Some find in him the descendant of those pirates who used to infest the river as far up as Memphis. It seems more likely his forbears were out-of-door, ne'er-do-well nomads of the pioneer days. His shanty boats, like Huck Finn's father's, may be seen moored in the willows or against the sandbars as far up and down the river as I have ever traveled. He squats on bars and bits of mainland subject to overflow, raises a garden and a patch of corn, steals timber, rafts it, and sells it to the mills, and relies the year round on fishing for a living. . . . They lead a life apart, uncouth, unclean, lawless, vaguely alluring. Their only contact with the land world around them consists largely in being haled into court, generally for murder.[5]

In summer 1917 on a trip to Vicksburg, home of a large shantyboat colony, American author Julian Street described the racially integrated riverfront settlement as a "heterogeneous assortment of an incredible and comic slouchiness." In the colony were many Black fish markets that advertised by dangling catfish from the rails and posts of their boats.[6] On the New Orleans *batture* and Louisiana bayous, many settlement residents were Cajuns or Blacks. No matter the ethnic origins, a special river complexion made shantyboaters easy to pick out in a crowd, according to Marshall. He compared the complexion to that of poor whites in areas of the South. "Not all betray themselves by their peculiarly listless river ways," he wrote, "but ninety-nine in a hundred show a curious similarity of color in the face. . . . It is apparent alike in the lightest Scandinavian and the darkest native of southern Europe. With a difference, it shows itself in the countenances of the river negroes, even."[7] Drawn at first to factory cities of the river valleys, shantyboat migrants rejected the regimentation of industrial life and sought freedom on the river. For Howells, "they all gave evidence of a tranquil and unhurried life which the soul of the beholder envied within him." In 1938, Burman wrote, "For of all free lives in this machine-riddled world, there is none so free as the life of the shantyman."[8]

The basic diet of river people consisted mainly of fish, turtle, cornmeal, bacon, hot biscuits cooked in a greased cast-iron skillet on an iron stove, and muddy river coffee consumed hot at breakfast and noon, and cold in the evening. Quinine, second in importance only to coffee, was a popular folk remedy to ward off malaria, commonly known as "the shakes," which plagued river communities. In part, Marshall attributed "the river complexion," as even the people themselves called it, to constant exposure to river weather. Vitamin deficiencies or malnutrition may have been a contributing factor, but he blamed excessive consumption of muddy coffee. "Made from the turbid liquid on which the cabin-boats float," he noted, "it is the exclusive non-intoxicating beverage on the stream."[9] Aboard the *Reece Lee* from St. Louis to New Orleans in 1915, William J. Aylward observed countless "River People." "One cannot but admit the undeniable charm of a life of perfect freedom, drifting as fancy dictates from place to place," he confessed, "but the price is high and each must pay. The sallow complexions, an air of lassitude, the misshapen figures of men prematurely old racked with rheumatism, malaria, and all the chills and fever that in the river vernacular come under the general head of 'the shakes'—these are part of the price of their lethal existence."[10]

Emma Koen Meacham, wife of an Arkansas delta planter, described shantyboat colonists as "idle, sallow, unwashed, underfed, outlawed, so far as the general public knew, constant companions to mosquitoes and malaria. Not being strong enough to make circumstances serve them, they become creatures of their environment, stagnant pools of life's highways or like static snags in life's river."[11] Reuben Gold Thwaites, director of the State Historical Society of Wisconsin, offered a more expansive description after a canoe trip down the Monongahela and Ohio rivers to Cairo in 1894:

Among the houseboat folk are young working couples starting out in life, and hoping ultimately to gain a foothold on land; unfortunate people, who are making a fresh start; men regularly employed in riverside factories and mills; invalids, who, at small expense, are trying the fresh-air cure; others, who

drift up and down the Ohio, seeking casual work; and legitimate fishermen.
. . . But a goodly proportion of these boats are inhabited by the lowest class
of the population,—poor "crackers" who have managed to scrape together
enough money to buy, or enough energy and driftwood to build, such a
craft; and, near or at the towns, many are occupied by gamblers, illicit
liquor dealers, and others who, while plying nefarious trades, make a pre-
tense of following the occupation of the Apostles.[12]

In 1910, writer Raymond S. Spears used the term "river trippers" to describe
houseboat nomads on the Mississippi and its tributaries. He divided them into
two categories: "short trippers" and "long trippers." Short trippers on the Upper
Mississippi stayed above St. Louis, and those on the Lower Mississippi did not
travel above the city. Long trippers floated thousands of miles to New Orleans.
Popular images typically lumped them into an amorphous mass of degraded
river trash. Burman's writings portrayed them as "primitive" elements in a
losing battle against "civilization." In St. Louis's Little Oklahoma, H. L. Shaw,
a river trader described as "the Rockefeller of the settlement," insisted that
water gypsies floated south because they were too lazy to stay behind and work.
"They'll stop in some Arkansaw [sic] swamp," he complained, "where they can
shoot a wild hog for meat and pass the winter there."[13] As a shantyboat woman
on the Ohio River noted in 1908, police profiled them in efforts to solve river
crimes: "'Pears like every time any of the shanty boat folks up the river gits into
trouble, they come down the river takin' pictures of all the other boat folks in
the hopes of findin' 'em."[14]

Sensationalized newspaper stories highlighted crimes in waterfront settlements, but the *Cincinnati Enquirer* in 1895 pointed out that "there are thousands
of hard-working miners, furnacemen, and laborers along the Ohio between
Louisville and Pittsburgh who own and live in shanty boats that are not only
safe and comfortable, but beautiful." The newspaper defended them against
unrelenting criticism that held them to a higher standard of behavior: "They
live and raise their families, are free from rent, and enjoy much more comfort
than thousands of hard-working men who are compelled to give up too much
of their hard-earned money for miserable shanties and hovels on shore. Why
not give the shanty boat an honest, square deal?"[15] In the early 1900s, travel
writer and photographer Clifton Johnson found similar sentiment expressed by

a Paducah farmer: "I been acquainted with a heap of 'em, and ninety percent of 'em are as honest and good-hearted as you could ask. It'd surprise you what fine and intelligent people there are among 'em."[16]

Clifton Edwards ("Ukelele Ike") was among the river people as a child. On June 14, 1895, the Hollywood actor, Vaudeville singer, and voice of Walt Disney's "Jiminy Crickett" was born in the waterfront colony where my grandmother lived at the time as a year-old baby. "The boat was tied to a clump of willows below the levee at Hannibal," he recalled, "and we were so poor that father, Edward Edwards, a fisherman, paid the doctor who attended mother by giving him a mess of carp and buffalo."[17] The Edwards family then floated to St. Louis's north wharf. Cliff's father, who spent time in the city's sanitarium, later drowned near Hannibal. He eked out a living as a fisherman who sometimes picked up work on the railroad. In St. Louis, Cliff sold newspapers at age ten and picked up coal along the railroad tracks in a desperate effort to heat their shanty on cold winter nights. The search for fuel and food was unrelenting. "We were dreadfully poor," he recalled, "and many times the six of us kids piled into the rag heaps we called bed and got rid of the gnawing hunger pangs by falling off to sleep."[18]

Hiram Jenkins, a former steamboat pilot and ex-Confederate soldier, lived in a Louisville shantyboat colony north of the city's waterworks in 1888. In his early sixties, he was a celebrity on the Ohio River between Cincinnati and Cairo. According to him, he traveled in a skiff from Cincinnati to New Orleans at age thirteen and paid for passage home months later by working as a cabin boy on a steamboat. He later worked as a deckhand on a slave-trading steamboat, and after "cubbing" on the Mississippi River he secured a license and piloted a steamer until a fight with a second pilot at the wheel led to a collision with a towboat and the subsequent death of the second pilot. After 1865, Jenkins fished and amassed a tidy sum of money as a merchant/junk dealer on the Ohio. According to some, he was a notorious river pirate at one time.[19]

Squatter settlements held birds of passage in high esteem because of their river experiences and storytelling prowess. Tales of the river followed them wherever they docked. They owned their own boats whereas many squatters rented a houseboat, usually from a better-off resident in the settlement. The most destitute, year-round squatters inhabited dilapidated boats, crude shanties, tents, or dugouts in the side of a nearby hollow. Some paid nominal ground rent to a railroad, lumber company, or the city's harbor and wharf commissioner if he caught them at home. Many were widows or were left high and dry by their husband. In St. Louis, some of the women worked in tobacco or garment factories, many were washerwomen, and a few were fortune-tellers and midwives. Rough-edged, many smoked short pipes and/or chewed tobacco, and they could brawl or brandish a shotgun or revolver with the same ease, confidence, and skill as men. The formality of marriage and divorce was ignored in many cases. Critics complained of the loose morals of women who jumped from boat to boat freely, but many women were destitute and did whatever they could to earn money and feed their children. They scavenged waterfront dumps for scraps of iron or steel to sell at junk shops, and scoured the shoreline for driftwood to sell to bakers and others.

In some cases, men hired a housekeeper for river trips. For a trusting woman strapped for money, bored, and eager to escape factory drudgery or an abusive husband, the offer of a job might entice her aboard if willing to risk a journey into the unknown. The romantic image of life on a houseboat appealed to rebellious teenage girls and young women eager to escape a bad marriage, but they were vulnerable. Male predators and womanizers operated on the river, promising a life of excitement and travel, but what they promised often fell far short of what they delivered. Consider the fate of Anna McGibbens, who left her husband in Fort Madison and ran off with Frank Piero aboard the houseboat of Andrew S. and Malissa Litwilder, of Muscatine. The four were living on the boat in Alton when McGibbens died in childbirth on January 11, 1905. No attempt to summon a physician was made until the last minute. The coroner found her emaciated body and that of her dead newborn in a dingy bed amid squalor. Ruling death from exposure and neglect, he snapped at Piero: "I would like to hang you, but there does not seem to be a legal way of doing it."[20]

In some cases, shantyboat midwives performed criminal abortions for desperate women in poor river communities, but the following is a case that ended in tragedy. Ida Clark, who in early 1905 lived with her husband, Henry, in a one-room houseboat on Four Mile Island across from the cement plant in Ilasco, advertised her services through the "grapevine" in the town, which had more than its share of poor women in desperate circumstances. Five or six Ilasco women claimed that she represented to them that for $5 she could perform an abortion or induce a miscarriage through use of medicines and instruments. According to Anna Rupert, Ida showed her a piece of wire about six inches long and claimed she had used it on herself to abort in 1904, insisting that she'd rather die than have children. Reportedly, Ida studied osteopathy and at one time practiced in Hannibal. Pearl Pryor, an eighteen-year-old woman from Barry, Illinois, who was about five months pregnant and an acquaintance of Ida's, sought her services after living in Ilasco for a period before returning to her father's home in Barry. This was not Pryor's first abortion. Two years earlier, a physician in Barry treated her for the aftereffects of an abortion. The Clarks met her at the Ilasco train depot and took her in a skiff to their houseboat on the island, where Pryor died from the procedure on May 16, 1905. The instrument used to abort pierced the bladder instead of the womb. In the Pike County circuit court, the Clarks were convicted and sentenced to fourteen years in Illinois penitentiaries.[21]

In 1908, Hal C. Green, a New York/Pittsburgh newspaper writer on an adventurous houseboat journey from Pittsburgh to New Orleans with his wife and two sons, stopped for a few days in O'Donnell Bend, near Osceola in the Arkansas delta. When he spotted a shantyboat with a sign, "Fortunes Told Here," he paid the occupants a visit in search of a story. A young, athletic-looking man about thirty or thirty-five years old with long curly hair, a closely cropped beard, and an arm missing below the shoulder invited Green into the boat in neighborly fashion. Green edged past two yelping dogs and a rooster perched on an inverted washtub on the porch. The interior of the "scrupulously clean" boat contained several guns, traps, a half-finished fishing net, a sewing machine, and a caged pet raccoon.[22]

A few minutes later, the cackling of chickens and barking of dogs announced the arrival of the young man's wife, wearing blue jeans and a boy's canvas cap and carrying a shotgun and a rabbit she shot. "Excuse my hunting costume," she said upon being introduced to Green. "When I saw your boat I thought it was a customer. I tell fortunes, you know, an' daresn't be 'way from the boat long. They just don't give me no rest." She told Green that although she did not announce her services in advance, two Black women who picked cotton on a nearby plantation came to her for readings the night before. "I tell 'em in three ways," she added, "by th' kairds, by the palms of their hands, an' by signs, an' I always get 'em right." When Green asked how the couple made a living, she spoke up: "We river folks has got to live. Now my old man there hunts an' traps an' runs the boat, an' I tell fortunes, that's my business, but I can make nets and seines, an' prepare bird's feathers for the market. Oh, we always eat three times a day, and sometimes four." Her husband expressed pride in her skills. "Yes," he interjected, "and she is pretty nearly as good a fisherman as I am. . . . She caught a catfish weighing four pounds an' a soft-shelled turtle last night. The cat went for our breakfast, an' the turtle will make our supper." He opened an ice box and showed Green three ducks and a turkey he shot the day before. "But there's one stunt we won't do," his wife interrupted, "we don't peddle no whisky. I bet we've had a chance to sell a hundred gallons since we left Cairo. People row out to us in the night and call us up in the hopes we got liquor. They's money in it, but Lor', I don't want no constable nor sheriff after us for bootleggin'." The couple was en route to New Orleans from Kansas City. In some of the towns, the woman read fortunes, but she emphasized that she complied with the law by taking down her sign where ordinances banned fortune-telling.[23]

Earlier, on Louisville's Towhead Island, Green met "Big George" Bush, a "gigantic" Black shantyboat owner and skilled fisherman who sometimes fished for clam shells or worked in a local factory. Fishermen often sought advice from Bush, widely respected on the river for his honesty, generosity, waterways savvy, and self-sufficiency. "No one ever meddled with his lines or nets," Green wrote. "Possibly a custom he had of coming out on his deck occasionally and shooting at a mark either with his shotgun, rifle or revolver had a discouraging effect upon predatory meddlers."[24] Shortly after Green tied up on the island, Bush, a longtime resident of Louisville, led a procession of shantyboats from the mouth of Beargrass Creek to deeper waters along the inside channel of Towhead Island. Bush landed his boat next to Green's, jumped ashore, and tied up his lines. Green, who befriended him, noted that the boat owned by Bush and his wife boasted the "whitest curtains and the snowiest linen in Shantyboat town." Their boat was "as tidy inside and out as the interior of a gentleman's yacht."[25]

A month later, Green ran into "Big George" again on the Ohio, this time in his freshly painted shantyboat, looking for better fishing waters near Brandenburg, Kentucky. Bush, proud of his boat's fresh coat of paint and new colors, let Green know he recently made a "killin'" on Beargrass Creek. While taking in his lines, Bush discovered that a refinery vat of lard burst open and the lard "had all run down in th' crick." "I just shoveled my ole johnboat plum full of it," he explained, "an' took it ovah to the soap wu'ks an' sole it for thu'ty dollahs."[26] He used the money to stock up on corned beef, smoked ham, flour, tea, coffee, and other provisions for lean times. In winters, he sometimes floated to Cairo and holed up in Arkansas, where he hunted and worked as a tour guide for hunters. After the lard bonanza, a white family headed by "Meandering Mike," as he was known in Beargrass Creek, tied up next to him. They were without food and in desperate shape. With a hungry toddler, the family sidled up to Bush, who explained to Green, "An' I couldn't let no baby go hungry when I had anythin' to eat on mah own boat."[27] Bush shared provisions he had laid in stock for himself and his wife, but "Meandering Mike" made no attempt to fish or do work of any kind. Everywhere Bush went on the river, the family tied up next to him. For about six weeks he fed the family. Then one night Bush slipped away quietly, pulled up the mouth of a creek to hide, and gave him the slip. "And that was the last we saw of 'Meandering Mike,'" wrote Green, "the man who had a good graft and lost it."[28]

No matter how high or low in the pecking order of a shantyboat settlement, many felt a common bond as river people who lent a helping hand to each other in times of need. "I have lived on the river all my life," a waterfront colonist observed in 1925, "and I have never seen a single case where folks were in need that other boats did not help them out."[29] There was an unwritten code of ethics and a tendency to stick together against outsiders. Unless strangers were known river pirates or tramps, residents asked few questions about them. If a thief or trouble-making stranger did show up, a leading resident might quietly tip off an officer who policed the waterfront beat. Or, while the stranger was sleeping, a delegation of residents might cut the lines to his boat and set him adrift.[30]

Births and deaths among river people at times went unrecorded as a result of their lifestyle, and marriages were often common-law. Census enumerators sometimes failed to count them. Of necessity, burials might take place on a lonesome hillside near the riverbank or in a secluded lagoon. A Memphis houseboat resident recalled the disaster when a levee broke north of the city in the flood of March 1903: "Lots o' people were drowned jis' like rabbits. . . . It was a dreadful, cold, stormy time of year, and thar was sickness an' accidents an' many deaths from the exposure. Thar was no way to git coffins—no way to git nothin'—and they had to sew the bodies up in sacks with sand enough put in to make 'em sink, and then they'd throw 'em in the river."[31] In the case of a hermit on an island or in an isolated marshy slough or bayou, no burial might take place at all. Buzzards, alligators, or huge rats with saw-like teeth disposed of the corpse. The Mississippi swept more than its share of "floaters" downstream, but no matter the town or city, Potter's Field was the final resting place for many. Such was the fate of "Aunt Bettie" Bailey, a Black woman who claimed to be one hundred years old when she showed up in the St. Louis waterfront settlement known as the Dock Street Addition to Little Oklahoma. Annie Young, a Black resident, took her into her shantyboat and cared for her until she died ten years later. Shortly before Bailey died, she reportedly muttered, "When I die, just don't have any services and let the city bury me, and if it won't, then go down and tell them to put this old body in the river and let it float away."[32]

Waterfront communities drew an eclectic population. Some were roustabouts, deckhands, day laborers, barbers, bee hunters, musicians, carpenters, cobblers, ex-slaves, steamboat pilots, ship caulkers, or willow-weaving makers of wicker chairs. Many were fishermen, including pearl hunters, and a few were artists, actors, lawyers, preachers, or photographers. In St. Louis, many year-round residents held steady jobs in rolling mills, quarries, factories, and lumber and railroad yards. The settlements attracted craftsmen who plied their trade on the river in seasonal fashion. Tax-evading tintype studios on the Tennessee River were common in Chattanooga. Travel writer John Leisk Tait, who visited a Mississippi River shantyboat community in 1907, found among its residents three paperhangers, three musicians in the orchestra of a leading theater, four watchmen, two ship carpenters, two painters, two employees of a macaroni factory, a house carpenter, a photographer, a plasterer, a blacksmith, and a talented landscape artist. Some on the lower river and the bayous collected Spanish moss used by northern manufacturers of mattresses. The swamps also provided a sanctuary for an occasional outcast to hide from authorities. In 1912, a flood relief expedition to Louisiana's Bayou Barataria found among the shantyboat population George Jacquin, an escapee from the Louisiana Leper Home, located on the Mississippi River in Carville, Iberville Parish. For several years, he lived as a fisherman in a screened-in shantyboat among friendly neighbors who helped him when he needed it. He preferred bayou life on a shantyboat to isolation and confinement in the inpatient treatment center for leprosy (Hansen's disease), which was thought to be extremely contagious at the time. The State Board of Health forced him back into the Leper Home.[33]

Thanks to button manufacturing in the 1890s in Muscatine, freshwater clam fishermen and pearl hunters dotted the waters of the Mississippi and many tributaries. As button factories appeared in many river towns, especially on the Upper Mississippi, fishermen dragged the river with crowfoot iron bars and four-pointed hooks to snag clam shells. On shore, they and their families boiled the shells to get rid of the mussels before shell buyers hauled them in wagons to factories. This created a vile stench in settlements where "clammers" tied up their mud-caked, flat-bottomed fishing boats and slept in houseboats or camped in pitched tents. An added incentive for shell diggers was the lure of finding dazzling pearls in the mussels. Professional buyers, some of whom were unscrupulous, traveled the rivers where there were productive clam beds to search for poor fishermen with pearls to sell. High-dollar pearls were unusual, but they fueled wild speculation as rumors swept the waterways. Pearl rushes sent frenzied hunters to Clinton, Iowa, as early as 1860, or the White and Black rivers in Arkansas in 1897, or rivers in Kentucky, Tennessee, and elsewhere in the early 1900s. On the Black River, a fisherman in 1914 sold a pearl for $25,000. On the White River, a particularly popular source of clam shells, a pearl found near Peel, Arkansas, brought $9,000 in the early 1920s. William Alexander Percy emphasized that the average river rat "seems to regard the White River as the Navajos regard the Canyon de Chelly—as a sort of sanctuary and homeland, and it supplies the clam shells from which he makes buttons."[34]

For Maggie Durley, cruelty at the hands of her husband, William Durley, a fisherman, clam digger, and pearl hunter, led to her death in Davenport in 1904. For a while, the move by the Black couple from St. Louis to a popular location for pearl hunters in the heart of the button industry paid off, at least for William. At the beginning of summer, the Muscatine Journal reported that Durley, "a colored clam digger of Rockingham township a few miles below Davenport," found a valuable pearl. A buyer offered $500, but Durley demanded $600 or he'd take the pearl to Chicago to find a buyer with a better offer. Reportedly, Durley sold a pearl to a Cincinnati buyer two years earlier for $1,750.[35] Maggie complained that her husband drank up all the money they had. Reportedly, they were chased out of Rock Island on account of William's cruelty to her. In Davenport, he fished, did odd jobs on the waterfront, and hunted for pearls.

Whatever money he earned, he kept from Maggie, who had little to eat and few clothes. On June 27, 1904, when she threatened to search for a job so she could have her own money and get something to eat, he beat and repeatedly kicked her with his heavy boots while she was on the ground. The beating left her paralyzed and hospitalized for a few days before she died and was buried in Potter's Field. Upon arrest, Durley had several pearls in his possession, which the sheriff confiscated. A local appraiser estimated that the pearl Durley was asking $600 for was worth only $50, if that much. Durley pleaded guilty to manslaughter and served a three-year sentence in the Fort Madison penitentiary.[36]

For shantyboat squatters near lumberyards, catching runaway logs on the rivers and returning them to companies was a way to earn money at times. Rises in the rivers often swept rafts of logs downstream, creating opportunities for those whose boats were in strategic locations. Many fishermen and others had pike poles, lines, and other equipment to tow logs from midstream to shore. The enterprise was popular, especially in backwaters. John Roxey, an enterprising resident of a Memphis houseboat colony, was among those in the business of catching logs. "Rafts and branded logs belong to the owner of the brand," he explained in 1903. "You see, all timber men have a way of branding timber on the butt of the stick with a stamp hammer or a hot iron."[37] A lone shantyboat owner might return a few logs for 25 cents each to hardwood mills on the nearby Wolf River, but unbranded logs were worth much more. On occasion, the business was profitable enough for Roxey to hire labor and pay the costs of a tow boat to return logs.

In December 1900, a near disaster for the Minnesota-based *Vernie Mac* tugboat rafter meant good times for shantyboat colonists when high winds whipped the boat about in a dangerous eddy near Memphis. The boat avoided destruction, but the convulsive eddy caused it to dump its tow of cottonwood and gum logs in the river. For Roxey, the near disaster was a bonanza. He returned nearly five hundred logs to two lumber companies on the Wolf River. "We got a line on 'em one morning early and herded 'em in," he recalled. "It cost us ten dollars for hired help and sixty dollars for a tug to take 'em up the river. When we delivered the goods the mill men handed us over two hundred and fifty dollars, which wasn't bad. We worked two days catching the timber and two days getting it into shape to tow."[38] John Lathrop Mathews, a Chicago reporter/waterways writer on a houseboat honeymoon from Chicago to New

Orleans, was in the Memphis colony and witnessed the massive dumping of logs. Shantyboat squatters were "deliriously happy," he wrote. Caught up in the excitement, he jumped into his skiff to try his hand at rounding up runaway logs. He and a shantyboat friend from St. Louis sprang into action. Each made $10, but not before Mathews's skiff overturned and dumped him into the cold waters. He clung to a log until he could maneuver it closer to the houseboat. His wife tossed him a line and pulled him out of the river.[39]

The logging industry contributed to the number of houseboats on the waterways. On the Upper Mississippi and its tributaries, crude shantyboat bunkhouses and floating kitchens housed and fed timber crews in Minnesota. Lumber companies towed wanigans to the northern edge of their logging operations along the rivers. Then, as lumberjacks cut their way through the pines, the mobile bunkhouses and cook boats drifted downstream with them to ensure they had easy access to food and shelter. On the Lower Mississippi, hundreds of farm laborers and small farmers from the Ohio, Missouri, and Mississippi river valleys went south in winter to cut timber in the cypress swamps of the Red River valley in Louisiana. At first, "swampers" from northern farms traveled by steamboat in late fall after the crops were gathered, but in 1896 a number of them opted to float downriver on sturdy houseboats instead. Once they reached the Red River, they journeyed on it to a point just above Bougere, Louisiana, where they followed the Little River to Catahoula Parish. Typically the lumber company paid $20 a month plus food and lodging, but the men, who worked in mud and water all day, found the cabins uncomfortable and unhealthy at night. Swampers persuaded the company to pay them $30 a month if they furnished their own provisions and a more comfortable, healthy place to sleep. They brought double-barreled shotguns to hunt abundant game in the swamps, and they planned to catch a tow back to their farms in the spring.[40]

In early October 1896, when a houseboat with six swampers and a cook docked in Vicksburg to buy provisions, a special correspondent for the *New York Sun* interviewed them about their work and journey. Of Aberdeen, Ohio, just above Cincinnati, they fished, hunted, and read on the way south. They were a hardy but rough-looking group who resembled backwoodsmen in their red flannel shirts, old clothing, and slouch hats, but they were not as rough as their appearance suggested. Among them was a young man who gave up teaching for cypress swamps in winter. He enjoyed the adventure of the trip, the camaraderie, and experiences that came with life on the river. The swampers' houseboat was cheap but neat and well-built. The front part was the kitchen, and in the rear were four bunks in two tiers on each side. Stored in the hold of the boat were barrels of flour, salted fish, salt pork, canned goods, and nuts. The newspaper correspondent asked why The Swamp King and its oil floats were painted bright yellow. Befuddled, he pointed out that of approximately thirty houseboats he saw go downstream recently, all but three were yellow. The names of some of the boats (Swamp Angel, Cypress Inn) suggested connections to Louisiana logging operations. When the correspondent asked if the color had special significance, a swamper replied that yellow was the cheapest paint available in Aberdeen.[41]

The Mississippi River attracted traders and others with labor, professional services, and commodities to sell. To sit on the levee and watch river traffic revealed fascinating snapshots of American life on the waterways. Whether showboats, circuses, floating saloons, patent medicine shows, or shantyboat preachers, there seemed to be no end to goods and services for sale. Even a "floating town" passed through St. Louis in November 1900. A fleet of houseboats that included a drugstore, printing office, tin shop, gunsmith shop, and general store stopped in heavily populated areas on the way downriver. Also aboard were carpenters, painters, even a physician. While the houseboats anchored offshore, a few of those aboard went ashore to distribute handbills advertising services and touting tax-evading advantages. The fleet stayed as long as sales were brisk, and then continued to the next stop downriver. A few traders operated general merchandise stores, and others peddled liniments, elixirs, quinine, and quack remedies from one river town to the next. Some of the more prosperous traders followed the river for business purposes only. On selling trips, they tied up their boat in shantyboat colonies but did not live in waterfront settlements. They usually owned comfortable homes and traveled without their family. When they set out, they stocked their boat with sugar, flour, coffee, meat, cornmeal, whiskey, tobacco, and other dry goods. As they sold their stock or traded for eggs, butter, vegetables, and farm produce at each stop, they replenished their supply until they reached their destination. Then, they sold the boat and boarded a steamer home. They soon bought another trading boat and planned the next business trip down the river. Less prosperous traders conducted business on their shantyboats with family aboard.[42]

The river was a popular artery for merchants in the illegal as well as the legal liquor trade. Whiskey boats, or floating saloons, operated on the Mississippi, usually in midstream between two states. Many did so with a federal license but without a state permit. Others had no license whatsoever. Waterfront residents rowed out in skiffs to buy liquor and maybe gamble on the boats. Or, the whiskey boats sold bottles of liquor to illegal "blind-tiger" hideouts along the shoreline. If law enforcement officers came on the scene, the boats sped to midstream, outside the jurisdiction of local authorities. Sheriffs and federal revenue officers were ever vigilant to shut down such operations that deprived the government of tax revenue or violated the moral strictures of the growing prohibitionist movement. By 1909, the illegal manufacture and sale of alcohol was widespread enough for Raymond S. Spears to call the Mississippi a "highway of lawlessness." He called attention to a booming bootlegging trade reinforced by "river law," a resort to firearms. Whiskey boats posed a challenge to authorities, especially in counties that passed local option laws in states that bordered the river. Governors sought greater cooperation with authorities on the other side of the river. In some cases, changes in the river channel led to changes or confusion in jurisdictional boundaries.[43]

The jurisdictional issues were especially important on the lower river. Mississippi, which virtually was a dry state by the end of 1908, sought stricter cooperation from Arkansas and Louisiana, including the exchange of jurisdictions, to keep smuggled booze from its predominantly Black labor force. Mississippi authorities found it easier to go after small-scale operations on shore. In 1897, Bolivar County sheriff W. J. Wooten uncovered a blind tiger on a shantyboat on the levee and went to make arrests near the steamboat landing of Australia. He arrested two Black men, but a third who tried to run away fired at a deputy. The sheriff tied together six sticks of dynamite and tossed them at his shantyboat. The explosion tore off half the boat. The fleeing suspect jumped into a skiff and rowed away, but when the sheriff fired at him he reportedly jumped overboard and drowned. More than two hundred men were convicted in the previous two years for selling whiskey without a license in Bolivar County.[44]

Whatever the merchandise, selling goods in trading boats was lucrative but posed life-threatening risks on account of river pirates and ruffians. On John L. Mathews's honeymoon river trip to New Orleans in 1900, he met the Thompsons, small traders from Indiana. They were docked in Shanty-boat Town on the northern edge of Memphis. During the stay, Mrs. Thompson gave birth to their child. Less than a month later, the Thompsons left Memphis ahead of Mathews and his wife. Thompson was under pressure to sell a lot of goods because of heavy expenses related to the birth of their child. For reasons of personal safety, most houseboat travelers avoided levee camps, where white contractors and foremen presided over the brutal exploitation of gang laborers, mostly Black sharecroppers and convicts housed in tents. Whippings and beatings of workers were common, and living conditions in the camps were horrible. The mix of gambling, alcohol, and prostitutes provided at times by contractors made the camps combustible at night after a twelve- to sixteen-hour workday. The camps were notoriously dangerous, but with Christmas only a week away Thompson was eager to find customers. On December 18 he tied up at contractor Hugh Morgan's levee camp at Arcadia Landing, Mississippi, near Lake Providence, Louisiana.[45]

There was an unwritten rule among shantyboaters never to answer a knock on the door after dark, but business near the camp was brisk, and Thompson threw caution to the wind. About nine o'clock, Lee Manning and John Wilson, Black levee workers, stepped inside. Posing as customers, they looked around at goods for sale and listened to a nickel-in-the-slot phonograph. One of them told Thompson there was a problem with the phonograph. When Thompson bent over to examine it, the partner grabbed Thompson's pistol from his hip pocket, shot him in the back of the head, tied up Mrs. Thompson, and stole money and whatever goods they could carry. When the criminals later returned to get more, they found that Mrs. Thompson had worked herself free. She hovered over her husband, who was seriously wounded but still alive. Manning and Wilson carried his body out and dumped it into the river. Mrs. Thompson pleaded for her life and that of her baby, but they suffered the same fate. The two levee workers beat her and tossed her and her infant into the river to drown. Then they set the boat ablaze and shoved it away from the bank into the river stream. When camp foreman Henry McCarina learned of the crime in the morning, he heard that a couple of workers in the camp had some new clothes, a Winchester rifle, and other items. He kept them under surveillance and notified authorities, who came to the camp and with help from nearby shantyboat travelers overawed the camp and arrested Manning and Wilson, who then confessed to the crime. Mississippi-style punishment was as swift and savage as the murders of the Thompsons. In an era of deepening racism, segregation, and frequent resort to mob justice and lynching, Manning and Wilson were lynched on the spot, their bodies riddled with bullets.[46]

Officials at the national, state, and local levels launched unsuccessful efforts to rid the nation's rivers of shantyboats, which at best were regarded as pests. In 1900, the National Board of Steamship Navigation urged a congressional bill to drive shantyboats off the river by bringing them under its control. Some states tried to eliminate or regulate them by passing licensing requirements, and so did local authorities. Shantyboat settlements attracted plenty of other unwanted attention. Contemporary accounts portrayed inhabitants as lazy, listless wanderers and hog stealers who were devoid of ambition and out of step with the march of modern capitalist progress. "The shanty-boatman proper is half laborer and half marauder," wrote Charles Buxton Going in 1895, "working when he must and stealing when he can. He is by turns an animal of prey, a scavenger, and a serf; partly hated, partly feared, and partly fraternized with by the lower classes along the river, but wholly an outcast to the farmer and townsman."[47]

Reporters poked fun at those who lived in shantyboat settlements and found them revolting and repulsive, yet they grudgingly admired, romanticized, and in some ways envied them. In some cases, reporters portrayed them sympathetically as inevitable casualties of civilization when authorities evicted them. In Burman's novels, shantyboat colonists of "Beaver Slough" were primitive, childlike, lazy, and superstitious characters prone to feuding, lying, and stealing. Moral reformers condemned wayfarers on the waterways for refusing steady industrial employment, but shantyboaters called attention to low wages as a disincentive for factory work. A woman on the Ohio River told Hal Green in the depression of 1907 that her husband "junked" and traded a little and sometimes made cigars in Cincinnati. They even went to Maysville, Kentucky, in hopes of finding work in the cotton mills, but "Lor', they're paying four days wages for six days' work," she complained.[48]

The interracial makeup of levee colonies disturbed newspapers and local authorities. Despite a tightly drawn color line in Memphis, a settlement at the confluence of the Wolf and Mississippi rivers was more flexible in race relations. In 1892, a reporter who visited the settlement observed that "social lines are not very tightly drawn in the village of the houseboats, and the homes of whites and blacks lie mixed indiscriminately, without regard to race, color or previous condition of servitude."[49] Racial miscegenation in waterfront communities often inflamed other residents of towns and cities. In 1893, a newspaper complained about a shantyboat community in Venice, Illinois, opposite St. Louis's north wharf, where Black and white residents dwelled. Denouncing young white women who flaunted the color line in utter disregard of "morals" and the law, the paper complained there were at least three known cases of miscegenation in the colony, where "a productive crop of cur-dogs and children roam at will."[50]

On August 4, 1895, the *New Orleans Times-Picayune* blasted a settlement on the city's *batture*, where approximately one thousand people, both white and Black, inhabited shantyboats between the Delachaise Street landing and the Carrollton line. The inflammatory article followed a tour of the settlement by a staff reporter and Alfred E. Clay, a Methodist minister who founded the New Orleans Waif's Home and headed the local chapter of the Society for the Prevention of Cruelty to Children. The tour's purpose was to highlight alarming conditions on the *batture*, which was regarded as public land under French Louisiana law. When the river was low, many "river rats" planted gardens and built chicken coops and pig pens on land accretions. The riparian settlements drew the attention of reporters, police, health officials, and child rescue officers like Clay, who guided the reporter on the tour, calling attention to degraded conditions, the plight of children, and the immorality and interracial makeup of the settlement's inhabitants. The resulting newspaper article celebrated Clay's record of removing endangered children from the settlements.[51]

In January 1896, six months after the newspaper expressed righteous indignation at the moral conduct and violations of the color line on the *batture*, a vigilante mob shooting and burning of an interracial couple took place. The victims were Pat Morris, a fifty-eight-year-old Irish laborer from Texas, and his Black sixty-eight-year-old wife, Charlotte (Lottie). For eight years, the couple and their eleven-year-old son, Pat Jr., endured threats and attacks by local mobs hell-bent on driving them out. When they first arrived on the *batture*, they lived in a shantyboat on the east side of the river at Southport, Jefferson Parish. Pat trucked cotton on the wharf while Lottie, born enslaved in Mississippi and sold as a child in Texas, sold homemade baked goods and operated a grog shop to feed and quench the thirst of nearby wharf and railroad workers. After a mob tore down their shantyboat and tossed its pieces into the river, the Morris family left Southport in 1891 and moved to the west bank of the river in Jefferson Parish. They joined a Black shantyboat colony on the Company Canal in Westwego, the site of a planned grain elevator construction project. With lumber that Pat gathered, he built a boarding house known in the area as the Catfish Hotel. For more than a year, Lottie managed the boarding house and Pat found steady employment as a construction worker near the grain terminals. After complaints against them by the superintendent of the grain elevator project and a saloon owner with an axe to grind against Lottie's business operations, a mysterious fire destroyed the Catfish Hotel in 1893.

The Morris family moved yet again to another nearby shantyboat, where Lottie rebuilt her business. Pat put the boat on stilts to help protect it from flooding, and Lottie opened a cook shop and sold cakes and sandwiches to construction workers and "luggermen" who fished for oysters on Barataria Bay. Soon she added another houseboat next to theirs that functioned as a dining area with sleeping rooms for two young Black women she hired to sell sandwiches and other baked goods to longshoremen on the wharf. The young women aroused suspicions of immoral conduct, and there were repeated complaints by the grain elevator superintendent that Lottie was illegally running a grog shop. He complained that construction crews were drunk all the time as a result. In a campaign of harassment, local authorities hauled Pat and Lottie into court several times on minor charges of drunkenness, disorderly conduct, trespass, and disturbing the peace. Shortly, Pat and Lottie were beaten by a mob and warned to leave, but they refused. At a time when Jefferson Parish was a hotbed of vigilantism, including lynching, rumors circulated on the wharf that the family was about to get "regulated."[52]

On the night Pat and Lottie were murdered, they hosted a party with music provided by a Black banjo player. Shortly after the party ended around ten o'clock, the family went to bed for the night, but a mob of twenty-five to fifty persons assembled on the other side of the levee. At first, one or two members of the mob set the front of the houseboat ablaze. Pat rushed outside and with difficulty extinguished the fire. He and Lottie, concluding that nothing else would likely be done to them that night, went back inside their boat. When someone in the mob started a second fire, they dashed out of the boat again, but rifle fire greeted them. A bullet pierced the right side of Lottie's neck and dropped her at once, and Pat was shot in the leg as he tried to retreat inside the boat. When the bloodthirsty mob approached the burning houseboat, eleven-year-old Pat Jr. rushed out the back door with his mother's blood stains on a button hole of his coat. He managed to escape, although a couple of bullets whizzed past his knee. He hid for the night under the Company Canal office building. The mob pumped thirty or forty shots wildly into the burning houseboat. When the charred remains of Lottie and Pat were gathered the next morning, Lottie's head was missing. The police chief concluded that someone in the mob grabbed an axe and beheaded her. Another souvenir from yet another lynching![53]

The *Times-Picayune,* despite its obligatory condemnation of the barbarism and firing of shots at the boy as he fled, bent over backward in its initial coverage to blame the victims rather than the perpetrators of the crime. The paper speculated that the mob simply wanted to burn the family out, but things got out of hand. Much of its early coverage highlighted the unsavory reputation of the victims, describing Pat as a hard drinker and Lottie as "a mammoth figure, weighing over 200 pounds . . . one of the most insulting women in the parish."[54] In a remarkably clear statement given to police, Pat Jr. identified Jerome LaFrance, a Jefferson Parish police officer, and John Gassenburger as armed members of the mob. Mass meetings were held in the parish to protest such brutal vigilantism, and a grand jury was impaneled but failed to find evidence for an indictment. A second grand jury indicted LaFrance and Gassenburger for murder and arson, but the cases did not go to trial. LaFrance, a native of Plaquemines with a special reputation for aggressive treatment of Black suspects, remained on the police force until death in 1898 ended his nine-year career. Pat Jr. was taken to Reverend Clay, who placed him in the new Home for Waifs at Beauvoir in Biloxi. In the case of Pat Jr., Clay's concerns for the safety and well-being of *batture* children were misplaced. The real threat came not from his parents or life on the *batture,* but from the systemic racism that fueled a fiendish mob and shielded from punishment the police officer and others who murdered the boy's parents and nearly killed him. After the charred remains of Pat and Lottie were scooped up, put into a box, and given to Lottie's sister, a quiet burial took place on the *batture,* next to where their burned-down houseboat lay in ruins. You might say that Reverend Clay inadvertently rescued another scarred shantyboat child, but the scars came from watching the murder of his parents by a mob that included a law enforcement officer.[55]

Whether seasonal nomads or year-round residents, waterfront communities resented harassment and condescending attitudes expressed toward them by child rescue agents, reporters, and others. Jerome Frank, preparing a 1911 report for the Illinois Board of Charities, asked a woman in Peoria if she thought her shantyboat was a fit place to raise children. "Why, I think it's much better'n livin' on the bluff," she shot back. "I used to live up there, and I tell you I never was satisfied with my house those days. Now I live down here, and I know it ain't so good as them, but I'm jest perfectly satisfied with it.'"[56] Ben Floyd, a junk dealer from Evansville, Indiana, expressed similar feelings in November 1900 when a reporter for the *New Orleans Times-Democrat* sought him out for an interview about the *batture's* shantyboat colonies. From a distance, the houseboats looked like old boxcars to the reporter as he approached the river's bend of the city. New Orleans was home to an estimated five hundred shantyboats with a population of two thousand. The reporter found Floyd, one of the city's more prosperous winter *batture* dwellers, sitting in a rocking chair in the front room of his boat at the foot of Cadiz Street. The four-room houseboat—seventy feet long, fourteen feet wide, and six feet high—was a cut or two above the average shantyboat. When asked about waterways migrants, Floyd replied, "Yes, I can tell you about them. I'm one of them myself. I've got the best boat on the river, and I know all there is about the business. I've been in it now for a long time, and I like it better every year."[57]

Floyd adopted New Orleans as his winter headquarters. He collected iron and scrap metal on the trip south and did not sell the items until he reached the city, where he supplied middlemen who in turn sold the items to local manufacturers. It was important, he noted, for houseboat owners to register their boats and renew each year. Those who didn't, he added, were the worst of the lot: "They are the fellows that stir up the fuss." Floyd defended the reputation of shantyboat people, who often got a bad name because of the criminal activities of a few:

I know the people make a lot of fun of us, but that's because they don't know who we are and how we live. Lots of them think we are all thieves and roustabouts just because some d___ fool now and then raises h___ and gets locked up. The fellows who do that, though, would land in jail no matter where they lived or what they worked at. We're just like everybody else. There are good ones and bad ones. I've been on the river now for ten years, and I believe that, take us as we come, we can size up pretty well with the fellows who live in town.[58]

Floyd acknowledged that many who live near rivers were hostile to shantyboat itinerants. As a junk dealer, he encountered the hostility because of deep-seated racist assumptions about those who sold junk to him. "It's fun to hear some of these fellows on the river growl when we tie up on their land," he mused. "You know, after we're registered, we can tie up anywhere we please except on a city wharf. A good many of the farmers don't like to have the shanty-boats stop at their places. And they have their reason for it, too. They say we trade with the 'niggers' and encourage them to steal iron and junk."

When asked how he gets back north, Floyd, who viewed town folks with "ill-conceived pity if not contempt," replied that he catches a tow from town to town where he stops. "It's a great life," he boasted. "It's the only life for those who've tried it. You can't leave it when you once get into it." Pointing to the evening skyline of New Orleans's tall buildings, he added, "It lifts you away out of and above all that. There ain't that many frills about it, but there's every sort of comfort. I wouldn't change it for a brown stone front in the best city from Evansville to New Orleans, and you wouldn't either, if you'd been at it as long as I have." As the sun set on the interview, a poignant moment captured the reporter's reflections when Floyd's little daughter came up. Floyd put her on his knee and lovingly kissed her. Then the three of them stepped outside on the riverbank and stared at the crimson colors in the western sky as the sun sank low. Taken by the beauty and humanness of the moment, the reporter wrote, "And all of it—beautiful as it was—was reflected in the eyes of a father and his little girl, as they stood last night on the river bank near their house, their home, their very life—the odd-looking little 'shantyboat' at the foot of Cadiz."[59]

2

Wealth Is Not His God

ORIGINS OF ST. LOUIS'S WHARF SETTLEMENTS

I went on this property a number of times, and when I first went there
I found a number of people living in various shanties, some of
them little river boats, and I have time and time again
removed them from the [Mary L.] Tyler property.

—ST. LOUIS ATTORNEY ROBERT COLLINS,
Swearingen v. City of St. Louis, 1900

~~~~~~~~

You couldn't get me to move from here. I like to be by the river
and I'm always happy when I'm near it. I go to sleep in my little flat-boat
on the water and feel as safe as any millionaire in his palace
and a good deal safer when a storm blows up.

—NATE SCOVILLE, *St. Louis Post-Dispatch,* 1894

The St. Louis levee, described in 1907 as "the birthmark" of the city and a "chapter in the history of the middle west," was not a levee in the truest sense. There was no built-up embankment, merely a natural waterfront paved with limestone. For all practical purposes, the levee in 1875 began at Biddle Street and extended south to Choteau Avenue. The busiest, most vibrant section stretched from the recently opened Eads Bridge south to Walnut Street, a half-mile distance, but by 1900 the entire wharf stretched more than nineteen miles, from the mouth of the Missouri River to the mouth of the Meramec at Arnold. In 1879–1880 the wharf received its first granite pavement. Of the city-owned 8.89 miles of the total frontage of 19.15 miles in 1910, only 2.69 miles were improved and available for steamboat landings. The central wharf (1.30 miles) was paved with granite and limestone, and the other 1.39 miles were improved with macadam. At that time, the busiest part

~~~~

stretched from the Eads Bridge south for about a mile and for about one-third of a mile to the north. The city leased much of its unimproved wharf to railroad, lumber, coal, and sand and gravel companies.[1]

Waterfront business wasn't as brisk as in the glory days of steamboats before the Civil War. Steamboats in postbellum America faced stiff competition from railroads, which gained powerful political influence and gobbled up waterfront space without paying wharfage or rental fees to the city. Fewer rafts of timber floated down the river, while railroads unloaded increasing tons of lumber on the levee. Wharfage fees collected by the city plummeted from $5,593.89 in 1894–1895 to $2,446.78 in 1896–1897. The steep drop partly was the result of the depression of 1893, but the role of railroads in the industrial transformation of St. Louis had much to do with it. The full-scale slaying of the pines in Minnesota and Wisconsin also accounted for falling lumber volume on the St. Louis wharf. By 1908, there were only seven raft boats commissioned on the Upper Mississippi and only five sizeable sawmills in operation between Keokuk and St. Paul. Reporting from the northeast Iowa river town of McGregor, the *Des Moines Register* noted that "the pineries are depleted, the thousands of saws that buzzed and screamed in the river towns are hushed, the mills are abandoned, and their doors are barred over, their army of workers scattered."[2]

The levee was not as wildly congested and chaotic in 1875 as it once was. The opening of the Eads Bridge in 1874 relieved some of the congestion, but steamboats still lined up for more than a mile along the central wharf, and crews of roustabouts and stevedores flocked to load and unload cargo and to sign on to work the packets. Edward King's travel account described the levee as a "kind of pandemonium" on both sides of the river:

> An unending procession of wagons, loaded with coal, was always forcing its way from the ferry-boats up the bank to the streets of St. Louis, the tatterdemalion drivers urging on the plunging and kicking mules with frantic shouts. . . . These wagons, in busy days, were constantly surrounded by the incoming droves of stock, wild Texas cattle, that with great leaps and flourish of horns objected to entering the gangways of the ferry, and now and then tossed their tormentors high in the air; and troops of swine, bespattered with mud, and dabbled with blood drawn from them by the thrusts of the enraged horsemen pursuing them. Added to this indescribable tu-

mult were the lumbering wagon-trains laden with iron or copper, wearily making their way to the boats; the loungers about the curbstones singing rude plantation songs, or scuffling boisterously; the nameless ebb-tide of immigration scattered through a host of low and villainous bar-rooms and saloons, whose very entrances seemed suspicious; and the gangs of roustabouts rolling boxes, barrels, hogsheads, and bales, from wagon to wharf, and from wharf to wagon, from morning to night.[3]

For convenience, large wholesale dealers and shipping companies located near the river, but the riverfront derived its cultural look from endless small retail businesses. Cheap shoe shops, secondhand clothing stores with pistols and knives for sale, and pushcart peddlers catered to levee dwellers and steamboat crews. So did crowded waterfront saloons. "Small groggeries are jammed so closely together that the bar-keepers can smell each others' breaths," observed the *St. Louis Republican*.[4] By 1882, when Mark Twain visited St. Louis for the first time in more than twenty years, the levee bore notable signs of declining river traffic. "Half a dozen sound-asleep steamboats where I used to see a solid mile of wide-awake ones," he wrote. "This was melancholy, this was woeful."[5] To be clear, groggeries still lined the riverfront, as Twain happily noted, but they attracted far fewer patrons than in the heyday of steamboats. The wharves were lonesome and empty by comparison, the atmosphere less frenetic. Twain conceded that St. Louis was "a great and prosperous and advancing city," but he lamented that "the river-edge of it seems dead past resurrection."[6]

Shantyboat settlements swelled with the rapid rise of industrial St. Louis. Dating back to the late 1860s and even earlier, transient flatboat dwellers were scattered loosely on the waterfront, but their numbers grew as hard times uprooted many of the Mississippi valley's down-and-out. The economic depressions of 1873, 1882, and 1893 (the Long Depression) added to homelessness and the size of settlements. For many of the uprooted, the waterfront offered a cheaper, far preferable option than the city's squalid, overcrowded tenements, rear-alley sheds, and shanties a few blocks away. A devastating report on housing conditions by the St. Louis Civic League exposed the state of rat-infested tenement housing operated by slumlords in overcrowded neighborhoods near the wharf. In a sad commentary on the unsanitary conditions of outdoor compartments and yard toilets shared by multiple families in the neighborhoods, the report pointed out that saloon owners with modern toilets estimated that one-third of their revenues came from men off the street who used the toilet and felt obligated to buy a beer in return.[7]

The north wharf (now the Near North Riverfront), home to the city's largest shantyboat settlement, was a patchwork of confusion when it came to sorting out ownership rights, squatters' rights, and jurisdictional matters. More than ten miles of the city's waterfront were privately owned. To illustrate the confusion, ownership of river frontage from the northern boundary of St. Louis to the central wharf alternated between private hands and the city in a broken manner. The city owned about three hundred feet at the foot of Bremen, part of which it leased to companies, but adjoining the strip on the south was a privately owned section that stretched nearly to Dock Street. The city's frontage then resumed near Dock and ran south for about two miles to Mound Street. Of that two-mile section, the levee between Branch and Chambers streets was paved. At the foot of Tyler Street, the Wiggins Ferry Company leased frontage from the city that included a sand landing, two inclines, and a hoist. Tracks belonging to the Terminal Railroad of St. Louis ran from Tyler to Mound Street. Private ownership then resumed from Mound to Mullanphy, where the Laclede Gas Light Company owned a coal landing. The alternating pattern of ownership continued in similar fashion from Mullanphy south to Biddle Street, where the central wharf began.[8]

By the early 1880s, St. Louis officials, owners of riverfront real estate, and companies that leased wharf space from the city grew annoyed by the settlements. A few squatters paid token ground rent to the harbor and wharf commissioner, but many refused. City officials sought to make greater use of the wharf for commercial purposes, but squatters often stood in the way. Eviction efforts by lawyers who represented the city or wealthy landowners had little lasting effect. To complicate matters, ownership rights to large parts of the north wharf were in dispute, especially where land accretions resulted from changes in the river channel. Riparian rights were often at the heart of three-cornered riverfront conflicts between the city, squatters, and wealthy property holders. City officers, invoking "adverse use and occupancy," pressed lawsuits for the quieting of title to disputed, neglected lots. In 1882, Harbor and Wharf Commissioner Charles Pfeifer made clear what was at stake: "The unsettled condition of the city's title to a great portion of the north wharf is interfering materially with the collection of revenue."[9]

On December 4, 1883, Harbor and Wharf Commissioner John Alt gave the Board of Improvements a list of squatters who refused to pay the nominal rent charged them by the city. He emphasized that for charitable reasons he and the previous commissioner let them remain on the levee because they were poor and homeless, but due to their unsavory character, the squatters were now a nuisance and impediment to waterfront businessmen. Several months later, Alt ordered fifteen longtime squatters to vacate the north wharf area at LaBeaume and Chambers streets. A company that leased nearby wharf space had asked them to move, but when they refused, the company had turned to the harbor and wharf commissioner for help.[10]

In November 1885 there were four flatboats, a shanty, and a tent occupied by squatters in a nearby settlement between LaBeaume and the foot of Tyler Street. In the crude shanty lived a Black family whose men were steamboat roustabouts. A shantyboat near the water's edge housed a Black family who collected and sold driftwood and raised chickens. Two other flatboats were the dwellings of white families whose men were steamboat deckhands. A Danish boat builder resided in the remaining flatboat, and in the tent lived Elizabeth Decker, a white woman, and her sixteen-year-old son. Her six-by-eight-foot wall tent was pitched east of a lumberyard, a few yards from the Wabash tracks. In the tent were a bed, trunk, table and two chairs, and other small items. A few boards laid loosely across timbers provided a floor. In poor health for years and deserted by her husband in East St. Louis, she lived off the small earnings of her son. Her daughter and Black husband lived on Eleventh Street. When Decker died at age forty-three in November 1885, black crape hung over the tent to mourn her death for a day and a half while her body lay inside the tent for viewing on a board supported by two chairs. Neighbors grieved, and occasionally a train sounded a horn or stopped briefly while a brakeman ran over to pay his respects before she was buried in Potter's Field.[11]

The boat builder in the settlement was Christian Anderson, a Danish immigrant. His flatboat, built with sturdy lumber and coated with thick tar, featured an eight-by-ten-foot sleeping room and a twelve-by-ten-foot dining room, part of which doubled as a kitchen and workshop. The exterior was painted white, and inside were modest furnishings, including a rusty wood stove, bed, and carpenter's bench. Anderson built small boats that cost between $6 and $10. On the north waterfront for fifteen years, he lived on a city-owned strip leased to the Wiggins Ferry Company but paid rent only now and then. Anderson's residence and boat-building business suited his lifestyle. When he accumulated a sizeable overstock, he built a sailboat, sold his flatboat home, and headed to New Orleans with a string of boats in tow to sell on the way. In New Orleans, he sold his sailboat and returned to St. Louis on a train. He then built a new houseboat on the north wharf and started the cycle over again. On occasions, more expensive houseboats docked in the neighborhood. Some were seventy-five feet long with three or four rooms. In 1884, a married couple lived there in *The Baby Mine* before moving to another waterfront settlement north of Harrison [Branch] Street. *The Baby Mine* featured carpeted rooms and a piano, which the woman played on Sunday afternoons to entertain squatters. An engineer for the N. O. Nelson Manufacturing Company once lived near Anderson in a boat that cost $700. "All my neighbors are respectable and behave themselves," Anderson emphasized. "We do not let any disreputable people in among us." If someone did slip in there who invited trouble, he let the police know to chase him out. He was aware that some squatter settlements had a rough reputation. "I hear they are sometimes noisy and troublesome at Harrison Street, where the railroad boys get the run of some of the houses," he told a reporter, "but I am happy to see that we are all law-abiding and do not attract outside attention."[12]

In the mid-1880s, wealthy property owner Mary L. Tyler, who had moved to Kentucky, hired St. Louis attorney Robert E. Collins to take care of legal matters related to a few pieces of her long-held real estate on the north wharf. One of the strips in city block number 2544, which appeared on plats for the first time in 1874–1875, extended from Buchanan Street on the north to Dock Street on the south, and was bounded on the east by the west wharf line. Lots on the irregular, triangular block number 2544 were much deeper from east to west near Buchanan than farther south toward Dock Street. When Collins inspected Tyler's wharf lots, he found that Christian F. Liebke had put enclosures on a section of her unattended property. Liebke stored piles of rafted logs on the strip for use in his nearby lumber mill. The mill, on land he leased from the heirs of George Buchanan, ran from Second Street to the river at the foot of Angelrodt

Street. After Tyler died in Louisville in December 1891, Collins brought a suit against Liebke on behalf of her estate.[13]

Among matters Collins was employed to take care of was the occupation of the property by squatters. "I went on this property a number of times," he later recalled, "and when I first went there I found a number of people living in various shanties, some of them little river boats, and I have time and time again removed them from the Tyler property." For eight years or more, he tried but failed to clear the property of squatters. As he explained, "The people that I would remove sometimes would move right back, and if they did not move back others would come in their place."[14] John G. Joyce, a civil engineer and surveyor who often passed by Tyler's wharf lots in the course of his work, made a sketch of the area, illustrating that between the east line of city block number 2544 and the river lay nothing but sand, bushes, willow trees, and squatters who named their community "Oklahoma."[15]

On April 9, 1891, the city of St. Louis seized a strip of land claimed by Martha J. Swearingen, whose wharf lots adjoined Tyler's on the south about fifty or sixty feet north of Dock Street. The city utilized Missouri's adverse possession law on grounds "that for more than ten years the property had been in the adverse use and occupancy" of Swearingen. Less than two weeks later, the harbor and wharf commissioner leased to Justin E. Joy part of the unimproved wharf at the foot of Dock Street for use as a lumberyard. In 1894, Swearingen, too, hired attorney Collins to remove squatters from her wharf property as she prepared to sue the city, Justin E. Joy, and the St. Louis, Keokuk & Northwestern Railway, which the city granted an easement on her property. Charles T. Farrar, a realtor and manager of Swearingen's property, recalled that squatters in houseboats and shanties were on her wharf property when he first looked after it in 1875. From time to time he ordered them off the property, which grew considerably from accretions caused by St. Louis's system of dikes designed to straighten out the riverfront. In Swearingen's suit in the city's circuit court on April 16, 1895, she claimed riparian rights to a strip about 150 feet wide and 1,500 feet long. She sought damages of $5,000 plus $100 per month for city rents collected from Joy. The circuit court awarded her a ninety-foot strip, part of what she claimed, but the Missouri Supreme Court threw out the award on appeal. Swearingen took the case to the US Supreme Court, which in 1901 ruled in favor of the city.[16]

Efforts against squatters on the north waterfront led to continued frustration. When M. J. Murphy took over as harbor and wharf commissioner in 1887, he was determined to crack down. One of his first official acts was to remove squatters near Brooklyn Street, an area they had occupied for several years, but the crackdown accomplished little. By 1894 more than one hundred families inhabited houseboats, shanties, and tents in "Little Oklahoma," which stretched south from the Knapp-Stout company's lumberyard at the foot of Bremen to Dock Street.[17] Some of the homes were comfortably furnished, while others were ramshackle huts. "There are some unique dwellings in this river-bank settlement," observed a reporter in 1901, "and the people seem to have vied with each other to see who would build the most grotesque place for his habitat."[18] Discarded streetcars found a home in the settlement by the late 1890s. Frank Leach built hulls around his Easton Avenue streetcar to float south with his family in the annual fall migration. "Beyond doubt," a bewildered reporter observed, "their houseboat will architecturally stand alone."[19]

The largest concentration of squatters was just below where the McKinley Bridge opened in 1910 to connect automobile traffic between north St. Louis and Venice. Some of the houseboats had a look of permanence about them. A "fish for sale" sign marked Bill Meyer's houseboat, one of the nicer ones. Meyer, a fisherman, tied up his boat at the foot of Angelrodt Street in 1884, found the fishing good, and decided to stay. Nate Scoville, a boat builder, soon moored his houseboat nearby. Many others joined the colony's "assortment of quaint things and quainter people." Meyer was among those who made notable decorative improvements to his houseboat, including carpets and window shades. Vines that ran from flower beds to the roof partly shielded it from the sun's rays.[20]

When a *Post-Dispatch* writer visited Little Oklahoma in April 1894, he met a cross section of its inhabitants from Mallinckrodt to Dock Street. Bertie and Rose Mosenthein and their brother Gus Steimel were among them. The writer noted that Rose could out-row most of the men in a skiff race on the river. Most of the colony's men were fishermen, but a painter, carpenter, fiddler, willow basket maker, sand elevator boss, and a floating saloon and grocery store proprietor, Louis H. Seibt, were among its residents. So was Harry Hanley, who owned a plumbing shop at Eleventh and Angelrodt streets but operated two trading boats. On profitable river trips at certain times of the year, he traded goods and provisions to trappers in exchange for furs. The inhabitants shared waterfront space with countless dogs, a rooster, and a ring-tailed monkey kept in a cage on a brightly decorated flatboat that once was a photography studio. Nelson Vaughn, the boat's owner, converted it into a circus boat but failed to make the business a success. He let go of all his animals except the monkey. "Pete," a fighting cock, chased children around the settlement, pecking at their bare feet. In a shack that was part tent, part hut built of boards, sheet iron, canvas, and rags lived Frank and Mattie Eden. When Frank saw the reporter taking notes, he mistakenly thought he was a census taker and spelled his surname in exaggerated fashion to make sure that he got it right. It was Eden, not Eaton, he insisted, rather irritated. Neighbors jokingly dubbed the Eden place the "Garden of Eden."[21]

As Herman Schwartz found out, the settlement frowned on disruptive behavior. Schwartz, who lived in a flatboat with his family, came home drunk one stormy night the previous winter and playfully fired shots at a poor family's boat. When neighbors discovered the source of the noise, they cut Schwartz's boat loose. He and his family found themselves afloat, tossed about on a storm-roiled river, until they landed on the Illinois side near Venice. Angry, Schwartz spent the winter sulking in a squatter colony in East St. Louis, but returned to Little Oklahoma in the spring. "A man who is crooked may live in Oklahoma," noted the *Post-Dispatch*, "but he's got to keep his crookedness mighty quiet."[22]

Due to seasonal migrations, Little Oklahoma's population thinned in late fall and winter but floated higher in spring and summer. Its boundaries were not sharply defined. They shifted on account of floods, waterfront development, and repeated evictions by city authorities. The eastern boundary was the river, and the northern edge was near the foot of Mallinckrodt Street. The settlement stretched south to Destrehan, Angelrodt, Buchanan, and Dock streets, and its western edge was bounded "by the finest collection of dumps in the Mississippi Valley."[23] Nate Scoville expressed a sentiment that was widely shared by fellow residents: "You couldn't get me to move from here. I like to be by the river and I'm always happy when I'm near it. I go to sleep in my little flat-boat on the water and feel as safe as any millionaire in his palace and a good deal safer when a storm blows up."[24]

Nor were Little Oklahoma's racial boundaries clearly defined. In a popular referendum in 1916, St. Louis passed a residential segregation ordinance that was declared unconstitutional the following year. Racial covenants soon followed. Although segregated housing clusters existed informally in north water-front settlements as well as other parts of the city, the lines of demarcation on the riverfront were not absolute. Even de facto segregation among occupants of houseboats and crude shanties often meant little in terms of daily interactions. As a favorite swimming spot, Little Oklahoma attracted boys from the city's rough streets and alleys. No matter how many times police chased them out, or how many whippings their parents gave them, poor Black teenage boys and their white counterparts swam naked together in the river, wallowed in the mud, and engaged in summer horseplay in the settlement.[25]

Little Oklahoma, the largest, most resilient squatter settlement on the river-front, was one of many such communities that dotted both sides of the Mississippi. In the mid-1870s and 1880s, shantyboat settlements formed in coves and inlets in south St. Louis, too. The date is unknown, but Louis Smith reportedly founded "Squatters' Town," or "Squatterville," around 1875. Floodwaters and high winds unceremoniously dumped him and his keelboat under the high bank of a bluff near the St. Louis Arsenal. After floodwaters rapidly receded, Smith awoke in the morning to find his boat stuck in mud far from the river's edge. Rather than endure the expense of moving his boat to the water, he opted to stay put. He sank down roots right where he washed up, near the soon-to-be shipping office of the fast-growing Anheuser-Busch Brewing Company. The brewery, which soon asserted ownership rights to the land on which Squatters' Town was located, filled in part of the flats in an effort to limit the colony's growth, and tried with limited success to impose rents. Many squatters who lived north of the arsenal agreed to pay, but the brewery faced opposition from those whose houseboats and shanties were in the southern parts of the settlement. A few paid, but most disputed Anheuser-Busch's claim of ownership. They insisted that the city owned the land. The next squatters were John Meyers, the "nabob" of Squatters' Town, and his wife. Meyers built a houseboat south of Smith's, and his father moved his boat next door. Other flatboats washed up from time to time in floodwaters, and the owners decided to stay. The Meyers hosted social gatherings and parties attended by at least thirty people. On account of damaged eyesight, John drew a monthly government pension and owned a boat estimated to be worth $250. Despite thick, troublesome swarms of mosquitoes, Squatters' Town seemed an attractive option for many. Its location under the bluff provided a measure of seclusion and protection against blasts of wintry air. At times, city residents fed up with predatory landlords and slum housing sought refuge in the settlement. As a boat builder put it, "You ain't bothered with landlords comin' around every month."[26]

The settlement reached as far north as Anna Street, but in the next decade city authorities ousted squatters north of Dorcas Street. From Dorcas south to Meramec Street, a distance of about a mile and a half, the riverbank was privately owned. Squatters' Town, one of two settlements on this section of the levee, was located mainly between Dorcas and Cherokee Street. In the mid-1880s, thieves and river pirates built nests there and drew police attention, but the shantyboat community for the most part was tranquil. There were no saloons or churches. Parents sent their children to nearby schools. Christenings, balls, weddings, and other gala events in the settlement reinforced a sense of community. A reporter who visited the colony in late fall 1887 noted that, except for complaints about mosquitoes, residents were happy with their homes. "Life without screens is a continual misery in summertime," the reporter observed, "and most of the people would rather do without houses than screens."[27] Like the Meyers family, most residents lived in Squatters' Town for a number of years. None expressed dissatisfaction with their living conditions. When the reporter asked "Old Man" Anthony Witt if he feared malaria on account of the swarms of river mosquitoes, the latter shrugged and motioned toward the city, "Yes, we gits malaria sometimes, but then they has malaria up there too."[28]

Fishing and collecting driftwood were the main occupations in Squatters' Town at the time. Nearby bakers bought cheap firewood from residents who collected it. Fishermen sold their catfish, buffalo, and river crappie to Soulard market vendors. Some of the men worked in the Busch brewery or other manufacturing establishments, and a few boat builders called Squatters' Town their home. The elderly did what they could to eke out a living and help each other. Witt furnished wood to Mrs. Layman, a widow, and did other chores for her on a routine basis. On occasions, fishermen pulled "floaters" from the river and received $5 from the coroner. On May 30, 1882, aged Joseph Roy and his wife were fishing in their skiff and spotted an object, put a rope around it, and towed it to shore. It turned out to be the badly swollen corpse of Zoe Watkins, whose mysterious disappearance nearly two weeks earlier had captured national headlines.[29]

Among the residents when a reporter toured Squatters' Town in 1892 were two women who were showboat actors and a Mexican resident known only as

Carlos to his neighbors. He and his wife performed balloon ascensions on the river. Will and Sam Kane were itinerant smokestack painters whose dangerous trade took them from St. Louis to New Orleans in their boat each year. The job required fastening an iron hook to the top of a smokestack and lowering themselves down as they painted. When not plying their skills on the river, they lived in Squatters' Town. Other skilled tradesmen occupied houseboats in the settlement. William Menard, a fisherman with a disability, knitted hammocks for sale. G. T. Moore, whose houseboat was a general store of considerable value, was "one of the oldest 'rats' on the great Western waterways." He sold a wide range of goods from grindstones to coffins and knew "every inch of the Mississippi from St. Paul to New Orleans, and has no mean idea of the Ohio and several of its tributaries." Residents were suspicious of newcomers until they proved their trustworthiness. They kept them under surveillance and ostracized undesirables. If ostracism was not enough, they ran them out of the settlement, one way or another. Other than the presence of three or four pet dogs per family that sometimes created problems between residents, there was considerable internal harmony. In reference to the typical resident of Squatters' Town, the reporter noted the absence of social distinctions and called attention to the lack of constant, competitive striving to accumulate more and more material possessions in the colony: "Wealth is not his god, and success not the ambition of his life."[30]

Below Squatters' Town lay another sizeable waterfront settlement of houseboats and shanties in a secluded area that enjoyed relative freedom from the sounds of the city. It was a bit difficult to access from anywhere except the river. Deep limestone quarries provided a barrier between the settlement and the heights of Broadway two blocks away. "It is easy to get lost on the way," noted a reporter. "Only one street leads directly to it from Broadway, and unless the visitor finds this street at first, he may wander for hours in a maze of quarries and brickyards, finding every approach to the river blocked by sheer precipices which drop down into quarries."[31] The rough boundaries of "Chickentown," established in the mid-1870s, extended from the foot of Marine Avenue on the north to Cahokia, Osage, Gasconade, and Meramec on the south, near Carondolet. Most of its residents lived between Marine and Cahokia streets. Jimmy McGinley, "a boxer of merit," owned a saloon in Chickentown, which featured cock fights on Saturday nights and Sundays.[32]

The leader of the settlement in the 1890s was "Big John" Lohrum, the proprietor of nearby limestone quarries where many of the settlement's men were employed. He was well connected as a city contractor and political appointee in the administration of Democratic mayor Edward A. Noonan, 1889–1893. Upon assuming office, Noonan appointed Lohrum as street commissioner, but the city council rejected the appointment. In 1891, the council approved Lohrum's appointment as the new superintendent of the nearby city Workhouse. Upon the patronage appointment, a *Post-Dispatch* reporter observed that he "can now work his quarry, which adjoins the Work-house, to suit his pleasure."[33] As proprietor of the quarries that lined the river from the Workhouse to Cahokia Street, Lohrum acquired a "neat fortune." A distance separated his "pretentious" two-story home in the southwest corner of Osage Street from Chickentown's houseboats and hastily built shanties. His property included a large barn where he stabled teams of horses and wagons for his quarrying operations. The nearby Workhouse used one of his quarries to secure a supply of crushed limestone for city streets. The guards, often drunk and corrupt, supervised the labor of prisoners at the hellhole. Police court justices banished prisoners to the Workhouse who were public nuisances, petty thieves, loafers, and perpetrators of other minor offenses. In some cases, judges simply did not know what else to do with vagrants, homeless individuals, and those addicted to alcohol and drugs. Hard quarry labor in ball and chains was the punishment for those without money to pay fines. Suicides, attempted suicides, and attempted escapes by inmates were common in the Workhouse, known for its brutal regimentation and lack of efforts toward rehabilitation. Housing conditions for male prisoners in the Workhouse were especially bad. In 1897, City Health Commissioner Max Starkloff condemned the overcrowded, vermin-infested institution's male quarters as "an outrage on civilization."[34]

Little changed to improve conditions. In 1898, nearly a dozen outraged Chickentown residents, who typically shied away from publicity, disputed the official version of a prisoner escape from the quarry. On July 21, James Clark, a rather feeble sixty-year-old prisoner wearing a ball and chain on his feet, escaped through the southeast gate of the quarry undetected by guards. The attempted escape ended in Clark's death after a guard fired a shotgun blast at him as he stood in waist-deep water at the river's edge. In a rush to print without adequate time to investigate, the *Post-Dispatch* at first portrayed Clark's death as a suicide, claiming he fled the Workhouse to drown himself in the Mississippi. According to this early version, Clark was driven by despair over his one-year sentence to work off a $100 fine imposed by Judge Thomas H. Peabody in the First District Police Court. Without friends on the outside or any hope of release, Clark chose suicide. The newspaper noted that many prisoners in the past tried to obtain knives or ate poison to end their life of physical and mental torment in the dreaded chambers of the medieval Workhouse.[35]

Upon further investigation, the *Post-Dispatch* called attention to suspicious circumstances surrounding the case. A reporter caught officials in the coroner's office and Workhouse in a web of contradictory accounts of the circumstances that led to Clark's death. By the time the reporter concluded his investigation, he questioned whether the decayed, decomposed body turned over to the city morgue by Workhouse officials was Clark's. The investigation took him first to the Workhouse, and then to Chickentown, the city morgue, and the coroner's office. As the reporter neared the Workhouse quarry to survey the scene from above where Clark's death occurred, Leopold Matt, the guard who fired the shotgun blast at Clark, ran him off. Matt insisted that nobody was allowed to observe prisoners at work. When the reporter dropped down along the river to talk to potential witnesses in Chickentown, he found a dozen steaming residents eager to tell their version of what happened. They rejected the coroner's ruling that drowning was the cause of death. The mate on a nearby government snag boat who also saw what happened confirmed the version by Chickentown's residents. The following details of the case emerged from their interviews with the reporter.

When Clark, hobbling along with ball and chain, reached the river, he turned north past a row of shantyboats. Adolph Betzhold, the teenage son of a Chickentown resident who was on friendly terms with Workhouse guards, spotted Clark and ran up the hill to summon them. Matt and two other guards took a shortcut down the bluff on a set of steps hidden in the weeds, and quickly closed the distance between them and Clark. Exhausted and fearful of a load of buckshot, Clark passed by the shantyboat of Annie Buechlein, who was outside at the time. Gasping for breath, he asked her where he might hide. Well-familiar with the unsavory reputation of the trigger-happy guards, she pointed ahead, urging Clark to hide behind a shed belonging to the Rencking Quarry Company. In hot pursuit, the guards showed up at Buechlein's shantyboat and caught a glimpse of Clark, who then walked into the water beneath where the quarry jutted out. The guard known in Chickentown as "Loophole Matt" because of his hot temper and quick trigger stepped onto a ledge overlooking Clark in the water below. From a distance of about twenty-five feet, Matt without warning fired at Clark, who immediately dropped under water and never came back up. As soon as Matt fired, he hollered, "I intended to shoot over his head." As far as Chickentown eyewitnesses were concerned, it was a case of cold-blooded murder. There was no possible way for Clark to escape as he stood waist-high in the river with ball and chain. The unnecessary shooting was the result of anger and poor judgment on Matt's part.

Shortly after Clark dropped under water, Nicholas Karr, the superintendent of the Workhouse, hurried down to Chickentown. Gathering as many residents as he could, Karr threatened evictions if they told newspapers or other officials what happened. So indignant were the eyewitnesses that they couldn't wait to tell the *Post-Dispatch* reporter what they witnessed. Guards at the Workhouse, they told him, were routinely drunk on duty. After gathering eyewitness accounts, the reporter went to the Workhouse to speak to Matt and Superintendent Karr about the incident, but was told that neither was available. On July 23, the investigation took the reporter to the city morgue and coroner's office, where Workhouse officials earlier that morning brought in a badly swollen, decomposed "floater" they claimed was Clark. No one else identified the body, but the coroner's office accepted it as Clark's and issued a speedy ruling that he died by accidental drowning. When the reporter viewed the corpse, he noted how discolored and disfigured the head was. Skeptical that a body in the water less than thirty-six hours would decompose so badly, he suspected it was the body of a much younger, more vigorous man. Another feature of the body he found troubling was that only one leg had a shackle attached to it. The other anklet was tied around the body's waist with a piece of cloth. Its rivet was missing. According to the Workhouse, Clark somehow knocked the shackle off his left leg and tied it to his waist so it wouldn't impede his escape. When last seen by Chickentown eyewitnesses at the point Matt fired at Clark, though, both of Clark's legs were shackled.

At the request of Workhouse officials, the coroner's office conducted a superficial examination of the body for bullet holes. Upon finding no evidence of bullet holes, the office issued its finding that the cause of death was drowning. When asked why a thorough autopsy was not performed, Deputy Coroner Henry Lloyd claimed he ordered Dr. Louis Wolfert, the official postmortem surgeon, to look for bullet holes. At first he insisted that he did not think it necessary to do a full autopsy because he hadn't seen the body yet and was unaware of its badly decomposed state. When he did find out, he directed Deputy Coroner Theodore Gast to instruct Wolfert to conduct an autopsy. Gast told the reporter that he called the morgue superintendent, Frederick A. Mack, to relay instructions for an autopsy to Wolfert. Mack claimed he complied, but Wolfert, when questioned, said the case was already closed. Upon that bit of information from Wolfert, the reporter dashed back to the coroner's office and again asked Gast what his specific instructions were. Once again, Gast made clear that he gave explicit instructions for Wolfert to perform an autopsy. "I suppose that he is doing that now," Gast added.

By going back and forth between the morgue and the coroner's office and talking to officials separately, the reporter caught them in a contradiction but kept quiet about it in their office. A few minutes later, with the reporter still there, Wolfert walked into the office and, when asked by Gast, confirmed he did not perform an autopsy. Wolfert turned to the reporter and joked that he was getting him into trouble. Then Wolfert insisted this was the first time anyone asked him to conduct an autopsy. Later, he changed his story, admitting that Mack gave him instructions but urged him to speak to Gast first. In Wolfert's view, the matter was a mere misunderstanding, but he offered no explanation as to why he closed the case and filed his report without an autopsy.

While the reporter was in the office, a phone call came from Superintendent Karr, who spoke to Mack. The reporter listened as Mack assured Karr that Clark's body did not have a single scratch on it. Mack instructed Karr to send someone to pick up the shackles as quickly as possible. Before the call ended, Mack repeated the same instructions. The reporter wondered why Mack seemed so eager for the Workhouse to pick up the shackles. In a final reflection upon the contradictions and questions raised by his probe, the reporter shared with the public his underlying suspicions: "Floaters are abundant in the vicinity of the Work-house." Two days later, Deputy Coroner Lloyd conducted an inquest on the floater identified by guards as the body of Clark. Without a jury and with precious few witnesses, Lloyd confirmed that Clark's death was the result of accidental drowning. In the end, the eyewitness accounts by Chicken-town residents meant nothing. The ruling stood without further investigation.[36]

When Chickentown first formed, residents in jest chose a mayor, but the tradition became an established serious practice. Each year, squatters chose a mayor to represent the interests and governance of the settlement. In 1905, the *Post-Dispatch* lampooned a number of the city's "Little Mayors," among them Louis Christmann, of Chickentown. "More carefree than all the 'little mayors' put together," Christmann was the voice of the settlement for eight years. The newspaper pointed out that despite the fluctuating population due to seasonal river migrations, "All acknowledge his rule while their boats are tied near his home on the river bank."[37]

On the Illinois side of the river, the construction of dikes in the nineteenth century to straighten the shoreline from Venice to East St. Louis led to land ac-cretions. These large accretions ("made land") drew shantyboats. At the time that Edward Stites moored his boat at Vaughn's Dike in East St. Louis in 1881, the riverbank was about a half-mile farther inland. When the river changed course over time, it left his houseboat on dry land. He hoisted the boat up on stilts and in the back opened a blacksmith shop on the property. The land ac-cretions did not fill in everywhere, leaving sloughs and marshy areas along the shoreline opposite St. Louis. Other flatboat dwellers joined Stites at Vaughn's Dike, including several Black workers employed at the cotton compress works in East St. Louis. Some were in desperate straits. Ben McCary, suffering from tuberculosis and lacking food and medicine, died in a leaky flatboat where he and his wife lived in 1884. She fished to provide their food, and did not ask neighbors for help. Finally, she called attention to her husband's plight, but by the time a doctor arrived it was too late.[38]

When Mary Schultz, a flatboat pauper at Vaughn's Dike, died in 1888, un-dertakers and county officials quarreled over what to do with her body while it decomposed on her boat. To save expenditures, the St. Clair County board of supervisors had passed a recent resolution requiring that all paupers' coffins be purchased from a coffin maker in Belleville. When Schultz's coffin arrived, the East St. Louis undertakers Benner and Kurrus refused to retrieve her body from the flatboat, prepare it for burial, and haul it to the cemetery. Angered that the board gave business to an out-of-town firm, the local undertakers insisted that the Belleville coffin maker would have to send someone with a wagon to retrieve the body and oversee burial. Questioned by a reporter about the shameful situation, Board Supervisor N. C. Boughan acknowledged in exasperation that it was disgraceful to allow a body to decompose, but he blamed Benner and Kurrus, who held firm in their refusal to retrieve the corpse. "Of course it is an outrage to let the body lie there without even having been washed," Boughan said, "but what I can I do?"[39]

Squatters clustered along a ten-mile stretch of Illinois waterfront from the village of Brooklyn south to East St. Louis, including the badly polluted Carr Slough just above Venice in Madison County. In 1900, about seventy-five residents lived in twenty-five houseboats near the Merchants' Bridge. Sometimes also referred to as "Oklahoma," its counterpart on the Missouri side, the settlement's numbers fluctuated. At times there were as many as fifty houseboats. East St. Louis riverfront squatters often drifted back and forth between the St. Louis Consolidated Elevator Company's grain elevator and the Pittsburg dump. "Shantytown" and "The Sand Bar" were among the clusters, but the largest settlement was between the grain elevator and the Eads Bridge. The little bay area, which consisted of about four hundred acres, was known as "Sandy Hook," or simply "the hook."[40] In summer, Sandy Hook held as many as fifty houseboats. Pete Bramlin tied up on the island as early as 1870. Charles Beiser, who operated a popular fish market, located there in 1893–1894. Like many others, he and his wife raised their children in the settlement. Some of the residents built workshops and sheds, raised chickens, and cultivated gardens on their plots. Most fished for a living, but numerous artisans and boat builders inhabited the settlement. A slough separated Sandy Hook from the Illinois mainland. Most of the time, the only access was by boat or by wading through marshy swampland. Many of the island's residents headed south in late fall. When a reporter visited the settlement in late October 1895, he found only half-burned stumps from bonfires they enjoyed shortly before floating to winter locations. Each spring, "It was an occasion of rejoicing and merrymaking as the shanty boats, singly, or in twos and threes, and ever and anon in such numbers as to form a little flotilla, came back to Sandy Hook."[41]

Area newspapers put a critical spotlight on squatter colonies. In the public's mind, violence, crime, and the river poor went hand in hand, but violent as well as petty crimes committed by or against waterfront dwellers were reflective of a broader pattern of violence in industrial America. For sure, the levee had plenty of violence and crime, but so did the rest of the city. When pressed by a reporter in 1907, the St. Louis police department acknowledged that the average rate of crime in levee settlements was no higher than in many parts of the city. To put violence into a broader perspective, the forced removal, harassment, and destruction of shantyboats and private possessions by police or waterfront gangs who did the bidding of police during evictions were acts of state-sanctioned violence. When millionaire developers and railroads and their detectives forced squatters off tiny strips of land on the levee that had been their home for fifteen years, it was an act of violence. In many cases, lawless, corrupt police officers harassed shantyboaters and roustabouts on the water's edge. For roustabouts, the whippings, beatings, and cussing they suffered on steamboat packets were part of a violent system of racial labor discipline akin to slavery. Violence was built into the everyday work routine aboard steamboats, as it had been for many roustabouts when they were enslaved. For the river poor who lacked money to pay fines in police court for vagrancy, peace disturbances, and other minor infractions, the brutality of the St. Louis Workhouse awaited. In short, violence was woven into the social fabric of American life. You might say it was the mudsill of the political process.[42]

Newspapers sensationalized crimes by shantyboat dwellers and roustabouts, but this is not to suggest that crime did not plague the river poor. In a waterfront colony at the foot of Potomac Street occurred one of the most vicious crimes in the history of St. Louis at Christmas 1894. The mysterious, shocking double murder rocked settlements on the south wharf. The first discovered victim was twenty-six-year-old Lizzie Leahy, of Alton. A neighbor found her on the bed of her shantyboat in a pool of blood with the back of her skull bashed in. Remarkably, Leahy lived for nearly a month afterward. Missing at the time was thirty-year-old Thomas George Morton, the stage name of the man with whom she lived in the boat. He became the chief suspect when police could not locate him for questioning. Morton, whose real name was Gilroy, was an entertainer from Newport, Kentucky, who once formed his own small traveling troupe in the Ohio River valley. An acrobat, singer, and dancer, he performed in Cincinnati concert halls and variety shows in the mid-1880s before leaving Newport with four other performers in a horse and wagon with theatrical scenery and props. He intended to perform in small towns, but by the time he reached St. Louis nearly broke, he divested himself of the show and props. He met Leahy, an actress who traveled in a patent medicine show. Her father was an Alton musician. Leahy took Morton to meet her parents and told them they planned to marry as soon as she could get a divorce from her husband, from whom she was separated. Around the first of November, Morton and Leahy tied up their boat at the foot of Potomac Street in St. Louis. Despite meager resources, they planned a new life together on the river.[43]

At the hospital, Leahy drifted in and out of consciousness, but when questioned during an interval of lucidity, she refused to identify her assailant. Police suspected Morton, but she denied that he attacked her. On December 29, officer Thomas Whalen, assigned to watch the houseboat in case the suspect returned, noticed that Morton's small black-and-tan terrier kept running back and forth from the houseboat to a spot about 150 feet away. A group of men nearby chased the dog away, but when they left he trotted right back to the spot, sniffing and scratching at the ground. Detectives, noticing that the soil at the spot was a bit loose, picked up shovels and began digging. Soon they found Morton's corpse in a shallow pit on the river's edge. The little terrier crouched by the corpse and howled.[44]

Police arrested Noble Shepard, an oily-tongued twenty-nine-year-old unemployed glassblower who lived in a tent near the victims' houseboat. Earlier, the couple had hired him to fix their houseboat's leaky roof. When police took Shepard to the city morgue to identify Morton, he remained cold and detached under questioning. At last he confessed but gave four slippery, contradictory confessions revised to fit the moment. In a web of lies, he claimed to have killed Morton in self-defense with a shovel after Morton threw a brick at him that hit Leahy instead. According to Shepard, Morton fired a pistol at him upon discovering that he and Leahy were intimately involved. Leahy, in a sworn statement taken by officers at the hospital, denied that she and Shepard were intimate or that she was drunk. A coroner's jury concluded that Shepard used a hammer and hatchet to kill Morton, whose pockets were turned inside out when his body was found. When Gilroy's distraught mother arrived from Kentucky to claim his body and effects, she mentioned to police that he carried with him a gold watch worth $125 and a family keepsake gold ring. The chief of police showed her a watch recovered by a detective from a pawn shop, which she identified as her son's.[45]

Shepard showed no remorse or sympathy for his victims. He mockingly wrote a song describing how he killed Morton, and he shared the verses jokingly with the chief of police and detectives. In late November 1895, a jury convicted Shepard of first-degree murder of both victims, but he never paid for his crimes. With an execution looming and an appeal to the state supreme court pending, he cut through a metal plate in his cell wall, crawled through a rat-infested sewer, and escaped jail on June 22, 1896. Despite tips, reported sightings, and a reward offered by the governor, Shepard remained on the lam for the rest of his life. On October 2, 1924, Governor Arthur M. Hyde received the first of two letters purportedly from Shepard, who offered to turn himself in if the governor promised not to hang him. When Hyde refused, he received a second letter in which Shepard declined to surrender.[46]

For waterfront communities under the watchful eyes of authorities, the murders and sensationalized gossip about levee love triangles, shantyboat hopping, and drinking invited further scrutiny as the settlements swelled. According to an estimate, at least a thousand shantyboat squatters lived inside the city limits of St. Louis in 1900. In the name of civic improvement and growth, waterfront industrial development, and public morality, authorities waged a steady campaign against them. As St. Louis and East St. Louis were transformed from river towns to industrial cities, squatters wedged on the shoreline wherever they could. Poverty, homelessness, and economic depression drove many of them there, but for others the river offered a practical working-class lifestyle they cherished in what was fast becoming a crowded, industrial urban society.[47]

3

The Roughest Life There Is

ROUSTABOUTS ON THE LEVEE

The life of a roustabout is the life of a dog.
—GEORGE ARNOLD, WPA interview, 1936

∼∼∼

I am actually ashamed of some of the things that I have actually done
in the way of working people beyond humanity,
that is the only way you could put it.
—J. HARVEY COOMER, interview, 1958

The St. Louis levee provided a major supply of roustabouts and other cheap labor to steamboat packets on the Mississippi River and its tributaries. The figure of the Black roustabout was the most enduring cultural symbol of the levee. From minstrel shows to magazines, newspapers, and literary writings, white American audiences couldn't get enough of the sentimentalized steamboat character. Romanticized images laden with racist nostalgia soaked popular culture between the Civil War and the Great Depression. For white steamboat passengers, "carefree," "jolly" roustabouts were entertaining figures who sang and danced for coins pitched by cabin passengers from the second deck. For steamboat officers, on the other hand, roustabouts, many of them formerly enslaved, were also beasts of burden and objects to be clubbed, cussed, demeaned, feared, and degraded. In many ways, the transition from slavery to freedom for roustabouts was a matter of "same mule, new rider."[1]

Steamboats resembled antebellum plantations in hierarchal structure and matters of labor discipline. High atop the enclosed Texas deck were staterooms and cabins for officers on one end and the modest quarters of Black chambermaids, cabin stewards, and their assistants on the other. Perched high in often

∼∼∼

plush quarters, armed, and well-schooled in the rough-and-tumble world of the waterways, a steamboat captain was lord and master of all he surveyed on the river and all whose labor he commanded on the decks below. He hired pilots and, in consultation with the clerk, managed the finances of the boat, which he often owned or partly owned. For nautical reasons, he showed deference only to the pilot, whom Twain described as "an absolute monarch who was absolute in truth and not by a fiction of words."[2] Captains entrusted labor discipline and efficiency on the main deck to white steamboat mates, who functioned as overseers of roustabouts and deckhands in much the way plantation overseers supervised labor of the enslaved. Mates also worked under the authority of pilots, and so did engineers. The latter oversaw Black firemen, who fed wood and shoveled coal into the engine room's boiler. Black captains of the watch, chosen by mates and resented by roustabouts, played a role similar to that of enslaved "drivers" under the plantation regime. Mates and watch captains coerced labor via whippings, verbal abuse, and beatings with clubs and iron bars. In some cases they got away with murder. "There is a saying on the river," observed steamboat captain Frederick Way Jr. in the early 1930s, "that a mate has to kill a nigger to get a reputation."[3]

The river resurrected dark images as an artery of enslavement and brutal exploitation for many; but for others, life as a roustabout on steamboat packets after 1865 presented new opportunities. Many roustabouts were freedmen formerly owned by or leased to steamboat captains for back-breaking labor on the big cotton boats. In spite of harsh working conditions akin to slavery on the packets, the river to many represented a more promising option than southern plantation agriculture. Such was the case of Moses "Old Mose" Phelps, who worked the New Orleans–St. Louis packet. At the time of his death at age one hundred on December 3, 1895, he was a blind beggar whose home was a tent in a shantyboat settlement near today's Mary Meachum Freedom Crossing on St. Louis's Near North riverfront. Peter Corn, a roustabout born into slavery around 1851 in Ste. Genevieve County, moved to St. Louis after doing farm labor and working in an iron factory near Potosi. In St. Louis, he shipped out as a steamboat roustabout. "Den I 'run de river' three straight years from St. Louis to Cairo and Memphis, and Baton Rouge, and New Orleans," he told a WPA interviewer in 1936. "I den quit de down trade and rested up and made de northern trip from St. Louis to St. Paul."[4]

In the antebellum heyday of steamboats, packets relied on German and particularly Irish immigrants to load and unload freight and passengers, but the postbellum trend was toward the use of Black crews. By 1900, the number of roustabouts shrank considerably, but an estimated four hundred still used St. Louis as their home base. The overwhelming majority were Black. When Black roustabouts in 1887 replaced a crew of ten whites who stormed aboard the Mississippi Valley Transportation Company's *Oakland* and clubbed and threw the mate William McDaniels overboard, the boat pulled away from the wharf afterward with a Black crew for the first time in the history of the St. Louis and New Orleans barge line. In 1880, there were 2,330 steamboat roustabouts in Missouri. It was not uncommon at the time for Black and white roustabouts and deckhands to work side by side, especially on smaller boats. White deckhands stored cargo in the hold of the boat or on deck under the supervision of a mate after roustabouts carried the freight aboard. Deckhands performed many tasks, including keeping the deck clean and using a weighted rope to take water depth soundings for the pilot. The bottom deck where low-fare passengers shared space with deck crews, livestock, and other freight required at least daily cleaning. In 1878, the *Post-Dispatch* oversimplified the racial dynamics of the relationship, but noted that white deckhands were "frequently found working shoulder to shoulder with their dusky companions with never the thought of the color line disturbing their minds."[5]

The demand for steamboat labor also drew a robust supply of stevedores, as well as deckhands, engineers, firemen, cooks, and cabin crews in St. Louis. Stevedores, often represented by labor contractors, unloaded and loaded cargo when steamers arrived and departed. Unlike roustabouts, they did not travel on the packets. Stevedores averaged about $1.75 per day in the 1880s. On big cotton boats of the Lower Mississippi, they made from $45 to $60 a month in the busy winter season. Most crews were predominantly Black and settled with families and homes in the city. A former roustabout and leader of a St. Louis crew of stevedores complained that roustabouts spent their hard-earned money on shooting craps and carousing. They blew their money so fast, he observed, that sometimes they were broke and forced to sign up for another boat the morning after they got paid. "Dey ain't no good," he exclaimed. "Dey's tough, I tell you, and when dey's in town dey libs around dem dives up dere on de levee and on Clabber Alley and Spruce street."[6]

The work of roustabouts required them to live near the wharf. A few with families lived in shantyboat settlements on the river's edge or in nearby waterfront neighborhoods, but the unmarried typically lodged in cramped, squalid dens or rooms above waterfront saloons for about 10 cents a night. Cold fried fish, pickled pigs' feet, bologna sausage and cheese, cast-iron skillet cakes specked with flies, and the floor or a chair with an old army blanket were often all they got for their money in Black entertainment taverns in the "Bloody Third" police district. "These groggeries are quite often hotels in a small way," the *St. Louis Republican* observed in 1875. "That is to say, the men sleep in the chairs and on the floor. The roustabout is well fixed who has a whole chair to himself, and a lucky dog is the one who gets a snug corner without a fight."[7] To ply steamboat workers away from saloons, the Bethel Mission at the foot of Olive Street, supported by steamboat companies and charitable donations, offered a full meal plus lodging for 20 cents in 1882. Segregated floors for sleeping held 120 beds for Black lodgers and 120 for white lodgers. The dining room was integrated. Although the restaurant soon closed for lack of business, the lodging continued for a number of years. Designed at first to benefit steamboat workers, the mission later catered to poor people in general.[8]

By the time roustabouts returned to St. Louis after a packet run, they were more than ready to cut loose in waterfront taverns. In 1882 there were eight thriving saloons on the block between Morgan and Chestnut streets, featuring pool rooms, gambling, dancing, and musical entertainment as well as lodging. With a nickel beer came snack foods at the bar. The district, which included Clabber Alley, Wildcat Chute, and other sections of Black nightlife entertainment near the levee, was notorious for its brothels, raucous and rowdy saloons, gambling dens, and violent nightlife. According to William Hoban, captain of the *Lora*, roustabouts upon returning from a packet often spent the first night in jail for drunkenness or passed out on the levee. "Night in the levee district was the wildest proposition I ever want to see," he recalled.[9]

To squelch vice, vagrants, and gambling, police routinely harassed roustabouts in saloons and poolrooms. Officers made "pop-calls" to catch the sleep-deprived nodding off in chairs. If both eyes of a seated patron were closed, he was a vagrant, subject to arrest and a fine. If a startled patron tried to run, police threw their nightstick at his feet to trip him up, sometimes causing injury. For penniless roustabouts, a fine imposed by a police court judge meant a sentence to the dreaded Workhouse for ball-and-chain quarry work. In W. C. Handy's autobiography, he recalled police harassment of a pool room where he hung out in 1892 while stranded and homeless in the city's waterfront district. "'Foot-working' was the usual criterion," he wrote. "Either your feet had to be swinging or moving, or your eyes had to be open when the policeman entered the room. Otherwise you were a bum." On one occasion, Handy was fast asleep when an officer popped in, but "some odd, subconscious instinct made my feet move at the approach of the dreaded steps." Handy, whose brother later faced similar harassment in St. Louis, told how a one-eyed patron fooled officers on pop-calls. "Most of the down-and-outers had a way of pulling their hats over their eyes so as not to attract attention to their eyes," Handy explained. "This one-eyed fellow, however, covered only his left eye. His right eye, which happened to be glass, he left exposed; and since it remained wide open when he slept, he was always safe from suspicion."[10]

Harassment and racial profiling of roustabouts by police took many forms. After a string of robberies in 1907, an anonymous informer tipped off authorities that for each of the past few nights two Black men from the levee went downtown and returned flush with money to the levee. The police chief ordered detainment of every roustabout aboard the *Peters Lee,* which was fully loaded and ready to pull out for Memphis. Taken to the holding pen at the Four Courts were sixty roustabouts. Captains J. F. Flanagan and D. M. Connors, superintendent and general agent for the Lee Line of steamers, were upset by the loss of their labor force. In response to complaints about the financial cost of the delay, the chief of police told them that if they could identify arrested roustabouts who made the upriver trip on the packet, he would release them. As a result, only six or eight roustabouts were released. The *Peters Lee* pulled out with a skeleton crew five hours behind schedule.[11]

In the 1870s and 1880s, roustabouts typically worked in tattered, low-quarter brogan shoes run-down at the heel, cotton pants rolled up at the bottom, a striped flannel shirt in cold weather or a cotton checked shirt in summer, and a beat-up hat. When dressed for a night of revelry in saloons, they preferred butternut peg-top trousers, widely flared at the hips and tight in the legs. They chewed tobacco, smoked blackened corncob pipes, and walked with a distinctive swagger in boots with three-inch pointed heels. A razor in the boot backed up the swagger. Many roustabouts bore visible scars from cuts, a broken or chewed-on nose, ear-pulling, and eye-gouging brawls. They generally lacked undergarments, bedding, or a cover to protect themselves from the cold. They had few earthly possessions, but often among them were a razor and a pair of dice. A writer on a steamboat from St. Louis to St. Paul described them as young and slender "animated scarecrows," "thinly clad in the weirdest and most picturesque lot of old clothes I ever saw."[12] Tom Gardener, a St. Louis police officer, admired their strength, endurance, and toughness. "They must be to live as they do," he said. "They go to work without a bite of food, work half a day up to the hips in water and let the clothes dry on them during the other half, sleep on a skid pile during the night, or, with the soft side of the levee cobblestones for a mattress and a tarpaulin for a canopy, they rest after a day's work."[13]

Steamboat owners took a cut of profits from saloon concessions that sold alcohol and tobacco on the packets. Bartenders extended credit to roustabouts, who did not get paid until packet's end. Roustabouts drew their pay at the guard window of the steamboat's bar after the clerk deducted debts for tobacco and liquor. A round-trip packet from St. Louis to New Orleans took from twenty-two to twenty-five days in 1887. Between paying their bar bill and gambling debts, roustabouts were hard-pressed at times to have any money at all when they walked down the gangplank at the end of a long run. Those who were broke might end up sleeping on a pile of sacks or rope on the docked boat, or in warm weather they might sleep under the stars on the levee. In cold weather, they scrambled to find free shelter on the levee for the night. Ben Lawson, who became a roustabout near Paducah, reflected on the notorious gambling that took place on the packets: "I got me a job and worked as a roustabout on a boat where I learned to gamble wid dice. I fought and gambled all up and down de Mississippi River, and in de course of time I had 'bout $3,000, but I lost it."[14]

A symbiotic relationship existed between roustabouts and saloon owners. Saloons were a vital part of working-class culture. They were a place to swap river stories and to discuss politics, wages and working conditions, and abusive mates to avoid on the boats. In some cases, owners provided check-cashing services, bailed roustabouts out of jail, and let them drink and board on credit, especially in winter and slack times on the river. At times, they served as intermediaries between Republican political clubs and Black voters. A few saloon owners functioned as labor contractors who bargained for higher wages on behalf of roustabouts, in part so they could repay their saloon debts.[15]

After roustabouts ran out of money, they looked to ship out on another packet. When a steamer bell clanged seven times on the St. Louis wharf—five short taps and two longs—it signaled that the mate was ready to hire a crew for the captain. Robert Zang, a St. Louis-born deckhand, mate, and pilot, recalled how prearranged signals aided him as a first mate in the 1920s when it came to hiring roustabouts. "We always had these head negroes who knew the men wanting jobs," he explained. "The men'd be lined up maybe forty or fifty of them out there and we'd pick out which ones we wanted. . . . We'd walk along and if there was one the head negro wanted, he'd scratch the back of his head—and that was good, see. And if he pulled his ear, why that'd mean he was passable but not too good."[16] If a "rooster" hoping to join a crew carried with him a spoon, it meant he was experienced, and his chances of getting hired increased. Although food served by Black cooks on packets generally met with approval by deck crews, eating conditions were primitive. Cooks did not distribute eating utensils when they ladled food onto roustabouts' tin plates. Of seventeen steamboats investigated by Surgeon Walter Wyman, of the US Marine Hospital Service in 1882, only seven provided a messroom where deck crews could eat. Commonly known only by nicknames, roustabouts in St. Louis averaged about $25 a month in the mid-1870s. By 1910, they made about $65 a month. They bargained over wages at the point of hiring on the wharf. If they objected to terms set forth by the mates, they made a counteroffer that was relayed to the steamboat captain, who either accepted it or looked for another crew at his price. Depending on the pay, quality of food, and mate's reputation, roustabouts signed on or refused in hopes of finding a better deal on the next boat that docked.[17]

Burman considered roustabouts "as vital a part of a steamboat as the engines or the paddle wheel." Once the boat cleared port, roustabouts were divided into two watches, one for the starboard and the other for the port side. When work was light, they worked six hours on and then enjoyed six hours off. Meals were served four times a day. One watch ate while the other remained on duty. In times of light work, roustabouts on their six hours off had leisure time to fill, but in times of loading and unloading heavy freight piles, they were expected to work as long as it required, even if it took twenty-four hours or longer. No matter how many hours they worked without sleep, roustabouts might be called on to swing out the gangplank for a load of freight. Or to perform a task that put their life in jeopardy. So broken and interrupted was their sleep, Burman wrote, "that when a roustabout I knew died, his black friends assured me the reason given by the doctors was that he was five years behind in his sleep."[18]

Fitful sleep for roustabouts often came between landings, which in some cases occurred at fifteen- to thirty-minute intervals. A report in 1873 noted that on cotton boats it was not uncommon for roustabouts to work thirty-six hours or longer without sleep, stopping only to eat. In warm weather, roustabouts slept on bales of cotton, coils of rope, sacks of wheat, an occasional hammock, or wherever they could sprawl out on the lower deck. In winter, they slept near the boiler for warmth in small rooms crowded with stacked bunks. On boats that didn't provide bunks, they crawled into spaces near the boiler to avoid freezing. Thirteen of seventeen Ohio River steamboats examined by Dr. Wyman in 1882 did not provide bunks. He explained what the absence of bunks in cold weather meant for roustabouts: "Forced to find some place where they will not freeze, the crew crawl on their hands and knees into the narrow space of three and a half feet between the boilers and the deck, and there lie and bake. It is either freeze or bake, and they prefer the latter. At first, they perspire freely, but soon the heat becomes so great that perspiration is checked; they become stupefied, or 'dizzy and crazy-like,' and when called upon for duty come out dry and parched, scarcely able for some moments to go about their work."[19]

At some of the farm and plantation landings on the river, especially in the South, roustabouts had to climb steep embankments with heavy loads. When the river was low, the steep banks were even more imposing and dangerous. In some cases, the sixty-foot gangplank didn't even reach the top of the embankment, and there was no graded roadway to the landing. The riverbank often caved in during heavy rains. For roustabouts trying to load a stubborn cow, ill-tempered Arkansas razorback, or other heavy cargo down a soft, steep, slippery embankment during heavy rains and storms, the dangers and difficulties multiplied tenfold. Captain Volney "Stogie" White, who in the 1920s and 1930s worked for the Cincinnati Greene Line Steamers, acknowledged the incredible endurance of roustabouts. On the Kanawha, a tributary of the Ohio, they sometimes shoveled coal from barges onto Greene Line steamers near Ironton, Ashland, and Huntington, West Virginia. Captain White remembered that "they [roustabouts] would be up twenty-four hours without a minutes sleep.

Working and singing all the time."[20] Roustabouts with legendary strength were celebrated and enshrined in river lore by steamboat captains. In 1952, Captain William L. "Steamboat Bill" Heckman Jr., of Hermann, Missouri, recalled "Calhoun," one of the strongest and most admired on the St. Louis levee. When roustabouts unloaded sacks of wheat for storage at the city's grain elevators, they were paid an extra penny per sack to carry the wheat all the way into the elevators. Some sacks weighed as much as 175 pounds, but Calhoun carried a sack on each shoulder while fellow roustabouts in awe struggled to carry a single sack per trip.[21]

Patterns of harsh, authoritarian abuse of roustabouts by white steamboat mates and captains grew out of slavery and deep racism that underlay the codification of segregation in the 1890s. More broadly, they were reflective of prevailing class-based attitudes toward labor, especially on the Lower Mississippi. Mates, known for creative profanity, cracked a whip, clubbed, and cussed roustabouts routinely. "There is many an amateur in the world who flatters himself that he knows how to swear," the *St. Louis Republican* exclaimed in 1875, "but he would hide his head in shame after hearing a steamboat mate let himself out on a gang of roustabouts."[22] Cecil Roberts, an English vagabond writer in search of work and adventure in the United States, was employed briefly as a "sailor man," an extra on the Diamond Jo Line's *Libby Conger* packet between Dubuque and St. Louis. He quickly learned the pecking order, explaining that mates had no choice but to cuss, threaten, and beat roustabouts if they hoped to get any work out of them. He characterized most roustabouts as "the very scum of the country."[23]

Roberts's justification of the abuse of roustabouts reflected popular views held by steamboat officers and the American public. Newspapers promoted dehumanizing images of roustabouts that legitimized their abuse. According to an old river axiom at the time, "You can't make a rouster work unless you club him." Singling out roustabouts in cities like St. Louis and Cincinnati, in particular, the *Paducah Daily News* in 1893 used animalistic imagery to describe those on the bottom of a packet's totem pole as among the nation's worst of all "depraved scoundrels," filled with "beastly desires" and "animal like pleasures." "Some of them are so low on the scale of humanity as to resemble, both in habit and appearence [sic], animals rather than humans," continued the newspaper. "Intolerably filthy, many of them never wash unless by accident they fall over-

~~~~

board, and only change their clothes when the old ones drop off from sheer rot. Living like dogs, acting like dogs, their existence is a miserable one."[24]

A beating was the penalty for hiding aboard ship to avoid work, a practice known among roustabouts as "rattin'." "Sometimes we have to beat 'em and sometimes they are revengeful, but not as a rule," a mate told a St. Louis reporter in 1887. "Generally they are good-natured and take a cursing or a beating without a whimper." Roustabouts most feared getting thrown off a boat somewhere along the river. "That breaks their hearts," the mate remarked, "and they'll beg for a whippin' rather than that. Usually after a clubbin' they are all right and work like slaves."[25] In June 1914, the captain of the Streckfus sternwheeler *Sidney* smashed a beer bottle against the side of a roustabout's face and threw him off the boat at a landing north of St. Louis on the first night of a packet bound for St. Paul. The injured roustabout set out to find a police officer, but the captain, described by a writer on the boat as a "brutal Hibernian . . . whose qualifications consisted in the power to inspire terror in all, from the first mate down," quickly pulled away from the waterfront to avoid questioning.[26]

Wyman, of the Marine Hospital Service, described life for deck crews on steamboats in 1882 as "the roughest life there is."[27] He singled out the harsh conditions, health hazards, and abuse of roustabouts. A mate interviewed by Wyman complained that he was cited in court for knocking out a roustabout with a stanchion, insisting he had a perfect right to do so. Appalled, Wyman pointed to a case in which Second Mate James Fountain murdered Gabe Morgan, a roustabout on the Cincinnati–New Orleans packet *Charles Morgan* as Morgan was lifting a coal box on May 2, 1881. Angered that Morgan didn't pick up the coal box quickly enough, Fountain drew a pistol and shot him as the boat prepared to pull away from the Louisville wharf. As other roustabouts watched in horror, Fountain threatened to kill others, but intervention by Captain Albert Stein's son prevented additional murders. Morgan was carried off the boat and taken to the Marine Hospital, where he died three weeks later. When police officers came aboard to investigate, Albert Stein gave the command to pull out while his son, Captain Harry Stein, intercepted them to prevent Fountain's arrest. The officers had to jump quickly off the boat as it pulled away. After months on the lam, Fountain was apprehended, convicted, and sentenced to seven years in the penitentiary, but the governor of Kentucky pardoned him for the cold-blooded murder. Soon, Fountain was employed again as a second mate on an Ohio River packet.[28]

Some steamboat companies deducted money from wages to support the Marine Hospital, where roustabouts could receive care, but the injured or sick at times had to fend for themselves if their condition threatened to delay a packet or add to its expenses if a Marine Hospital wasn't nearby. On June 6, 1895, an employee of the St. Louis Elevator Company's Elevator B at the foot of Choteau Avenue called the city dispensary to report a Black male writhing in pain on the levee. An ambulance found William Morgan, a roustabout on the St. Louis & Tennessee River Packet Company's *City of Savannah*. A large sack of grain had fallen on him while he was loading freight, badly injuring a leg. When First Mate Andrew Goudy saw that Morgan was unable to work, he ordered him off the boat, claiming he didn't have time to take him to the dispensary. The steamer pulled out and left Morgan lying there.[29]

Writer Willis Gibson in 1903 disputed that roustabouts were exploited and ill-treated. In his view, they were men of leisure, aristocrats of sorts who lolled about the levee with the power to get mates fired and to pick and choose when they worked. According to him, roustabouts worked only one boat a month and laid off the rest of the time. At a time when the average monthly pay was $40, they pressed their advantage by holding out for $60, maybe even $90 in the fall when there was increased steamboat traffic and high demand on cotton boats of the Lower Mississippi. Gibson did admit that roustabouts worked day and night aboard the steamers, "a sort of work no white man could stand." They constituted "a powerful machine, answering to the slightest inclination of the mate's will," but he insisted that mates had to watch them carefully lest they slough off and pose a dangerous threat. "The least sign of flinching in a mate is not only fatal to discipline, but to his safety," Gibson argued, "for the roustabout is by nature quarrelsome and revengeful, a brooder over fancied wrongs."[30]

Among the "fancied wrongs" was a white mate's murder of a Black roustabout witnessed by Jennie Arnold, daughter of Wesleyan Methodist missionaries on the Mississippi, while her family's gospel steamer was docked near Memphis. The *Rosa Lee*, which operated in the cotton trade between 1887 and 1892, docked below them as roustabouts swung the gangplank to shore. As they loaded and unloaded cargo, a box of damaged oranges burst open and was set aside. One by one, the roustabouts, most of them white, grabbed an orange to eat as they passed by the box, but when a Black roustabout helped himself to an orange, the mate picked up a hatchet and without warning struck him on the temple, killing him on the spot. As Arnold wrote, "The captain ordered his men to dig a grave on the shore among the trees. Others picked up the dead man, and, dropping him in, shoveled the dirt upon him and left, the whole proceedings occupying perhaps ten minutes. Mamma and some of us girls went and prayed over his lonely grave—the body still warm."[31] Jennie's sister, Julia A. Shelhamer, remembered that they and their mother found boards and placed them at the foot and top of the grave after the *Rosa Lee* pulled away. Their sister, Helen, painted an inscription on a board. "The moaning winds sung the requiem over his lonely grave," Julia mourned, "while the dashing waves of the Mississippi kept time to the tune."[32]

The relationship between roustabouts and mates was strained at best. In 1904, Captain William Hoban, of the *Lora*, recalled his experiences as a second mate before he became a captain. His brutally frank recollections captured the prevailing racist and classist attitudes toward roustabouts and matters of labor discipline:

> The only way to get a nigger to work was to use a hickory club, and I guess I've been arrested a thousand times right here in St. Louis for beating them, either out on the trip or here at the levee. . . . You've seen the roustabouts go on a trot over the gangplank with their hundred and fifty pounds. Well, the hickory's what did it. . . . A mate runs his risk though, and I've been slashed at and shot at, and had clubs and bricks used on me by niggers, but was just lucky in not getting killed.[33]

Admiralty statutes offered roustabouts a legal recourse to sue abusive steamboat officers for damages and unpaid wages. Aggrieved roustabouts did press suits to assert their rights, and courts sometimes awarded favorable judgments to them. In 1885 an admiralty court determined that steamboat officers were legally responsible for beating and clubbing a roustabout, but the practice continued. Claimants often were at a disadvantage because it was hard to get other roustabouts to court for testimony. The judgment sometimes came down to the word of a Black roustabout versus the word of a white mate or captain. To avoid prosecution under the statutes, some mates behind the scenes delegated beatings to a favored white deckhand. Steamboat owners resented federal meddling in labor and race relations, complaining that authorities encouraged frivolous lawsuits over trivial incidents and phony vengeful accusations. They argued that roustabouts were in such a low, degraded state that beatings and whippings were necessary to compel them to work. With few exceptions, this underlying premise went unchallenged by judicial authorities, particularly in southern courts. The doctrine of assumed risk ("blame the victim") prevailed in American courtrooms when it came to job injuries at the time. If you worked on a steamboat, you knew the dangers when you signed on. Therefore, you assumed the legal risk. No matter how dangerous the conditions, your employer was not at fault. You and your family were not entitled to legal compensation in the event of injury or death.[34]

Even when roustabouts and deckhands successfully sued steamboat companies, the appellate courts, typically conservative and probusiness, often overturned judgments awarded by local juries. A jury in Judge Daniel Dillon's St. Louis Circuit Court on March 27, 1890, awarded $2,000 in damages to James Edward Jones, a Black roustabout, for injuries he sustained while loading coal on the St. Louis, Naples & Peoria Packet Company's steamer *Calhoun*, and for subsequent kickings and beatings at the hands of the second mate on May 22, 1888. The second mate had set up two temporary fifteen-inch planks parallel to each other about three or four feet above the boiler's large coal bin to facilitate dumping coal into the bin. The planks rested on three end-to-end coal boxes on one side and the steamboat deck on the other. Jones called the mate's attention to a defect in the plank on the deck end. Only about seven inches of the broken-off plank rested on the support. The mate cussed Jones and ordered him onto the plank, insisting it was safe. To carry a full coal box, which held approximately four bushels and had a handle on each side, required a team of two men. When Jones started onto the plank with a fellow roustabout on the other handle of a full coal box, the defective plank gave way. Jones tumbled headlong into the bin as the coal crashed down on him. The load of falling coal mangled his left hand so badly that it later required amputation of his middle finger. For several days afterward on the packet, whenever the captain and first mate were off watch, the second mate took revenge on Jones, whose hand was still bleeding and whose arm was in a sling. He ordered Jones to pick up and carry sacks of wheat. When Jones didn't do it to his satisfaction, the mate cussed, kicked, and clubbed him on the back and ribs, mocking his injuries.

The suit requested $10,000, but a juror who meticulously calculated the damages pushed for an award of $17,000. After deliberations, jurors trimmed the figure to $2,000—$1,500 for the finger and $500 for the abusive treatment meted out by the mate afterward. The *Post-Dispatch*, which pointed out the reluctance of most roustabouts to sue steamboat companies, concluded that the ruling would set a precedent. On January 27, 1891, however, the St. Louis Court of Appeals overturned the circuit court's judgment and ordered a new trial. By then, nearly three years had passed. In the meantime, Jones endured much pain and suffering, including the loss of his finger and livelihood. It's possible that he and the packet reached a settlement, but more likely he abandoned his pursuit of justice in the courts.[35]

Steamboat packets were fraught with dangers that threatened the safety of all those aboard, but roustabouts were in a particularly vulnerable position. They were put into precarious loading and unloading situations, often at night without adequate lighting or sleep. US Steamboat Inspection Service reports were spotty or misleading when it came to roustabout drowning cases on the packets. In many instances, there was no inquest, investigation, or even mention of death. In 1882, surgeon Wyman urged a more aggressive role for the Steamboat Inspection Service to guard against abuses, but was skeptical that the federal government would offer meaningful protection to lowly roustabouts. He took it on himself to investigate two drowning cases on the same steamer on the same night near Hanging Rock, Ohio. His findings suggested the links between dangerous working conditions, reckless mates, and drowning deaths. Green Osborne, of Glasgow, Missouri, was the first Black roustabout to lose his life that night. Later, a second drowning occurred. Upon interviewing three eyewitnesses aboard the steamer, Wyman learned that the second victim was a son [John] of Malinda and Isaac Woodson, secretary of the colored Mason's lodge in Hannibal and former Civil War sergeant in the 56th US Colored Infantry. Both drowning victims were in their early twenties.[36]

At the time of Osborne's drowning, the crew was loading pig iron from a coal barge that lay between the steamer and shore. Two planks, three feet apart and about eighteen inches wide, were stretched between the boats. Roustabouts walked onto the barge via one of the planks and returned to the steamer on the other, carrying pig iron. The deck of the steamer was higher than that of the coal barge. The twisting and swaying of the barge made loading extra difficult and dangerous, especially in the context of fatigue and a mate who yelled at the crew to run, not walk, with the pig iron onto the steamer. Osborne missed the plank and fell into the water between the boats. Other roustabouts were afraid to stop working and try to rescue Osborne. As an eyewitness told Wyman, "The mate walked up and looked over the guard and said, 'Well, pick up your iron and get out of the way; the man's drowned now; needn't be standing around.'"[37]

The mate had a terrible reputation among experienced roustabouts in St. Louis, who refused to work a boat that employed him. Later that night, the steamer was towing upriver a barge loaded with coal. The crew was loading coal from the barge while they were underway on a pitch-dark night. Handheld lanterns, one at the front of the boat near the gangplank and another at the head of the barge near the coal pile, provided the only light as they worked, two men to a coal box. The light didn't extend to the outer side of the barge or the back side of the coal pile. A roustabout who was working behind Woodson described what happened: "The mate caught hold of him and told him, 'Hurry along, ___ ___ you'; and so he was hurrying along where he couldn't see, and went too far, and just walked off the side of the barge. . . . No, sir; neither of these men had been drinking anything. The boat slowed up a little and stopped her headway, but didn't back, and nothing was thrown overboard."[38]

The relationship between mates and roustabouts often was at the heart of dissension and conflict on the packets. Tennessee-born Henry Scott, a longtime St. Louis roustabout, acknowledged there were abusive mates but downplayed their overall prevalence. "The mates are generally good to us," he insisted. "They hustle us up, but we're used to that. Once in awhile, there is a mean mate on one of the boats, but the boys never go out with him if they can help it."[39] In a 1936 WPA interview, George Arnold had a far more critical memory of the working conditions and abuse of Black roustabouts. Born into slavery on April 7, 1861, in Bedford County, Tennessee, he reflected on his experiences as a roustabout in the 1870s. He first shipped out on a sternwheeler packet on the Ohio and Cumberland rivers between Nashville and Evansville, Indiana. Later, he went to Cairo and worked for three more years as a roustabout on the *El Dorado*, a St. Louis and Cairo packet to Cincinnati. "The roustabout is no better than the mate who rules him," Arnold recalled. "If the mate is kindly disposed the roust-about has an easy enough life. The negroes had only a few years of freedom and resented cruelty. If the mate became too mean, a regular fight would follow and perhaps several roustabouts would be hurt before it would be finished." In Arnold's assessment, "The life of a roustabout is the life of a dog. I do not recall any unkindness of slavery days. I was too young to realize what it was all about, but it never could have equalled [sic] the cruelty shown the laborer on the river boats by cruel mates and overseers."[40]

Mates commanded men to work harder and efficiently. From each crew of roustabouts, a mate picked a Black captain of the watch to help organize and supervise their work. It was up to mates to ensure that loaded freight was evenly distributed to facilitate the smooth running of the steamboat. They had to detect strains from an unbalanced load that might threaten the structural integrity of the boat's hull in shallow waters. If roustabouts tried to hide from work aboard ship, it was the mate's responsibility to root them out, no matter the danger: "If the roustabouts hid in the excelsior pile beneath the main deck (stored there for plugging leaks in the hull), it was the mate's responsibility to crawl in there and force the men out, sometimes at the risk of a knife slash or bullet wound."[41]

Roustabouts faced countless hardships as they toiled in all kinds of bad weather. They often got wet and muddy, and sores covered their bodies when the packet took them through areas of heavy mosquito infestations. An over-loaded steamboat in low water might spell extra trouble if cold weather set in while they were stranded. A number of roustabouts were badly frostbitten when their stranded boat ran out of fuel and provisions on the Red River in 1873. To make matters worse, several had smallpox. In December 1886, Isaac Preston, Charles Deal, Bill Nevlin, Ed Tripp, William Parnel, Julius Hall, James Handley, and Charles Johnson, roustabouts on the *Mattie Bell* on the Illinois River in Pearl, suffered frozen feet, ears, and hands. Unable to hobble without great pain, they were sent by train back to St. Louis. The legs of four of the men required amputation.[42]

Patience wore thin on packets, especially those that lasted two or three weeks. The hierarchical workplace was highly masculine and often violent. Tempers flared from mosquitoes and mates' constant cussing, pushing, prod-ding, and pouring out racist epithets. Quarrels in tight quarters under trying conditions sometimes were settled with knives, fists, razor blades, or revolvers. On the *India Givens* packet from St. Louis to Hamburg, Illinois, a mate and roustabout drowned after the latter knocked the former overboard and jumped into the river to continue the fight. On August 8, 1892, a quarrel between Tom Connors, a white deckhand, and Black roustabout John Sneed on the *Arkansas City* in Helena ended on the riverfront when Connors shot and killed Sneed.[43] Some of the mates carried sticks, iron bars, or canes reinforced with lead. "I am actually ashamed of some of the things that I have actually done in the way of working people beyond humanity, that is the only way you could put it," confessed J. Harvey Coomer when he later reflected on his career as a steamboat night watchman, mate, and captain. A mate with six facial scars from knife slashes who worked the Ohio and Mississippi rivers confessed: "It was the worst kind of inhumanity, but we were country boys, and we just didn't know any better."[44]

Unsettled grudges extended from landing to landing. Roustabouts turned on each other as well as the mate, ship captain, and Black captain of the watch. In some cases, roustabouts' hatred and resentment of watch captains were legacies of slavery. Used by slaveholders who doled out special favors to them, drivers were tasked with getting more work out of their fellow enslaved in the plantation regime. Many steamboat watch captains came out of slavery with experience in the role. Like white mates who oversaw them, they often had horrible reputations for brutality. Antoine "Frank" Valle, a former driver born into Missouri plantation slavery, developed a reputation for abusing roustabouts on the *Lady Lee*. On July 16, 1881, abuse of Emmett Jones on the Missouri River near Kansas City cost Valle his life. His mistreatment of Jones dated back about three years to a steamboat on the Lower Mississippi, but the immediate catalyst for murder grew out of a *Lady Lee* incident in which they were taking on a load of wood. Valle struck Jones with a piece of wood, knocking him unconscious and nearly severing his ear. When Jones regained consciousness, the mate tied his ear to the side of his head so it wouldn't fall off. Jones left the boat for medical treatment in Glasgow and afterward headed for St. Louis to exact revenge. With the side of his head heavily bandaged, he boarded the *Lady Lee* in harbor at the foot of Olive Street, caught Valle asleep in a hammock, drew a pistol, and shot him twice at point-blank range. The city's criminal court convicted Jones of premeditated murder, and the Missouri Supreme Court upheld the conviction. Jones, age twenty-six, was sentenced to be hanged on January 18, 1884, but the day before, Governor T. T. Crittenden commuted his sentence to life imprisonment.[45]

On August 13, 1895, a shooting spree by a Black roustabout on the St. Louis levee grew out of a grudge against a captain of the watch on the *City of Cairo*. George Newson, alias Sam Fowler, who joined the crew on the previous packet to Memphis, balked when watch captain Lou Davis ordered him to work faster as they loaded grain. The two exchanged words, and Davis threatened to throw him off the boat. A fight followed in which Davis gave Newson's face a beating. Another roustabout, Charles Garner, clubbed Newson with a stick of wood. At the behest of Captain William McClatchey, the mate threw Newson off the steamboat near Cairo.[46] Newson returned to St. Louis on a train and plotted revenge. His moment came as a hundred passengers filed down the *City of Cairo*'s gangplank on the St. Louis wharf. He fired a hail of bullets at the steamboat, seriously wounding Davis in the back. The steward and two other roustabouts received less serious bullet wounds as they stood talking on the wharf. Newson fled but was arrested and charged a week later.[47]

In July 1905, the Nashville-based Ryman Line sent the *J. B. Richardson* to St. Louis to initiate a new packet to service Calhoun County, an Illinois peninsula of apple and peach orchards between the Mississippi and Illinois rivers above their confluence. On Ryman steamers, roustabouts enjoyed a respite from being cussed incessantly. In 1885, after a religious conversion at a tent meeting by popular preacher Sam Jones in Nashville, Captain Tom Ryman initiated changes in the way he operated his steamers. When contracts for bar concessions expired on his boats, he did not renew them. Instead, he ended the sale of alcohol and tobacco, giving up his share of profits from the lucrative saloon business. His boats, blazoned with scripture appropriate for those who worked the packets, were an anomaly. He hired soft-spoken mates who refrained from cussing roustabouts. Known for his sympathies for the downtrodden after his conversion, he built a mission for steamboat workers next door to his office on Broad Street in Nashville. He hired a minister to hold nightly services at the mission, as well as a night school teacher to educate steamboat workers and their families. He built a Gospel Wagon for neighborhoods without churches. One of the most successful businessmen in Nashville, he died in December 1904, but his son continued the practices. When the *J. B. Richardson* began the

Calhoun County packet out of St. Louis, it did so without the sale of alcohol on board and without the cussing and racist insults by mates as they prodded roustabouts to work faster.[48]

Roustabouts adopted a number of strategies to gain higher wages and better working conditions. At times after agreeing to terms with a mate on the packet, they "jumped" him by stepping back ashore as the boat pulled away. The tactic forced the boat to land again and either concede to their fresh wage demands or lay over until a new crew could be found at an acceptable rate of pay. In response to aggressive bargaining tactics and strikes, steamboat captains who earlier replaced white crews with Black ones routinely threatened to replace Black "rousters," or "roosters," with southern and eastern European immigrants. Captain Henry Leyhe, who with his brother William "Buck" Leyhe, ran the St. Louis-based Eagle Packet Company, dismissed a crew of roustabouts in March 1904 after they "jumped" the mate. Rather than accede to higher wages, he stormed uptown in search of a new crew. He found forty Austrians at a labor agency willing to work the *Grey Eagle* for $45 a month, the rate previously agreed to by the displaced Black roustabouts. Despite Captain Leyhe's warm praise for the Austrians and repeated predictions by steamboat officers that other packets would replace Black roustabouts with white ones, such threats came and went without lasting success.[49]

Three years later, the Eagle Packet Company found itself in a wage conflict in St. Louis that led to the "drowning" of a roustabout. A spokesman chosen by a crew of roustabouts identified as Priest Dedman, better known on the levee as "Crying John," voiced demands to officers of the *Grey Eagle,* which was loaded with general merchandise bound for Commerce, south of Cape Girardeau. A fight broke out on the spot between Dedman and First Mate Andrew McClatchey. According to the roustabouts, McClatchey hit Dedman first, and Second Mate Joseph Langevin and Captain Buck Leyhe joined the fracas. Leyhe was known for his quick temper when it came to labor matters. According to the police report, he and the mates tossed Dedman overboard, but Leyhe insisted that Dedman fell into the river and drowned when he tried to leap from the *Grey Eagle* to a wharf boat next to the steamer.[50]

An ugly scene developed when roustabouts found out that Dedman was dead. They held that either Leyhe or one of the mates struck him with a long pike, picked him up by his head and feet, and threw him overboard. Dedman was swept away by the current so quickly that no one had a chance to rescue him. A crowd of nearly one thousand angry roustabouts and supporters gathered on the levee, cursing and yelling threats at the boat's officers, who blocked initial efforts to investigate. Police arrested the two mates, who upon reaching jail implicated Captain Leyhe. The police returned to the boat, where the crowd was waiting for Leyhe to come out. After he surrendered, police took him to jail with great difficulty as protesters tried to rush them. Only the officers' drawn pistols held the surging crowd at bay. The mates were released without bond, but the captain was charged and released on a $20,000 bond. Leyhe was ordered to appear in circuit court in October, but apparently the charges were later dropped. It was customary at the time for steamboat operators to pay roustabouts $75 per month during the hottest part of summer, but when the *Grey Eagle* pulled out the next day for Chester, Illinois, a crew of twenty-five roustabouts shipped out at wages of $110 per month plus an extra penny for every sack of potatoes or grain. In the immediate aftermath of what happened to Dedman, other St. Louis roustabouts stuck together, insisting on $90 per month plus a penny a sack. The packets acceded to their demands.[51]

When roustabouts took collective action, they did so typically without formal organization. In November 1901, a crew of them deserted a boat in Alton and made their way back to St. Louis in protest against abuse aboard ship. When the nationwide railroad strike of 1877 sparked a general strike in St. Louis, hundreds of roustabouts, although not unionized, responded to cries from white unionists to join the strike. They and other levee workers joined and in some cases led strikers as they marched from factory to factory, shutting down operations until the demands of all workers were met. A workers' collective influenced by the German Revolution of 1848, Paris Commune of 1871, and the Marxist First International briefly ran the city. The Paris Commune came to St. Louis, if only for a fleeting historical week. A spirit of class solidarity across racial lines was prevalent but proved fragile in the end. Major newspapers helped to drive a wedge in the strike's interracial coalition, differentiating between "respectable" white unionists and the Black levee "mob." According to the *Missouri Republican*, "The cluster were simply communists, who, when they talked, showed their teeth like wolves."[52] The *Globe-Democrat* regarded the levee strikers as "bummers, tramps and human rats," and the *Post-Dispatch* complained that "self-constituted committees made up of stevedores, hoodlums,

idlers and lazy Negroes, paraded through portions of the city notifying laborers at various points that they must quit work, regardless of whether they are
receiving too much wages or too little."[53]

On July 9, 1891, Samuel Gompers, president of the young American Federation of Labor (AFL), sought to harness militancy on the St. Louis waterfront and
steer it into more conservative channels by commissioning George L. Norton
as a general union organizer. Norton, the AFL's first Black organizer, was general secretary of the Marine Firemen's Protective Union No. 5464 in St. Louis.
Born in 1852 to enslaved Tennessee parents, Norton and fellow Marine Firemen's officer Peter Pearl co-owned a saloon and restaurant at No. 3 North Levee.
Norton began to organize longshoremen, roustabouts, marine engineers, and
firemen, but Gompers received complaints from other unions that Norton was
organizing white and Black workers into the same union. As an organizer, Norton refused to bend to pressures for racially segregated locals.[54]

On March 28, 1892, Gompers cautioned William P. Newell, secretary of
St. Louis's newly formed Marine Engineers' Protective Union No. 5622, not
to rush hastily into a strike to settle years of grievances overnight. A couple of
days later, nearly 150 Black marine firemen and 100 engineers struck to protest
discriminatory wage rates by the Anchor Line, one of the two largest steamboat
companies operating between St. Louis and New Orleans. The engineers and
firemen demanded wages equal to rates paid by the rival St. Louis & Mississippi
Valley Transportation Company's line of steamers. About one thousand longshoremen (one-third of them white) and six hundred newly unionized Black
roustabouts joined the first strike of its kind on the Mississippi River. By the
first of May, the number of roustabouts on strike reportedly reached nearly one
thousand. Strikers demanded union wages and a closed shop. In an atmosphere
resembling that of religious camp meetings, nearly two thousand strikers and
their wives sang levee songs and spirituals as they patrolled the wharf to prevent strikebreakers from loading or unloading steamboats.[55]

Union officials drafted demands that steamboat companies recognize the
Roustabouts' Union (Inland Seamen's Protective Union), hire only union roustabouts, and pay them $45 per month (or $1.50 per day) plus board. The demands called for longshoremen to receive a raise from 17½ to 25 cents per hour,
and for engineers to make between $90 and $125 per month, depending on the
size of the boat and the number of boilers. Union representatives delivered the

demands to steamer captains, who blamed saloon owners Pearl, Norton, and Joe Haywood for the roustabouts' militancy. Norton and Pearl's saloon served as a recruiting center for the Roustabouts' Union. Norton's wife helped to maintain an orderly, dignified atmosphere while he and other unionists signed up new members. She threw out a handful of roustabouts when they refused to heed her ban on profanity in the meeting.[56]

Haywood's tavern at No. 9 Washington Avenue, where many roustabouts lodged, served as an additional strike headquarters. Haywood, a former roustabout who headed the local Longshoremen's Association, gave impassioned speeches, exhorting roustabouts to pay 25 cents in dues for a union card and the promise of a brighter future. The *Post-Dispatch*, in a facetious reference to the French Revolution, mocked him as the "[Georges] Danton of the 'river niggers' revolution."[57] Among those who delivered rousing speeches in the saloon was John Willis, a fifty-four-year-old roustabout. Willis emphasized that under slavery he was bought and sold five times. Like many, he could not read or write. For far too long, he complained, roustabouts accepted whatever the master doled out. Urging others in the saloon to join the union, he proudly noted that the strike represented the first time roustabouts organized through the AFL to get more of what their labor was worth.[58]

On April 6, executive committees representing roustabouts and longshoremen reached an unsigned agreement with Captain Isaac Mason, president of the Anchor Line company, the main target of the strike. Mason, the newly elected president of the St. Louis Merchants' Exchange, agreed to pay longshoremen at 25 cents an hour, roustabouts at $35 a month plus board, and engineers from $90 to $125 a month. In the compromise agreement, Mason reserved the right to hire nonunion labor. He and Pearl, president of the Roustabouts' Union, publicly announced that the strike was settled.[59] Briefly, the wharf became a chaotic place again. Merchants, upon hearing of the settlement, sent loaded wagons and carts to the waterfront. Drivers of wagons, carts, and drays cussed and yelled at each other as they jockeyed for space on the crowded wharf. Police tried to direct traffic, but in the stampede and confusion there were collisions, damaged freight, and near fights. Roustabouts, to expedite the movement of goods, even carried freight from the wagons directly into the holds of the steamboats. The Anchor Line's *City of New Orleans* pulled away from the wharf in the evening, loaded to capacity.

The settlement unraveled the next morning. When roustabouts and long-shoremen showed up on the cobblestones for work, the first mate on the *City of Providence* refused to hire Tom Crawford, a member of the union executive committee who negotiated the settlement. As a labor contractor, vice-president of the Longshoremen's Association, and roustabout, Crawford was highly pop-ular among waterfront workers. A veteran of twenty years on the river, he worked closely with AFL organizer Norton to coordinate the strike and pres-ent demands to steamboat companies. In retaliation, Captain Mason refused to reemploy him. When roustabouts learned of Crawford's plight, they walked off the boat in protest and gathered in Union Hall to discuss the situation. They decided to resume the strike until the Anchor Line rehired Crawford.[60]

The police worked with owners to restore order on the wharf and to pro-tect strikebreakers and steamboats. Fearing Crawford's presence on the levee might rally strikers, Sergeant Walter Gregory cornered him in a saloon and ordered him to go home and stay away from the levee until the strike ended. Crawford protested, but Gregory gave him no choice. Without Crawford's in-spirational presence, many strikers returned to work. On April 8, about six hundred white and Black longshoremen showed up on the wharf for work. The *Post-Dispatch*, noting that about half belonged to the union, concluded that the strike was virtually over, but it dragged on. Confrontations between strikers and strikebreakers led to violence, bloodshed, and arrests while the Anchor Line steadily gained the upper hand. A lack of discipline, coordination, and desperately needed support from AFL headquarters plagued the strike, which from time to time was called off by one of the unions only to be renewed again. In time, the boats operated at near capacity with scab roustabouts, engineers, and firemen. When the river flooded in May, the company cut wages of the strikebreakers to $1 per day.[61]

As the strike faltered, Norton took note of the critical need to organize roustabouts and other waterfront workers on the Ohio and Mississippi rivers. At his request, the AFL Executive Council authorized expenditures to send him to New Orleans for a month to continue organizing in an effort to discourage roustabouts, firemen, and engineers from working the Anchor Line steamboats targeted in the strike. In response to a complaint by the whites-only Car Driv-ers Union in New Orleans, Gompers urged Norton to bend to southern racial traditions and not overstep his authority in regard to segregated locals.[62] By the

~~~

time Norton returned to St. Louis a month later with little to show for his efforts, the steamboat companies had weakened the strike considerably. To drive a wedge between engineers and the other groups on strike, Captain Mason told engineers he objected to their association with roustabouts and longshoremen via the AFL. On June 2, he ordered commanders of Anchor Line boats to fire AFL engineers and firemen, who in response renewed their strike, backed by union roustabouts. A new round of confrontations between strikers and scabs followed. "We are not to blame in this matter, and Capt. Mason can lay his loss upon no one but himself," a chief engineer on the *City of St. Louis* asserted. "The engineers are paid $120 per month and we are satisfied with our salary, but we do not propose to pull out of the American Federation of Labor Union. . . . Capt. Mason is endeavoring to break the union up and we will then be compelled to work for just what we can get." When engineers met a week later, they expected assistance from Gompers, who reportedly was coming to St. Louis to intervene in the strike. They were disappointed when he did not show up. They were also angry at the Pilots' Association, which supported the steamboat companies.[63]

Roustabouts' support for the strike broke down completely on July 1, 1892. They had held out for nearly three months, but desperate, they flocked to the wharf to go back to work. Only a few found boats willing to hire them under any terms. Without lasting ties to the city's trade unions or significant political influence, they were at the mercy of steamboat companies, which refused to fire strikebreakers. The engineers vowed to continue the strike, but they and the roustabouts were bitter at the AFL's lack of support. They blamed Gompers for not coming to St. Louis at a critical time, complaining that he might have adjudicated the strike and saved them trouble and money. They accused him of deliberately avoiding a commitment to the strike's success.[64]

Gompers did show up in St. Louis, but not until a month after the strike collapsed. There was considerable bitterness and finger-pointing. The city's Trades and Labor Union president, Henry Blackmore, of the conservative Carpenter's Union, complained to Gompers about the activities of A. S. Leitch, a commissioned AFL general organizer and editor and publisher of the *Union Record*. Leitch and Norton worked together before and during the strike. Gompers refused to comment publicly, but upon returning to AFL headquarters he revoked the commissions of organizers in St. Louis and urged the central body to choose Leitch's replacement. Blackmore took over as general organizer, and the fledgling Roustabouts' Union collapsed.[65]

Whether unionized or not, roustabouts learned the value of collective action to get higher wages and concessions from steamboat packets. They were blasted and belittled for their efforts. In 1909, when steamboat operators threatened again to replace Black roustabouts with Greeks and Italians, the *Hannibal Morning Journal* cheered: "The roosters of color are not to be had at reasonable wages. Most of them at best are shiftless and willing to work only when they feel like it. There are plenty of them, goodness knows, but they won't enter the service unless paid an exorbitant wage."[66] Steamboat captains blamed labor unrest on anyone and anything except its underlying causes. At a time when alcohol was under attack nationwide by temperance reformers and corporations that linked labor inefficiency to its use, the levee haunts of roustabouts drew fire. The Steamboat Managers' Association sought ways to shut down levee saloons without driving roustabouts farther from the wharf. Some roustabouts became addicted to cocaine and other narcotics in an effort to ease the effects of the brutal punishment their jobs inflicted on them. Their use of cocaine, readily supplied by drugstores, especially in New Orleans, drew public attention. In some cases, mates reportedly gave it to roustabouts so they would work harder and faster. The growing addiction problem was an open secret, but the need for labor and profits took priority over roustabouts' welfare. As the *Post-Dispatch* explained, "Many of the Negroes are addicted to drugs, but as long as they can stand up and work they are useful."[67]

Like many in shantyboat communities, roustabouts were not driven by the clock or factory-like discipline. The Industrial Revolution turned America into an increasingly regimented, bureaucratized society, but roustabouts cherished control over their own time and leisure between packets. It galled critics that roustabouts did not bend to a disciplined, temperate lifestyle. Much to the chagrin of steamboat captains and critics, their work rhythms were more in line with preindustrial patterns, determined less by the clock and more by tasks at hand. But mates on the packets were certainly conscious of the clock. Their jobs might hang in the balance if boats fell behind schedule. The packets required punishing manual labor, but when many roustabouts left the steamer afterward, they enjoyed bouts of idleness, leisure, and hard drinking and carousing until they ran out of money and hired on to work another packet.[68]

According to one estimate, the average service of roustabouts on packets was about five years. Most roustabouts were young, but they were older than their years by the time they left the river. Steamboat operators blamed their short work life on hard drinking and carousing when they weren't working the packets. Roustabouts pointed to the backbreaking demands, punishing regimentation, lack of sleep, and unhealthy nature of the work. "The boats break a man down," reflected Henry Scott, a St. Louis roustabout. "There are some men who stand it year after year, but the most of us get stove up and in bad health. If the pay wasn't what it is none of us would go out, for we're away a whole lot, have to work day and night, and get broken down from the heavy carrying."[69]

4

The River Gives Up Its Dead Slowly

SEASONS, CYCLES, AND THE RIVER'S FURY

As a child I feared this river and respected it more than I feared God.
As an adult now I fear it even more. . . . Mighty, muddy, dangerous,
rebellious, and yet a fathering kind of river.

—EDDY L. HARRIS, *Mississippi Solo*, 1988

Even the dreaded "low water," with all the dangers of "snags" and
sunken wrecks is not so much to be feared as one of the great ice sweeps
which, with its glittering teeth, will in a few moments grind to atoms
hundreds of thousands of dollars' worth of property.

—EDWARD KING, *Southern States*, 1875

Life on the waterways was fraught with dangers from natural sources. From ice gorges to floods, levee breaks to convulsive eddies, tornadoes to hurricanes, the wrath of Mother Nature poured forth at times to remind even the most seasoned river expert who was in charge. Those who lived on the river adapted to its wild, moody cycles and the hidden threats beneath its surface. In 1900, Clarence Jones, a young St. Louis shantyboat peddler, expressed deep respect for the Mississippi: "I have been on the river three years. The first year you don't like it very well, but you think it's easy. The second year you have your doubts about how much the river could do to you if it tried. The third year you're in love with it but you ain't got no doubt you're afraid of the river every minute, sleepin' or wakin'."[1] For writer Julian Street in 1917, the "grandeur," "beauty," and "stately" yet "placid" nature of the upper river flowing between tall bluffs stood in contrast to the Lower Mississippi's "countless wooded islands," "drama," and "mystery." "The lower river is a temperamental mistress," he wrote. "At one moment she is all sweetness, smiles, and playfulness; at the next vivid and passionate. Even when she is at her loveliest there is always the possibility of sudden fury: of her rising in a rage, breaking the furniture, wrecking the house—yes, and perhaps winding her cold arms about you, in a final destroying embrace."[2]

In St. Louis, levee settlements bustled with activity each autumn as residents fortified their boats for the winter or repaired them for the migration south. The fall ritual in Little Oklahoma, a meeting place for outside hunting parties who floated south with shantyboat migrants, often brought reporters on the run in search of a story. In late November 1900, John Kritzler predicted a mild winter in Chickentown, noting to a reporter that the bark on a nearby tree was no thicker on the north side than on the south. "I have lived here nine years," he boasted, "and I have never been sick in all that time." The reporter also caught up with Jim Neely at the foot of Meramec Street. All the other birds of passage in Chickentown had cleared out for the winter, but Neely was still getting his boat ready. At age eighty-two, he was still locked into the seasonal rhythms of the annual migration with his trammel nets, shotgun, and steel traps. He planned to fish on the way downriver until he found a good cove or inlet where he could hole up for the winter and subsist by hunting and trapping. With no rent to pay, fishing and doing odd jobs on the St. Louis waterfront enabled him to get by until winter. "You seldom see a houseboater looking for charity," he noted. "I'm a little bit late, but I couldn't get away as quick as these other fellows. I'm getting old and I can't get around like I used to."[3]

Henry Schroeder and his wife were among those in Little Oklahoma who remained year-round in the settlement. For the 1900–1901 winter, they pulled their houseboat onto shore and boosted it atop logs. A huge stack of driftwood was piled against the kitchen end of their boat, and smoke was billowing out the roof through a stovepipe when the reporter arrived. Mrs. Schroeder sat relaxed on the front porch as she smoked a short pipe, confident they were prepared for the coldest of winter. Nearby, a woman from the far north in a houseboat appeared unsettled in contrast as overhead sounds of Canadian geese momentarily diverted her eyes. Her husband, after a recent spat, had left her. As he pushed his boat toward midstream and headed for a southern destination, he reportedly left her with these parting words: "You stay in St. Louis and rustle for yourself awhile and I'll never pester you again." The woman accepted her fate stoically. She turned away from the reporter, resumed fortifying her shantyboat, and made ready to face winter alone.[4]

The breakup of ice gorges posed a frightening threat to steamboats and those who lived and labored on the river. "Even the dreaded 'low water,' with all the dangers of 'snags' and sunken wrecks," wrote Edward King in 1875, "is not so much to be feared as one of the great ice sweeps which, with its glittering teeth, will in a few moments grind to atoms hundreds of thousands of dollars' worth of property."[5] A rapid overnight rise in the river and enormous ice floes at the confluence of the Missouri and Mississippi rivers in February 1903 sank four houseboats on the Illinois side and forced ten inhabitants to flee across twenty feet of ice. At about 3:30 in the morning, John A. Arthur heard his wife scream as their houseboat lurched forward and jerked away from shore. Mrs. Arthur snatched their baby and hurried toward shore on the ice but fell. F. C. Collins, who already had escaped safely, rushed back onto the ice to help her while Mr. Arthur crossed the ice to safety with their other child. Families stood on shore and watched their homes and belongings disappear into the gloomy abyss of the river. In Mrs. Arthur's haste to save her baby, she darted out of the houseboat without shoes and suffered frozen feet. In Chickentown in February 1905, John Stanton and his thirteen-year-old son were eating supper in their houseboat when disaster struck. Without warning, two huge cakes of ice caught the boat in between and crushed its hull. The boat sank in four feet of water, but father and son escaped unhurt. Several other cabin-boats in Chickentown were damaged, and two nearby steamers, the *Laura* and the *India Givens*, were caught by the ice breakup but survived.[6]

Ice gorges were particularly bad in the winter of 1909–1910, when the river recorded its highest winter level in St. Louis in twenty years. Nearly one hundred construction workers on temporary support structures on the city's McKinley Bridge project barely avoided death on December 31, 1909, when an ice jam nearly six feet high crashed into the structure. Some of the men, along with a derrick, falling timbers, and hoisting engines, fell into the river. Others heard the cracking of timbers and leaped onto a steel structure in time. Thanks to Captain John Short and the ice-cutting capabilities of his tugboat, the difficult two-hour rescue operation saved many lives. When Gus Steimel, from his houseboat in Little Oklahoma, spotted the threatening ice gorge breaking up, he ran across the ice to warn the crew. About halfway to the bridge, he nearly lost his life when the ice separated. He clung to an ice cake until rescuers reached him an hour later. A series of ice jams followed by breakups, fast drops in the river level, and then formation of new ice gorges in the weeks ahead left a path of waterfront wreckage in its wake. Whether damaged grain elevators, steamboats, ferry boats, wharf boats, rowing club boathouses, or shantyboats and yachts, property losses on the riverfront were staggering, but there were no reported deaths.[7]

Ice gorge breakups routinely swept away shantyboats, with or without the inhabitants. In 1927, Wilson Crist, a seventy-one-year-old shantyboat fisherman on the Ohio River in Aurora, Indiana, recalled terrifying close calls with ice gorges. In his view, they represented the greatest danger to those who lived on the river. Ice jams were capable of pulling willow trees out by their roots if boats were tied to them. "One night in January I heard the ice crushing against my boat," Crist remembered: "It was tied up in the mouth of a creek, and I knew that the ice jam in the creek was washing out. I grabbed a part of my clothes and rushed out on the ice-cold bank barefooted. Scarcely had I hit the bank when my boat broke loose and I stood there and heard the ice in the river grind it to pieces between large cakes of ice. All I had left was the few clothes I grabbed in my hand. . . . In emergencies we always grab for our clothes and a few of the bed clothes if possible. In winter we always make sure that we have matches somewhere in our clothes. A fire built from drift-wood on the bank will keep us from freezing to death until morning." In another close call when ice tore Crist's boat loose, he stayed on it in hopes he could save it by steering between ice cakes safely. "When the ice began to crush my home it looked as if I was a goner," he recounted, "but I tore a plank loose from the boat and used it as a bridge to walk from one large cake of floating ice to another. In this way I finally reached the shore. The banks were lined with people watching me make my escape."

On another cold night of bad weather, when Crist's young son was sick, it wasn't an ice gorge but a steamboat that rammed their shantyboat and burst the hull. When water began to pour in, Crist picked up his son and started to run out of the boat, but he worried that the bad weather might worsen his son's condition. He put his son back in bed, propped up the boat so the water would drain away from him, and stood in the cold water while he repaired the damaged hull and pumped out the water. "I had kindling hanging from the ceiling," he remembered, "and after I finished I built a fire and dried out the boat and my clothing." Despite the perils of river life and the loss of five boats to ice, Crist endorsed life on the waterways: "Yes, while the river sometimes seems cruel and rough to us, at other times she is mighty kind. The river has always given me a living. When you go out and draw in your nets and find that you have a hundred pounds of pretty cat and buffalo fish, it makes you forget all the hardships. Best of all, there is something about the great stream that seems to soothe the sorrow of the past and makes us happy and contented."[8]

For seasonal waterways migrants who got a late start or encountered delays in the fall, river travel was particularly dangerous on the Upper Mississippi if the river iced over earlier than usual. On December 29, 1879, an ice gorge forced Washington Lambert, age eighty, to dock his flatboat in St. Louis. He and his wife were on their way from Wisconsin to Bird's Point, an island and steamboat landing in the Missouri bootheel across from Cairo. The aged couple ran out of food, and Mrs. Lambert became desperately sick and weak. By the time Lambert docked their boat on the north wharf, he and his wife were in critical need of food and medical assistance.[9] John Davis and his wife were well-accustomed to dangers on the river, but for some reason did not head south early enough in the fall of 1902. In October, they rowed down the Missouri River in a small boat from Kansas City until the river emptied into the Mississippi. From there, they rowed upriver to Canton, where John worked to earn some "flour and coffee" money before heading to St. Louis. By the time they left Canton, large floating ice cakes posed a threat on the river. In Quincy, Illinois, they were caught in a grinding ice jam, and their boat was thrown up onto a huge cake. They waited for the ice to break, and when it did on December 27, they simply rode a floe down the river until it melted. With an oar and pole they warded off floating chunks of ice along the way. A week later they docked in Little Oklahoma, but a scarcity of wood for heating denied them a safe winter harbor in the settlement. They continued south of the city limits until they found a suitable cove sheltered by a nearby cliff with plenty of tangled driftwood left by the previous year's floods and freshets. They pitched a dog tent (eight feet long, six feet wide, and five feet high) under the cliff. Davis, a woodsman, took his axe and secured wood for their small stove inside the tent. Soon they had a rousing fire and settled in with a few eating utensils and a mattress on the ground. "The home is so small," remarked a reporter who interviewed them, "that one feels constrained to go outside to sneeze."[10]

Ice floes and stormy weather also delayed Harve Turner and L. Murphy, who in late October 1909 left Sioux City en route to New Orleans but ended up stranded in December in St. Joseph. They intended to tie up their houseboat and skiff in a settlement at the foot of Francis Street, but huge ice cakes on the fast-moving Missouri River destroyed their skiff. Without the skiff, they were unable to reach shore. The current swept them past St. Joseph about twenty-five miles. At last they managed a landing at Atchison and walked back to St. Joseph, where they were expecting a letter with money. Upon finding no such letter awaiting them at the post office, they were without funds and separated from their houseboat twenty-five miles away. With the temperature near zero, Murphy and Turner stepped into the police station and asked for a bed for the night.[11]

For year-round squatters in St. Louis levee settlements, the winter challenges of scraping by until spring were daunting at best and fatal at worst. Disease and starvation stalked the waterfront in the season of influenza, pneumonia, and other viruses. In January 1924, seventy-two-year-old Julia Pennceno was a casualty of the freezing cold weather. A Black washerwoman who lived in a shantyboat at the foot of Malt (Mott) Street for a number of years, she fell ill and was unable to keep a fire going. She died in an ambulance en route to the city hospital.[12] In January 1898, an ambulance took Hazel Cavanaugh and her two children, Albert and Hannah, from their houseboat at the foot of Bremen. Cavanaugh and her son had pneumonia, and Hannah suffered from malaria. James, her husband, had worked as a railroad switchman in Waterloo until he lost his job. In search of work, he took the family to Winona, Minnesota, but found none. He and his family set out down the Mississippi in a houseboat, reaching St. Louis in November. James took sick upon arrival, and the family ran out of money at the worst time of the year.[13]

During the Christmas season, the *Post-Dispatch* often published a list of "deserving" destitute persons in need of charity based on recommendations by police districts. Not surprisingly, residents of levee settlements were often among those in need. In the spirit of the season, the newspaper called attention to children of needy parents to encourage city-wide donations for toys and other gifts. On December 12, 1904, a *Post-Dispatch* "agent" of Santa Claus visited a Chickentown family. Afterward, an article, "Christmas Fairy Is Her Only Hope," put the spotlight on Josephine Gerard, a nearly fourteen-year-old girl born and raised in the settlement. "We always wanted a Christmas tree like mamma told us the rich children up over the hill had in their houses," she remembered. For years, her father, Charles Gerard, was regarded by neighbors as the "King of Chickentown." He worked for wages at a carriage factory, and the family did alright in their two-room shantyboat until a historic tornado tore through downtown St. Louis and East St. Louis on May 27, 1896. Josephine explained to Santa's agent what happened as a result of the tornado: "After the cyclone we got poor. That awful day, when our house was most blowed in the river, my papa walked home in the rain and storm. He wouldn't wait uptown for he thought that maybe mamma and I and baby brother, George, had been killed. His legs got wet, and he has had the rheumatism ever since. For eight years he has not walked much and mamma had to go out washing. Some weeks she could make $4, but that was when she worked for good people." On the previous Christmas, someone posing as Santa had showed up at their shantyboat with a tree and promised to return on Christmas Eve with gifts and candles to light the tree. Upon his return, he lit the candles, but his Santa's beard caught fire and so did the gifts. "It was the only chance we have ever had to have a sure enough Christmas," Josephine lamented.[14]

A week before Christmas 1900, the *Post-Dispatch* ran a front-page story about a needy shantyboat family on a sand spit near Venice. Al and Rose Tunis with their five children, dog, fish box, and trammel nets docked near the Merchants' Bridge in October. Al was a fisherman, but with winter upon them he left his family on the boat with what little money and provisions they had and set out to seek employment in an area sand and gravel pit where he once worked. He left information about how to reach him by mail, and told Rose he'd return soon, hopefully with news of a job. Days turned to weeks. Rose sent two letters to him without a reply. The money and food Al left her and the children ran out. "For a week they had lived on flour mixed with lard and fried," noted the *Post-Dispatch*. Then the flour and lard ran out, too. Desperate after three days without food for the children, Rose was standing on the riverbank wondering what to do when she heard shouts of joy back at the boat. Her husband, who fell ill while away, had come home with joyous news the week before Christmas. His new job would start the next morning.[15]

The fortunes of waterfront squatters often rose and fell with the river's cycles. In Paducah, John "Quickstep" Newman, a Black fortune-teller, awoke in the night to find himself adrift on the rising Ohio River in February 1902. Frightened, he jumped from his houseboat into a skiff without his shoes and rowed ashore. When the boat was found near Metropolis, Illinois, authorities assumed the worst, but Newman turned up safe among friends.[16] When floodwaters rose in St. Louis in May 1892, a reporter and a captain of a tugboat chartered by the *Post-Dispatch* to survey conditions on the wharf noted the threat to Little Oklahoma: "The little shanty town of Oklahoma, behind the C.B.&Q. embankment at the foot of Destrehan Street, was wretchedly anxious last night over the threatening attitude of the river, which is just within reach of the top of the fortification which has kept them from being drowned out for nearly a week past." Justin Joy's lumberyards between the CB&Q tracks and the tracks of the Merchants' Terminal at the foot of Harrison Street were partially submerged. At the foot of Dock Street, floodwaters backed up through a trestle under the CB&Q tracks and covered an area about two and a half blocks long. About fifteen houseboats and shanties were flooded. "The wretched families dragged their little household effects to Harrison Street on the south," observed the reporter, "and left their homes deserted."[17]

At times the river's unpredictable wildness caught even seasoned river experts off guard. On December 20, 1895, the Mississippi rose by eleven feet overnight in St. Louis. "This is the biggest sudden rise I ever saw at this season of the year," remarked Captain Ralph J. Whitledge, assistant harbor and wharf commissioner.[18] The rapid flooding temporarily wiped out portions of Little Oklahoma, prompting the *Globe-Democrat* to note that the flood was more effective than the previous summer's attempts by police to evict squatters. Little Oklahomans scrambled to pack their utensils, repair their boats, and take other emergency measures. They pitched tents on higher ground and crowded together, ten or twelve to a tent. A few sought shelter at a police district substation, while others kept an eye on their property as best they could in the cold December rain, slush, and rampaging floodwaters. A squatter watched helplessly as the river swept his capsized boat away. Four residents were rescued when their houseboat sank. Nate Scoville, who spotted a capsized houseboat being swept away, risked his life by climbing aboard to try to save lives. All the windows and doors were locked shut, and there was nothing he could do. Only the stovepipe was visible as the houseboat submerged.[19]

A year later, Scoville's own houseboat was in trouble as high winds, heavy rains, and rare winter flooding combined with icy January temperatures to make life miserable in settlements for two weeks. His houseboat, one of the nicer ones, sprang a leak and sank as winds and high waves lashed it about. Fortunately, he and his family had already removed their household contents. The next day, they battled furious blasts of cold air to pull their submerged houseboat from the water. A new houseboat owned by Ed Digney also sank, as did a small one that belonged to Joe Heintz. A family in a tent with a wooded floor was forced to move twice in the same day to escape wintry floodwaters, which also forced out George W. Anderson, an elderly man who had built a small dugout in the side of a gulley. As was customary in squatter settlements, other residents took care of those rendered homeless.[20]

Three months later, when the annual rise came in April 1897, spectators and newspaper reporters flocked to the north wharf, drawn by dire flood forecasts. Dr. H. C. Frankenfield, chief of the US Weather Station in St. Louis, singled out Little Oklahoma as an area likely to be decimated by floodwaters. Those in shanties and unseaworthy shantyboats were most at risk. Shantyboats capable of floating were not in as much danger as long as their moorings remained secure. They typically tied up to solid structures and put out gangplanks to dry land. If they had plenty of slack in the moorings to accommodate rising water levels, they simply floated atop the waters until levels receded. On occasions, they collided with other objects when whipped about by high winds and rampaging waters. An elderly woman nearly perished when her boat broke, struck a log, and sank in five feet of water with only the roof visible, but a young man in a skiff rescued her.[21]

Shantyboat residents remained undaunted and philosophical in the face of dire warnings. The throng of onlookers brought cheer to Little Oklahomans, who began to fill the "growler" in the early morning as they waited. Men, women, and children sat around drinking in small groups. With rising floodwaters only feet away, Aaron Dockens, a seventy-three-year-old Black resident born in Arkansas, remained calm as he sat on a stool, smoking a clay pipe in front of his shantyboat at the foot of Dock Street. Asked if he was worried, he took a long draw on his pipe and replied: "When she comes up it is time to think about going, but I am not afraid of the water. I have been fighting floods and building levees all my life. If she does come up I will wait until I am forced to go before I do so."[22]

Nearby landlords or companies that leased wharf space from the city complained that when houseboats tied to moorings during floods, they often ended up stuck on their property as trespassers when waters receded. Boat owners worked to return their homes to the water's edge, but acknowledged the validity of complaints by owners of lumberyards and other businesses on the wharf. There was little that houseboat owners could do under the circumstances until the floodwaters dropped. Nevertheless, on the very day a *Globe-Democrat* reporter visited the flooded settlement in April 1897, landlords in the area notified houseboat owners that they intended to cut the ropes to their moorings, ignoring requests to wait until flood conditions improved and it was less risky to move the boats. The reporter returned from the north wharf with grudging respect and admiration for squatters, who took pride in their shantyboats under adverse conditions. Interiors of their boats were clean and "pretentious in the way of furniture and fittings." Several featured organs and other musical instruments. Emblazoned on the exterior of a Little Oklahoma houseboat was a sign proclaiming that a "Phenomenal 6-year-old violinist" dwelled therein. "These people represent an evolutionary adaptation to environment which at the present time has most decided advantages," the reporter observed. "Instead of a reeking tenement in a narrow street, the open sweep of the river gives them breathing space."[23] A month later, with floodwaters still threatening, onlookers returned to the north wharf. Little Oklahomans in houseboats were still afloat, but the other shanties were washed away. Residents set their furnishings out on the nearest dry street. Exhausted, some napped on their beds in the open air while the onlookers gawked at them.[24]

In the face of life-threatening crises, resourceful waterfront dwellers adapted to conditions with stoicism and resolve. When an excursion boat transported paying sightseers to view the city's south waterfront in the devastating flood of 1892, only a half-dozen houseboats in Squatters' Town were still afloat and fit to live in. The rest were partially or entirely under water. Evacuees shared tents on higher ground nearby. Barbara Vogel's houseboat, although tied to moorings, sank to the bottom, but she seemed to take it in stride. With excursion boat sightseers looking on, she extended a ladder from the roof of her houseboat to the shoreline and busily hung out her wash to dry.[25] Amid flooding in 1898, women in the Sandy Hook settlement in East St. Louis devised a creative, collective way to hang clothes on wash day. Under circumstances that were hardly routine, the women turned a routine task into an entertaining activity driven by percussive music with the aid of a highly skilled rower and an agile, fearless woman of the settlement. A reporter described the scene:

> In one of the large boats it seems there was a union meeting of washerwomen from surrounding boats. Three or four tubs were ranged in a row at the back of the boat, and while as many housewives of the place played music on the washboards two pretty and plump maidens hung out the clothes on a line stretched from the back of the boat to a friendly willow several yards down the stream. One of the damsels bent on the oars and pulled the skiff so deftly that the other girl was not jolted or jarred from her upright position so necessary in pinning the clothes to the swinging line. The scene was witnessed by a number of railroad men, all of whom are ready to wager that Miss Sallie Long, who had charge of the boat, can row a stroke as steady in a skiff as any man in St. Louis.[26]

With the river rising in July 1902, Edward Whitfield, a Dubuque fisherman moored in the Venice squatter settlement near the Merchants' Bridge, left his sick wife and two children temporarily to run an errand uptown. As he was returning home, he stared in disbelief as his houseboat snapped loose from its moorings. The rising river swept it and the attached skiff downstream with his family. He kicked off his shoes, plunged into the river, and swam as fast as he could in a feverish effort to catch up with the runaway boat. Gradually he closed the distance, but the boat was on a collision course with the Eads Bridge. To no avail, his wife did everything she could in her weakened condition to steer the boat toward shore. Exhausted, Edward yelled to her from behind. At last she heard him. He put forth a final burst of energy to catch up with the boat but lacked strength to climb onto it. His wife reached out to him with one of the sweeps and helped to pull him aboard. He lay on the boat briefly to catch his breath, then managed to land it safely at Sandy Hook.[27]

~~~

For squatter settlements, floods were a routine part of life. When the river flooded, lumber was often afloat in the saw mills and lumberyards that surrounded Little Oklahoma. Runaway logs added to the dangers. The main threat to houseboats came from driftwood and debris, but owners felt secure as long as they could tie up to moorings. "Let 'er come," mused an old-timer in the face of rapidly rising floodwaters in June 1903. With his shantyboat tied to the railroad tracks, he added, "I have enough slack in my towline to lift 'er to the top 'o the water tower. Floods don't scare me."[28] In south St. Louis, flooding in June drove at least a hundred families from shantyboats and houses between Gasconade Street and the mouth of the River des Peres. On the north wharf, rising waters created a deep pond of backed-up water between nearby railroad tracks and Little Oklahoma. Later the water covered the tracks, but about a day earlier squatters set their belongings on the tracks and nearly forty boys floated rafts on the pond. Two of the boys, ages fourteen and sixteen, carelessly floated out beyond the line of houseboats. The current swept them toward a large scow piled high with logs. William Gleason, a Little Oklahoman who recognized the dangerous predicament the boys were in, jumped into his skiff and rowed quickly out to save them from drowning. When he pulled them safely to shore, the father of sixteen-year-old John Havermeyer was there to greet his son "with a half-dozen cuffs on the side of the head and sent him home."[29]

When a dangerous thunderstorm and high winds struck the north wharf in August 1904, fifty Little Oklahomans sought shelter under a railroad bridge over a small cut at the foot of Mallinckrodt Street. Among them were George A. Miller and his wife and sixteen-month-old child, of Muscatine, who never made it from their houseboat to the bridge. On the way, Miller's wife suffered a three-inch gash on her forehead from flying debris. She and her husband dropped to the ground and lay flat, holding their toddler between them until the storm's fury abated. Their houseboat suffered damage, and so did others.[30] A month earlier, a terrifying experience during a severe storm in south St. Louis might have killed a houseboat family had it not been for the intervention of a government tugboat. Hugo A. Preller and his wife, Gaynie, river photographers from Columbus, Kentucky, were docked on the northern edge of Squatters' Town when the thunderstorm hit. High winds and waves whipped the boat about until it tore loose from its moorings and drifted toward the middle of the turbulent flood-high river in the blinding rain. From the deck of a government tugboat, Captain John Henry caught a glimpse of the houseboat and set out on a rescue mission. Due to the storm's intensity, he lost sight of the boat temporarily, but heard faint cries for help. When he blew the whistle of his tugboat and yelled, Preller answered. Soon, the tugboat pulled alongside. Deckhands secured the houseboat to the tug and landed with it safely.[31]

On May 27, 1896, the most destructive tornado in American history at the time ripped through downtown St. Louis from the southwest and crossed the river near the Eads Bridge. Leaving behind 137 dead and countless injured, the storm then ravaged East St. Louis, where it killed an additional 118 residents. The wharf on both sides of the river was filled with wreckage and ruin, but fared better than first feared. St. Louis's harbor boat, anchored at the foot of Lucas Avenue when the tornado hit, was blown a distance of three and a half miles. Though damaged considerably, the boat was repairable. And despite substantial destruction of riverfront property, steamboats, and shipping interests, the loss of life there was minimal compared to other devastated sections of the city.[32] In the chaos of the storm's deadly swath, it was nearly impossible to get a clear sense of the number of fatalities, especially on the waterfront. On account of their itinerant lifestyle, shantyboats were the hardest to account for. According to a newspaper source, an estimated sixty-four shantyboats with approximately three hundred residents aboard disappeared in the tornado. Fortunately for residents of Little Oklahoma, the tornado did not score a direct hit on the north wharf. Squatter settlements in south St. Louis, too, were fortunate to have been spared the worst of the storm. Although Chickentown and Squatters' Town were near the swath of the tornado, their location provided them a measure of protection. Shielded by high bluffs, the settlements' residents remained in their houseboats and watched debris fly over them above the bluffs, but they escaped the worst of the fury that destroyed so many others.[33]

T. J. Stinson, head of the freight office of the Iron Mountain & Wiggins Ferry Company at the foot of Carroll Street, pointed out that all the shantyboats were evicted from the area near Carroll Street a day or two before the cyclone. The evicted squatters grumbled, but the evictions likely saved their lives. Stinson assumed they went to the Illinois side about a mile or two farther south. The St. Louis grain elevator at the foot of Chouteau Avenue suffered serious damage, and about twenty houseboats near it on the day of the tornado were missing the next day. As the *Post-Dispatch* noted, "The river gives up its dead slowly." From Stinson's lookout perch on the river, he was in a good position to view everything that floated past. "I can say without the least exaggeration that not less than twenty-five of these [house]boats floated down bottom side up."[34]

Even under normal weather conditions, drowning incidents were common. Many of the victims were children. In 1896, the *Post-Dispatch* urged the creation of a public bath to reduce the number of drowning victims among children who, despite parental warnings, swam and bathed in the river. A bill to that effect had been introduced in the previous year's Municipal Assembly, but a lack of funds was cited as the reason for not implementing a public bath at the time.[35] At the foot of Krauss Street, "Uncle" Eb Jackson, formerly enslaved in Louisville, took great pride in his adeptness at pulling "floaters" out of "Dead Man's Eddy," where an estimated 90 percent of river corpses in St. Louis were found. The river's current made a sharp break from the main flow and with a mighty force swept back sharply toward Krauss Street. For twenty-five years, until his eyesight dimmed badly at age eighty-three, he earned money by what he called "reachin'." There was enough money in "reachin'" for Jackson to eke out a living. "Sometimes I gets $10 and $20 fer a floater," he explained, "den at other times dey only gives me 15 cents." He worked hard to preserve corpses as best he could, but often received little for his efforts. Black corpses plucked from the river paid little; the money was in plucking dead white women from the river. "Ef you want ter make money, reach out some white gals and women," Jackson told a reporter. "Dere's money in dem almost every time. Dere's allus some'un lookin' for 'em, and dey allus give a poor man a little somethin' for the trouble that he has to sarve 'em."[36]

Near the end of January 1895, a number of unidentified persons aboard a shantyboat were sucked into a dark, watery grave by a violent whirlpool just below Bougere's Landing in east central Louisiana's Concordia Parish. According to Frank Bougere and other eyewitnesses, two men were rowing the small flatboat, which had an attached bateau and two skiffs. A woman with a baby in her arms and children aboard the flatboat were heard crying when it struck a spur that jutted out from the bank. The boat, thrown into a notorious convulsive whirlpool nearby, was sucked into the vortex and went down quickly with those aboard. Hours later, an oar surfaced and floated downriver, and the next day a box and the bateau made it to the top, but the bodies remained submerged.[37]

In August 1906, Little Oklahoma was abuzz with news of the drowning of Bertha Riley, age twelve, whose body was fished out by residents Clarence Durham and George Ortkas near the foot of Destrehan Street. Bertha, angry at her father because of his threats to send her to a corrective institution on account of her wildness, was indifferent to death. According to her ailing stepmother, she was a street-tough who fought boys and stayed out late on the streets or did not come home at all. She wore trousers, bobbed her hair, adopted a coarse street dialect, and repeatedly cursed her father and stepmother. Regarded as an incorrigible who was expelled from school, she had whacked her father with a pole a few nights before her drowning and told him she hated him. Shaler Nelson and others who saw her wading in the river and diving off a slippery log on the day of the drowning warned her, but she retorted that she was unafraid. They claimed she inherited her mother's untamed love of the river and its wildness. Five years earlier, her mother, who preferred to sleep on the riverbank on summer nights, had drowned herself in a suicide at the Chain of Rocks.[38]

Though much maligned, roustabouts and shantyboat residents performed many acts of heroism to save lives on the river, whether on steamboats or in waterfront colonies. On countless occasions they risked their own lives to save victims from drowning. When a young white woman, Sadie Stevens, fell from a gangplank of the excursion steamer *City of Providence* in St. Louis on September 1, 1909, George Bradley, a Black roustabout known on the levee as "Shanty Boat," dived into the river immediately upon hearing her scream. He nearly drowned, and so did two other roustabouts, in a futile attempt to rescue Stevens.[39] The history of the steamboat packets reveals countless acts of bravery on the part of roustabouts in times of crises, disasters, and tragedies. The same is true of those who lived in shantyboat colonies. In the catastrophic flood of 1927, which devastated the Lower Mississippi valley, the Arkansas and Mississippi delta bore the brunt of Mother Nature's fury when the system of levees designed by the US Army Corps of Engineers failed between Cairo and New Orleans. The swollen river mocked the engineers, who assured that the levees would hold. Shantyboaters were among those killed or uprooted, but generally they were better prepared to deal with floods than those who lived on land. Many joined rescue efforts to pluck refugees from trees, cabin roofs, and levees where they were stranded and without food. In Greenville, Mississippi, where 90 to 95 percent of the fertile area's cotton plantation labor force was Black,

William Alexander Percy, the aristocratic head of local relief efforts who otherwise despised shantyboat people, grudgingly gave the White River "bootleggers" their due in the flood disaster: "No one had sent for them, no one was paying them, no one had a good word for them—but they came. Competent, devil-may-care pariahs, they scoured the back areas . . . and never rested until there was no one left clinging to a roof or a raft or the crotch of a tree."[40]

With life on the river came risk and acceptance. The fate of those who lived and worked on the waterways was often determined by the river's rise and fall, by its seasons and cycles. To live in the moment and to trust the river gods was to roll the dice. The next roll might bring calamity or death from a tornado, flood, whirlpool, ice gorge, or a submerged log. In the face of every disaster and setback, denizens of the levee slowly but resolutely put the pieces of their life back together. No matter how much Lady Luck was smiling, life and labor on the temperamental river was not for the faint of heart.[41]

5

The Pride of St. Louis

KING OF LITTLE OKLAHOMA

A beer glass of egg-nog, swallowed at a draught like a glass of beer,
would surprise some stomachs, but it did not trouble the
internal economy of the Little Oklahomans.

—*St. Louis Post-Dispatch*, 1897

~~~~~

I have been King here for nine years.

—CAPTAIN LOUIS H. SEIBT, *St. Louis Post-Dispatch*, 1897

On Christmas morning 1897, a *Post-Dispatch* reporter hustled to Little Oklahoma at 10:30 to witness a celebration hosted by its leader, Captain Louis H. Seibt. Routinely lampooned in print as "King" of the colony, and called "Fritz" or referred to as "Dutch Fritz" by his "royal" subjects, Seibt brewed five gallons of eggnog for the festive affair. He sent word out the night before that he would provide holiday cheer. At the sound of a bugle, his subjects were to gather in his saloon for toasts and rounds of free eggnog. A few thirsty patrons jumped the gun. They showed up at daybreak, but Seibt sent them back to their houseboats and shanties. The community was still, no one stirring when the reporter arrived, but shortly Seibt summoned "Humpty Hum," trusted courtier and bugler. From a horn nearly as big as its blower, a loud blast beckoned residents to the saloon. "If the scene had been a country church yard," the reporter observed, "the dead would have been awakened."[1]

Seibt filled a dozen tall beer glasses with eggnog, and a dozen patrons stepped up to the bar. At his command, "Raise Up," each lifted a glass and quickly belted down a stiff drink of eggnog. "Fire and fall back!" He barked. At once the first rank fell back, and Seibt filled a dozen more glasses. Then the second rank stepped up to the bar for a repeat of the ritual. Residents who did not heed the bugle blast soon heard another. A few still did not respond, but Seibt dispatched a courier to roust them out for toasts. Once everyone downed a glass of eggnog, he exhorted them: "Step up and take your medicine again. This must all be drank up."[2] Afterward, the reporter noted in astonishment: "A beer glass of egg-nog, swallowed at a draught like a glass of beer, would surprise some stomachs, but it did not trouble the internal economy of the Little Oklahomans. On the contrary, one epicure declared [after downing five glasses] that he could not tell he had drank any egg-nog."[3]

Seibt, a Prussian immigrant, came to the United States shortly after the 1870–1871 Franco-Prussian War. Salt rheum patches—ugly scars from wartime saber cuts on the top of his head—and three or four bullets lodged under his skin were testimony to his battle-tested toughness. He clerked in a rag shop, worked as an ice cutter on the Mississippi, and shipped out as a roustabout on steamboat packets. In January 1880, a daughter, Emma, was born to him and his common-law wife, Mary Wender, whom he officially married in East St. Louis on July 2, 1882.[4] In early 1888, an incident during a railroad strike in the Louisville & Nashville yards of East St. Louis resulted in Seibt's beating at the hands of Illinois state representative George S. Bailey. A member of the local of the Switchmen's Mutual Aid Association, Bailey served the district and the United Labor Party in the legislature. He and Seibt, who at the time was an ice cutter on the river, provided two conflicting versions of the assault. According to Seibt, he was working nearby when a railroad worker told him someone in the yards wanted to see him. Without asking questions, Seibt followed him to the switch house, where Representative Bailey and two other men waited. Bailey confronted Seibt, accusing him of working for the Furlong Secret Service Company to help break the strike on behalf of the Chicago, Burlington & Quincy Railroad. Bailey, the subject of two attempted assassinations since elected in 1886, charged that Seibt knew the identity of whoever fired a shot at him during the strike.[5]

Seibt claimed that Bailey hit him with a blunt object and knocked him out. After Seibt regained consciousness, he staggered into the police station in East St. Louis and swore out a warrant for Bailey's arrest. At the station, Seibt suffered seizures and convulsions related to the blow. The police feared he might die, but he was much improved by the next day. Officers arrested Bailey, who admitted that he hit Seibt but insisted that he hit him for a good reason with his fist, not a blunt object. According to Bailey, Seibt came to the switch house shanty in the yards at his own initiative, suggesting he held information as to who fired shots into Bailey's home about a year earlier, striking the crib where his infant slept. Bailey did not believe Seibt, whose suspicious behavior suggested that he was trying to blackmail someone for money. When Seibt vigorously denied the charge and called him a liar, Bailey punched him twice, insisting to the justice of the peace that he had sufficient provocation. When Seibt failed to appear at the hearing, the judge dismissed the case.[6]

Around that time, Seibt became a widower left to raise his daughter, Emma. Soon afterward, he docked his shantyboat in Little Oklahoma, where he fished for a living until he secured a dramshop license from the office of City Collector (and future Mayor) Henry Ziegenhein. The city issued the license for six months. After Seibt's application for a one-year federal liquor license was approved and paid in advance in July 1893, he opened a fully licensed saloon and grocery store on a new boat he bought and painted green. His financial investment in the waterfront store/saloon, the only one in the growing settlement, paid off as business boomed. On Sunday afternoons the saloon sold as many as thirty-five kegs of beer. The profits enabled him to diversify into the skiff rental business as well. By mid-decade, he presided over a fiefdom of squatters on the north wharf. Seibt did his best to keep a lid on trouble in the saloon, but on November 4, 1893, a raucous argument among a group of hard-drinking men led to a fight and killing outside the saloon after Seibt kicked them out.[7]

The murder brought greater police scrutiny, but Seibt enjoyed a thriving business until new state excise tax legislation stopped him in his tracks when he sought to renew his city license in January 1894. The 1893 law imposed a new tax on saloons and mandated stricter requirements that a license application be supported by two-thirds of property owners in the area where the saloon was to operate. Seibt, who owned no waterfront acreage, failed to meet the new requirements. Excise Commissioner Nicholas M. Bell rejected his renewal application when the Schulenburg-Boeckler Lumber Company opposed it. Elizabeth Schulenburg, who lived in California, owned the nearby property. Seibt protested that it was impossible for him to get her permission from such a far distance, but the lumber company asserted its right to speak on behalf of her family interest in the matter. As a result of the license application's rejection,

Seibt forfeited half of what he paid for a full year in advance to obtain the federal liquor license. Indignant, he complained of unfairness, pointing out that his boat was connected to the city only by way of a long gangplank. He closed his saloon briefly but continued to sell groceries. "Everything was lovely," he later recalled, "but when the excise law was passed it knocked everything in the head."[8]

As Seibt fumed, he decided to continue operating his saloon near the foot of Mallinckrodt Street in defiance. Police arrested him repeatedly and slapped him with heavy fines, but he hired a cheap attorney on retainer. He appealed each fine and won every appeal, he later bragged. Emboldened by Seibt's success, competitors in the settlement at the time, Ellis Davis and Jeremiah Burroughs, launched a saloon-boat operation offshore. In June 1894, they set up a saloon on a flatboat anchored about fifty yards offshore at the foot of Buchanan Street and briefly did a thriving business until police shut down the operation. Determined to clamp down on flatboat saloons, Charles Speck, the internal revenue collector in St. Louis, denied a retail liquor license to a firm that aimed to sell whiskey on a flatboat near the government works at St. Genevieve. In June 1894, Joseph S. Miller, the commissioner of internal revenue, upheld Speck's action, emphasizing that the only boats eligible for liquor licenses were steamboats.[9]

Seibt, who previously played by the rules, embarked down the "highway of lawlessness." Adopting a new strategy in the face of police harassment, he went to Carondolet and paid for construction of a gasoline excursion steamer, which he named the *Pride of St. Louis*. He returned to the shantyboat settlements and in a bumboat kind of operation sold offshore liquor and onshore groceries to waterfront dwellers. As he proudly explained, "I dropped anchor a little way out from shore. All the shantyboat people had skiffs and there was no falling off in the patronage of my bar." If police showed up to arrest him, he quickly raised anchor and sped away. "I could cross the river in four minutes with that boat," he boasted.[10]

Seibt's moorings were still in Little Oklahoma, part of which was on property owned by Edward Mallinckrodt, a chemical manufacturer, pharmaceutical supplier, and philanthropist. Mallinckrodt, ex-governor David Francis, the Maffitt and Franciscus Real Estate Company, and lumber businessman August Wilhelm Schulenburg planned with city officials a waterfront industrial development project that led to police evictions of squatters, including Seibt, near the foot of Mallinckrodt Street in June 1895. Seibt and others with seaworthy houseboats relocated to nearby locations on the wharf. He and his fifteen-year-old daughter, Emma, moored in a new spot near the foot of Destrehan and Angelrodt streets. On December 10, 1895, Emma married John Schreiner, a paperhanger. About a month later, Seibt married Schreiner's mother, a widow who reportedly brought a sizeable sum of money to the marriage. The four of them lived on the *Pride of St. Louis*, but John was soon stricken with typhoid fever and nearly died. When he recovered well enough, Seibt hired him as a bartender.[11]

Seibt operated his saloon without a license, at times on shore and at times on the river, but grew weary of the cat-and-mouse game with police and hit upon a new plan. He convinced a brewery to lease a strip of land from the Schulenburg family who owned it. The brewery then subleased the strip to Seibt. Now with the brewery's support, he had the requisite two-thirds majority to secure a saloon license in June 1897. With a license proudly displayed on the wall of his saloon and grocery store, Seibt took further steps to consolidate his fiefdom. On the strip he subleased were about twenty houseboats and several shanties without hulls. Now a landlord by virtue of the sublease, he notified all inhabitants that unless they paid him 50 cents a month in rent, they would have to move elsewhere. If they stayed, he promised to provide them with protection and other services.[12]

The first test of Seibt's landlord authority came from Black squatters when he sought to relocate his saloon and supply store. Hard rains made the settlement's narrow lanes impassable and virtually cut off access to his business. Seibt desired to move closer to the railroad tracks, where patrons could step from the cinders and enter his saloon on a gangplank without getting their shoes muddy. A shantyboat belonging to John Ramsey, a Black counselor and spiritual adviser in the settlement, occupied a spot where Seibt intended to relocate his saloon. Ramsey balked when Seibt indicated he wished to swap living locations with him. Ramsey, "a rag picker on week days and preacher on Sundays,"[13] had a small following in the settlement. He launched a campaign to protest Seibt's collection of ground rent. The campaign resonated among a few who believed they had as much right to their living places as Seibt did. Ramsey filed a suit against him and refused to pay rent. According to a reporter, a growing number of supporters secretly supported the "no rent" movement. Tensions escalated when Seibt marched over to Ramsey's shantyboat to order him and his followers out of the settlement because of nonpayment of rent. When Ramsey refused to comply, a heated argument broke out. Ramsey whipped out a knife and chased Seibt back to the saloon, where the bartender's intervention prevented further escalation. Ramsey threatened to kill Seibt, who, after the fracas, kept "a small cannon strapped to his hip."[14]

At Seibt's behest, police arrested Ramsey, who was fined $5, but the preacher continued to resist Seibt's authority. Seibt threatened possession of his shantyboat, but Ramsey retorted that his wife owned it. Seibt gave Mrs. Ramsey thirty days' notice to vacate. In late November 1897, Seibt filed a suit for $10 against Ramsey, who insisted that neither he nor his brethren would comply with Seibt's mandate. A reporter noted that "the reverend gentleman backs up his earnestness with the display of a revolver."[15] After Seibt won the suit, police officers ejected Ramsey from the settlement. In desperation, Ramsey offered 10 cents a month in rent if he could stay, but Seibt and the officers rolled his shantyboat into the river. "The blacks are out of my kingdom for all times to come," Seibt reportedly proclaimed. As the case suggests, racial tensions lurked beneath the surface, but the color line was not always so rigidly drawn in the sand and mud of waterfront settlements. Ramsey moved his shantyboat to the nearby Dock Street Addition to Little Oklahoma, which featured a mixture of Black and white squatters with a heavier preponderance of Black inhabitants. The dispute was fraught with racial tensions, but a reporter who covered Seibt's ejection of Ramsey emphasized that the color line was not at the heart of the conflict.[16]

According to Seibt, the faction led by Ramsey stood in the way of his plans to beautify the area and open a beer garden the following summer. Seibt intended to plant two hundred willow trees to create a little grove where he could seat patrons at tables and chairs under a canvass roof to protect them when it rained. Editor William Arste, of the *Waterways Journal*, scoffed at the plans for the grove, "where a grasshopper would starve to death in a week unless he could live on the sand which is there."[17] At Seibt's behest, however, a few tenants were already busy cutting willows upriver and hauling them by boat to the settlement. Seibt claimed he ejected Ramsey and his followers so that no malcontents would raise objections when he applied for a license to run a summer beer garden. Seibt had other ambitious plans to build three bathhouses where patrons for a nominal charge of 5 cents could rent a towel and bathing suit and swim without fear the police would chase them away. He envisioned using his trim-built steamer to pilot St. Louis residents from the city wharf to his garden spot, "thereby saving them from the walk from Broadway and Angelrodt streets over unromantic mud heaps and garbage pits, and the debris of canned goods."[18]

In a *Post-Dispatch* interview while the case against Ramsey was underway, Seibt recounted his history in Little Oklahoma. "I have been King here for nine years," he proudly asserted, emphasizing that his waterfront business was entirely legitimate. He claimed he was arrested and acquitted fifty-three times during his operations in the settlement. "I am a licensed captain myself," he boasted. "Here is my picture in my captain's uniform. I was a roustabout once, and I have climbed up to be a captain."[19] While Seibt and the reporter stood on the waterfront for the interview, an itinerant Black shantyboat owner docked and asked Seibt how much he charged to tie up his boat in the settlement. Seibt replied that the charge was 25 cents to tie up, and 50 cents if he wanted to pull his boat up onto the land itself. When the traveler indicated he just wanted to tie up there, Seibt consented, stressing that all he expected in return was that he buy what he needed at his grocery store and saloon. The stranger at once entered the saloon and bought a beer. "You see that's the way we treat them. They treat me right and I treat them white," he insisted as he shook his fist in the direction of Ramsey's shantyboat, "but if they get gay and say they have as much right here as me, why I show them."[20]

Seibt played up the harmonious nature of the settlement, which included a number of European nationalities: "No one steals here. You can leave your ax or your pocket-knife on the ground, and it will be safe." The residents, he noted, were roustabouts, carpenters, fishermen, factory and railroad workers, and other "men of independence and freedom, who prefer not to be cramped up in tenements and alley dens."[21] When trouble did occur, it mostly came from outside the settlement, Seibt pointed out. "Everybody tends to his own business and lets everybody else's business alone," he stressed. "So there ain't any trouble. A policeman comes along through here, but he never has anything to do unless some bum comes down here from uptown and raises a row."[22]

An occasional self-imposed cast-off from the world of the upper middle-class drifted into Little Oklahoma. Such was the case of attorney Eugene

Bruemly, who fled his family and law practice in Ionia, Michigan, after un-requited love broke his heart and contributed to personal financial ruin and embarrassment. He fell apart, lost his position in a law firm, and disappeared in disgrace and humiliation. He opened a law office in Colorado and did well until a fire destroyed his office. He showed up in Little Oklahoma in January 1897 and took a job for wages in a St. Louis glue factory and slaughterhouse. Well-mannered and respected for his intellect, Bruemly bought a boat next to Seibt's saloon and kept to himself with his typewriter and law books. Devoutly religious, he attended services at the Niedringhaus Memorial Mission, which provided religious, educational, and athletic activities to the north waterfront. Bluemly showed no inclination to contact his family in Ionia, but a brother-in-law tracked him down after a lengthy search. At first, Bruemly was unmoved by pleas to return home, but when told that his sister was slowly dying of a disease, he left with his brother-in-law after a year in the settlement.[23]

Winters in St. Louis's shantyboat settlements meant added deprivation, suffering, and illness. Disease hit Little Oklahoma hard a couple of days after the 1897 eggnog Christmas celebration. Seibt summoned Dr. Edward F. Randall, of the North End Dispensary, which serviced the emergency medical needs of the poor. Randall treated Seibt's sixty-year-old bodyguard, Thomas Stewart, as well as the bugler, Humpty Hum, and "Squirts," who was dubbed the court jester by a reporter. All three of Seibt's loyal friends were quite sick. Randall sent Stewart to the city hospital in critical condition. A reporter noted, "His [Stewart's] ailment is the result of starvation. Times are hard in the squatter settlement."[24]

When tensions between the United States and Spain over Cuba escalated in early 1898, Seibt gathered men of the settlement around him to announce he would form a volunteer company for combat. Promising to provide recruits with arms and ammunition, he enrolled fifty-two volunteers. "Every one of them is heart and soul in the movement," he assured. "I fought in seven battles of the Franco-Prussian War. In the settlement are 13 experienced seamen. We are going to have drills daily." Seibt sent the following message to the secretary of the navy: "Sir—Louis Seibt of Little Oklahoma stands ready to march on Cuba with 100 fearless men at the first bugle blast. Our sympathies are always with the Stars and Stripes." The *Waterways Journal* noted derisively that the plan to raise a Little Oklahoma naval fleet of shantyboats bound for Cuba "will be carried out to the letter if the potent influences of beer and other booze work all right."[25]

With a ship captain's spyglass, Seibt kept an eye on the waterfront, sometimes using his boat to help search for drowning victims. He bought several houseboats and rented them to those looking for a place to live on the north wharf. Knowledge of the river earned him added respect in the settlement. His influence extended beyond his own leased acreage, as other Little Oklahomans and wharf inhabitants patronized his saloon and grocery store. When patrons suggested he provide music, he opened a little concert hall where his followers gathered to drink and dance.[26] The transformation of the grove even earned the grudging respect of editor Arste, who earlier scoffed at Seibt's plans for the area. Arste, perhaps a bit tongue-in-cheek, acknowledged the time and money Seibt put into the grove: "It is a living illustration of what can be done by man in causing the waste places to blossom like the rose. . . . Through an artistic arrangement of rapidly growing trees, a beautiful grove has sprung up as if by magic, where the weary can find rest, the hungry be fed, and the thirsty be supplied with the most delicious beverages."[27]

Seibt's financial picture was bright in the summer of 1898. His saloon/store, grove, and beer garden in Little Oklahoma did a booming business. He left in late October to spend the winter in the Mississippi delta, where the *Pride of St. Louis* was chartered to tow cottonseed on the Yazoo River to the Greenville oil mills. He first stopped by the office of the *Waterways Journal* to let Arste know his plans. Later reports indicated that Seibt was laid up in Greenville with his steamer for sale, but by March he and his steamer were in Little Oklahoma, where family troubles greeted him. The marriage between Emma and his son-in-law/bartender was on the rocks. In an argument over wages, Schreiner pulled out a revolver and fired at Seibt, who was uninjured. The dispute was settled without further violence, Schreiner continued to tend bar in the saloon, and Seibt found new uses for the *Pride of St. Louis*. When the celebrated gunboat *Nashville* visited St. Louis six weeks later, the city swelled with out-of-town visitors eager to tour the boat that played an important role in the war against Spain. Mayor Ziegenhein, members of the municipal assembly, and other dignitaries hosted a banquet for the officers, and there were many other patriotic festivities to welcome and honor the men aboard the gunboat. Seibt used his boat to carry sightseers and passengers to various points on the riverfront, including the excursion boats on the Illinois side of the river.[28]

Another squabble with his son-in-law over money turned violent in late

June 1900. Schreiner, who by now was separated from Emma and failed to support her, exploded in anger when Seibt confronted him. Schreiner fired pistol shots at Seibt, who ducked behind the bar. Schreiner fled but kept firing on the way out. Bullets shattered beer glasses and the mirror behind the bar. He hopped into a skiff as a nearby police officer heard the shots and came running. Schreiner fired at the officer from fifty feet off shore. The officer returned fire, but Schreiner escaped. At Seibt's behest, the officer arrested his other bartender, Ed Lindeman, for handing his pistol to Schreiner to use against Seibt.[29]

Soon after the ruckus, Seibt decided it was time to sell his investments and leave Little Oklahoma. On August 3, the *St. Louis Republic* ran a story titled "King Seibt Quits Oklahoma's Throne." Seibt found a buyer for his business operations. His decision to sell may have come from police pressure, but he claimed he intended to travel to New Orleans for rest and relaxation. A few days later, however, he was nabbed in a police raid across the river in Venice. The Madison Ferry Company earlier warned him and his followers not to squat on its riverfront property. The company alerted Venice police officers, who then broke up the party in a shantyboat camp near the Merchants' Bridge. They charged Seibt with selling beer without a license. He denied the charge but was locked up to await the October grand jury. Police torched the camp but spared the houseboats, warning occupants to vacate in a few days or face arrest. Venice police believed that Seibt was trying to establish a foothold on the Illinois side of the river.[30]

In Little Oklahoma's heyday, Seibt reigned as its king. He brought a degree of stability to the settlement and earned the respect of its inhabitants. His grocery and saloon, which he sold to George H. Smith, not only did a thriving business but served as an important working-class cultural institution on the levee. After his departure for New Orleans in the autumn of 1900, he never again achieved the notoriety and financial success that life in the settlement brought him. Nor was the settlement as stable after he left. On his leisure trip down the Mississippi, he made it as far as New Madrid before deciding to turn around and go back. Homesick for St. Louis, he sold his steamer and bought a smaller gas-powered boat for the return trip. By the first week in December, he was in St. Louis, where six years later he lost Emma to tuberculosis. He made a living as a junk peddler near the north wharf until his death on August 6, 1926.[31]

Seibt's departure from Little Oklahoma left a power vacuum. The settlement was plagued by internal conflicts and lost a considerable degree of cohesiveness after he left. As a steamboat pilot, Seibt spoke with an authoritative voice. He enjoyed credibility with police and other local authorities, even though he at times was the subject of derision and ridicule in newspaper articles. Soon after his exodus, minor fights broke out within factions vying to fill the vacuum. His sister, Lizzie Miller, and her daughter, Annie Kelly, tangled when Kelly tried to assert authority. When Kelly, dubbed "Queen Bess," threatened to whip her mother, a brawl ensued with friends of Miller coming to her aid. When police arrived, all of them jumped into the river in an effort to avoid arrest. Miller blamed her daughter, who ended up with a black eye and a fine of $5 in police court for starting the ruckus. "Annie has acted most disrespectful towards me of late and given scandal to our friends," Miller explained to the judge. "She started in to club me Sunday, and, of course, my friends came to my assistance."[32]

Two weeks earlier in the Dock Street Addition to Little Oklahoma, a Black successor to Seibt briefly emerged. Lulu Collins, the twenty-two-year-old sister-in-law of John Ramsey, whom Seibt had evicted from his strip three years earlier, led a faction that came to power briefly after Seibt's departure. She entered what she admitted was a marriage of convenience to John Collins, a forty-six-year-old ash cart peddler with a little money, but loud domestic arguments that disturbed their neighbors and brought police to the settlement ended their brief reign. Lulu and John were arrested on peace disturbance charges after an argument in which she beat her husband and slammed furniture around their shanty. John, who warned that her loud voice disturbed neighbors, threw her out of the house and started smashing dishes. A police court judge fined Lulu $5 but let John go.[33]

Gus Steimel emerged as the largest landlord with a degree of power in the settlement. Born in 1869 in Emporia, Kansas, to army surgeon F. C. Steimel and Mary Hürlimann, a Swiss immigrant, Gus moved to St. Louis with his mother and siblings in the late 1870s after his father abandoned the family. Mary remarried but divorced again, and in the mid- to late 1880s she moved with her children into a houseboat in Little Oklahoma, where Gus bought his own boat and married on April 30, 1894. Three years later, however, he sued his wife, Nellie, for divorce and married twenty-two-year-old Ora Viola Doyle on December 21, 1912. They had two children, Mamie Fay and Velma Pearl, but at age twenty-eight his wife died at the foot of Buchanan Street in 1919. Little Oklahoma remained Gus's home until he died of lobar pneumonia in his houseboat at age fifty-eight on January 7, 1928.[34]

Steimel, described by a 1900 census enumerator as a real estate speculator, established squatters' rights to a valuable one-acre tract in Little Oklahoma. When he tried to impose a ground rent increase on William Bareiter in the late fall of 1900, he hit a stumbling block. Bareiter, who under a previous lease paid a nickel every two weeks to locate his houseboat on Steimel's lot, balked when the lease expired and Steimel raised the rent to a dollar a month. Steimel threatened to evict him, but Bareiter objected to what he felt was arbitrary discrimination against him because his lease was shorter than others.[35] The dispute created turmoil in the settlement. Bareiter received a summons to appear in court to show good cause as to why he should be exempt from the rent increase. He recognized Steimel's right to charge rent but retorted that he would rather use his boat for kindling or move to a more democratically run community than submit to arbitrary tyranny. Steimel made clear that other squatters would be hit with the same rent increase when their leases expired, but Bareiter still objected. "Most of our neighbors pay nothing," he complained. "A few who occupy the narrow strip owned by the Bremin [sic] brewery promise to pay 25 cents a month, but the collection is not made often."[36]

Resentments against Steimel over ground rent increases may have played a role in an incident in which he was shot in August 1901. He was bathing in the river near the Merchants' Bridge when the current swept him downstream to one of the bridge's piers. He grabbed hold of the pier and caught his breath before continuing down the river toward his houseboat. Minerva Hill, a houseboat resident in the settlement, shot him with a pistol load of heavy bird shot in the scalp and left arm, inflicting painful flesh wounds. Whatever Hill told police convinced them to arrest Steimel at first, but they quickly released him and took him to get medical treatment for his wounds. Hill complained that bathers in the area had been harassing her lately.[37]

Bill Meyer, one of Little Oklahoma's most financially successful residents for twenty-five years, also enjoyed stature in the settlement. Owner of a popular fish market, he built affordable boats with a business partner, Sandy White. Meyer kept a cow, chickens, and hogs on his property. Because of new sidetracks and fill dirt put in by the Burlington Railroad nearby, his houseboat, one of the nicer ones with more attractive furnishings, resembled a regular house.

Hailed as "King" of the settlement at the time, Meyer reportedly had considerable money in a bank, but robbery was not the motive of an attack in which he was stabbed in his houseboat at the foot of Angelrodt Street. Charles Shaler Nelson, who lived with his wife and two children in a houseboat at the foot of Destrehan, burst through the door of Meyer's houseboat on October 17, 1906, and attacked him as he sat at the supper table with his wife and her teenage daughter Laura. Having reportedly warned Meyer previously, Nelson accused him again of having a clandestine affair with his wife.[38]

Mrs. Meyer screamed a warning to her husband. In the attack, both men ended up on the ground outside the houseboat, where she kicked Nelson hard in the jaw and Laura jumped on his back to prevent him from doing further damage with the knife. Nelson ran away, loosened his skiff, and rowed to the marshy areas on the Illinois side to hide from authorities. Meyer, who had back problems and rheumatism, made it to the North End Dispensary with the help of his wife. He was sent to the hospital in serious condition with several knife gashes, but he recovered from his wounds. Sandy White attributed the attack to a "Frogtown vendetta" by those who resented Meyer's success. According to White, financial jealousies prompted a few Little Oklahomans to convince Nelson that Meyer was having intimate relations with his wife. "Bill's prosperity has made some of these 'geeks' sore and they planned to 'do him,'" White told a reporter.[39]

About a month earlier, someone broke into Meyer's boathouse at the foot of Destrehan and did mischief. One of his boats sank to the bottom of the river, and the attached skiff was cut loose and set adrift. After considerable difficulty, the sunken boat was raised and the skiff retrieved, but to White the vandalism was the result of Nelson's misguided anger at Meyer, who had befriended Nelson and given him a job at one time. A week before the assault, Meyer found a note left on a pump handle at the boathouse. The writer of the note indicated that he was an ex-friend who planned to get even for an unspecified wrong. Meyer, described as "a good type of rivermen along the levee—ruddy faced, heavy set and of slow but picturesque speech," laughed off the threat.[40]

When Nelson, charged with assault to kill, was brought to trial in the St. Louis Circuit Court, the "unwritten law" became his defense. His lawyers argued that he had a right to attack Meyer because Meyer was messing around with his wife. Meyer denied intimate relations with Mrs. Nelson, but Shaler made clear that he warned Meyer repeatedly to stay away from her. Married for seven years, Nelson in fact insisted that he stormed Meyer's houseboat on the evening of the attack only to warn him again, not to stab him. According to Nelson, only when Meyer tried to smash a chair over his head did he whip out his knife in self-defense. When Mrs. Meyer's testimony corroborated her husband's, Nelson's attorneys tried to discredit and embarrass her by getting her to admit that she and her husband were not legally married. Her admission laid bare the dependent status of women in seeking marriage, whether legal or common-law, at the time. On the stand, she noted apologetically that with two children, "I had to get someone to support them and me."[41]

The defense attorneys put Mrs. Nelson on the stand at the end to make a dramatic revelation that turned the case. As jurors and courtroom spectators strained to hear, she confessed in a low voice that she and Meyer, whom she had known for thirteen years, were seeing each other secretly. According to her testimony, she wrote a note to Meyer one day with a heavy lead pencil that left an impression on a piece of butcher paper under it. Her husband discovered the butcher paper and confronted her. On that basis, the jury acquitted Nelson.[42]

Little Oklahoma had its share of internal conflicts in the decade after Seibt's departure, but it retained enough cohesiveness to remain as St. Louis's largest houseboat colony. In 1902, an estimated four hundred to five hundred squatters still called it home. Despite encroachments from developers, city officials, civic planners, and other squatters, Little Oklahomans fought tooth and nail to hang on to their wharf space. Whether the encroachment came from the city or from developers or from a fellow shantyboat squatter, residents of all waterfront settlements stood ready to resist. As the *Post-Dispatch* observed, "It is bad form, in Shantydom, to 'jump' another man's mooring place, and a 'stake jumper,' like his brother pirate, the 'claim jumper,' may have to fight to maintain his hold."[43]

6

Ain't Got No Place to Lay My Haid

RIVER FIDDLERS, RAGGERS, AND ROUSTABOUTS
IN RAGGED TIME

I slept on the cobblestones of the levee of the Mississippi.
My companions were perhaps a thousand men of both races.

—W. C. HANDY, *Father of the Blues*, 1969

~~~~~~

To sit on the bow of a packet on a moonlight night,
listening to the black roustabouts pouring out the pent-up sorrows
of their race in song, was an experience which even the dullest
and the most hardened could never forget.

—BEN LUCIEN BURMAN, "Music on the Mississippi," 1956

Music was an integral part of life on the levee. Steamer bells, show-boat calliopes, factory and freight train whistles, and a mate's endless profanity at roustabouts on the gangplank provided props for songs. For those who toiled and lived on or near the shore, the river put the moans and anguished cries of back-breaking labor and hard living to a rhythm and rhyme. You could feel the beat in the hustle and bustle of the wharf, the ragged time of "coonjine," the raucous, rowdy levee saloons, and the river's tumultuous cycles. In the gentle lapping of waves on the ancient shore at night, you could hear tender ballads and lonesome laments—tales of heartache, sorrow, and loss. If you paused long enough to listen to a levee train whistle as it faded in the night, you could hear the blues and lonesome, fading echoes of a lost lover or loved one. The distant, rhythmic call of a whippoorwill down the shoreline or a far-off steamboat whistle stirred wistful feelings and a longing for a better life. From minstrel shows, cakewalks, "coon songs," ragtime, blues,

~~~~

and "coonjine" of Black roustabouts to vaudeville, spirituals, Irish jigs, sea chanteys, and Appalachian folk ballads from the British Isles, the sand, mud, and cobblestones of the St. Louis wharf furnished rich soil for the cultural cross-fertilization of music that shaped the cultural history of the Mississippi River valley. As members of a casual, transient labor force on the waterways, roustabouts and shantyboaters helped to create, cross-fertilize, and transmit music in ports and steamboat landings. Whether in St. Louis, St. Paul, Memphis, or New Orleans, the levee fostered creativity and inspired songs that were shared across racial lines by Black roustabouts, white deckhands, and shantyboat migrants on the waterways. Jazz scholar William Howland Kenney credits levee culture in St. Louis, later a dynamic center of jazz and popular music, for shaping the roots of riverboat jazz.[1]

Singing and dancing were a rich part of the work culture of roustabouts on steamboat packets and the wharf. In an otherwise critical portrayal, a St. Louis newspaper in 1875 observed that a roustabout's "redeeming qualities are his cheerfulness under adversity, and his genius for singing rude melodies."[2] Members of St. Louis's high society routinely came to the wharf just to listen to roustabouts as they sang plantation melodies and bawdy levee songs while toting heavy loads of freight up and down gangplanks. Roustabouts sang as they rocked from side to side to shift and balance burdensome freight from shoulder to shoulder. They did so in perfect synchronization to a rhythmic, shuffling dance trot on the gangplanks. They often made up songs as they worked. They had songs for sacks, songs for cotton bales, and songs for every kind of cargo. W. A. Curtis, a writer/passenger on the *Sidney* in June 1914, described the role of music and the rhythmic dance trot on the gangplank at landings between St. Louis and St. Paul:

> Whenever we made a landing, the hall porter, a German mulatto, and the bootblack, with violin and banjo played on the upper deck, while the roustabouts unloaded and loaded. Trotting across the gangplank and into the warehouse went the roustabouts in perfect time to the music, flinging their feet out side-wise in most curious half-circles, bearing burdens that threatened to crush them. Poor, consumptive-looking mulattoes trotted along under great barrels of molasses that big white men could not lift, and every now and then some fellow, bent double with an enormous load, would

pause in an ecstasy and execute a double-shuffle on the gang-plank. The roustabouts did their work five times faster under the influence of music than they would have done without it.[3]

Thanks in no small part to the role of roustabouts in shaping levee culture and Black folk traditions, St. Louis was the epicenter of ragtime music, which flowered in the 1890s. W. C. Handy's experiences on the city's levee in 1892 included hearing a roustabouts' tune that by the mid-1890s became popularly identifiable as a ragtime song. He recalled hearing "The Bully," or "Looking for the Bully," played, too, by riverboat bands in St. Louis. Soon to be enshrined in popular culture, the song about a murder was performed on stage by "Mama Lou," who belted out bawdy levee songs at the Castle Club, Sarah B. "Babe" Connors's notorious St. Louis nightclub, bordello, and variety theater at 212 South Sixth Street. After hearing Mama Lou sing the song, a boyfriend of Canadian-born vaudeville "coon shouter" May Irwin brought it to her in 1896 for integration into her Broadway show, *The Widow Jones*. Irwin recorded it in 1897 and made the song a commercial success. The lyrics highlighted the murder of a levee roustabout by a rival roustabout. The song contained many verses, but the opening verse and chorus will suffice here to set up the murder:

> Have yo' heard about dat bully dat's just come to town?
> He's round among de niggers a layin' their bodies down.
> I'm a lookin' for dat bully and he must be found.
> I'm a Tennessee nigger and I don't allow
> No red-eyed river roustabout with me to raise a row,
> I'm lookin' for dat bully and I'll make him bow.
>
> Chorus:
> When I walk dat levee round, round, round, round,
> When I walk dat levee round, round, round, round,
> When I walk dat levee round,
> I'm a lookin' for dat bully an' he must be found.[4]

At the Castle Club, a popular spot for roustabouts and music that traveled on steamboats in the river valleys, Mama Lou performed a number of songs that became hits after they fell into the hands of capitalists in the music business, including "Ta-ra-ra Boom-de-ay," "There'll Be a Hot Time in the Old Town To-night," and others. Faye Templeton, a contemporary American actress in musical theater and comedy as well as a singer and songwriter, credited the Castle Club with the sweeping popularity of "coon songs" and ragtime in the 1890s. Roustabouts exerted a strong influence on the music that played in the night-club. As Templeton explained, "The boat hands from the south often sit down at the piano and play some melody picked up somewhere far down the big river."[5]

Murder ballads and songs about heroes and antiheroes flourished in a violent city with a rough-edged levee culture. A good example is a song that grew out of the infamous 1895 Christmas evening murder of Billy Lyons, a "levee hand," by his friend Lee Shelton ("Stack Lee," or "Stag Lee") in Bill Curtis's saloon, a popular roustabout hangout at the corner of Eleventh and Morgan. The murder gave birth to more than four hundred versions of "Stacker Lee," "Stagger Lee," "Stagolee," and other variants of the ballad. Lyons and Shelton, a carriage driver, gambler, and flashy pimp with a white Stetson hat and a rap sheet dating back at least eleven years, were drinking together when an argument over politics erupted. After Shelton struck and damaged the front of Lyons's hat, the latter snatched Shelton's Stetson from his head and refused to return it unless compensated for the damages. Shelton whipped out a .44 revolver, shot Lyons in the stomach, picked up his hat, and walked coolly out of the saloon. Shelton's defenders claimed he shot Lyons in self-defense and pointed to Lyons's unsavory character, but after a hung jury in the first trial, Shelton was convicted of second-degree murder and sentenced to twenty-five years in the Missouri penitentiary. Paroled in 1909 but returned to prison in 1911 after committing armed robbery and assault, he died of tuberculosis in the penitentiary on March 11, 1912.[6]

Soon deeply woven into American folklore, the song turned Shelton into a cultural icon. It is unclear who wrote it, but it was already popular when ragtime pianist Charlie Lee played it at a meeting of the Negro Press Association in Kansas City in 1897. The song likely traveled with roustabouts on the packets, spreading into the Mississippi delta and beyond. In 1910, published sheet music of the song appeared, and a Texas woman told song collector John A. Lomax that roustabouts sang it while loading and unloading steamboats. Will Starks, a blues balladeer from the Mississippi delta, first heard the song in 1897 from a man who said he learned it in levee camps near St. Louis. In a 1911 article in the *Journal of American Folklore*, sociologist and song collector Howard W. Odum included two versions of lyrics popular in southern states. Each version contained multiple verses and different melodies:

Stagolee was a bully man, an' ev'y body knowed,
When dey seed Stagolee comin', to give Stagolee de road,
Oh, dat man, bad man, Stagolee done come.

Stagolee killed a man an' laid him on de flo',
What's dat he kill him wid? Dat same ole fohty-fo'.
Oh, dat man, bad man, Stagolee done come.

or

I got up one mornin', jes' 'bout four o'clock;
Stagolee an' big bully done have one finish' fight:
What 'bout? All 'bout dat raw-hide Stetson hat.

Stagolee shot Bully; Bully fell down on de flo',
Bully cry out: "Dat fohty-fo hurts me so."
Stagolee done killed dat Bully now.[7]

Many subsequent versions bore little resemblance to the details of the murder. Given the explosion of ragtime in St. Louis in the 1890s, the song as originally written may well have been a ragtime number or at least a fusion of blues and ragtime. The first recordings were jazz foxtrot instrumentals in 1923 by white dance bands and orchestras—Fred Waring's Pennsylvanians and Frank Westphal & His Regal Novelty Orchestra. Cora "Lovie" Austin, a Black jazz and blues pianist, recorded the first version of the song with lyrics in 1924. Soon afterward, Ma Rainey recorded it to the melody of "Frankie and Johnny," with Louis Armstrong on the cornet. In 1928, Cliff Edwards ("Ukelele Ike") recorded "Stack O' Lee," but the classic, most recognizable recording came that year when Mississippi John Hurt did a finger-picking blues/country version that took Stack to the gallows.[8]

In 1897, musician and entrepreneur Tom Turpin, who played piano at the Castle Club when Mama Lou sang there, published his landmark composition "The Harlem Rag." His father, a local Republican politician and businessman, operated The Silver Dollar, a saloon where ragtime pianist Scott Joplin was hired to play soon after he arrived in St. Louis in the mid-1880s. Joplin went back to Sedalia for several years, but after returning to St. Louis in 1901 he wrote some of his most well-known songs, including "The Entertainer," while playing at Tom Turpin's Rosebud Bar. In 1900, Turpin, who took lessons from one of the city's top German-American pianists, opened the saloon complex at 2220–2222 Market Street in the heart of St. Louis's Black entertainment district. He advertised the saloon as a "Headquarters for Colored Professionals." Open day and night with two bars, upstairs lodgings, a gambling room, and a cafe in the rear, the complex, which took up a large share of a city block, became a cultural oasis for itinerant and local ragtime musicians until it closed in 1906.[9]

Critics of the music's "ragged time" and syncopated beat complained that the piano thumping style grossly violated the standards of European classical music and appealed to the uneducated, uncultured lower classes. The appearance of "Harlem Rag" in published form in 1897 partly undercut such criticisms. In the meantime, the culture created by roustabouts on the levee spread farther into Black neighborhoods, such as Mill Creek Valley and Chestnut Valley. Nearby Black elite entertainment clubs and hot spots absorbed the music being created and transmitted on the waterways. Ragtime soon was in high demand in the city, and enjoyed greater acceptance from critics. The exciting beat especially thrilled young people eager for rebellious expressions of original music or adaptations of earlier genres.[10]

The music's ragged time was rooted in the work rhythms and river culture of roustabouts. To keep tons of freight moving as quickly as possible, white steamboat mates chose a roustabout to set the pace of work by singing. The designated roustabout started a song with a rhythm that was in sync with the body movements of the gangplank dance trot to shoulder crushing loads of cargo. Many of the song structures were in the tradition of field holler songs on slave plantations. On the chorus, other roustabouts in "call and response" fashion joined in, making up lyrics as they went along:

I live in the kiln where the brick was burnt.

Chorus: O! Don't you tole me.
But who threw the brick was never learnt.
Billie Patterson rode by,
Chorus: O! Don't you tole me.
O! Bill, your horse will die,
Chorus: O! Don't you tole me.
If he dies I'll have his skin,
Chorus: O! Don't you tole me.
If he don't I'll ride again.
Chorus: O, yes I tole you.[11]

Music was plentiful on steamboats, which employed Black stewards, cooks, cabin attendants, and chamber maids, as well as firemen and roustabouts. Firemen often sang as they shoveled coal or muscled wood into the fiery hell of the steamboat's furnace. Packets usually had a banjo, guitar, or piano aboard for evening entertainment. Black stewards often put together a band of crew members to entertain passengers, whose luxurious conditions on the upper decks stood in sharp contrast to the conditions of roustabouts, firemen, low-fare passengers, and deckhands below. In 1875, Edward King described an evening of entertainment aboard the *Great Republic* en route to New Orleans: "In the evening, there is the blaze of the chandeliers, the opened piano, a colored band grouped around it and playing tasteful music while the youths and maidens dance."[12] Upper-deck cabin passengers pitched coins below to encourage roustabouts and crew bands to sing and perform dances commonly featured in minstrel shows. Captain William Hoban recalled that roustabouts danced the jig, pigeon wing, and the buck and wing. When roustabouts sang, they at times improvised their own percussion on the chorus by clapping hands, slapping knees, and making popping sounds by hitting their mouth with an open palm:

"Roll Out"

I hear dat bell a-ringing,
I see de Captain stand,
Boat done blow'd her whistle,
Roll out! Heave dat cotton—

Roll out! Heave dat cotton—
Roll out! Heave dat cotton,
Ain't got long to stay.

When they rested, they "patted juba":

Juba in, juba out,
Juba, juba, all about,
Dinah, stir de possum fat;
Can't you hear de juba pat?
Juba![13]

Journalist Lafcadio Hearn, who wrote about Cincinnati's levee life, captured many of the roustabouts' song lyrics and called attention to the cultural role of their music. On the levee, he heard spirituals and field holler songs by the formerly enslaved from east Kentucky and Virginia, as well as songs with bawdy, profane lyrics about levee life. With a band playing in a racially integrated dive on Cincinnati's Sausage Row, Black dancers amazed him with their gracefulness and perfect rhythmic coordination, "patting juba," stamping feet, and dancing wildly with arms intertwined. Hearn also noted the influence of Irish working-class music on Cincinnati's Black levee culture. He pointed out that Black roustabouts sang Irish songs with an Irish accent to perfection.[14] Among the most melancholy songs popular among roustabouts leaving port on the Ohio and Mississippi rivers was "Let Her Roll By." Roustabouts often sang it as their sweethearts stood on shore and waved farewell as the steamer glided down the river:

I'm going away to New Orleans!
Good-bye, my lover, good-bye!
I'm going away to New Orleans!
Good-bye, my lover, good-bye!
Oh, let her go by!

She's on her way to New Orleans!
Good-bye, my lover, good-bye!

She bound to pass the Robert E. Lee,
Good-bye, my lover, good-bye!
Oh, let her go by!

I'll make dis trip and I'll make no more!
Good-bye, my lover, good-bye!
I'll roll dese barrels, I'll roll no more!
Good-bye, my lover, good-bye!
Oh, let her go by!

An' if you are not true to me,
Farewell, my lover, farewell!
An' if you are not true to me,
Farewell, my lover, farewell!
Oh, let her go by![15]

The St. Louis levee provided a creative fountain for the blues. W. C. Handy's "Saint Louis Blues," written on Beale Street in 1914, came on the heels of his "Memphis Blues," which helped to launch the commercial popularity of the twelve-bar blues with a three-line lyrical structure. "Saint Louis Blues" grew out of homeless nights on the St. Louis levee in 1892. Cheated out of two weeks of wages by a Black labor contractor on a job in East St. Louis, Handy was nearly nineteen years old, musically literate, and from a deeply religious Alabama family, but he was stranded and hungry with no money and so lice-infested that he tossed away his shirt and undergarments. "I slept on the cobblestones of the levee of the Mississippi," he later recalled. "My companions were perhaps a thousand men of both races."[16] Destitute outside a white saloon one night, Handy was drawn inside by the sounds of a singer accompanying himself on a guitar to an old familiar song, "Afterwards." Two lines of the second verse had long appealed to Handy: *Sometimes my heart grows weary of its sadness, sometimes my life grows weary of its pain.* At first, he hesitated to step into a white saloon, but the pull of the music was too powerful. "Moved suddenly by the familiar tune," he wrote in his autobiography, "I forgot that I had no shirt under my coat, that I was a miserable sight and that I shouldn't have been in that place under any circumstances." The bartender treated Handy rudely at first, but "when he found that I too could play the guitar and sing that song as well as others, he changed his tone. When I had finished a second selection, the crowd in the saloon took up a collection, gave it to me, and invited me to come and sing often. I did not accept the invitation, but I did buy a change of clothing."[17]

Handy slept in a horse's stall at the racetrack, on a vacant lot with hundreds of others at the corner of Twelfth and Morgan streets, and in a poolroom chair in the Black entertainment district. He also slept on the levee, where he heard "shabby guitarists picking out a tune called 'East St. Louis.'" The song had many one-line verses like this one, sung repetitively: "I walked all the way from old East St. Louis, and I didn't have but one po' measly dime."[18] On the cobblestones one night, Handy overheard an intoxicated woman muttering as she stumbled past him in the darkness, "Ma man's got a heart like a rock cast in de sea." Curious as to the meaning of the words, he asked a nearby woman, who interpreted them for him: "Lawd, man, it's hard and gone so far from her she can't reach it." Twenty-two years later, the drunk woman's words ended up in the lyrics of "Saint Louis Blues" when fragmented memories of the levee inspired the musical composition and words. In the opening line, Handy wrote: "I hate to see de evenin' sun go down." As he noted in his autobiography, "And if you ever had to sleep on the cobbles down by the river in St. Louis, you'll understand that complaint."[19]

From sad love stories to bawdy tales of carousing and violence, songs about steamboat wrecks and races, and spirituals and songs of deliverance from bondage, roustabout music grew out of the harshness of life on the river in slavery and freedom. In the early 1880s when writer/artist Joseph Pennell boarded the *Mark Twain* steamer in Memphis bound for New Orleans, he was captivated by the singing of roustabouts as they loaded the boat. One of the roustabouts began in a low tone, and soon others followed. Pennell overheard these lyrics in the final verse of one of their songs:

Oh, Moses, he strutch out he's rod,
Oh-o-o-oh de Red Sea.
And de Childern's Isr'el pass ober dry shod.
Oh, de R-e-d Sea.
An' Pharaoh come follerin' down
By de R-e-d Sea.

Wid all de sojers in de town
By de R-e-d Sea!
An' dar de Lord confounded 'em
By de R-e-d Sea!
An' all de waters drownded 'em
In de R-e-d Sea!
Dis de way dat folks begin
By de R-e-d Sea,
An' dats de way dey tumble in
In de R-e-d Sea![20]

Many songs were work-themed. For a lonely roustabout kicked off a steamboat packet hundreds of miles from home on a dark shoreline, this popular bluesy song on the river held special meaning:

"Ain't Got No Place to Lay My Haid"

Ain't got no place to lay my haid,
Oh baby, ain't got no place to lay my haid,
Oh baby, ain't got no place to lay my haid.

Out on de col' an' frozen groun',
Oh baby, out on de col' an' frozen groun',
Oh baby, out on de col' an' frozen groun'.

Steamboat done put me out o' do's,
Oh baby, steamboat done put me out o' do's,
Oh baby, steamboat done put me out o' do's.

Steamboat done lef' me an' gone,
Oh baby, steamboat done lef' me an' gone,
Oh baby, steamboat done lef' me an' gone.

Don' know what in dis worl' I'm gwine tuh do,
Oh baby don' know what in dis worl' I'm gwine tuh do,

Oh baby don' know what in dis worl' I'm gwine tuh do.

Sweetheart's done quit me an' gone,
Oh baby, sweetheart's done quit me an' gone,
Oh baby, sweetheart's done quit me an' gone.[21]

Roustabouts on Paducah's *Joe Fowler* sang about the celebrated brawn and prowess, both physical and sexual, of "Stavin' Chain," a legendary rooster often referenced and transformed into a sexual hero by blues artists such as Lil Johnson, Jelly Roll Morton, Big Joe Williams, and others. In the steamboat world of roustabouts, "evuhbody ought to be lak Stavin Chain."[22] For men whose bodies ached everywhere and whose shoulders were rubbed raw until they bled from carrying barrel staves, livestock, and sacks of grain, potatoes, and other crushing freight that sometimes weighed 150 pounds or more, exploitation of labor was at the core of their lyrics:

Run here, dog,
And git yo' bone.
Tell me what shoulder
You want it on.[23]

Or, in a variation that further expressed low regard for the life of roustabouts on steamboat packets:

Nigger he ain't got no home
Makes his living from his shoulder bone.
Break a line, buy another
Nigger die, hire his brother.[24]

Roustabouts continued to influence Black music, even though the number of packets and roustabouts sharply declined in the 1920s. In the First World War era, music on the St. Louis riverfront underwent a shift toward riverboat jazz and dance music, thanks in large part to the German-American steamboat family of John Streckfus Sr., a fiddle player whose sons were musicians as well as captains. When it came to overseeing music on the boats, Streckfus trusted his son Joseph to make many of the decisions. In the 1890s and early 1900s, the Columbia Excursion Company and the Eagle Packet Company operated excursion boats profitably on the St. Louis riverfront. As steamboat freight traffic declined, Streckfus repositioned his Acme Packet Company to enter the excursion business to offset falling revenues from packets. In 1901, he oversaw construction of a custom-designed boat, the *J.S.*, which featured a large maple dance floor that held nearly two thousand patrons. Streckfus wanted lively dance music tailored to his specifications and designed to attract white middle- and upper-class dancers to the boat at night. After the *J.S.* burned in 1910, he bought the Diamond Jo Line of steamboats. Under the new name of Streckfus Steamboat Line, he and his sons converted packet boats to excursion steamers that operated on the Mississippi as well as the Ohio. The company's focus was on St. Louis, St. Paul, and Pittsburgh as summer ports and New Orleans as a winter port for harbor cruises.[25]

In 1907, Streckfus hired seventeen-year-old Fate Marable, of Paducah, to replace Charlie Mills as a pianist aboard the *J.S.* Both pianists were Black. For purposes of musical advertising, Streckfus insisted that Marable, whose mother taught him music theory and how to play the piano, learn to play the excursion boat's steam calliope. On the first trip from Rock Island to New Orleans, Marable played with Emil Flindt, a white violinist from Davenport, but he later added two other white members from Paducah to what became the four-piece Kentucky Jazz Band. Under his leadership, they played ragtime on the old Diamond Jo boat, the *Sidney*. After the horrible race riot in East St. Louis in 1917, Marable broke up his racially integrated band as the grip of Jim Crow tightened further on the Streckfus boats and elsewhere. Streckfus ran a tight ship, imposing curfews on the musicians. He and his son Joe dictated musical arrangements and every aspect of music aboard their boats, demanding that musicians attend daily rehearsals, read sheet music, play commercially arranged popular as well as traditional songs, and mostly avoid improvisation. No original music was tolerated. Captain Joe Streckfus, who attended rehearsals, even dictated the number of beats for specific dances and allowed no deviations, insisting that every fourth song in the set list be a waltz.[26]

The era's Great Migration of southern Blacks to northern cities included several New Orleans jazz musicians recruited and hired by Marable and Captain Joe Streckfus. Among them was Louis Armstrong in 1918, who joined Marable's Metropolitan Jaz-E-Saz Orchestra to play dance music with a powerful rhythmic drive on the *Sidney, Capitol, St. Paul,* and *J.S. Deluxe.* Although New Orleans musicians recruited by Marable did not read music, they agreed to learn under his tutelage aboard the excursion boats on which they worked and often slept. After Armstrong and drummer Warren "Baby" Dodds left the band in 1921, fewer New Orleans musicians were willing to work in St. Louis. As a result, Marable recruited more young Black musicians from St. Louis to play in their home port.[27]

As leader of a large orchestra, Marable navigated the transition from ragtime and the blues of roustabouts to jazz and popular dance music aboard the Streckfus Steamers until 1940. He bent to Streckfus's specifications but negotiated a small space for improvisational freedom that incorporated the New Orleans traditions of many of his orchestra members. The instrumental synthesis that resulted retained elements of the rhythmic singing of roustabouts. Although Marable earlier included white musicians in his orchestra, the bands he fronted on Streckfus excursion steamers in the interwar period were Black and unionized into segregated locals of the American Federation of Musicians. The composition of Marable's orchestra changed from time to time as band members left to play with Cab Calloway, Fats Waller, King Oliver, Duke Ellington, or other great band leaders.[28]

Black excursionists were allowed aboard Streckfus boats on Monday nights only. On the other six nights of the week, the orchestra and the boat's roustabouts were the only Blacks on board. Black patrons booked reservations through Jesse Johnson, a Black St. Louis booker, as per arrangement with Streckfus. New Orleans drummer Warren "Baby" Dodds remembered how special those Monday nights were:

> The boat was packed and we got such a kick out of it because it gave us a free kind of sensation for working. We worked all the week for white people and this one night we could work for colored. It gave us an altogether different sensation, because we were free to talk to people and the people could talk to us, and that's a great deal in playing music. We were less tense because it was our own people. I especially loved it because I made a big sensation with my shimmy beat. I used to shimmy and drum at the same time, shake all over. The colored people had never seen anything like that.

I used to have a bunch around me backed up five or six deep; and Louis Armstrong would have a bunch five or six deep backed up around him. It was a wonderful thing, and we were the two sensational men on the boat, Louis and I.[29]

Known for his own authoritarian manner, Marable and members of his orchestra were confined by the musical structure imposed by Streckfus, but the adapted riverboat jazz that grew out of the structure retained elements associated with the Black folk music of roustabouts. Marable noted in 1945 that "jazz was the outgrowth of Negro life in New Orleans. It developed from the chants of roustabouts loading cotton boats, singing with perfect rhythm as they lifted the bales." Danny Barker, a New Orleans jazz guitarist, songwriter, and banjoist, further connected the dots between roustabouts and jazz: "This is how the riverboats got music on them. Those boats had roustabouts on them, and half of those roustabouts played guitar, and nearly all sang. Well, when those boats went up the river, the roustabouts were on the lower deck, and the passengers, the gamblers, et cetera, stayed up on the upper deck. But when the people on the upper deck heard the singing and playing of the roustabouts, they would come downstairs, and that gave Strekfus [sic], the owner of the boats, the idea of putting music on the boats."[30]

Streckfus provided white upper-class patrons on the boats with reassuring and all-too-familiar racial and class images from the nineteenth century. The company used the employment of Black dance orchestras in the age of jazz to tap into images of caricatured roustabouts singing, working, and entertaining white passengers on steamboat packets. Highly professional riverboat jazz musicians clad in tuxedoes hardly resembled roustabouts in tattered, muddy work clothes and beat-up hats, but the company's literature promoted imagery that harkened back to minstrelsy and the golden era of steamboats. *Streckfus Steamers Magazine* interpreted the Mississippi River for passengers and would-be passengers, often drawing on Mark Twain's literary characters as points of reference. The magazine even produced "Jim" in the form of a fictionalized roustabout who fulfilled minstrelsy stereotypes. The imagery must have reassured residents of Hannibal, described by "Baby" Dodds as "a hard place." In Ralls County, whose eastern boundary is the Mississippi and whose northeast corner touches the city limits of Hannibal, a newspaper expressed the vilest racist condemnation of jazz in 1925: "Those tum-tum-tummy songs were a flareback to barbarism. It is the sort of music that it is favored in the best mid-African society where the women with rings through their noses beat on drums while the men stamp the ground with the skulls of their enemies dangling around their necks."[31] Dodds remembered that on the orchestra's first nighttime excursion out of Hannibal, not a single patron danced. The sight of a dignified Black orchestra stunned the town's white patrons. They sat and stared in stubborn, sullen silence at band members who did not conform to the roustabout caricature. "I think the first time it was a surprise for the people," he recalled. "They had never before seen Negroes on the boat. They saw Negro roustabouts but had never seen a Negro with a tie and collar on, and a white shirt, playing music. They just didn't know what to make of it." On a subsequent trip, he quickly added, Hannibal patrons "were the most dancingest people I ever found on the boat."[32]

In 1897, when patrons suggested musical entertainment at Louis Seibt's saloon, beer garden, and grove in Little Oklahoma, he added a small concert hall for dancing and listening to music. As a former roustabout, ice cutter, and steamboat captain, he was attuned to music popular on the levee. He brought in river fiddlers, ragtime pianists, and organ grinders who made the waterfront shantyboat settlement their headquarters in the spring. One of the most popular fiddlers in waterfront communities from St. Paul to Dyersburg, Tennessee, was John F. Beeman. Born in 1841 in Cayuga County, New York, he was the son of a German ship engineer/machinist who moved his family from Ashford, New York, to Richland, Wisconsin, in the mid-1850s. In Montbello, Wisconsin, John married Hannah Reichart, "county belle," and they moved to a farm in Winona, Minnesota. When Hannah experienced chronic health problems, they bought a shantyboat. With their children, they drifted down the Mississippi in hopes that Hannah's health would improve with fresh air and a change in lifestyle. According to Beeman, river life proved an elixir for her ailments. He claimed she was cured by the time they docked in St. Louis. They continued their float south until they reached the mouth of the Obion River about 120 miles north of Memphis. They sold their houseboat, bought a yawl, and rowed up the Obion/ Forked Deer River to Dyersburg, where they spent the winter among Black and white sawmill workers. From then until Hannah's death in St. Louis on January 3, 1889, the Beemans were river gypsies, one of the best-known couples in waterways settlements. John entertained levee dwellers and river "pigs" who steered huge rafts of white pine logs from Minnesota and Wisconsin to lumberyards in Hannibal, St. Louis, and points below. On board a large raft boat, fiddlers like Beeman performed in the center of the raft as river pigs sang, danced, and engaged in boisterous laughter.[33]

The Beemans lived in St. Louis's Little Oklahoma at the time Hannah died in 1889. John tried afterward to settle down but grew restless with the fall colors and honking of southbound geese. The river was in his blood. He returned to Dyersburg, but played many gigs in the St. Louis area. With one or more of his sons, he docked at the Merchants' Bridge on the Illinois riverfront in Venice.[34] With an impressive repertoire of fiddle tunes, Beeman picked up extra money for "luxuries" by entertaining toe-tapping riverfront dwellers. With an ear to regional political sensitivities, he included "Dixie" or "Marching Through Georgia," depending on where he performed. He played a rousing rendition of the Irish folk song and jig "The Irish Washerwoman." Patrons of Seibt's saloon in Little Oklahoma, Jimmy McGinley's tavern in Chickentown, and other settlements in St. Louis drank, swapped river stories, and listened to his music. They danced a lively jig to Beeman's music at one moment, and at the next, tears filled their eyes as he put them in a dreamy state with "Home, Sweet Home," a parlor ballad popularized in the Civil War. A newspaper noted in 1894 that he "could scrape a melody out of his old violin that would fit any dance the boys and girls of [Little] Oklahoma would start up and after his arrival dances were given weekly if not oftener."[35] Waterfront squatters couldn't wait for Beeman's houseboat to dock. "Children love the old man," a reporter observed in 1905. "They become his friends in whatever cove he lands; in every floating village, he is 'grandpa.' He plays for them and tells them wonderful tales of the river— the great wonderful river which they live on but know so little about."[36]

In the winter of 1904–1905, the "Ancient Mariner of Shantyboatmen" made what he claimed was his fortieth consecutive migration south. His youngest son accompanied him in a larger shantyboat with coops of chickens and pet pigeons. In Venice, Beeman noted that his boat, fiddle, and pigeons were his dearest treasures in life. "I sorter like the river," he reflected. "I have lived on it so long that I guess I'll die on it."[37] During a flood in June 1908, a neighbor was trying to escape high floodwaters when he heard groans in an unmanned shantyboat floating aimlessly in the Carr Island slough. Inside, Beeman lay unconscious. Last seen four days earlier, he was without food or drink. After lingering for several months, he died of carcinoma of the mouth and blood poisoning on November 20, 1908.[38]

Folk ballads and jigs were popular in shantyboat settlements, where musicians, especially fiddlers, were in high demand. When Captain Edward Pillsbury reunited and reconciled with his wife, Katie, and stolen houseboat in an East St. Louis squatter settlement on Christmas Day 1901, it was a joyous occasion that called for a music-filled celebration. Only the day before, he brought charges against Abraham Paltrow for stealing his houseboat and his wife in Alton, but when he located his boat and remorseful wife alone on the East St. Louis waterfront, he notified squatters of a party at their houseboat. Captain Pillsbury, whose *New Haven* steamer operated a packet on the Missouri River, hired one of the best fiddlers in the settlement to provide the entertainment. When a young man in the shantyboat settlement sang "Oh, Whistle and I'll Come to You, My Lad," a Scottish tune by Robert Burns, Captain and Mrs. Pillsbury joined in the singing of the chorus.[39] Other songs by the fiddler included "Absence Makes the Heart Grow Fonder" and "Arkansas Traveler." There were many adaptations of the latter song's lyrics, but by 1900 the popular version had turned into a swipe against Arkansas hillbillies. For houseboat squatters, the song's dialogue between a poor Arkansas squatter and the Traveler, an educated outsider, held special appeal because of the way newspapers, magazines, and town folks demeaned and despised them.[40]

The Appalachian "Cripple Creek," a lively fiddle song later recorded by Gid Tanner and His Skillet Lickers in 1929, was popular among shantyboaters, but writer and song collector Ben Lucien Burman pointed out that many songs he heard in waterfront colonies were "mournful" and often "grim." He once came upon a scene in which an old woman, badly sick on a boat, seemed to be on her deathbed. "Her family and neighbors, all Holy Rollers, sat around the bed and chanted in hypnotic rhythm the strange ritualistic Appalachian folk song 'O Death'":

What is this that I can see
With icy hands taking hold of me?
I am death and none can't tell
I open doors to Heaven and Hell.

I'll fix your feet so you can't walk.
I'll lock your jaws so you can't talk.
I'll close your eyes so you can't see.
This very hour come and go with me.
chorus: O, Death, O Death, O Death.
Please spare me over till another year.[41]

Among the ballads, jigs, gospel hymns, and songs popular in waterfront settlements was a lament that spoke to the antagonistic relationship between shantyboats and steamboats. From the perspective of waterfront squatters, the following incident reflected the bad blood between them and steamboat pilots. In late June 1903, Josephine Whitehouse was standing on the front of her houseboat north of the Lee Line Steamers' warehouse in Caruthersville when the *Stacker Lee* barreled past at full speed near shore. Huge waves ripped loose one of the Whitehouse cabin-boat's fastenings and upended Whitehouse into the murky waters of the Mississippi. Fortunately, her husband and others rescued her. She suffered bruises on her shoulders and back and swallowed a lot of water, but escaped without serious injuries. Her experience was one of many that fueled resentments against pilots as expressed in song by the fictional Aunt Vergie in a high-pitched nasal tone in Burman's 1929 novel, *Mississippi*:

Oh, I don't like a steamboat man,
Oh, I don't like a steamboat man
He'll swamp you, he'll torment you,
He'll drown you if he can.
Oh, I don't like a steamboat man.[42]

When a St. Louis reporter toured Squatters' Town at the foot of Dorcas Street in 1892, he admitted that its residents didn't conform to prevailing images of "river rats" in squatter colonies. He met two pretty young actresses— Lou Mitchell, "a dashing blond," and Anna Stillman, "a petite brunette." Mitchell and Stillman wrote and performed character sketches in riverboat shows. Reportedly, one of their sketches was about to be sold for a considerable sum of money. "Life in Squatters' Town never gets monotonous," observed the reporter. "There are balls and parties every week at which the elite of the settlement turn out en masse." Hosts of the parties and dances put out large board pathways so that attendees did not track mud into their houseboats. Women dressed in their finest clothing. The settlement's plentiful musicians provided the music. Stillman and Mitchell were "the reigning belles," and young men competed for dances with them. At times there was not enough space in the houseboat, but the reporter noted that "it is not a rare sight to see half a dozen couples enjoying the dizzy waltz on the roof of the cabin to the strains of violin and mouth-organ music furnished by Squatters' Town musicians."[43]

In 1916, the Hop Hollow colony on the Alton riverfront hosted a dance that featured a number of fiddlers. Among the invited guests were several shell diggers and their families and friends from upriver. Many were good fiddlers who called the figure-dance (square dance) to these lyrics in the traditional Missouri and Arkansas fashion:

> Honor your pard, lady on the left
> Jine eight hands and circle to the left;
> Retrail back in a single line,
> Lady in front and 'gent behin';
> Swing your pard and alimand [sic] Joe,
> Right and wrong and around you go.
> Hook and crook and the finger ring,
> Now turn yer lady on the double swing,
> Pound yer cinnamon, and roll yer dough,
> Swing your partner and do si [sic] do.
> First couple out to the couple on the right,
> Now pop the whip 'round yer lady tight;
> Break to the left and fall to the right.
> Hickory is the best of wood,
> Dancing does the ladies good;
> Around the gent—don't be too slow,
> Four hands up and around you go.
> Break and swing the left hand girl;
> Four hands up and one more yard—
> Break away and swing your pard;
> Four hands up and one more whirl,

Break and swing to the left hand girl;
Six hands up and another whirl—
Now break away with a left hand swing;
Chase the rabbit, chase the squirrel,
Chase the purty girl 'round the worl',
Hook and crook and the finger ring
Take yer lady on the double swing;
One foot up and one foot down,
But keep the ladies going 'roun and 'roun,
Six hands up and Hullo ding!
Promenade to yer seat and let the ladies rest their feet.[44]

In summer 1898, Seibt's saloon in Little Oklahoma became the center of a new dance craze and cultural fad among a subset of white working-class teenagers. Influenced by Irish jigs, hoedowns, and waltzes as well as African American ragtime and cakewalks, the subculture originated in north St. Louis and spread like a wildfire throughout the city. "Raggers" were known for their distinctive dancing, mode of dress, dialect, and toughened gang swagger. As the *Post-Dispatch* explained, "In addition to keeping up with the fashion in the wearing apparel, he or she who would be a ragger must master the ragger's dance, the ragger's walk, the ragger's slang and the ragger's unwritten laws of etiquette and propriety."[45] Jack Oliver, "King of the Raggers," tended bar five nights a week and lodged in Seibt's saloon. When a reporter asked Oliver to define a ragger, he replied: "Well, he's a whole lot. He's a swell dresser, a swell dancer and he's a good scrapper. Sometimes he don't look for a scrap, but he won't get out of the way. He's gotta know how to walk and he's gotta know how to talk. And, he's gotta have a pettie [girlfriend] which knows all them things, only he does the scrapping for her." Oliver set the dance floor style in a blue ragger suit and brindle hat. The coat was single-breasted with three rows of buttons on each sleeve, twelve in each row. The double-breasted vest, which sat low toward the waist, featured two double rows of buttons, four in each row. A dozen buttons adorned the bottom of each leg of the pants, which measured twenty-four inches around the knees as well as at the bottom. The shirt was white with a turned-down collar, pleated bosom and silk puffs, and suspenders. A ragger carried a rubber eraser to clean spots off his shirt, and his feet were squeezed into tan, pointed-toe shoes. A good pair of suspenders was also required. As Oliver explained, "We gotta do that to make the pants hang right. They gotta be good ones, too. No fifty c's. About a dollar I pay."[46]

A black tie made from a piece of ribbon worn by a "pettie" was part of every good ragger's attire. From behind the bar at Seibt's saloon, Oliver pulled out a piece of two-inch black ribbon worn by his pettie and demonstrated to a *Post-Dispatch* reporter how to fashion it into a tie. "He adjusted his collar," the reporter observed, "and deftly fashioned the ribbon into a four-in-hand knot. The ends were tucked under the shirt front about six inches below the collar."[47] Oliver spent about $40 to dress himself in the ragger way, but to stay ahead of countless imitators, he added new wrinkles to the style of dress in order to maintain his status. Most raggers didn't make much more than $40 a month, so they had to cut corners and scrimp on other things to afford the subculture attire. As he pointed out, the stakes were high: "If a ragger wants to stay up in front and keep some other guy from coppin his pettie he's gotta do this every three months. That's a whole lot in a year, specially if you ain't woikin." It cost much less to outfit a ragger's pettie. A white shirtwaist, black skirt, spring-heel shoes, and a sailor hat did the trick. "Well, the goils ain't so swell as the boys," Oliver explained. "You see they're nearly all woikin' goils and they gotta give their money home. The boys wear the flashy paint and the goils spoit the pretty mugs and the swell shapes. Say, any goil whit a little waist and a good pair of stilts can be somebody's pettie right sudden if she goes in the right company."[48]

The "look" was not the only distinctive feature of raggers. Second in importance was the dance technique. With the *Post-Dispatch* reporter as his audience, "King Jack" stepped from behind the bar to demonstrate dance steps on the sawdust floor. First came the "short-step glide." Oliver "straightened his shoulders, kinked his elbows, threw out his chest and chin and 'glided.' He meandered across the saloon by a series of heel-and-toe movements which caused not a muscular tremor above the knees." Then followed a demonstration of the ballroom glide. Oliver "stuck out his right arm to a horizontal position, made as if encircling the waist of his 'pettie' with the left, and floated around the sawdust floor. His feet were never more than six inches apart, and he looked like an automaton with only the feet working." Oliver explained that "your pettie puts her head on your shoulder, her right arm around your waist, and her left mitt lays in this one [right hand] out here."[49] To become a full-fledged ragger required more than the clothes, glide, spiel, and gum-chewing partner. A ragger rolled his own cigarettes, and had to "lick" another ragger to establish his bona fides and gain acceptance. When asked to name the Queen of Raggerdom, Oliver scratched his head briefly and named Jessie Gillespie, his partner. "Jessie is the best dancer and knows the lady raggers' glide better than any of them," he boasted. "She's only 18, but she's got 'em all skinned . . . say—come down here [Seibt's saloon] Sunday and see it."[50]

Raggers became all the rage in St. Louis, especially after a feature article on Oliver as "King of the Raggers" appeared in the Sunday edition of the *Post-Dispatch* on July 31, 1898. The cultural fad caught on at first among white working-class teens in north St. Louis who held jobs and could afford to dress in the style that Oliver showcased. The rage spread to south St. Louis, the West End, and across the river to the Columbia Excursion Company's excursion boats, which featured dance bands and entertainment. As "Rag" Mantell, discerning winner of several ragger dance contests, observed, "Uppin' Nort Sent Louis they're more graceful . . . They hold the woman away from 'em 'n' take it slow 'n' keep still 'n' chin the ladies in a corner after the dance."[51]

Seibt's saloon became the center of ragger cultural gravity. Business boomed as his waterfront beer garden became a popular hangout for about two hundred raggers and their "petties" on Sunday afternoons. Oliver's newfound status attracted a few who were eager to knock "King Jack" off his throne and challenge his claim to the title, both on and off the dance floor. On August 7, 1898, a week after the *Post-Dispatch* put the spotlight on the "King of Raggers" at the saloon, a second Sunday edition article featured Oliver, the ragger craze, and his challengers. While the reporter was in the saloon for a follow-up interview, Oliver pulled out a letter from Petey White, a challenger in Carondolet. White, who derided Oliver for wearing buttons at the bottom of his pants, invited him to prove his claim to the throne by competing against him in a dance contest for an amount up to $50. "Petey White! Wonder what laundry he smokes at," snorted Oliver behind the bar. He then turned to a serious ragger in the saloon: "Say, Blondie, whatdayutink of this spiel? Here's a guy which wants to do a medal twist in summer?" Blondie stepped up to the bar, read the letter, and laughed with Oliver at White's challenge. "Now, whoever heard of a medal twist in hot weather?" Oliver scoffed. "I'm right here to take care of mesel against all comers, but I ain't going to run whit no cheap screws like this Petey White."

As he explained, "If he was a ragger . . . he'd know that no good man is going to take chances whit his reputation on the rough floor of one of them summer garden pavelions [sic]. When a man goes to bet $50 on his style and grace he's gotta have wax under his feet and plenty of room."[52]

Oliver was aware that many raggers in the saloon were angry over his claim to the title. George Riley, who headed a group that met nightly in a saloon near Fifteenth Street and Cass, was known in the neighborhood as "Kid Lavigne" because of his fighting prowess. (Lavigne was a popular boxer of the time.) He claimed that dark green, not outdated blue, was the winning color of a ragger's suit. Before he left Seibt's saloon, he criticized nearly every feature of Oliver's mode of ragger dress. Jimmie Reardon and Louis Gill disputed that there was a king or queen of raggers. "If yer want ter put somein' in the poiper about raggers jes' say dey never has no money," asserted Reardon. "I tell you how dey gets to dance. Dey sends de loidy up an' she rags aroun' an' by an' by she cops out some guy dat'll stand fer a quarter touch. Well, she comes down to de door, gets her feller and up dey go. . . . To look at him you'd tink he owned a bank, an' not comin' in cause his goil made a touch." Gill insisted that raggers didn't use the word "petties" anymore and didn't want a king, even one with buttons on his pants. He said he never heard of Oliver, accusing him of trying to make a name for himself. Gill warned what might follow as the result of Oliver's claim to the throne. "I wouldn't be dat feller Oliver fer money. You know what dey'll do to him? Ever' place he goes, dey'll say: 'Are you dat King Oliver?' and sump'n'll start. I knows, 'cause de fellers are all sore at him makin' a talk 'bout bein' it and settin' de style. He'll wish it never happened."[53]

Later that Sunday afternoon after the second article appeared in the *Post-Dispatch*, trouble erupted in Seibt's saloon. Jack and his younger brother Bert Oliver were tending bar when a party of raggers took offense at a remark by the younger brother. Whatever Bert said apparently violated an unwritten code among raggers. The gang left the saloon and gathered nearby to decide how to respond to the affront. When the gang returned, one of them stepped forward and calmly but with ragger swagger let Bert know he took offense at the remark. Before the gang's spokesman could finish, Bert drew a pistol and so did Jack. The brothers ordered the gang out of the saloon. Someone fired a shot behind the gang to hurry them along. About 9:00 that evening, the gang returned and shot up the saloon. A bullet caught Bert Oliver in the shoulder, and stray bullets nearly struck occupants of nearby shantyboats. With the aid of a friend, Bert fled the saloon and sneaked through dark alleys to elude the gang searching for him. At last he made it to the North End Dispensary for emergency treatment. Police arrested a couple of young suspects.[54]

On Saturday night, August 20, less than three weeks after the *Post-Dispatch* "discovered" Jack Oliver and introduced the subculture to readers for the first time, raggers made their stage debut at Koerner's Garden, which regularly hosted cakewalks and other popular dance contests. Attendees poured into the Garden from all parts of the city, including the wealthy West End, to get a look for themselves. When the curtain lifted, there were nearly forty young men and women on stage. Each young man wore a soft felt hat with dents made by five fingers, a white shirt with a turned down collar, a four-in-hand tie, low-cut vest, long coat, and "the most marvelous wide trousers that one ever saw."[55] Each young woman wore a shirt waist, and some featured stylishly cocked picture hats. All were poised and self-assured as Reuben Welch, manager of Koerner's, called each couple by name and introduced them to an enthusiastic audience. When he called their names, the couples gracefully waltzed forward in their distinctive ways. The appreciative crowd cried for more. Three couples gave distinctive ragger versions of the cakewalk, a popular African American dance once featured at gatherings of plantation slaves before the Civil War. Minstrel shows helped to popularize the dance, which in the hands of Black vaudeville musicians became a ragtime dance. Its inclusion of women in the 1890s opened up new avenues for improvisation, adaptations, and stage excitement. The Koerner Garden audience went wild during the kissing scenes in each cakewalk. The night closed with a ragger square dance. Jack Oliver attended but did not play a prominent role in the evening's festivities. His brother Bert was still in serious condition after being shot two weeks earlier. Jack, mindful that members of the gang might still be after him, refused to attend until Welch agreed to pick him up and take him home in a carriage.[56]

Koerner's Garden hosted raggers again the following Saturday night as the craze swept St. Louis. The *Post-Dispatch* took credit for bringing public attention to raggers and their dancing. The paper showcased them repeatedly in its Sunday edition. Antonio Bafunno, director of Bafunno's Concert Band, composed a ragtime or cakewalk march, "Queen of the Raggers," to honor the newspaper for discovering raggers. On September 4, 1898, the Sunday edition included part of Bafunno's musical score in an article featuring seventeen-year-old Lottie "Gladys" Clark, "Venus of Raggerdom."[57] Ragger dance contests became celebrated events. Leland Melroy at the Fourteenth Street Theater ran an advertisement to hire twenty ragger couples as quickly as possible. Saturday night "medal twists" were held at Bell's Hall on the corner of Eleventh Street and Franklin Avenue. Petie Quinn, a rival to Jack Oliver, came away from a ragger contest at Bell's Hall on September 24 with a friendly assessment of him. "Jack Oliver ain't so swelled like some might think," he admitted. "No, that guy's all right. Mean him hadda couplee bowls 'n he settem up to me fren's whitout kickin' about th' change."[58]

So celebrated was the craze that at the invitation of the *Post-Dispatch*, Oliver attended the highly exclusive annual Veiled Prophet grand ball and pageant on October 4, 1898. He met city dignitaries, debutantes bedecked in diamonds and jewels who were on a secret list of invitees, and other members of the social and political elite. Conceived after the 1877 general strike, the Veiled Prophet, shrouded in secrecy, was created as a cultural tool by white elites determined to remind challengers who was in charge of the city. In a single evening, Oliver went from his lodging place in Seibt's shantyboat saloon to the city's most extravagant ritual and gala event of the year. Surrounded by high society, including former Mayor and ex-Governor David R. Francis, King Jack met the secretly chosen Veiled Prophet and witnessed his crowning of Miss Marie Scanlan as the Queen of Love and Beauty.[59]

By inviting Oliver to the Veiled Prophet ceremony and by promoting raggers, the *Post-Dispatch* subtly coopted the craze. The names of Spider Meyers, Rag Mantell, Petie Quinn, and other contenders for Oliver's throne appeared regularly on the pages of the newspaper. For more than a year, a special ragger column appeared under the name of Petie Quinn in the paper. As a contributor, Quinn dispensed pearls of ragger wisdom and commentary on politics and nearly any subject imaginable. One of the columns contained a song, "Petie Quinn's Pettie," and another included a lengthy poem, "I Rather Be a Ragger." The first verse captures the essence of the song:

I wouldn't be a soldier,
A sailor er a king.
I wouldn't be a copper, a

Mayor er anything
To carry guns er cutlasses
Er wear a heavy crown—
S-a-a-y!—I rather be a ragger 'n'
Bum Around Th' town.[60]

Almost overnight, raggers were feted and in high demand. In September 1898, Oliver, Quinn, and other celebrated raggers provided the featured entertainment in St. Charles's Klondike Park. Along with vaudeville and musical comedy acts, a "ragger cakewalk" highlighted an evening of entertainment on the West End. In a concert at the St. Louis Exposition coliseum on October 26, touring bandmaster John Philip Sousa played Bafunno's "Queen of the Raggers," a composition that celebrated the subculture. Lottie Clark, the feted queen, and Jack Oliver, Petie Quinn, and other raggers attended as celebrities.[61] Wealthy West End residents hired them to provide entertainment at private parties in their homes, and ragger dance contests found their way to political functions. On December 4, 1898, the Ninth Ward's East End Republican League Club hosted a dance contest as part of the night's entertainment at Concordia Turner Hall. Jack Oliver and Jessie Gillespie, his pettie, were among the featured.[62]

Lottie Clark, the "Venus of Raggerdom" who preferred to go by the name of "Gladys," was an attractive, ambitious seventeen-year-old working-class girl who, since leaving school, worked in bag factories and department stores. Weary of the limited jobs open to most working-class teenage girls, she dreamed of a life on the theatrical stage. She was married, but according to her she never spent a night with her husband under the same roof. Marriage was a mere convenience that kept police from sending her to the House of the Good Shepherd. After disobeying her mother by staying out late at night to go dancing, she ended up before the Police Matron at the Four Courts, who threatened to put her into the Good Shepherd's home. The choice was simple: either get married or go to the home. Lottie exhibited all the coarse trappings of ragger gang culture in dialect and swagger but held herself to high moral standards. Aware of her beauty, she resented popular attitudes that stereotyped working-class girls in theater and entertainment. "Some people don't think goils ought to go on the stoige," she told an interviewer. "They say it's unmoral 'r something like that, but I think they're jealous. I don't think there's anything wrong about it. I kin be as good on the stoige as anywhere else. 'N say there's good coin in it, too. Some o' these snuff boxes gets $50 a week, which is more than a goil can make stripping tobacco 'r sewing bags fer 10 weeks."[63]

In a few years, celebration turned to condemnation and attempts to suppress the subculture. Fifty young women who worked in the Stobie Cereal Mills went on strike in 1901 to protest a foreman who called them a "bunch of raggers" when they refused to stop dancing in the warehouse. A divorce litigant even cited as grounds for divorce the fact that his wife was hanging out in low-class dance halls popular among raggers. In 1902, a *Post-Dispatch* entertainment columnist who reported that a St. Louis temperance organization banned raggers at an upcoming ball denounced ragging as "one of the most intemperate things that ever came down the social pike."[64] Neither did raggers receive a warm welcome on excursion boats that catered to the comfort and safety of upper-class patrons. The boats wanted dancing, of course, but nothing that would offend bourgeois sensibilities. Captain Harry Brolaski in 1905 ejected ten male raggers from the *Corwin H. Spencer* in Alton, accusing them of "wiggle wiggle" dancing. When the ejected raggers stoned the boat in retaliation, Brolaski grabbed one of them and turned him over to police, but dropped charges on the stipulation that he never step onto his boat again.[65]

Franklin Fyles, a drama critic for the *New York Sun* who also wrote for the stage, noted the presence of raggers at the Louisiana Purchase Exposition in 1904. Writing from St. Louis, he noted derisively that raggers were drawn to the amusement resorts of the Arizona camp with its mining exhibits, saloons, and dance halls. During the exposition, the camp featured vaudeville, burlesque, and plenty of drinking and dancing. He compared the customs and manners of inhabitants of the mining Southwest to those of St. Louis levee dwellers. In an explanation of the ragger phenomenon to reading audiences beyond St. Louis, he wrote, "The 'ragger' is a local type. . . . He is to St. Louis what the Bowery Boy is to New York."[66]

In the music, liquor, and laughter on the wharf, where nightly dancing took place in its barrelhouses and shantyboat saloons, there poured forth sounds of temporary release from a hard life often determined by the roll of loaded dice. Music and dance on the cobblestones of the levee and rooftops of shantyboats added an exciting dynamic to St. Louis's cultural life from below. Seibt's popular saloon on the north wharf brought disparate elements together by providing a mixture of toe-tapping fiddle music, ragtime, and ragger dancing. On a nighttime visit to the central wharf at the southwest corner of Chestnut Street, a *Globe-Democrat* reporter in 1907 pointed out the abundance of musical talent, emphasizing that Black levee musicians sometimes found careers in vaudeville or on showboats after being "discovered" on the wharf. The reporter investigated when the sounds of a badly tuned piano lured him to the darkened rear caverns of a levee restaurant. He noted that the low dives on the levee were eating places that served alcohol and featured dancing in the back. In search of the musical sounds coming from the rear, he made his way through the restaurant into passageways that led into a world alien to him in terms of race, class, and culture. "Dusky forms glide around the floor and keep time with the spasms of the pianists," he wrote. "The smoke is thick; still, they are all happy."[67]

Little Oklahoma, Foot of Destrehan Street, *St. Louis Post-Dispatch*, November 25, 1900.

Captain Louis H. Seibt, "King Louis I of Little Oklahoma,"
St. Louis Post-Dispatch, September 24, 1897.

Two African American men and a houseboat, undated. From the collections of the
Herman T. Pott National Inland Waterways Library at the University of Missouri-St. Louis.

CHICKENTOWN MUST GIVE WAY BEFORE
THE MARCH OF MUNICIPAL PROGRESS

LEW CRISMAN.

Chickentown, *St. Louis Republic*, July 28, 1904.

Roustabouts, circa 1900. Missouri Historical Society Collections.

Child fishers of the Mississippi, *St. Louis Post-Dispatch*, September 14, 1930.
Self-supporting shantyboat sisters, ages ten and seven, whose fishing business supported
their widowed mother on Memphis's Mud Island in the Great Depression.

Watching a sternwheel steamboat pass, circa 1900. Earl S. Miers River Photograph Collection, 33011, Tennessee State Library and Archives, Tennessee Virtual Archive.

Roustabouts rolling barrels of Apples from the Eagle Packet Company wharf boat in St. Louis with Captain Henry Leyhe in a straw hat looking on. Undated photograph by Louis Rosche. From the collections of the Herman T. Pott National Inland Waterways Library at the University of Missouri-St. Louis.

Shantyboats at Naples, Illinois, undated.
Courtesy of David and Sally Polc, Hannibal, Missouri.

Roustabouts on the deck of a steamboat, circa 1900.
Earl S. Miers River Photograph Collection, 33012, Tennessee State
Library and Archives, Tennessee Virtual Archive.

Nora Gamache in her standoff with Anheuser-Busch and the city
of St. Louis, *St. Louis Post-Dispatch*, July 10, 1903.

Houseboat along the Ohio River at Rochester, Pennsylvania, 1940.
Library of Congress Prints and Photographs Division, FSA/OWI Collection.

Patent medicine peddler "Espanto the Clairvoyant Medium."
Courier (Waterloo, Iowa), October 3, 1904.

Roustabouts loading hogs along the Tennessee River, 1905.
From the collections of the Herman T. Pott National Inland Waterways Library
at the University of Missouri-St. Louis.

"The Unwashed Washed." The young residents of Little Oklahoma during
the flood of 1903. Missouri Historical Society Collections.

Rose Mosenthein, women's sculling champion of the world. Sketch by historian
Victoria Bynum based on a photograph that appeared in *Leslie's Weekly*
at the time of the 1895 international regatta in Austin, Texas.

Roustabouts on the *Tennessee Belle*, circa 1923–1942. Inland Rivers Photography Collection, Cincinnati and Hamilton Country Public Library, Ohio.

Loading freight on the New Orleans levee from a Bob Blanks packet in 1905.
Inland Rivers Photography Collection, Cincinnati and
Hamilton County Public Library, Ohio.

Woman holding child on houseboat stranded on the banks of the Mississippi River,
circa 1930 or 1931. Photographer Lewis Wickes Hine, Library of Congress Prints
and Photographs Division, American National Red Cross Collection.

Shantyboat family, Louisiana, Missouri, circa 1914.
Online Steamboat Museum, Dave Thomson Collection.

7

The American Fondness for Humbug

MEDICINE BOATS, SWAMP HEALERS, AND SHOWBOATS

For several years "Espanto" had been traveling up and down the river in
his boat selling humbug remedies to blacks and whites, working all sorts
of quack medical dodges, and making a comfortable fortune out of it.

—JOHN LATHROP MATHEWS, *The Log of the Easy Way,* 1911

Dr. Patti dressed well, having many suits of handsome cloth, and his
appearance, nearly always in a stovepipe hat, was most prepossessing, and
his wonderful physical energy was set off with a most attractive mentality
that, in any line of conversation was as bright as the lightning's flash.

—*Vicksburg American,* 1906

Whether in wagons or houseboats, traveling medicine show "doctors" were important figures in American popular culture at the turn of the twentieth century. Medicine shows typically featured musicians, magicians or illusionists, blackface minstrels, and vaudeville, stage, and circus entertainers. The shows incidentally provided employment to blues artist Gertrude Ma Rainey, vaudeville's Clifton Edwards, and other theatrical performers, but the underlying purpose was to sell patent medicines. Between acts, a doctor with a stovepipe hat, patriarchal appearance, and persuasive sales pitch hawked magic elixirs and miracle cures that promised the moon. If you had an ailment, the good doctor had something to fix you right up—a cure for every sniffle, dreaded disease, and ache and pain. Patent medicine manufacturing produced "toadstool millionaires," and newspapers grew addicted to revenue from wonder drug advertisements with sensational testimonials. The ads promoted blood purifiers, endless miracle salves and panaceas, and tonics and pills for nearly every affliction. Whether "Cocaine Toothache Drops," "Mrs. Winslow's Soothing Syrup," "Peruna," "Swamp Root," or some other concoction, many patent medicines contained a high concentration of booze. Some were commonly laced with morphine, opium, or cocaine. A number of parents who administered patent medicine to their infants and children later cursed the day they spooned the first dose. Samuel Hopkins Adams, a muckraking journalist, played a major role in exposing the industry in a 1905 series of articles in *Collier's: The National Weekly.* "Gullible America will spend this year some seventy-five millions of dollars in the purchase of patent medicines," he wrote. "In consideration of this sum it will swallow huge quantities of alcohol, an appalling amount of opiates and narcotics, a wide assortment of varied drugs ranging from powerful and dangerous heart depressants to insidious liver stimulants; and, in excess of all other ingredients, undiluted fraud."[1]

In 1906, the Pure Food and Drug Act inaugurated federal regulation of such cure-alls and began a modest crackdown on beverages and extracts containing alcohol. "Lemon ginger," manufactured by the Collins Brothers Medicine Company, of St. Louis, contained 57.8 percent alcohol. The internal revenue commissioner's office noted that the concoction, which more closely resembled a liqueur than a medicine, was subject to a liquor tax. Federal enforcement of the new regulatory legislation was weakened by the lobbying work of the Proprietary Association of America, the trade association of patent medicines. Officials on regulatory boards often sympathized with or were in the hip pocket of the patent medicine industry. Newspapers, reluctant to surrender a lucrative source of advertising, often did the bidding of the trade association. Courts watered down the legislation and softened fines on the industry. In 1920, a chemical analysis of Hostetter's Bitters by the American Medical Association revealed that the popular remedy contained 25 percent alcohol, down from 43 percent in 1906.[2]

Despite warnings and early federal regulation, the demand for patent medicines remained high. Medicine shows were a common feature of life in the West, rural South, and Midwest. Larger troupes typically traveled in wagon caravans, but a single wagon, street corner, or shantyboat sufficed for a lone elixir peddler like shantyboat doctor John Pearly, the fictitious central character in Burman's *Steamboat 'Round the Bend.* The Mississippi basin attracted its share of smooth-talking peddlers on the waterways. Small-scale medicine shows, if they didn't use music, sometimes featured services in the "crafty arts" that promised magical Egyptian amulets, cures for drunkenness, removal of a bad witch's spell or voodoo curse, love life consultations, even stock market tips. The market in shantyboat communities and delta areas where freedmen picked cotton or cut sugar cane was quite profitable. Hundreds of patent medicine peddlers, fortune-tellers, clairvoyants, and voodoo practitioners did a brisk business in river cities such as St. Louis, a major center of patent medicine manufacturing. In 1888, Aaron Dockens, a Black shantyboat resident on the city's north wharf, brought charges against Prince Alexander, "King of Voodoo," when a magical coal amulet he bought failed to win back his white wife, who left him. The Court of Criminal Correction sentenced Alexander to six months of hard labor in the Workhouse. When an ordinance in Alton required fortune-tellers to pay a draconian licensing fee, an unlicensed fortune-teller in a shantyboat community threatened in 1908 to cast a spell on the city attorney, who threatened her arrest repeatedly. In Pittsburgh, "Madam Clifford" sold patent medicine from her shantyboat in the early 1910s by advertising her services as a palm reader and clairvoyant on the riverfront.[3]

Patent medicine manufacturers in the Mississippi valley used the river to advertise and market their goods. In 1900, the Lightning Medicine Company, of Muscatine, sent agents to New Orleans in a freshly outfitted houseboat to distribute free samples and promote the company's remedies. With bright advertising inscriptions covering the boat, traveling agents marketed the company's remedies to those who lived in towns and settlements on the Lower Mississippi. In many cases, nostrum peddlers in medicine boat shows on the river hired a Black banjo player or other assistant. They took advantage of superstitions and self-doctoring patterns among the poor. With great hoopla and fanfare, they pitched elixirs to shantyboat communities and freedmen on delta cotton plantations. To encourage the appearance of authenticity, they sometimes hired an indigenous person or two to travel with the show, or they featured impersonators to peddle quack remedies such as the Kickapoo Indian Medicine Company's "Sagwa" and other tonics.[4]

Talent was limited at best in some of the smaller shows, and drug and alcohol addictions at times afflicted performers and peddlers alike. In early October 1902, the owner of a medicine boat in Little Oklahoma advertised for an energetic, honest young boy to sign on as an assistant for small wages on a six-month trip south for the winter. Less than two months later, J. H. Hamilton, who operated a medicine houseboat for a St. Louis wholesale drug company, docked in Helena, Arkansas. A morphine addict, he was too sick to conduct business when he arrived. His young assistant fell ill, and they both suffered from lack of food. The police found Hamilton pitifully helpless and took him to jail for treatment by a physician, but it was too late to prevent death.[5]

In St. Louis, Blake Brothers (Wilson L. and William S.) was among the companies that manufactured, marketed, and distributed patent medicines. The company advertised nationally, sold its products in drugstores, and oversaw a mail distribution network. For about 22 cents a bottle in a drugstore, you could buy Blake's Anti-Bilious Pills for dyspepsia, headaches, and liver ailments. Blake Brothers remedies included Marsh Tonic, Nerve and Bone Liniment, Complete Cough Cure Syrup, and "Malaraine" for swamp fever and malaria, but its top seller at 50 cents a bottle was "Chickasaw Oil," touted as a cure for rheumatism, neuralgia, headaches, sore throats, tooth aches, swollen tonsils, stiff joints, insect bites or stings, sprains, stomach ailments, cramps, diarrhea, and "All Manner of Pains." The company assured mothers the product was safe for colicky babies if they diluted it with sweetened milk or warm, sweetened water: "However strong it may appear in taste it can be given the most aged and infirm, as well as the youngest babe with perfect safety."[6] Billy expanded the company's customer reach by peddling tonics in a "wild and wooly" boat with "Chickasaw Oil" and "doctor" painted on its exterior walls. Well known on the Lower Mississippi, he later converted to a gasoline-powered boat. When John Lathrop Mathews tied up his houseboat in Shanty-boat Town on the north side of a Memphis sandbar for ten days in late November 1900, he was two boats down from the "Chickasaw Oil man." According to Mathews, Blake was among the best-known peddlers on the river.[7]

On a trip down the Mississippi in a skiff, writer Raymond S. Spears in 1905 met one of Blake's agents south of Helena. John Pierce, former sheriff of Caruthersville, invited Spears to float with him for several days on his houseboat. According to Pierce, an agent who among other items sold Blake's Chickasaw medicines, most of the company's sales took place on the river. Pierce admitted there were "rascals" as well as legitimate peddlers of patent medicine on the waterways. He told Spears about a case in which a peddler showed up at his boat late one evening north of the mouth of the Red River. The peddler, who appeared jumpy, confided that angry nearby Black customers were chasing him. He explained that on an afternoon of brisk sales on a nearby plantation, he ran out of a popular "belly wash." He then mixed liniment into a formula and sold it to a woman as a tonic. She drank it and died almost immediately.[8]

One of the slickest, slipperiest, and most successful medicine boat peddlers on the Mississippi was William "Billy" Netterfield Jr., better known as "Doctor Espanto." Born in Indiana, he painted houses in Minneapolis-St. Paul before abandoning his wife to set out down the river. Divorced in 1890, he first tried farming and painting in the Missouri Ozarks near Cuba in Crawford County. In 1892, he married Anna Naomi (Taylor) Whitson, of English township, Iowa County, Iowa. The *Bland Courier,* an Ozarks newspaper, later remembered them as "wonderful people" and noted that Netterfield was a successful painter. Restless, the Netterfields leased out their farm and moved to St. Louis. Billy made friends in Little Oklahoma and found a partner with whom he formed a patent medicine outfit. Around 1895, they floated down the river in a houseboat to pitch patent medicines for a company. According to Dr. John D. Seba, a physician in Bland, Netterfield intended "to swindle the ignorant and superstitious negro" who lived along the river. On the first run down the Mississippi, likely as canvassing agents for the Espanto Remedy Company, of Davenport, and the Mexican Amole Soap Company, of Peoria, Billy and his partner fared well. Soon afterward, Billy bought out his partner and ran the business with Anna, who joined him on the houseboat. They no longer pitched for companies. They compounded their own formulas and sold them on the river. From then on, Billy assumed the persona of "Doctor Espanto" in the Mississippi River valley.[9]

While Mathews was docked in Memphis in his honeymoon houseboat in late 1900, "Espanto, the Mexican Indian" was in the settlement, too. Mathews did not meet him at that time, but learned much about him from Clarence Jones, a young St. Louis river trader who formerly was Espanto's assistant. Jones told Mathews stories about the flamboyant huckster, "much that we were glad to know when at Lake Providence we came on the track of this wily individual, and at Vicksburg where we actually met him." Mathews described Espanto as "a small man, very dark of face," but Jones revealed that he dyed his hands and face to darken his appearance. Netterfield took the name of Espanto after learning of superstitions among freedmen, who held indigenous medicines in high regard. He grew shoulder-length hair and sometimes braided it in a queue worn down his back. Signs painted on his boat advertised services as a "doctor" with "Mexican Indian Medicines" aboard to treat ailments. Mathews characterized him as "a universal genius who had discovered the American fondness for humbug and was making full use of it." In Vicksburg's shantyboat community on the Yazoo River in January 1901, Mathews befriended him and asked to take a picture. Espanto unbraided his hair and let it flow freely down his back "as he wore it when on 'medicine duty.'" He wore an old-fashioned frock coat, a wing-collared shirt, and a flowing tie. The skirts of the coat flapped in the river breeze as he posed on his medicine boat for the picture while Anna peered at Mathews from the boat's doorway.[10]

The Netterfields were spiritualists who believed it possible to communicate with spirits of the dead through séances and other means. They were part of a thriving movement that reached its peak at the turn of the twentieth century. Espanto cultivated a mystique as a trance medium and clairvoyant, impressing delta freedmen. Some feared him, suspecting he possessed voodoo powers, but they preferred him over other "doctors" if he was at their disposal. The mystique was good for business. "They come miles to get his charms and remedies," Jones told Mathews.[11] Jones acknowledged Espanto's shrewdness, but Anna was "the real brains of the firm" who ran "the medicine part," compounding the formulas and tending to the mail business: "She's a mighty nice, motherly old lady, and was very good to me. Billy puts up the front, fixing his hair and his complexion to look like 'a Mexican Indian'—as he styles himself." Espanto, who owned an impressive collection of pistols and Winchester rifles, was an expert marksman and showman. His marksmanship added to the mystique. As Jones made clear, "He is a dead shot, and has some fine pistols and guns."[12] Espanto was popular among white and Black river people who preferred to treat themselves rather than pay fees to a licensed physician. Mathews described him as "rather taciturn, but hospitable and willing to help those who needed it." In towns away from the shore, however, Espanto's prosperity rankled some. As Mathews put it, "For several years 'Espanto' had been traveling up and down the river in his boat selling humbug remedies to blacks and whites, working all sorts of quack medical dodges, and making a comfortable fortune out of it."[13]

In March 1899, Espanto got into a scrape with Louisiana authorities in Lake Providence, a lucrative market on account of its vast cotton plantations and large Black labor force in East Carroll Parish. He ran an advertisement in the local newspaper touting his national reputation and medicines prepared by his own company free of harmful drugs. "Special attention given to Chronic, Nervous and Private Diseases of Men and Women," read his advertisement, which also touted the affordability of his services, including free consultations and examinations. For about six weeks he did a brisk business on the Lake Providence levee. According to Jones, Espanto "took in over a thousand dollars in ten days, and then the other doctors got the marshal after him for practicing medicine without a license." On March 8, the marshal jailed Espanto, who claimed to be a physician of the allopathic or homeopathic school. Espanto easily put up $100 cash bail and promised to return to fight the case in court. "Then he went back to the boat and went to work again," Jones remembered. "He made that one hundred dollars up in no time."[14]

When the marshal learned that Espanto continued to treat patients on his houseboat while awaiting trial, he returned to the levee to re-arrest him, but found himself staring down the barrel of a Winchester. Insisting that the waterfront belonged to the federal government, Espanto warned that the marshal had no authority to arrest him. Anna, as her husband's Winchester froze the marshal in his tracks, pulled in the lines of their boat and off they went, but not far. They tied up just below the town's official limits, beyond the marshal's legal jurisdiction. When word spread on the levee that Espanto got the best of the marshal in the standoff, customers flocked to the medicine boat. As Jones recalled, "That advertised them so that they took in a good many hundred more in the next week. Billy didn't go back for trial and the judge was mad that he hadn't put the bail at five hundred dollars. Billy would have given that just as easy as one hundred."[15] The local newspaper complained that Espanto broke his promise to return for trial. Calling attention to his expertise with Winchester rifles, the paper speculated that he likely would not hesitate to use one if pushed too far. All the paper could do was to express bewilderment at the gullibility of the area's Black population: "It is strange how the colored people will flock to such quacks and pay all kinds of prices for a lot of trash with the belief that they can be cured."[16]

Espanto's slick powers of persuasion, whether among Blacks or whites, educated or uneducated, were not to be underestimated. He leased out his Crawford County farm again in August 1901 and floated south with Anna to sell patent medicine, but the following year he convinced a *St. Louis Republic* reporter that he, "Don Espanto," was on a diplomatic mission on behalf of a syndicate of

Mexican investors interested in buying large apple orchards in Cuba, Missouri. On a stop in St. Louis, Espanto informed the reporter that he was en route to Cuba to buy several thousand acres of land. Promising other investments would soon follow, Espanto explained: "We Mexicans have a little money to spare, and we find that Missouri offers a good field for investments. We have bought properties at several points . . . but our largest holding outside of Mexico will be at a point between Cuba and Springfield, Mo."[17] Calling attention to plans underway for the St. Louis World's Fair in 1904, Espanto promised that many visitors from Mexico would attend. The reporter was fooled by him: "Don Espanto is an Aztec and wears long hair, done up in a knot when away from his home. He has been to Washington on Government missions, and on his return trip through St. Louis will confer with World's Fair officials."[18]

In 1903, Mathews caught up with Espanto again in St. Louis's shantyboat settlement on the north wharf, where Espanto was visiting friends. By now, the Netterfields had sold their houseboat. "No more river for me," Espanto told Mathews. "I have bought a good farm out in this State and my wife and I will live in peace the rest of our lives." A resident of Little Oklahoma who was part of the conversation afterward added as an aside, "Too many places he can't go back to."[19] Espanto's travels as a spiritualist patent medicine peddler were far from over. From Louisiana and Texas to northern Iowa and the Dakotas, he raked in money as a vagabond deliverer of spirit messages and seller of patent medicines compounded by Anna. They sold their farm in Cuba and moved to St. Louis, where Espanto advertised as Dr. William Espanto Netterfield. He conducted mail-order business and continued as a medium, spiritualist lecturer, and flashy patent medicine peddler on the road. In Waterloo, Iowa, where he was quite popular, the *Courier* described him as "a man of deep and wide experience in both the spiritual and physical parts of man."[20] Espanto convinced the *Courier* he was a native of Mexico City with a medical degree from there and a diploma from a leading medical college in the United States. "Quiet and unassuming in manner," wrote the editor, "but intensely keen and a thorough master of his profession, the doctor impresses the observer as being one of those persons who are brought into the world for the special purpose of ministering to and alleviating the sufferings of mankind."[21]

In St. Louis, a regional center of spiritualism, the Netterfields were active in spiritualist societies as well as the Socialist Party of America (SPA). Like many women who were spiritualists, Anna was devoted to the Socialist movement and women's suffrage. She shared the speakers' platform with well-known Socialist activist Kate Richards O'Hare, Florence Wyman Richardson (president of the Equal Suffrage League of St. Louis), and others. Billy may have convinced Anna that he shared her socialist convictions, but members of the SPA's St. Louis chapter were skeptical. In 1906, squabbling over a municipal platform plagued a meeting of the local, but the main dispute erupted when members from the First Ward endorsed Netterfield as the party's candidate for the house of delegates in the municipal assembly. After bitter arguments, the local tabled the nomination and encouraged First Ward members to give further thought and consideration to selection of their nominee.[22]

The Pure Food and Drug Act in 1906 brought scrutiny of Netterfield by medical authorities. Dr. John Seba alerted the Iowa State Board of Examiners and the Missouri State Board of Health, and notified Iowa newspapers in the Waterloo area that he was a quack. In September 1907, Espanto pleaded guilty and was fined $300 for practicing medicine without a license in Spirit Lake, Iowa, but he was undeterred. As the *Bland Courier* noted two years later, "This would-be Indian Doctor Espanto has been chased by nearly every state board of health of the west."[23] The medical authorities were not the only ones bearing down on Espanto. So was Anna, who grew suspicious of his frequent travels to St. Joseph, Missouri. Rummaging through his belongings, she found an intimate letter from Scottie Rutherford, whose husband, a musician, was often away from home. Espanto boarded at their home when in town on business. After Anna filed for and received a divorce, he married Rutherford in 1909 in Bowie County, Texas, where he did business. His new wife was a lecturer in the St. Joseph Spiritualist Society.[24]

Anna gave up patent medicine manufacturing to become a general agent for the newly organized Florida Everglades Land Company in 1913. She moved to Fort Lauderdale, where she ran a real estate business on behalf of land sharks, speculators, and promoters of land development in Moore Haven. After marrying Judge John A. B. Shippey in June 1917, she dropped out of the real estate business but remained active in Socialist and spiritualist circles. She and her new husband, whom she converted to spiritualism, hosted séances at their home until the marriage fell apart. Banned from their home but not divorced, she fell on hard times. In 1930, the year Judge Shippey died, she was accepted as a charity patient at the Broward County's Haven of Rest for the aged in Dania, where she died in 1933.[25]

Despite efforts at federal and state regulation, Espanto dodged authorities and did a thriving business in patent medicine until his death in 1936. He played the dodge to the last, telling a 1930 federal census enumerator in Cassadaga, Florida, the site of a spiritualist camp in which he and Elsie Selecman, his fourth wife, were married and spent winters, that he was born in Louisiana to Mexican parents who were descendants of the Aztecs. He served as trustee of the Mississippi Valley Spiritualists Association and attended its annual camp meetings in Clinton, Iowa, where he and Elsie kept a summer home. After an investigation by the US Post Office Department, the federal crackdown against mail fraud in the patent medicine business shut down his operations in 1935. At age eighty-one, Espanto was charged with fraudulent use of the mail to sell fake medicines from his headquarters in "a wee cabin in a small winter Florida resort." The *Washington Evening Star* described him as "one of the cleverest quack doctors who ever flimflammed the American public."[26]

Another boat doctor widely known in shantyboat settlements on the Mississippi was Dr. William Patti. A well-traveled, self-described naturalist, botanist, and homeopathic lecturer born in 1824, he touted natural herbs instead of narcotics-laced elixirs. According to him, his father was a chemistry professor in the Botanical Medical Laboratory of the Royal University of Bonn in Prussia. Reportedly, at age eight he began to work with his father, gathering and gaining knowledge of plants and herbs. The Imperial Natural Cure Society of the university later recruited him to search for rare botanical specimens in different parts of the world, including central Africa. He immigrated to the United States on September 6, 1860, and became known below Memphis as the "swamp healer."[27]

Notwithstanding the questionable veracity of Patti's autobiographical assertions to newspaper reporters, he traveled the Mississippi from its headwaters to New Orleans in search of plants useful in compounding herbal remedies. He operated as a blockade runner against the Union fleet in the Civil War, taking medicine and supplies to Confederate forces. After the war, he located on the Memphis waterfront until around 1872. He operated a medicine boat show, at times hiring a traveling Black banjo player to help attract customers. New Orleans became his headquarters. In 1880, he and his family lived in St. Mary

Parish, but they spent much time peddling herbal remedies on the river. In 1884, they led a traveling medical troupe that included J. E. Gilfillan, purportedly a Native American doctor, and several young Black youth "whose singing acted as a sort of sedative, to soothe the patients into taking their medicine, or prepare them for the skillful examination of Mrs. Patti."[28]

Patti told newspaper reporters that he gathered herbs to furnish chemical firms with raw materials they needed for pharmaceutical production, and that he maintained extensive connections with large wholesale druggists in New Orleans and Memphis. His search for medicinal plants took him to swamps in Louisiana, Mississippi, and Arkansas. He claimed that he filled contracts with firms in Germany, by whom he was well-compensated for his efforts on the banks of Lake George and the Congo, Nile, and other African rivers. He claimed to have met the well-known explorer Henry Stanley, who headed the Emin Pasha Expedition in central Africa. For several days before Stanley met Pasha in 1888, Patti purportedly stayed with Stanley, who was suffering from jungle fever. According to Patti, he treated Stanley with medicinal herbs until he recovered. Touting herbal remedies for popular afflictions, Patti developed an "Indian Blood Purifier," a tea to get rid of children's worms. His own favorite treatment for coughs, colds, and cholera was "Louisiana Live Oak." In his medicine boat shows, Patti hawked homeopathic remedies that he compounded to treat rheumatism, tuberculosis, dropsy (edema), and nearly every known illness. In 1886, he returned to Memphis, where he opened a doctor's office near the riverfront. The "old comet," critical of modern medicine, gave lectures on health, climate, and naturalist approaches to treating diseases, but the State of Tennessee passed a law in 1889 designed to put "quack" doctors out of business and to limit medical competition. The legislation, backed by the Tennessee State Medical Society, was part of a national trend toward professionalization and standardization. Patti was a victim of the battle between two schools of medicine at the time. As a homeopath, he emphasized the importance of fresh air, diet, and use of herbal remedies. His approach was popular in rural areas, where mainline doctors were often held in low regard and where people preferred to spare expense and treat themselves with popular remedies.[29]

The *Vicksburg American* noted that Patti was a fascinating, colorful character of robust physical and intellectual stature with solid family connections. Harris Dickson, a local judge, novelist, and short story writer, was impressed after an engaging conversation with the venerable botanist. Patti's daughter, Jennie, was educated and married to Henry Lee Alexander, a bookkeeper for the Livermore Foundry and Machine Company in Memphis. Ada Patti worked as a dressmaker for B. Lowenstein and Bros. in Memphis, and Mary McQuinn lived in Memphis with her husband, Thomas, a Canadian immigrant ship builder. Dr. Patti's sister, Mary Roth, resided in Natchez with her husband, George, a local realtor. "Dr. Patti dressed well," the newspaper observed, "having many suits of handsome cloth, and his appearance, nearly always in a stovepipe hat, was most prepossessing, and his wonderful physical energy was set off with a most attractive mentality that, in any line of conversation was as bright as the lightning's flash."[30]

In 1891, Patti was the first to be prosecuted under the new Tennessee law for practicing medicine without a certificate from the State Board of Medical Examiners. He was arrested, jailed in Memphis, and convicted in the Criminal Court of Shelby County. Denied a new trial, he was granted an appeal to the Tennessee Supreme Court but apparently did not prosecute the appeal. He moved in briefly with his daughters Jennie and Ada in Memphis, but was soon back on the river, performing medicine boat shows in Mississippi and Louisiana. His daughters, worried about him at his advanced age, tried but failed to persuade him that he was too old to continue medicine boat shows. Life on the river was what he loved, however, and he refused to give it up. By now a widower, he traveled with a Black assistant and two other boats tied to his shantyboat. In early summer 1906, the "Old Wonder Doctor" at age eighty-two set out from Vicksburg to Greenville but mysteriously disappeared near the Yucatan Island plantation about forty miles south of Vicksburg. A shantyboat fisherman found two of his houseboats on a sandbar and the other one partly submerged nearby. The fisherman contacted D. W. Aiken, of the nearby plantation, who notified authorities. Blazoned on the side of one of the boats was "Dr. Wm. Patti, Botanist and Specialist." When Vicksburg's police chief received the news, he paid a visit to the local shantyboat colony to search for clues. Under suspicion at first was an elderly fishing couple and their teenage daughter, Maude Newton, from Rock Island, Illinois. On the river since 1897, they had met Patti two months earlier when he befriended them in the colony on the Yazoo Canal north of Vicksburg. He even offered them use of one of his boats. The Newtons considered an invitation from Patti to travel south with him, but conflict erupted when he charged them in city court with using their daughter for immoral purposes. Angered, the Newtons countered that he made romantic overtures toward Maude, who rejected his advances. Earlier, Patti pawned his gold watch to buy Maude a pair of shoes. According to the Newtons, their daughter's rejection of Patti fueled a spiteful complaint against them. In a bitter court confrontation, Judge Dickson dismissed Patti's charges for lack of evidence.[31]

Upon questioning, the Newton family admitted they were furious at Patti, but expressed concern that he may have been murdered. After the police chief ruled them out as suspects, the finger of suspicion pointed toward Patti's Black traveling assistant. Known in the shantyboat community only as "Jack," the assistant disappeared, rumored to have in his possession a diamond ring that aroused suspicions. Unfounded rumors led Natchez police to lock up Jake White, an unsuspecting Black lumber camp worker coming up the river in a skiff from Waterproof, Louisiana. Purportedly seen sporting a large wad of money and a cigar box filled with jewelry, White was held in jail overnight and released after police checked out his story and found only 90 cents in change on him. In the cigar box was nothing but fishing tackle.[32]

About a month after Patti's disappearance, son-in-law Henry Lee Alexander received a letter from Brook's Landing, near Grand Gulf, Mississippi, indicating that the decomposed body of an old man was found in a sand and mud grave on a sandbar. The victim was shot in the hips. Alexander boarded a steamer downriver and identified the body as that of his father-in-law. The remains were taken to Natchez for burial. "Jack" may have been the murderer, but he may have been innocent and disappeared for fear he'd be lynched as a mere suspect by a mob of vigilantes. Other rumored suspects included two anonymous fishermen who reportedly followed Patti when he left Vicksburg. Patti's murder remained an unsolved Mississippi River mystery.[33]

Smaller medicine boat shows in the postbellum South were patronized mainly by freedmen in plantation agriculture who sometimes bought admission tickets with chickens, eggs, corn, flour, or other food. Other shows catered to white audiences. Performers sometimes became obnoxious and were driven back onto the river by indignant townspeople and marshals with shotguns. In a few cases, river pirates followed medicine boats and raided towns and plantations while owners attended the shows. Afterward, the pirates split the stolen booty with the troupe. Writer Raymond S. Spears noted that "many a town has been 'skinned alive' by river thieves, and the character of some of the river plays was worse than that of the thieves and pickpockets."[34] In a 1909 article on the history of boat theaters on the Mississippi, he used the following case to dramatize the hucksterism that underlay some of the small-scale medicine boat shows in the past. In three shantyboats at the mouth of the St. Francis River north of Helena lived a gambler, medicine-man, river fiddler, and house painter and his wife. All were broke after trying a number of ways to earn money, including picking cotton, fishing, and collecting driftwood and junk. The riverfront wayfarers formed a troupe and staged a few medicine boat shows. The gambler knew a few card tricks and once played second fiddle in a troupe that performed in the Indian Territory. The medicine-man played a banjo, and the house painter's wife sang while he took tickets and policed audiences. After a morning rehearsal, two of them went into town to advertise, and that night they performed to a $10 house. By the time they split up a week later in Helena, all of them had pocket money. "Many a river-man, hounded by bad luck and down to the point of killing other men's hogs," wrote Spears, "has recouped his fortunes by a monologue or lightning-change entertainment." Such small-scale, impromptu shows feasted on unsophisticated river audiences. On occasions, a patent medicine company propped up a struggling boat theater by paying the salary of an actor or singer. In return, the troupe performed a drama that featured a patent medicine peddler who came on the scene just in time with the right miracle tonic to save an ailing heroine's life. The low quality of smaller shows prompted Spears to conclude that "acting is the last resort of a river grafter."[35]

Spears was harsh on river entertainers, but he drew a distinction between low-budget performances and expensive showboats that underwent a resurgence in the late nineteenth century. Whether the *Golden Rod, New Sensation,* the *Cotton Blossom,* or other theater boats financed by heavy capital investments, elaborate "floating theatres" on the waterways brought high-quality musical entertainment, vaudeville, comedy, dance, acrobatic and magic acts, and blackface minstrelsy to the waterfront, especially in small, isolated towns that lacked a theater or opera house. "We avoid the cities and larger villages, tying up wherever we see a footpath leading down to the water or a spire of a church through the trees," Captain Augustus B. French, owner of the Cincinnati-based

New Sensation, told a Minneapolis reporter in 1889. "The cities usually have amusements of their own, but the little hamlets scattered along the bank of the river have no pleasure beside an occasional singing-school."[36]

French, as an orphan in Palmyra, Missouri, took a job as a cabin boy on a Mississippi River steamer. Soon he traveled with a small motley troupe on a flatboat to give shows in river town halls. The Civil War knocked him off the river and sent him into the grocery business in Clarksburg, Ohio, but in 1878 he sold his business and invested in a traveling tent show. In Waterloo, Ohio, he married Callie B. Leach. With her support, he built the original *French's New Sensation*, which without an accompanying tugboat to tow it was operated by a long sweep on each side and a steering oar in the stern. In 1886 he bought his first tug and replaced the original showboat. The purchase of a tug made scheduling easier and allowed them to hire agents to advertise shows ahead of time. By then, he and Callie had transformed a modest circus-like show into a top-notch vaudeville production with a brass band, orchestra, and calliope. When the *New Sensation* docked, a ten-pound canon on the hurricane deck fired five or six times to attract attention. The boat, which seated an audience of about six hundred and employed nearly twenty-five actors and musicians, was among several theater palaces on the waterways. Captain French, a banjo player and ventriloquist, performed magic acts, assisted by Callie, who in 1888 secured a steamboat pilot's license in New Orleans and soon thereafter a master's license. Captain Callie managed the theater, played the calliope, wrote skits, acted in bit roles in shows, and piloted the steamer that towed the *New Sensation*. In April 1892, Harbor No. 28, of the American Association of Masters and Pilots of Steam Vessels in St. Louis, initiated her as the first woman into the association. After her husband's death in 1902, "Aunt Callie" continued to operate the showboat until 1907.[37]

Floating theaters often traveled as many as six thousand miles in a season. Typically, the *New Sensation* left Pittsburgh in May and traveled up the Kanawha River to put on shows for West Virginia coal miners and their families before entertaining audiences in other towns in the Ohio and Mississippi river valleys. Among the showboat's best customers in the Mississippi delta and Louisiana bayou country were Black agricultural workers, especially during sugar cane grinding season in November and December. Captain French, who enforced racially segregated seating on his boat, sometimes offered special cheap shows to attract poor people on the river's edge. If they lacked money to pay admission, he sometimes accepted whatever commodity of value they offered. In many cases, showboats hired an agent in a gasoline-powered launch to travel well ahead of the boat to distribute publicity handbills and take care of wharf fees and advance preparations. Beginning in 1904, Ben and John W. "Billy" Menke, soon-to-be showboat owners from Cincinnati, hired on as advance agents for the *New Sensation*. In 1911, they bought their first of seven showboats, the *Sunny South*, and with Brad N. Coleman as a partner took the show on the waterways in the renamed *Floating Hippodrome*.[38]

Showboats and the steamers that towed them arrived on waterfronts to great fanfare and jubilation. The sounds of calliopes and a small cannon shot stirred excitement. William Alexander Percy, a Harvard-educated lawyer and poet born in 1885, recalled what it was like as a barefooted child to hurry with his grandfather to the levee when a *Floating Palace* approached Greenville, Mississippi: "The blast of the calliope way up the river had electrified the countryside. All the Negroes, all the children, and half the adults were swarming to the levee. From the thick of the laughter and shoving and pointing, he and I would watch the magnificent apparition sweep down the center of the stream, black smoke pouring from its funnel and white plumes of steam from the calliope." About a half-hour before showtime, the calliope played again, and a free outdoor concert or parade through town by band members or acrobats drew waterfront onlookers onto the boat to pay admission to the main entertainment. Percy's excitement and anticipation mounted as showtime neared: "Waiting for dark and the show to begin was unbearable. At last the calliope would hit a high note and hold it, until you almost burst, then dash into 'Dixie,' and we would rush down the levee, squeeze onto the gangplank, buy our tickets, and at last, at last, enter—Elysium." The showboat experience remained etched in Percy's memories: "Such a grand, exciting smell of sweating people, everybody eating pink popcorn and drinking pop, such a dazzle of lights, such getting stepped on and knocked over and picked up, and at last the show, the beautiful, incredible show. . . . Show-boat! I never heard of such a name in my time. Everybody knew it was the *Floating Palace,* and worthy, a thousand times, of its title."[39]

Ellsworth Eugene Eisenbarth exemplified a showboat owner who made the transition from medicine show to improve the quality of entertainment on the waterways. In the 1880s, he held Wild West "Indian" medicine shows in the middle Atlantic States and Ohio Valley. Traveling in a wagon, he billed himself as a "Healer and Entertainer." On tour, he met Julia Ann Henderson, a wealthy West Virginian whom he married in 1886. He did well financially and soon launched a river show, "Eisenbarth's New Wild West and Floating Opera," which he conducted through the mid-1890s. His wife urged him to upgrade the quality of shows in the late 1890s. Contemptuous of medicine shows and vaudeville as distasteful and low-class, she pressed him to deliver first-class cultured drama to river audiences. She offered to pay for construction of a top-notch showboat if he granted her final say-so over the programs. He consented, eager to join her in bringing educational drama to waterways audiences. In the late 1890s, they founded the "Eisenbarth & Henderson Mammoth and Combined Uncle Tom's Cabin Company."[40]

In early 1900, their new showboat, *The Eisenbarth-Henderson Floating Theatre, Temple of Amusement,* and accompanying steamer took to the waterways. With calliope, band, and orchestra, the boat brought top Shakespeare plays, fine musical entertainment, and other melodramatic productions to audiences on the Ohio and Mississippi rivers. Contrary to warnings that river audiences would not support educational productions, crowds turned out in full force for *The Merchant of Venice* and *Hamlet*, Goethe's *Faust*, and Harriet Beecher Stowe's *Uncle Tom's Cabin*. The showboat's band and orchestra, comprised of some of the best musicians on the river, put on free open-air concerts at each landing.[41] After a towboat accidentally rammed and destroyed the showboat at Grand Tower, Illinois, Eisenbarth and Henderson built an even larger boat, *The Eisenbarth-Henderson Floating Theatre—The New Great Modern Temple of Amusement.* The new boat entertained audiences on the Ohio River and the Mississippi from Clarksville, Missouri, to New Orleans and offered shows at landings on the Illinois River north of St. Louis. Eisenbarth continued to operate the showboat after his wife's death in 1906. He held his last show in 1909, when the Needham-Steiner Amusement Company bought his showboat and re-christened it the *Cotton Blossom*. The boat, one of the largest on the Mississippi, carried forty-eight members, including actors, deckhands and steamboat crew, a sixteen-piece band, and a ten-piece orchestra. The *Cotton Blossom* had its own printing plant for tickets, handbills, newspaper advertisements, and other publicity. Under Needham-Steiner, the theater boat shifted from Shakespeare to vaudeville and traveled up the Mississippi as far as Keokuk, Iowa. After a single season, the owners sold the boat to the "Showboat King," Ralph Emerson, who added pizzazz by hiring master magicians and sensational acts. Shortly after he sold his half interest in the showboat, an ice gorge in 1917 crushed the *Cotton Blossom* in Mount Vernon, Indiana.[42]

The connections between patent medicine shows and showboat entertainment also can be found in the family of English immigrants Sam and Violet Nell Bryant. Violet was a musician and opera singer who convinced Sam to peddle "Doctor Bryant's Magic Elixir" as an "Indian" remedy composed of herbs and roots manufactured backstage in a medicine show. They and their ten-year-old son, Billy, lit out in a wagon to perform shows across the Midwest and into the American Southwest. Billy warmed up the crowd by singing, dancing, and telling funny stories. Sam then pitched the product while Violet provided soft background music on guitar. After setbacks, they made their way back to New York. In 1900, they were out of money in Buffalo when they responded to an advertisement for a vaudeville act with the *Water Queen*. They joined the showboat in Augusta, Kentucky, and put on a family entertainment act in Ohio river towns. By 1902, however, the Bryants were back to hawking patent medicine, this time on the Ohio River in a shantyboat they bought in East Liverpool, Ohio. Their shantyboat sank in 1906, at which time Sam borrowed money from a bank to build the family's first showboat. Later, success enabled him to buy a much larger floating palace, *Bryant's Showboat*. Until 1943, three generations of the family provided popular entertainment in the Ohio and Mississippi river valleys, including New Orleans in fall and winter.[43]

From patent medicine shows to saloons, gambling, music, fortune-telling, cockfighting, and showboat entertainment, the cultural world of shantyboat squatters and roustabouts came under fire from Protestant missionaries who condemned it as sinful and self-destructive. Determined to eradicate sin and to provide social uplift among the river poor, religious forces took to boats in an effort to bring salvation to those they considered badly in need of a good old-fashioned dose of hell-fired holiness on the levee.

8

In the High Waters of Sin

MISSION BOATS AND RIVER PREACHERS

In many river towns the poorer class of people live in houseboats. . . .
Here is the advantage of the floating chapel. All races
and colors are allowed to enter it.

—DR. I. R. B. ARNOLD, *The Times* (Philadelphia), 1895

They [Rev. A. S. and Clara Orne] visit the houseboats along the river
and associate with the levee roustabouts trying to redeem
them from the sin so prevalent among these classes.

—*Quincy Daily Herald,* 1906

Hen shantyboat settlements swelled in the late 1880s, they caught the watchful eye of Protestant missionaries determined to clean up the behavior of levee dwellers, cure a social problem, and save a few souls while they were at it. Influenced by the Social Gospel movement, many ministers endorsed social activism among the poor in hopes that application of Christian principles to solving social problems would clean up the slums of industrial America. With a sense of urgency, Salvation Army preachers picked their way past cobbler shops and pushcarts to the cobblestones of the St. Louis levee to confront wayward sinners. Captain Eugene Hansmann, who formerly preached at the Bethel Mission, operated the St. Louis Central Home of Rest on the north wharf in the mid-1890s, where a bed and a bite to eat came with a stern lecture and a sermon. In many cases, preachers and missionaries came from outside the settlements, but in others they came from within. Nearly every crew of Black roustabouts included at least one preacher. Roustabout preachers held services in humble churches on the waterfront. Burman, writing mainly of the Lower Mississippi, described the shanties in which they conducted services: "The churches in which they officiate are pathetic: a bare little room with an old packing crate for a pulpit, and paper hanging in long mouldering strips from the broken walls. So poor are these churches that if it chances to be night, sometimes the preacher before commencing a sermon must take up a collection to buy kerosene for the oil lamp, so that the services may not be ended by darkness."[1] Under the Black ministry of Rev. Paul Kates in St. Louis in the 1890s and early 1900s, the Mt. Pleasant Baptist Church hosted regular services in a humble shanty in the Dock Street Addition to Little Oklahoma. Most of its parishioners were Black, but white shantyboat residents also attended. Kates and his family lived in a shantyboat in the settlement where he preached.[2]

Unwilling to trust conversion to poor settlement preachers, outside missionaries mounted a naval attack on the seamy, sinful side of levee life. Missionaries took to the Father of Waters and its tributaries in gospel shantyboats, skiffs, and floating chapels to peddle religious elixirs and apocalyptic visions to squatter colonies and others in the Mississippi valley, described by Thomas Ruys Smith as a "spiritual battlefield."[3] Some of the evangelists represented mainline churches, while others espoused millennialism or represented obscure sects or fanatical cults. In May 1889, a group of interdenominational leaders in St. Louis initiated an evangelizing project that was the brainchild of Free Will Baptist minister Morrall A. Shepard. A real estate agent of substantial means from Lebanon, Illinois, Shepard pumped his own money into the project, but donations poured in from supporters across denominational lines. The treasurer of the project's board of directors was William C. Wilson, head of a real estate firm and treasurer of the First Presbyterian Church's board of trustees in St. Louis.[4]

On Sunday morning, November 3, 1890, a ceremony on the north wharf at Bissell's Point took place to showcase the nearly finished construction of the *Free Will Baptist Floating Bethel*. The plan was to launch the large boat in the war on booze and sin in Mississippi valley levee communities. With crews of devout Christian workers and a large gospel tent aboard, the two-story flatboat aimed to stop for a week in selected river towns. Tent meetings were to be held on shore, and daily services to be conducted on board for shantyboaters, roustabouts, and others. In the bow of the boat was a large church bell to summon waterfront dwellers. From the flagstaff flew a large banner, "God Is Love." On the stern was painted, "F.W.B. Floating Bethel." Some of the boat's workers were to distribute literature along the shore. According to the plan, once the missionaries finished a winter in New Orleans, a steamer would tow the missionary boat to St. Paul in the spring. Then the boat would bring them back to St. Louis, evangelizing to "Hallelujahs" as they went along. For the launch, the boat was towed to the foot of Carr Street, where services opened to great fanfare on December 13, 1890. The project's planners figured that with an abundance of sinners on the St. Louis wharf, it would be best to devote two months of the winter to Little Oklahoma and other settlements before floating south. The project did not survive its first year. The wear and tear of the river took a toll on the boat and those aboard it. The only person converted in Cape Girardeau reportedly got drunk the next night. By December 1891, Shepard sold the boat in Cairo and abandoned the mission.[5]

Dr. Irwin Rodolphus Byron Arnold, of Wheaton College, was a pioneer of floating chapels on the waterways. In 1888, at the behest of Dr. Joseph E. Roy, secretary of the American Mission Society of Chicago, he embarked down the Mississippi from Clinton to explore possibilities for missionary work, especially among freedmen. A streamer flew from the boat's flagstaff that read, "Remember the Sabbath day and keep it holy." Accompanying Arnold were his wife (Adelia Nichols Arnold) and five daughters and two Wheaton College theological students, George Bond and Jonas Brooks. Arnold, a talented musician and teacher, was a former newspaper editor and publisher of *The Reformer* and the *Free Methodist* in Sycamore, Illinois. The *Post-Dispatch* described him as "a gifted writer, a deep thinker, a thorough scholar and a genius." Adelia, from nearby Brush Point in DeKalb County, was a teacher from a devout abolitionist family of Wesleyan Methodists. She was guided by a strong commitment to educate freedmen. Like her husband, she found racism offensive and objectionable. On the proselytizing trip down the Mississippi, she was invited to Black schools and churches. In Memphis, she and Dr. Arnold dined with white northern teachers at the Lemoyne Normal Institute for Black students.[6]

By May 1889, the Arnolds made it to Vicksburg, where they employed a steamer to tow them to Cairo and then up the Ohio River to Pittsburgh. Arnold reported favorably to Dr. Roy, pointing out that many people did not live within miles of a church. Arnold endorsed a floating chapel to reach those on the riverbanks:

> In many river towns the poorer class of people live in houseboats. Whole towns along the Mississippi are on the water. . . . Most of these people seldom or never hear the Gospel. . . . As a rule, the people are very poor and are unable to pay a pastor, although enough money is squandered in whisky and other vices to support a college. In some districts the church and school house are one building, and the colored people are not allowed to attend either. Here is the advantage of the floating chapel. All races and colors are allowed to enter it.[7]

In 1890, the Arnolds undertook the crusade aboard a new boat, custom-built in New Martinsville, West Virginia. The 30-by-110-foot boat featured a printing office, small classroom, kitchen, dining room, storeroom for books and literature, chapel with a seating capacity of five hundred, and sleeping rooms. Beginning on the Ohio River, the Arnolds joined the winter migration of shantyboats south. They also evangelized on the Illinois River and sometimes used Nashville as headquarters while on the Cumberland, where Ryman steamers towed them free of charge.[8]

Prior to the crusade, Arnold was a noted lecturer in Kansas, Nebraska, and Illinois who employed a stereopticon to illustrate lectures on ancient history, Bible geography, temperance, and other topics. His tent lectures and shows featured music by his wife and daughters, whom he taught to play a number of string and brass instruments. At times a quartet or duo traveled with them. Arnold used two stereopticons, or "magic lanterns," which projected images upon a canvass. Typically, while audience members were being seated, he projected images of local, state, and national interest upon a canvas to capture their attention. Once the lecture began, he replaced the images with lyrics to a hymn, for example, and projected a picture to accompany the hymn on a separate canvas. Temperance was often the focus of his lectures. To reach the poor, he showed images of how alcohol damaged the stomach. "These poor creatures get just enough papers to see that patent medicines are on the market," Arnold told a reporter, "and they'll buy them and do without something to eat."[9]

For fifteen years, the Arnolds persevered on the rivers, despite hardships, dangers, and near disasters. When the Mississippi River iced over in December 1901, they were trapped in Quincy, where Dr. Arnold gave lectures at the YMCA, Soldier's Home, and other venues before continuing to Hannibal in March. A crusade on the Upper Illinois River, 1895–1896, was especially beset with problems. With C. H. Nichols, one of Adelia's brothers, aboard as business manager, the Arnolds nearly perished when a heavy wind storm tore the boat from its moorings and damaged it badly in Henry. A dramatic rescue saved them. Thanks to local missions, boat repairs put them back on the water, but they could only float at a snail's pace down the river in early March 1896. Caught by an unexpected freeze north of Lacon, they were trapped in midstream when the boat was iced in after floating only five miles. To make matters worse, the Arnolds sometimes received a frosty welcome. The temperance message did not resonate with saloon keepers and town officials who supported them. Dr. Arnold requested but was denied police protection from disorderly elements in Spring Valley. Local rowdies told him that if they could not drink on Sunday, he should not be allowed to hold public lectures on Sunday.[10]

In time, deepening religious differences between Arnold and his family ended their river missionary travels together. After working at the Hebron Rescue Home in Cleveland, Adelia felt a rekindled commitment to missionary work among poverty-stricken Blacks in the South. She refused to accompany her husband on future river trips. In February 1906, she left him in Cleveland, where he served as an assistant pastor at the Euclid Avenue Baptist Church and operated the Stereopticon and Film Exchange. The rift became public. Complaining that he was too worldly, and that she and their daughters did most of the missionary work ashore while he showed secular images on stereopticons aboard the boat, she and their daughters left to undertake evangelizing on behalf of the Repairer Mission in Atlanta. Dr. Arnold filed a divorce suit on April 23, 1906, emphasizing that his wife and daughters were under the influence of a sect of Black Holiness fanatics. According to Adelia, their parting was amicable, and she was stunned by the news of the divorce filing. Undaunted, Dr. Arnold continued as a tent lecturer in Ohio and elsewhere. He promoted temperance among Cleveland's newsboys, and he continued to represent the Stereopticon and Film Exchange. He preached on the Allegheny River, but the family strife ended fifteen years of missionary work on the Mississippi.[11]

In more fixed waterfront settlements, there was at least one resident self-styled preacher. In the St. Louis area, Judson D. Woolever felt the call to preach from his own shantyboat on the east side of the river at Venice. Known as the "young circuit minister," he soon met sixteen-year-old Martha Verweyst. At age twenty-eight, he married her in January 1907, but after a brief honeymoon he told her he intended to preach in an itinerant lifestyle on the Mississippi. Less than three months after they married, he came home from fishing one afternoon to find Martha and her trunk and clothing gone. She went back to her parents. "When I married Mr. Woolever," she told a reporter, "I was sure I loved him and thought it great fun to live on a houseboat. But he soon got tired of me. After I get my divorce I will be careful not to try any more romantic marriages." After the divorce, Woolever took in his lines, and down the river he went to evangelize.[12]

Mississippi River traffic bore an eclectic assortment of missionaries from different sects. Among them were Edson White and Seventh-Day Adventists aboard the *Morning Star*, Rev. A. L. Durbin, of the Swedenborgian Church of the New Jerusalem, faith healer "Brother Isaiah" in a shantyboat on the New Orleans levee, and communal "Christian Brethren" millennialists with L. T. Nichols aboard the *Megiddo*. Many waterfront colonies on the Lower Mississippi were drawn to the vibrant Holiness movement, which was rooted heavily in Methodism. "Holy Rollers" typically gathered in the shantyboat of their colony's preacher for a service that began with a hymn. "Soon the tempo of the music quickens," wrote Burman in a description of such services. "Hands begin to clap in explosive rhythm. And as the excitement increases, and the clapping of hands grows louder, faster, the worshippers leap wildly into the air, to show their devotion to the Lord. At such moments, the preacher begins the curious 'talking in tongues,' and though like his flock both reading and writing may be far beyond his powers, he and his parishioners firmly believe that he is speaking the Greek of St. Paul and the Hebrew of Moses, and sometimes even the Egyptian of Pharaoh."[13]

The Holiness movement changed the life of Noah Barnett, an old Ohio River fisherman at the mouth of Mill Creek in Cincinnati's "Shanty Town." He worked as a janitor, repairman, and general assistant to Rev. Thomas Wright, who operated the *Shantytown Mission* houseboat and did work for the Mount of Blessings's "God's Bible School" in the riverfront community. The popular mission boat had a seating capacity of three hundred. Wright, employed on the river in his younger days, was not only a minister but a close adviser to the shantyboat settlement in temporal matters, too. In 1908, Barnett praised the Holiness movement for what it had done for him in the past seven years: "It's made a man of me . . . an' I was pretty tough material to work on; drinkin', out breakin' an' doin' nothin' like I should for myself. An' what that mission has done for me, it has done for hundreds of others—yes, sir—snatched 'em in out'n the drift in the high waters o' sin, as you might say."[14]

No matter their theology, missionaries faced skepticism among river people. "I ain't much confidence in 'em. Some are only fakirs," a levee dweller in Memphis told writer Clifton Johnson. "I've seen considerable much of ministers, and I've made up my mind that generally, ashore or afloat, they've taken up their callin' as a business and are workin' for what thar is in it. They beg every time they look at you. The mo' money you got, the bigger Christian you are. Yes, sir, you shove up five dollars to the preacher, and you c'n drink and cuss and rip and tear all you please."[15] George "Pa" Stanton and his wife, "Aunt Ann," were known as "Good Samaritans of the river folk" on account of their charitable deeds on the Ohio between Louisville and Madison, Indiana. "Aunt Ann" tended to the sick in their shantyboats, and even poor townspeople came to the riverfront to see her when they were ailing. Sometimes she brought the sickest to stay in her own twelve-by-twenty-foot houseboat until they recovered. Rarely did she receive compensation. "It's our religion though," she explained in 1925. "We don't go to church. We ain't got fine clothes to show off. There's people in this town that go to church every Sunday all dressed up, who wouldn't give a hungry man a mouthful to eat. But not me—not on your life."[16]

The most well-traveled evangelist on the waterways was Dr. A. S. Orne, an ordained ex-Congregationalist minister and social worker from a well-off farm family in Wolfeboro, New Hampshire. For ten years before taking to the waterways, he invited controversy wherever he preached in the northeast. He was assigned a church in Wentworth in 1887, but the Concord Congregational Ministerial Association soon stripped him of his license for repeatedly injecting holiness doctrines into his sermons in violation of church doctrines and practices. In 1890, he returned to Wentworth and holed up in an old broken-down hotel for four days to preach fiery sermons in the slums. A gang of rowdies who took exception to his sermonizing hurled insults and stones, hanged him in effigy, and ran him out of town. Undaunted, Orne returned a few months later despite threats that he'd be tarred and feathered if he dared to come back. After a service, a crowd of about fifty men pelted him with rocks and rotten eggs. He and his followers fled town via an alternate road to avoid ambush and tarring and feathering. The Massachusetts State Parental Home Association appointed him as an agent and advocate for the creation of a special home for neglected children of indigent parents in June 1892, but removed him after he denied medical treatment to his own infant daughter, who died of typhoid fever. He treated her by anointing her with oils and prayers. "Unfortunately, there is no law under which the pious and prayerful Orne can be punished," a newspaper complained. "His case is a sad illustration of what there is in human nature. Heathen have sacrificed their children to show their faith. Pious Mr. Orne sacrificed his daughter to show his faith." Orne attacked the Home Association, bragging that he raised most of its money, and defended himself against critics: "I do not believe in physicians or their treatment. Furthermore, I am not of this world, and I try to follow the word of the Scriptures, and as God did not heal my child, I believe He has another object in taking her away."[17]

Influenced by the teachings of Rev. Albert B. Simpson, a Canadian-born theologian and ex-Presbyterian minister who in 1887 founded the Christian and Missionary Alliance in Old Orchard Beach, Maine, Orne criticized the failure of churches to reach out to those on the bottom rung of the social ladder. His "in-your-face" style jeopardized his safety before angry crowds who didn't appreciate his message or abrasive methods. He set up independent, nondenominational missions in Dover and Pennacook, New Hampshire, before moving to Brooklyn, where he co-founded the Bethany Mission on April 4, 1895. With a judge's permission, Orne held services every Sunday in police court. With a determined band of followers, he marched into slums and saloons, singing and spreading holiness doctrines. After a public falling out with the mission's co-founder, Orne, a widower who had recently remarried, boasted that Jesus Christ was leaving the building with him as he severed his ties to the mission. On May 4, 1896, he and his wife, Clara, with two young sons from his previous marriage, set out from Haverhill, Massachusetts, in a "Gospel Wagon" with the inscription "Stop Sinning" on one side and "Seek Salvation" on the other. For the next twenty years they crisscrossed the nation in wagons, boats, and trains as well as on foot to spread holiness and conduct sociological uplift work.

Well-informed, they called attention to crime, pauperism, and moral decay in slums, in particular, and urged adoption of children's courts and industrial homes for delinquents. They preached, sang hymns, and met with charitable organizations, mayors, and governors. There was hardly a county jail, tenderloin district, house of refuge, work-house, roustabouts' saloon, or shantyboat settlement they didn't visit. Widely recognized for his pioneering advocacy of juvenile courts and industrial homes, Orne lobbied city and state officials to adopt initiatives on behalf of delinquent, neglected children of the poor. He reminded crowds and organizations that he and Clara began their work penniless, emphasizing that generous contributions furnished them with the necessities of life as they traveled from town to town.[18]

When the Ornes reached St. Louis in the late fall of 1897, they stayed in the heart of the Morgan Street slums near the levee. Bearing credentials and letters of recommendation from mayors familiar with their work, they conducted services on city streets. At the Workhouse, Clara preached to female inmates, and her husband held services for the men. They gathered research material for a study of juvenile offenders in penal institutions. When Reverend Orne toured the Workhouse with guard Minnie Gammeter, he asked if any juveniles were incarcerated. Gammeter named Jessie Wilson, a thirteen-year-old girl in the Workhouse on an unspecified charge with an indefinite sentence. Gammeter believed it a shame that Wilson was confined there, and suggested the Humane Society might better serve her. Wilson told Orne that her crime was that of homelessness. Her mother was in the insane asylum, and her drunken father was "no good." Wilson went to live with an aunt, who made her feel unwelcome. A police officer found Wilson on the street playing with her dog and asked her where she lived. Hopeful that the officer might find her a better home, she replied, "I have been staying with my aunt, but she don't want me anymore."[19] Instead, Wilson was arraigned in police court and banished to the Workhouse.

On Wilson's behalf, Orne spoke to an agent of the Humane Society of Missouri who pledged to do everything possible to place her in a better environment. He learned there were several seventeen-year-old boys in the Workhouse, and he met two girls, ages seventeen and eighteen, who expressed remorse for whatever their petty crimes were. Based on their desire to reform, he spoke to Mrs. M. E. Otto, who promised to try to transfer them to the Hephzibah Home for Friendless Girls, which she managed. He continued his investigations and sociological field work on crime and juvenile delinquency in St. Louis through the winter. He cited state, local, and national statistics to bolster his case for juvenile courts and industrial homes. In January 1903, he met with Mayor Rolla Wells and visited the Workhouse again as well as the jail and House of Refuge, which since 1854 housed children who committed crimes or simply were "tramps" on the streets. The House of Refuge used forced labor and meted out cruel punishment to the children, including lashes and solitary confinement. At times, it was indistinguishable from the Workhouse. Classes were held in the evening after the children finished six or eight hours of work. To relieve overcrowding, managers of the House of Refuge indentured children to area farmers and businessmen who needed a cheap source of labor.[20]

The Ornes were introduced to shantyboat squatters and roustabouts on their extended stay in St. Louis, which became a popular stop on their proselytizing journeys. Their experiences and observations of conditions on the levee convinced them to shift their focus to waterfront settlements. They sold their wagon and team of Missouri mules and bought a fifteen-foot-long skiff and a tent and cooking equipment. On July 6, 1903, the Ornes set out from Glendive, Montana, to pursue their brand of uplift among the river poor. Their evangelizing took them down the Yellowstone to the Missouri River near Buford, North Dakota, and then down the Missouri to St. Louis, where they joined the shantyboat stream to New Orleans. Their maiden voyage was not without controversy. Incendiary remarks about the Methodist Church by Orne, a self-styled crank, inflamed a group of nearly fifty "Methodist cowboys" in Bismarck who threatened to lynch him from a lamppost. In 1906, the "Shanty Boat Evangelist" and Clara were camped on the waterfront in Davenport when a reporter found them for an interview. They were en route from St. Paul to New Orleans. "Ten years ago 'mama' and I got interested in shanty boat life," Orne reflected, "and after doing a little missionary work among the shantyboat people, the thought came to us, 'Why not start out down the river and work among these people right along?' So we got a tent and a skiff and cooking outfit and started. And we have spent a good part of each year at it ever since." As the *Quincy Daily Herald* put it, the "strange little white-bearded peripatetic pastor" and his wife devoted themselves primarily to saving the souls and children of shantyboat squatters and roustabouts, "trying to redeem them from the sin so prevalent among these classes."[21]

The eccentric evangelists weren't always welcomed by local officials. In Chattanooga, the mayor refused to allow Orne to address a mass meeting on the subject of crime and juvenile courts in April 1905. The police chief refused to let him talk to officers without proving his credentials. Orne did visit the jail, where he complained about housing white and Black prisoners together. Arguing for social and racial uplift within Jim Crow, he urged segregated industrial homes to train Black children. The First Congregational Church of Chattanooga invited him to deliver an Easter Sunday morning service, and the A.M.E. Church hosted a special service that featured him as speaker. Invitations from these two Black churches were not enough for Orne, who was stung by the chilly reception from city officials. In vindictive remarks afterward, he grumbled that God would punish the mayor. The Ornes nursed hurt feelings in a remote location on the Tennessee River before continuing to Nashville, where they received a hearty welcome from officials.[22]

Whether in St. Louis's waterfront district, a Pentecostal mission in Nashville, or on Front Street in Muscatine, Orne's sermons and lectures highlighted crime by juvenile "tramps" in the nation's slums. Often acknowledged as the "father of the juvenile court," he pushed state support for compulsory school laws and industrial homes for delinquents. He also prescribed a good dose of the Holy Ghost and attacked the worldliness of modern churches. Well-traveled on the nation's rivers, the Ornes stopped in St. Louis a half-dozen times in the course of their travels, their final visit in 1911. In fact, Orne at age fifty-eight nearly died of malarial fever in the city hospital in October 1908. Ailing when he and Clara arrived from Kansas City, he was in critical condition by the time they tied up their skiff on the St. Louis waterfront. Although he later returned to the river, death seemed imminent at the time. "I think my work is nearly over," he told a reporter.[23]

Orne was suffering from kidney disease in May 1916 when he and his wife arrived in Morgan City, Louisiana. They decided to row their boat to Natchez. In a weakened state, he rowed until they reached the mouth of the Red River, where he collapsed. His wife took over the oars for a couple of hours against the strong current of the Mississippi. The Betsy Ann, a steamboat packet and mail carrier that hauled freight between Bayou Sara and Natchez, came upon them and took them aboard. The steamer transported them to Natchez, where Orne died penniless in the city hospital. The local chapter of King's Daughters paid for his funeral and burial in the city cemetery, and invited Clara to stay in their Home temporarily. For twenty years, she and her husband traversed nearly every state on foot or by boat, wagon, steamer, or occasional train. The final years were devoted to reaching roustabouts, shantyboat squatters, prostitutes, and levee hoboes. The Ornes gave up a comfortable lifestyle in New England to pursue missionary work and social uplift among the lowly. Even critics acknowledged the sincerity and passion with which they pursued their calling.[24]

Mission houseboats and "floating exhorters" remained common features of life and traffic on the Mississippi River and its tributaries. On August 7, 1921, a houseboat covered with biblical quotations in large lettering carried the family of E. D. Jamison, a Pentecostal preacher from Moore, Montana, on a waterways gospel mission. A self-styled "messenger of God," formerly of Elsberry, Missouri, he set out on the Upper Missouri from Fort Benton with New Orleans as a final destination. The *Boat of God* contained a single room with a built-in table and cupboard and beds that were suspended from the ceiling, lowered and raised by a rope and pulley. There was a porch on each end of the boat, which was powered only by oars and the river's current. On board were his wife and three daughters under the age of seven, as well as a hen and three baby chicks. The Jamison family left behind a comfortable farm home to undertake the mission. For three years until they reached the Crescent City on August 7, 1924, Jamison distributed religious literature and preached in waterfront settlements from atop his houseboat. He performed casual carpentry work and did other odd jobs to earn money to support his family en route to New Orleans on the mission.[25]

In November 1928, river adventurers Kent and Margaret Lighty were awakened early one morning when a sharp object hit the front porch of their houseboat in Hickman, Kentucky. Half asleep, they stumbled to the door to see a houseboat tying up next to them. Tall red letters on its bow greeted them: "Only Jesus Saves." On the port side and starboard were the words "Get Right with God," and the word "Bibles" was plastered wherever there was room. The boat's name was *Maranatha* (The Lord Cometh).[26] A friendly river preacher and his freckle-faced son aboard were from the Ohio valley. They sold Bibles and distributed literature, tightly rolled and bound to throw easily from their boat to others. In most cases, the preacher, who had a Bible-selling business on the side, chatted with waterfront squatters, but at times he merely distributed leaflets. On occasion someone might buy a Bible from him, or in a more settled shantyboat colony an inhabitant might buy one for the entire colony to use. The preacher held services and baptized converts in the river. He warned the Lightys to beware of sinful Louisiana. "Down there, he told us, the people were going to perdition and they liked it," the Lightys wrote. "New Orleans was to blame, of course, with its foreign influence. A city of many vices, dancing straight into the fires of hell, it was a burden to him, and in a sense he had to gird himself up each autumn for the tribulations of winter in the Southern bayous."[27] During prohibition, river preachers were suspected of close ties to revenue agents searching for moonshine stills on the islands and along shore. When the Lightys reached Memphis in 1928, they heard about a preacher who had a cozy arrangement with revenuers. For every tip provided that led to an arrest, he received $5. Shortly before the Lightys arrived, a preacher who hung around Mud Island long enough to gather intelligence was suspected after authorities raided a number of stills and made arrests on the island. After someone mysteriously fired a couple of bullets at his houseboat one night, he got the message. When morning broke, he was gone.[28]

Perhaps the most bizarre waterways evangelist was James Sharp, the self-styled "Adam God," who did hard time in the Missouri State Penitentiary after a 1908 shoot-out with Kansas City police in front of city hall. The path that elevated him to leadership of a tiny fanatical cult and led to a dank prison cell began in a childhood of petty crime on the Mississippi River. According to Sharp, born in 1857 near Lebanon, he ran away from home as a boy. For thirty years he was a gambler and thief. "The first meanness I did," he recalled, "was on the Mississippi River, when I picked pockets of people on the steamboats, cutting their pockets with a razor."[29] In 1887, he married Melissa F. Roper, born in Mountain Grove. Sharp, a self-described drunk, left the river to farm and get away from whiskey, but the whiskey followed him until a night in 1903 when a meteor fell near him in northwestern Oklahoma's Woodward County, Indian Territory. Shaken, he repented and changed his life, convinced that the falling star, which "came with a great noise with the wind of a tornado and rumblings of thunder," was a sign from the Book of Revelation. He and Melissa, who also repented, sold their Oklahoma farm and took to the road as self-styled agents of divine prophecy to sound the trumpet, gather followers, and preach that God would appear in the flesh. Their views scared off their older son, but Lee, "the boy preacher," remained with them on their travels.[30]

On April 17, 1905, the Sharps ("Adam and Eve") and John Aitken, a recent street convert who professed to be "Almighty God," paraded naked down the streets of Oklahoma City, singing and shouting "hosannas" and "hallelujahs" and warning that the world was coming to an end. When an arresting police officer asked if they were ashamed of themselves, both professed to have entered a blissful state of peace in their public nakedness. "God Almighty required it of us," Mrs. Sharp explained, "and he never asks us to do anything we would be ashamed of. It was the command and we fulfilled it. We understand all this. You do not."[31] When the Sharps refused to quit singing in their jail cell, police turned water hoses on them. James later claimed that he was immortal, having died under police torture that night: "No human being ever underwent such tortures as I did there in my cell," he insisted. "I would have swallowed a quart of strychnine that night, but it would not have done any good. I lay there, and groaned in agony until finally I felt the life die out of me and I was immediately born in the flesh once more. . . . That was the old body dying and the new one being resurrected, and this body of mine is immortal. I cannot die."[32]

Questioned by a judge and insanity commission, James indicated that it was Aitken who commanded them to take off their clothes. Denying insanity or use of cocaine or other drugs, he assured the judge: "What we did today will all work out for good. We are not like other people of this would [sic]. There has been a reign of night for nineteen hundred years. Christ spoke of this night. It must be controlled that people may have perfect peace. There will be no jails—no crime—all love, exactly like in the Garden of Eden. It will all be made manifest."[33]

The judge sent Aitken to an asylum and sentenced the Sharps to thirty days in the county jail. James soon turned on Aitken, whom he came to view as the Serpent who tempted them in the new "Garden of Eden." A physician on the commission called attention to Aitken's mesmerizing influence on the Sharps, concluding that separation would break his power over them. A police matron took charge of eleven-year-old Lee, who, according to Melissa, "was stolen from us and placed in a reform school."[34]

Upon release, the Sharps resumed their mission in wagons and shantyboats to recruit followers who would obey and surrender all material goods to James. The group lived off new followers and money collected on street corners and waterfronts by preaching and singing. Melissa, "a handsome young woman of magnetic personality,"[35] believed that material possessions would be irrelevant in a restored Garden of Eden. According to her, she and James walked naked in Oklahoma City because as the new Adam and Eve they were free of original sin and as pure as they were before their expulsion from the original Garden of Eden. James, who sported a long, coarse beard, claimed to be a prophet with healing powers. In summer 1906, a county attorney near Oklahoma City filed peace disturbance charges against them when neighbors complained about lewd, lascivious activities in their tent and wagon colony on a recent convert's farm near a public road where many of its nearly fifty colonists wore no clothes. James and a core group of diehard followers were arrested, among them brothers John J. Pratt and William Lewis Pratt, of Edina, Missouri, and Lewis Pratt's wife, Della (Jones). Authorities dropped the charges when James agreed to leave the area with his followers.[36]

In wagons and shantyboats on the Arkansas and Missouri rivers, the Sharps and their followers ran afoul of authorities time and again. In Kansas City, two years before the deadly confrontation with police, John Pratt was hauled into juvenile court with three of his school-age children. When a judge asked why the children did not attend school, Pratt replied: "Because they are not of this world; they are of the spiritual world. They are my disciples. They aid me in the dissemination of the gospel. They are at school in heaven." The judge ordered him to put the kids in school or the court would assume custody. A newspaper warned that Pratt "is evidently insane and should not be permitted to run at large as he is liable to become dangerous and may commit some atrocious deed."[37]

To escape repeated harassment, the Sharps and the Lewis Pratt family set out for the Pacific Northwest with plans to settle in Canada, but Canadian authorities blocked two attempted entries. On one attempt, there nearly was an armed confrontation with mounted police inside the border. By the time the Sharps and Pratts found their way to the Upper Missouri River in the fall of 1908 and exchanged their horse and wagon for a shantyboat, they were armed, angry, and bound for Kansas City. They vowed that authorities would never take them alive if they tried to seize the children. A farmer near Bowbells, North Dakota, took pity on them in their destitute condition and offered them a meal. With revolvers in holsters buckled onto their hips, they stacked Winchester repeaters in a corner before they dined at the farmer's table. Testy, Melissa told their hosts what happened at the border and displayed her "mammoth" revolver: "By God, we'd like to see them do it again."[38]

The families preached in waterfront settlements on the Missouri River, and the children sang for donations. In November, they left St. Joseph just as cakes of ice appeared on the river. When they tied up on the Kansas City riverfront, they took to the crowded streets and missions to proselytize among the poor. On December 8, 1908, George M. Holt, a juvenile probation officer investigating a child abduction case, observed Melissa using the children to solicit money near city hall. When he asked why the children were not in school, she told him to mind his own business.[39] She and the children went to the Workingmen's Mission to warn James and the others. When Holt followed them into the mission, James waved a pistol in his face, ordered him out, and cracked him behind the ear with the revolver. The children then set upon Holt, who was bleeding as he started toward the police station. James dropped his revolver, then picked it up and tried to shoot Holt, but the cartridge failed to explode. Singing hymns, the cultists moved closer to the police station, defying anyone to stop them from preaching and singing. All were armed, including the two oldest Pratt daughters. Before Holt finished warning police, gunfire broke out. When Officers Harry E. Stege and Albert O. Dolbow stepped out into the street, they were met by a volley of bullets that killed Dolbow and wounded Stege in the arm. Other police rushed into the fray. James shot and killed Officer Michael P. Mullane. Sergeant Patrick Clark, who ran outside without a firearm, tried to knock James's revolver out of his hand but took a bullet in the back and suffered a cut to his right eye from a knife concealed in James's other hand. Officers arrested Melissa and severely wounded Lewis Pratt, but James, whose hands were slightly wounded by gunfire, escaped and went into hiding. To avoid recognition, he slipped his hands into his overcoat pockets and ducked into a barbershop, where he got a haircut and sheared off his long beard.[40]

Della Pratt retreated with Lulu Fay, who was nearly fourteen, and Lena, age twelve, to their shantyboat on the riverfront. After a long shotgun standoff with police, she and her daughters slipped into their canopied skiff with a Winchester repeating rifle and pistols. Della rowed the skiff toward midstream to the cheers of sympathetic waterfront onlookers. Police at first were under orders not to fire, but as Della's escape seemed imminent, an officer was authorized to shoot holes in the bottom of the boat. As Della pulled on the oars faster amid ice floes, the officer fired, reportedly at the bottom of the boat, but a bullet killed Lulu Fay. Della returned fire with her Winchester, scattering levee onlookers. Once she exhausted her ammunition, she and Lena jumped into the icy river, but police in a river ferry plucked them from the water to face charges. A couple of days later, police arrested James, who was hiding in a haystack near Olathe, Kansas. The gun battle left Officers Mullane and Dolbow dead. Officers Stege and Clark recovered, but Clark lost sight in his right eye. Unrepentant, Lewis Pratt died from his wounds, indicating to the last that he wished he could have killed more police. An innocent bystander was also killed in the crossfire. The Sharps and Della Pratt were arraigned and charged with first-degree murder. The surviving Pratt children—Lena, Mary (age ten), and Dewey (age eight) reportedly were taken to live with an uncle in Kansas City. When questioned, they insisted that their religion granted a right to kill police officers who tried to keep them from preaching.[41]

James, convicted of second-degree murder, was sentenced to twenty-five years in the Missouri State Penitentiary. He entered prison on July 13, 1909, and served fifteen years. Della was released on grounds of insanity. She went to Sherman, Texas, where the bedraggled state of her children drew the attention of authorities. She was committed to the North Texas Insane Asylum on May 10, 1909, and her children went with relatives. Charges were dropped against Melissa after she served eleven months in the county jail. At first, neither woman expressed remorse, but by the time of Melissa's release she acknowledged that the armed actions were wrong. By now she was a sympathetic figure and model prisoner to her jailers. She moved to Jefferson City to be near James in the penitentiary. She earned money as a washerwoman and lobbied for executive clemency. Thanks to Governor Arthur M. Hyde's commutation of his sentence, James left prison on November 8, 1924.[42]

The Sharps returned to Kansas City, where Della Pratt reunited with them. By the following July, the three prepared a shantyboat with a canvas-covered scow on which they planned to float down the Missouri and Mississippi rivers. James insisted that he did not plan to preach anymore, that they just wanted to make a little money to get by on: "We are going to float down the river and make our way by working along its banks. . . . Cotton picking starts in August and we can make some money at that."[43] The three left Kansas City in July 1925, but after a year on the boat they left the Mississippi when James suffered health problems. A tent on a rubbish dump at an abandoned mining claim in southwest Joplin became the Sharps' new home, where they combed alleys as junk pickers. They barely scraped by, but never lost their religious zeal. In 1931 James told a reporter that prison taught him restraint, but flashes of the old "Adam God" were still there. "A great power is now at work within me," he remarked, "and shortly I will be guided to move mountains and to raise the dead."[44] A familiar figure in Joplin who called himself "The Reverend," James delivered street-corner sermons. Despite several heart attacks, he danced a jig before every sermon to show his vitality. On March 9, 1946, a day after dancing a jig, the "immortal" Sharp died at eighty-nine.[45]

No matter their theological perspective, the message of river preachers often went unheeded in squatter settlements, but missionaries in gospel wagons and houseboats remained undeterred in the face of storms, floods, moccasins, mosquitoes, alligators, harassment, and unrepentant wharf dwellers. Sometimes their efforts came at great personal sacrifice. In the "Adam God" case, blind faith and fanaticism went horribly awry when it clashed with police authority and led to murderous outcomes, but in a never-ending war on sin, missionaries trolled the waterways for wayward souls to save from the ways of the levee.

9

Neither Pumpkin nor Paw-paw

LITTLE OKLAHOMA'S SCULLING CHAMPION OF THE WORLD

Little Oklahoma is at present just about the proudest spot in the broad
state of Missouri. Its attitude distinctly declares to the world that it is
neither pumpkin nor paw-paw, but a solid little corner of national fame.

—*Waterways Journal*, 1894

~~~~~~

Rather small and lithe in build, she is as graceful in her boat as a water
sprite, and makes a pretty picture. . . . In street costume she looks exactly
like hundreds of other girls one sees in the streets—a comely, shapely
little lady. Not until she dons her racing suit of black knickerbockers and
stockings and white and purple sleeveless blouse that her
well-developed muscles assert themselves.

—*St. Louis Globe-Democrat*, October 15, 1894

St. Louis's north wharf settlement of Little Oklahoma boasted a world champion athlete. Long buried in American sports history is Rose Mosenthein's 1894 capture of the women's sculling championship of America in a race on the Mississippi River. No flash in the pan, she won the women's world championship the following year at an international regatta in Austin, Texas. Had the 1904 Summer Olympics in St. Louis included women, she likely would have competed. Rowing clubs in America denied membership to women, but male rowers in St. Louis recognized her skills on the oars and nurtured her in competitive sculling. A pioneer in women's competitive rowing, Mosenthein's childhood resembled that of many children in waterfront squatter settlements, and her mother's gritty struggle to raise children with an absent father was all too common. Even as the city cheered and celebrated the national championship race on the river, waterfront developers and city

~~~~

officials waged an ongoing campaign to get rid of the river community she represented. Likewise, powerful business interests in the mid-1890s moved to take possession of nearby Mosenthein Island, which her mother inhabited and farmed as a squatter for several years.[1]

Rose was born on January 13, 1873, in the Coffey County frontier town of LeRoy, Kansas. Her mother, born in 1850, was Mary Hürlimann, who emigrated from Switzerland in 1869. Rose's father was Ferdinand C. Steimel, a German-born army surgeon who emigrated around 1852. In the Civil War, he enlisted in the 32nd Ohio Infantry and served as a hospital steward until discharged on November 20, 1864, due to a herniated disc he suffered in Natchez. After the war, Steimel opened a physician's office and drugstore in a number of towns, including Chillicothe, Missouri. After his office in Chillicothe suffered devastating fire damage in December 1868, he moved to Emporia, Kansas, where he built an office and drugstore. At the beginning of 1869, Hürlimann arrived, married him, and gave birth to their son, Gustave (Gus), in October. Dr. Steimel made an unsuccessful bid as a Democratic candidate for coroner of Lyon County that year. Shortly after they relocated to nearby LeRoy, he abandoned the family. In October 1873, when Rose was nine months old, Mary filed a divorce petition in the Coffey County district court. Dr. Steimel fled the state for the Oklahoma Territory en route to Los Angeles. Later newspaper reports mistakenly claimed that he died when Rose was a child, but he opened a practice in Los Angeles and spent the final years of his life in the city's Sawtelle Veterans' Home for Disabled Volunteer Soldiers.[2]

Mary left Kansas with her two children, but by the time she met Charles L. Mosenthein in St. Louis she had remarried, divorced again, and given birth to a third child, Edward Krause, around 1876. Charles, who emigrated from Germany in 1874, operated an upholstering shop in north St. Louis for furniture manufacturer William Prufrock. Charles adopted Edward, who assumed the name of Mosenthein. Rose, too, went by the name of Mosenthein, but her legal name remained Steimel. Charles and Mary added three more children of their own—Bertha (1878), Otto (1879), and May Belle (1886). In 1885, they lived on a houseboat on the wharf between Harrison (Branch) Street and the Dock Street Addition to Little Oklahoma, but Mary and Charles soon went their separate ways. From neighbors, Mary bought an old houseboat, the *Baby Mine*. With her children, she moored it at the foot of Buchanan Street. According to her son Otto, she grew up on the shore of a lake in Switzerland and enjoyed living close to water.[3]

With hard times knocking at the door in 1889, Rose was sitting on the front porch of their shantyboat one day, worrying how her mother was going to make ends meet now that her stepfather was not around. A rather crusty-looking stranger on his way downriver in a boat stopped to chat with her on the north wharf. The stranger mentioned that personal circumstances forced him to abandon a fertile island upriver a few miles where he grew corn and vegetables. Upon hearing the plight of Rose's family, he was sympathetic. He urged her to take squatter's possession of the island and to encourage her mother to file for a homestead certificate to farm it. The island held a promising future for anyone willing to endure flooding and other rough elements of island living in order to farm its nearly 365 fertile acres. The island had grown considerably due to changes in the river's channel. Within earshot, two men at once hopped into their skiff and sped north toward the island. With an immediate shrug of his shoulders, the friendly stranger sighed that it was too late: "Them fellers is a-goin' up thar now. They have been watchin the place for a long time."[4]

Rose, who was sixteen years old, slipped into her family's small skiff and set out in a fierce race to beat the two men to the island. They were experienced oarsmen with a considerable head start, but she, too, was river wise and skilled. Her skiff, lighter than theirs, was more maneuverable against the current, high waves, and floating debris. Aware she was gaining on them, they poured it on, but when she overtook them they pulled up their oars and abandoned the race to the island, known by some as Willow Bar Island and by others as Goose Bar Island. Rose's mother soon laid a squatter's claim and moved her houseboat to the island, which she farmed. According to Otto, she used medical knowledge gained from her first marriage to practice medicine—likely as a midwife—in squatter settlements on the north wharf until the local medical society shut her down. Gus did not move to the island, instead remaining on a houseboat in Little Oklahoma at the foot of Buchanan Street. Neither did Bertha, who stayed with Gus in his boat and took care of housekeeping until he married in 1894. She, too, married and lived with her husband in a houseboat at the foot of Angelrodt Street. She often visited her mother and siblings on the island. Years later, Bertha recalled giving birth to her daughter while marooned on the island by large ice floes.

~~~

With the help of her children, Mary Mosenthein built a three-story house, two-story barn, and other outbuildings on the island. She put up fences and planted crops without horses or plows, according to her son Otto. They endured hardships, particularly floods that drove them from the island three times, but they always returned. On one occasion they took refuge on the roof of their house for a week until floodwaters receded. When government engineers showed up one day to survey the island, they were surprised it had grown so much. Otto, when asked its name, proudly replied, "Mosenthein Island."[5]

Rose's life took her up and down the north wharf from Little Oklahoma to Mosenthein Island. Her rowing skills impressed waterfront observers, and she was an outstanding swimmer and diver. With impressive physical strength, an engaging personality, self-discipline, and an attractive appearance, she was popular on the north levee. She, too, bought a houseboat and became known in the early 1890s as the "belle of Little Oklahoma." She managed to avoid the pitfalls of early pregnancy and marriage common to many poor teenage girls on the riverfront and elsewhere. When Rose was about twenty-one, her rowing skills caught the attention of the Central Rowing Club (CRC) as well as Fred Koenig, an American amateur rowing champion who represented the Western Rowing Club at the time. The CRC, incorporated in 1891 with seven charter members, grew to 125 members by 1894. The city council agreed to lease wharf space to the club for a new boathouse and headquarters at the foot of Palm Street on the north wharf. On October 13, 1893, the club held its first meeting in the new boathouse equipped with aquatic and gymnastic sports equipment. Dedication festivities at the new headquarters took place on April 29, 1894, just as Rose's sculling prowess was gaining attention.[6]

Rowing clubs were all-male organizations, but with Koenig's coaching and a racing shell furnished by the CRC, Mosenthein mastered the technique of rowing in a long, narrow, and much lighter racing shell with a sliding seat and specially designed oars. Before long, she competed in practice against other rowers in the club. In fact, she beat most of the men who rowed against her.[7] Her soon-to-be rival, Tillie Ashley, of Hartford, Connecticut, described the intricacies of sculling, pointing to the importance of balance and technique: "When you first get into one [sculling shell] you feel as though you were trying to sit on top of a bubble of quicksilver. . . . It is about sixteen inches wide at its greatest beam and is something in the neighborhood of thirty feet long. It is very shallow and would upset in a minute if it were not in motion or balanced by an experienced hand at the oars."[8] Ashley's first experience in a shell came at the invitation of male rowers who wanted to get a laugh. It was awkward at first: "The long outriggers for the oars, instead of the oarlocks I had been used to, the long light oars with the spoon blades and the extreme lightness of the boat were very strange. I caught a few crabs at the start, but I was careful not to work hard, so that when I missed a stroke I did not shoot back and sway the boat. The sliding seat made matters worse until I caught the swing of it."[9]

In early August 1894, Ashley met Fred Koenig at the National Association of Amateur Oarsmen's regatta in Saratoga Springs, New York, where Koenig won the national championship in single sculls. Ashley, known on the East Coast as the women's sculling champion, was in Saratoga with Edwin Newton Atherton, a champion rower who competed in the regatta. When Koenig suggested to Ashley that he could help arrange a match in St. Louis against Mosenthein for the women's sculling championship of America, she was thrilled. A. G. Bromley, captain of the CRC in St. Louis, sent Ashley a formal invitation to race Mosenthein in St. Louis or Hartford. Ashley preferred the match be held at Point of Pines in Boston Harbor, but since the CRC offered to pay Ashley's transportation and hotel expenses, she agreed to race in St. Louis.[10]

Highly regarded as New England's best women's athlete and rower, Ashley was four years old when her "poor but honest" family emigrated from Christiana (Oslo), Norway. They settled in Boston, but as a young woman she relocated to Hartford. Like Mosenthein, she was an excellent swimmer and diver with several medals in swimming and skating. After observing Ashley's rowing, Atherton introduced her to sculling, taught her its intricacies, and urged her to enter competitive races. She struggled at first, but soon became an outstanding competitor. She even gave Atherton a run for his money in headlong training competition. Under his tutelage, she trained vigorously on the Connecticut River for the upcoming race on the Mississippi.[11]

St. Louis promoters took care of Ashley's travel expenses and conducted publicity to generate interest in the upcoming match on Sunday, October 14, 1894. The city of St. Louis was ready to show pride in its young, talented athlete from the shantyboat settlement on the north wharf. Races of any kind on the Mississippi drew throngs of bystanders to the shoreline, and this particular race was special. Two women competing for a championship medal in a rigorous male-dominated sport was sure to ignite public interest.[12] Ashley and Atherton, her manager, arrived in St. Louis on October 3. Had they come ten days earlier, they might have watched as Mosenthein defeated Captain A. G. Bromley by forty yards in a quarter-mile exhibition race at Post-Dispatch Lake in Forest Park. The race was a tune-up for a quarter-mile exhibition match between Ashley and Mosenthein in Forest Park a week before the championship race on the river.[13]

On October 7, between twenty and twenty-five thousand spectators lined Forest Park for the exhibition race. Newspapers paid much attention to the nonconventional dress of the two athletes. Ashley wore a black satin blouse, knickerbockers with black silk hose, and a black cap. Mosenthein, wearing a white cap, was clad in a white blouse with royal purple sleeves and knicker-bockers and hose. In a preliminary match, the women's managers faced each other. Atherton surprised Koenig, who was gracious in defeat. Koenig chose the outside lane but ran his boat into the bank on the narrow, curvy course. Afterward he did not use that as an excuse for the loss, conceding that Atherton would have beaten him anyway. Mosenthein won the coin toss for her race and chose the outside lane. Atherton skillfully navigated the inside lane against Koenig, but Ashley struggled with it. She was nearly even with Mosenthein after the first two hundred yards, but Mosenthein forged ahead when Ashley veered into the bank and never caught up again. Although both women practiced on the course several times and pronounced it satisfactory before the exhibition, Ashley blamed her defeat on lack of familiarity with the course.[14]

The stage was now set for the championship race on the river a week later. If the spectator turnout in Forest Park was an indication, the city of St. Louis was ready to show up en masse on the riverfront. Little Oklahoma certainly stood ready to cheer and support its pride and joy. The agreed-upon race was a mile-and-a-half straightaway from the CRC's boathouse at the foot of Palm Street near the Merchants' Bridge to about two hundred feet north of the Eads Bridge. The Globe-Democrat described twenty-one-year-old Mosenthein as "the more comely" of the two athletes. "A decided brunette," she was five feet, eight inches tall and weighed 125 pounds for the match. Twenty-three-year-old Ashley, "a very pretty blonde," held a thirteen-pound weight advantage, and rowed thirty-six strokes a minute, compared to Mosenthein's thirty-four. Mosenthein's biceps measured eleven and a half inches, and her forearms were ten and a half inches around. "Rather small and lithe in build," the newspaper observed, "she is as graceful in her boat as a water sprite, and makes a pretty picture. . . . In street costume she looks exactly like hundreds of other girls one sees in the streets—a comely, shapely little lady. Not until she dons her racing suit of black knickerbockers and stockings and white and purple sleeveless blouse that her well-developed muscles assert themselves." The newspaper attributed her strength and competitiveness to her shantyboat life in Little Oklahoma: "Constant life on the river, with its exposure to all kinds of weather, has made her body as staunch as iron."[15]

An estimated crowd of fifty thousand spectators lined the riverfront on a cool afternoon to watch the race, which was scheduled to start at 4 p.m. A rather stiff breeze blew but not enough to affect the race. The river, usually deserted on Sundays, was crowded with craft of every kind and size from excursion boats, tugs, and ferries to houseboats and skiffs. Spectators swarmed all over the Eads Bridge, and Little Oklahomans turned out in force to cheer their "belle." Crews from the CRC and the Modocs, a rival St. Louis rowing club, attended the contestants to help mark the course and to be available in the event of an accident. It took longer than expected for patrol boats to clear the course to the Eads Bridge. According to the *Globe-Democrat*, Ashley appeared nervous, but Mosenthein remained calm and collected during the delay. At 4:29 p.m., the starting gun fired. Mosenthein shot ahead at once with a steady stroke while Ashley splashed a bit. At the end of a quarter-mile, Mosenthein led by a couple of lengths and was going strong. At a half-mile, Ashley trailed by fifty yards. Showing signs of distress, she lost heart, quit, and pulled her shell off the course to her Modoc attendants, who took her aboard while Mosenthein crossed the finish line at a leisurely pace. As she neared the Eads Bridge, she stopped rowing momentarily to salute jubilant spectators crowded above. Her time was 12 minutes, 13¾ seconds.[16]

At the moment Ashley abandoned the race, a deafening roar resounded on the river. In scenes reminiscent of the legendary steamboat race between the victorious *Robert E. Lee* and the *Natchez* in 1870, small cannons fired, tugs and steamers whistled, and spectators whooped and hollered to see who could make the most noise. When Mosenthein rowed ashore, throngs of supporters lurched forward to congratulate her and try to shake her hand. So eager was the crowd that a police officer drew his revolver to keep lunging fans back as she boarded a tugboat to return to the CRC's boathouse. At a public reception that evening, Captain Bromley presented her with a handsome gold medal as an emblem of the female sculling championship of America. According to a newspaper, she also received a purse of $500.[17]

It is a safe bet that Louis Seibt's floating saloon in Little Oklahoma did a brisk business that night. If the nation never heard of Mosenthein or Little Oklahoma before the race, they surely did afterward. Newspapers from all over the country covered the match. William Arste, editor of the *Waterways Journal*, wrote that "Little Oklahoma is at present just about the proudest spot in the broad state of Missouri. Its attitude distinctly declares to the world that it is neither pumpkin nor paw-paw, but a solid little corner of national fame."[18] Mosenthein's victory tapped into St. Louis's western regional pride and cultural resentments against the East Coast. "Let the effete East realise how it is bound to be downed by the vigorous West," Arste jubilantly declared. He praised the sculling champion for giving the shantyboat settlement reason to be proud. "Some roses 'by any other name might smell as sweet,'" he added, "but not so with Rosy Mosentheim—no, not by a whole Little Oklahoma jugfull."[19] Arste relished sticking a thumb in the eye of Eastern elitism. He noted that for quite some time the East boasted that it was the home of the female sculling champion of America. "But the good folks of Little Oklahoma just grinned at the pretension," Arste noted, "and, pointing to the modest little shanty-boat that now rests on the water at the foot of Angelrodt Street decorated all over with blue ribbons, said that right inside there they possessed a champion who could out scull any woman in the world, much less Miss Ashley of Connecticut."[20]

Ashley and Atherton did not take defeat well. They skipped the reception and ceremony afterward at the boathouse and caught the next train to Connecticut. Upon arriving home, they offered excuses for the defeat in an interview. Atherton, insisting that Ashley was a faster rower, charged that someone tampered with her boat at the exhibition race in Forest Park. He asked for a rematch on neutral ground. Then, offering an excuse that would have prompted several rounds of hearty toasts in Seibt's saloon, and no doubt sent peals of laughter ringing from boat to shantyboat on the waterfront, Atherton blamed Ashley's loss on river traffic interference in the championship race. In short, he blamed Little Oklahoma. "Miss Mosentheim [sic] lives in a river settlement above St. Louis, known as 'Little Oklahoma,'" the *Hartford Courant* explained, "inhabited principally by rough fishermen. They crowded the course with their small boats, and Mr. Atherton says he withdrew Miss Ashley from the race before it was finished because he saw it was impossible for her to win."[21]

Soon, Koenig sent Atherton a letter to inform him that he was in communication with John Crotty, rower and manager of the annual regatta in Austin, Texas. Koenig invited both Atherton and Ashley to compete in the 1895 international regatta that would include rowers from England and Australia. Koenig assured them that their travel and lodging expenses would be defrayed. Ashley would meet Mosenthein in a rematch for the world championship and a valuable diamond ring.[22] The rematch came a year later, but in the meantime Mosenthein and Ashley stayed active. Mosenthein stopped into the office of the *Waterways Journal* in April 1895 and told editor Arste that she and Ashley might have a rematch soon. At the time, she was practicing on the river for an exhibition match against Henry Koeneman at Silver Island under the auspices of the CRC. In August, Mosenthein took on a talented nineteen-year-old challenger, Anna Fabian, of Caronodolet, who was well known in south St. Louis as an expert rower. Mosenthein defeated her in a match on Creve Coeur Lake. The contestants did not race in a shell, but rather in a working river skiff as requested by Fabian. The race was close in the first half, but Mosenthein's endurance and experience paid off as she surged ahead in the final half.[23]

As the national women's sculling champion, Mosenthein inspired pride in St. Louis, and never more so than in Little Oklahoma. Her celebrated status was not enough, however, to spare her or some of her friends from harassment and forced evictions in June 1895. She complied and moved her new shantyboat at the foot of Angelrodt Street to Mosenthein Island, but when many squatters refused to comply with eviction notices, she could only watch as police and waterfront gangs terrorized them and tore down their shanties. The evictions came at the behest of riverfront developers and city officials who sought to clear a section of Little Oklahoma.[24]

On Austin's Lake McDonald (Lake Austin) in November 1895, the international regatta was held in which Ashley met Mosenthein in a rematch on neutral ground. The first-time inclusion of women in the competition meant added publicity and interest in the regatta. Joseph G. Miller, one of many St. Louis residents to attend, described the match as a "contest between the wild and wooly west and the effete East."[25] The *Hartford Telegram* was confident Ashley would get a fair shake in Texas, unlike St. Louis, where the newspaper insisted "she never had a chance to win from the first stroke, as the betting men booked her to lose, and the course was patrolled by boats to cut her out at the critical moment."[26] In the mile-and-a-half race for the world championship, both rivals started well and stayed even for a distance, but when Ashley began to steer a bit wildly, Mosenthein surged ahead and led the rest of the way to capture the championship ring and $150 purse. Ashley closed the distance between them somewhat, but when Mosenthein recognized the spurt, she poured it on to finish at a time of 15 minutes, 17½ seconds. Ashley did not have enough energy left at the end. The *Galveston Daily News* observed that Mosenthein "glided over the water with a stroke that was as steady and regular as the swing of a pendulum."[27]

Afterward, Ashley attributed her two losses to Mosenthein in St. Louis and the loss in Austin to the warmer climate of the South. Although the races took place in October and November, Ashley believed that she faced a climate-related handicap. She pressed for yet another rematch, confident she would win "if the race were rowed in the north or even at some halfway place."[28] She and Mosenthein remained active in sculling matches against male and female competitors in their respective regions, but they never faced each other again in a race. In 1900, Mosenthein accepted a challenge to meet Ashley in a world championship match on the East Coast, but the negotiations fell apart when she learned she would have to pay her own travel and hotel expenses. Ashley's promoters did not offer to cover travel and lodging expenses the way St. Louis promoters did for her in 1894. The two rivals made one last effort in 1903 to face each other in competition. Ashley, the subject of a feature article in the *Baltimore Sun* on May 24, 1903, boasted, "I don't believe any other American girl can row as fast as I can."[29] The article never mentioned Mosenthein, who upon learning that Ashley was billing herself in the East as the women's sculling champion of America, responded. Mosenthein challenged all competitors—but Ashley in particular—to compete in a race held in conjunction with the Southwestern Rowing Association (SRA) regatta in St. Louis at Creve Coeur Lake, July 25–26. She pitched the idea to the Western Rowing Club's John J. Schaab, president of the SRA, who, though skeptical of its practicality on short notice, agreed to present her proposal to the board and perhaps schedule the special race at a later date.[30]

In an extensive newspaper interview, Mosenthein, now thirty years old, shared her perspective on sculling. Asked if she recommended the sport for women, she replied, "Well, if it were not so expensive in the matter of getting a shell and so inconvenient in getting a place where practice could be obtained, I should say it is the best of sports. . . . It is great physical exercise. It develops the wind, and muscles, keeps the eye alert and gives plenty of fresh air and sunlight. Besides, it makes one quick to think and act and gives independence." She added, "If ever a girl who is fond of rowing ever tries a single scull and has somebody to coach her until she gets over the rough places, she will never want to get into a clumsy, ungrateful skiff if the shell is available."[31]

Mosenthein, recently inactive in competition, no longer had a usable shell but was confident she could get one, train for the match, and defeat her opponent yet again. She preferred to meet Ashley in St. Louis but emphasized that she'd gladly compete against her anywhere. Mosenthein, who kept in shape by rowing a skiff on the river, expressed a willingness to meet her opponent on short notice. When asked about Ashley's claims to the championship, she insisted that Ashley had no right to bill herself as champion. Mosenthein emphasized that she defeated her eastern rival all three times in head-to-head competition: "Just why she should be claiming the championship I do not see, unless it is because she thinks I am out of the game. She has no legitimate right to the title until she challenges me, and either beats me afterward or I refuse to row."[32] In Mosenthein's opinion, it was Ashley's lack of mental toughness and discipline, not her rowing skills, that kept her from winning the championship races. She explained: "Miss Ashley rows in splendid form in practice. She could have beaten me had she done as well in her actual races. In every event we have rowed, however, she has shown that she loses her head and her form with it. I beat her out that day [in Austin] by a length, and at the finish she was all gone. She couldn't reserve enough to keep her pace when I came on with a rush. It was the same with the race we rowed at Post-Dispatch Lake and on the Mississippi here. I outfinished her every time."[33]

When the subject of the 1895 regatta came up, Mosenthein reflected, "I was then about 23 years old and as hard as nails, being outdoors all the time." She then made a startling revelation about the Austin race. A representative from Ashley's camp approached her the night before and offered her $150 to throw the race. "Miss Ashley was crazy for the championship, as it would have been a good drawing card for her in the East," she reflected. "I would not consent to the arrangement and when the race came off put forth my best efforts."[34]

At the time of the revelation, arrangements were pending between St. Louis promoters and Ashley for a match at Creve Coeur Lake in August. The match never materialized. At a time when many newspapers hailed Ashley as the women's sculling champion of America, she bypassed St. Louis in August, perhaps embarrassed by the public disclosure about the attempted bribe. Instead, she went to San Francisco, where she tried to carve out a name for herself in rowing. She issued challenges to rowers on the West Coast, but soon dropped from the public eye.[35]

While Mosenthein was training for the regatta in Austin, her mother faced possible eviction from the island that by then bore the family's name. Until Mary settled there around 1889, the island held little or no appeal on account of flooding. Hers was the only family on the island, which, due to changes in the river channel, now included nearly 550 acres with improvements and cultivation by the family. The island now attracted powerful financial interests. Many in the area assumed the federal government owned Mosenthein Island, but on August 22, 1895, St. Louis investors Julian Laughlin, W. S. McMullen, Robert L. McLauren, and Edward W. Rannels created the Bellefontaine Improvement Company (BIC), capitalized at $100,000, to assert ownership rights based on a series of transfers of the original deed dating back nearly one hundred years.[36]

It is unclear how representatives of the company presented themselves to Mary, but later she claimed they fraudulently misrepresented that the government intended to flood the entire island. In exchange for her signing a quitclaim deed, the company paid her $2,100 for improvements she made to the island. "We did not purchase the island from Mrs. Mosenthein," Laughlin emphasized, "for she never owned it. We paid for the improvements, rather than go to the expense of a lawsuit to get possession."[37] The company announced that it had no immediate plans for the property, other than to put a fence around the island to keep out squatters. Its assertion of ownership was for speculative purposes only. "We expect the island to become valuable when the river is deepened," Laughlin explained, "and will retain it with that idea."[38] As part of the arrangement with Mosenthein, the company agreed to lease forty acres to her to cultivate and to let her use the rest of the island for grazing purposes.[39]

The BIC's designs on the island collided with the St. Louis Stamping Company and other interests tied to Frederick G. Niedringhaus. A powerful St. Louis tin manufacturer, real estate magnate, and former Republican representative in the US Congress, he and his brother, William, held vast acreage and manufacturing interests across the river in Granite City. They built a stamping and enameling plant as well as a steel works and rolling mills plant in Granite City in the 1890s. They, too, claimed ownership rights to the island, based on deed transfers dating back many years. They insisted that Mosenthein Island, west of Gabaret Island, belonged to Illinois, not Missouri. In June 1898 in the circuit court of Madison County, Illinois, Niedringhaus interests won a suit against the BIC and Mary Mosenthein, arguing that Willow Bar Island was an accretion of Gabaret Island, which was on the Illinois side of the Mississippi. Mosenthein hired attorneys to represent her interests in the suit. She pointed out that the BIC fraudulently induced her to quitclaim her squatter's interest in the island. After she testified in the case, a sympathetic columnist for the *Edwardsville Intelligencer* wrote: "Her testimony evidenced a wonderful perseverance on her part in an endeavor to provide for her family. She took the island a wilderness and transformed it into a productive field, and has remained there constantly, surmounting innumerable obstacles."[40]

The BIC lost its appeal in the Illinois Supreme Court, but while the appeal was pending, the company went after Mosenthein to recover what it paid her to quitclaim her interest in the island. In May 1899, the BIC filed a suit against her, alleging that the lease she signed in 1895 contained a stipulation that she not cut down willow trees or other timber on the island. The suit charged that in July 1897 she violated the lease agreement by clearing a number of acres and cutting down trees. Otto Mosenthein recalled years later that before the family settled on the island a basket-making company came to the island to cut down willow trees and haul them away. He emphasized that one of the reasons for the island's growth in the first place was the family's policy not to cut down young willow samplings on the edges of the island. "When high water came in the spring," he explained, "the trees would fall over the bank and form a natural willow mat which deflected the water away from our land. Before we came, the bare land was regularly washed away, taking about as much each spring as had been deposited the previous summer."[41]

The BIC sought triple damages plus costs for trees valued at $1,927. The circuit court of St. Louis ruled against Mosenthein, awarding the company a judgment of $1,927, but she filed an appeal. She insisted that since the island was in the middle of the Mississippi River, only the federal government had jurisdiction in the matter. While her appeal was pending, she and the company reached an amicable settlement in October 1899 at the same time the Illinois Supreme Court issued its ruling in favor of the Niedringhaus interests against the BIC.[42] According to both Otto and his sister Bertha, the Niedringhaus interests allowed their mother to remain on the island until around 1903 or 1904. Bertha recalled that her mother, in failing health, accepted an offer of a house from Niedringhaus in exchange for giving up her squatter's claim to the island. "But instead of buying a nice home," Bertha remembered, "Mother bought a little shack near Chain of Rocks because she did not want to be away from the river."[43]

Rose Mosenthein faded from public view in her thirties, but remained a familiar face on the waterfront. She was a pioneer in American women's rowing at a time when rowing clubs were all-male organizations. In the late nineteenth century, elite women's colleges in the East began to offer rowing but generally not as a competitive sport. Popular attitudes toward women at the time scorned the notion that they were cut out for physically demanding competition. To those in aquatic sports, Mosenthein was a source of inspiration who made herself available on the St. Louis riverfront for coaching advice on rowing, swimming, and diving. She never moved farther than a few blocks from Little Oklahoma, where her brother Gus remained for the rest of his life. At age thirty-four on December 24, 1907, she married Jerry Buckley, a St. Louis police officer who later worked at the Mallinckrodt Chemical Works. Only five years later, she contracted tuberculosis and suffered for months before moving in with her sister Bertha, who cared for her in her final days. A few weeks shy of her fortieth birthday, Rose died in the middle of the night on Christmas 1913. In a brief obituary, the *Post-Dispatch* reminded readers that she once was the women's sculling champion of America. Much like the history of Little Oklahoma, however, her role in sports history was soon buried and forgotten.[44]

10

The Ruthless Advance of Civilization

WATERFRONT EVICTIONS

This is my home and I intend to defend it. . . . If anyone attempts to pull
my houseboat off without due process of law, I'll kill the one who attempts
it. . . . I'm an American woman and have just as much right to government
land as any rich company with millions of dollars to back it.

—NORA GAMACHE, *St. Louis Post Dispatch*, 1903

Well, as long as I have a shotgun and a 38-caliber revolver around you
can say for me that the Warrens will be living right here on Sandy Hook,
Sheriff or no Sheriff. . . . Land along the river where there is no improved
levee is mine if I take it. . . . The river is our native country.
We live on the river. We are not going to leave it.

—ANNIE WARREN, *St. Louis Post-Dispatch*, 1905

Shantyboat settlements bedeviled local authorities, waterfront developers, and moral reformers of all stripes. To rid the riverfront of squatters posed an intractable, costly problem. As long as poverty, racism, and shameful conditions in St. Louis's slums remained, the waterfront continued to attract squatters, who employed a variety of tactics to slow, postpone, or defeat efforts to eject them. In many cases, they took the path of least resistance. If their boats were seaworthy, they relocated to a new riverfront spot but sometimes returned later. In other cases, they demanded financial compensation. Some who purchased a strip of waterfront property without a deed from someone who fraudulently claimed to own it insisted to no avail that they owned their spot on the river. Squatters sometimes chipped in a dollar apiece to hire an attorney to defend their rights and resist evictions, but the specter of violence loomed over the service and enforcement of eviction notices by authorities, who often timed evictions to take place in late fall/early winter after many residents floated south for the winter. The strategy benefitted city officials, but it meant that the evicted were homeless with a freezing cold winter staring them in the face.

Preparations for the 1904 World's Fair laid bare the class implications of the city's wharf policies toward houseboats. When reports reached St. Louis in January 1903 that members of the Pastime Club of Winona were building a large houseboat to take them to the fair, St. Louis officials bent over backward to accommodate them. According to reports, clubs in St. Paul and towns on the Upper Mississippi also planned to arrive in large houseboats for the fair. The St. Louis Harbor and Wharf Department gave assurances that harbor space would be provided for mooring the houseboats without fear of evictions. "As a general rule, the Harbor and Wharf Department discourages squatting of houseboats along the river front," noted Edward A. Hoberg, chief clerk of the department. "If the request came, however, it would be an easy matter to assign a certain space in an accessible portion of the city for the houseboats of visitors to the World's Fair. They would not have to pay wharfage fees if they occupied this allotted territory, and would be in no danger of being disturbed."[1]

Although the US Census Bureau announced in 1890 that the frontier was closed, frontier influences and customs endured. Shantyboat communities clung to a set of frontier principles and folk law when it came to squatters' rights. In the history of the frontier, the recognition of squatters' rights played an important role in the development of backcountry settlements. Land ownership and economic independence were at the heart of Jeffersonian republicanism in the early republic. Squatters who laid claim to unused land and made improvements on it expected rights of ownership. Burman described shantyboaters as "America's most rugged individualists,"[2] but his highly misleading characterization ignored cooperative traditions among them. Patterns of collective action to defend squatters' rights guided them as they laid claim to property that they occupied and improved for many years. In battles against land speculators, absentee landlords, and critics who viewed them as shiftless and lawless, squatters developed their own communities with a system of folk laws and governance enforced by the threat of collective action. State legislatures bowed to frontier realities by accommodating squatters and acknowledging their role in the development of frontier settlements. Although the enactment of statutes recognized the principles of squatters' rights, such laws and the courts that interpreted them also restricted the use of adverse possession against legal holders of property.[3]

Shantyboat residents identified with the American Revolution and republican ideals. Nearly every family displayed an American flag in their boat. Claims by Burman and others that shantyboaters were foes of government gave a false impression. Until Prohibition, river gypsies expressed abiding faith in the national government but regarded local sheriffs and officials with animosity and disdain. At times, squatters refused to recognize the authority of local sheriffs who came with eviction papers in hand. As far as squatters were concerned, sheriffs were in the hip pocket of local elites and corporations determined to rid the waterfront of shantyboats for their own financial gain. In an industrial age dominated by corporations and robber barons, the adaptation of squatters' rights to an urban waterfront presented a thorny problem. How to balance the rights of private and municipal ownership with squatters' rights posed a dilemma to city authorities exasperated by repeated efforts to break up shantyboat colonies. So exasperated, in fact, that in June 1895 St. Louis police resorted to extralegal, terroristic measures to remove a large cluster of squatters from a section of Little Oklahoma. Police served eviction notices to about two hundred squatters near the foot of Mallinckrodt Street. The property consisted of three strips owned by chemical manufacturer and pharmaceutical supplier Edward Mallinckrodt, ex-governor David Francis, and lumber businessman August Wilhelm Schulenburg. Through the Maffitt and Franciscus Real Estate Company, they planned a waterfront development project with city officials that spelled trouble for levee dwellers. The interlocked interests hired a company to pump sand and water from the river to fill a squatter-occupied hollow. The goal was to convert the low ground between the Chicago, Burlington & Quincy railroad tracks and the Merchants' Terminal tracks into a new industrial site.[4]

When a reporter visited Little Oklahoma on the eviction deadline of June 12, the settlement of houseboats, tents, and crude wooden shanties was a beehive of activity. The area to be cleared was occupied by two hundred residents in forty or fifty houseboats. Sounds of saws and hammers filled the air as residents repaired their boats or built new hulls for them while children played in the sand and weeds. Referring to Little Oklahoma as "that peculiar community of human flotsam and jetsam," the reporter wrote, "As usual with these happy-go-lucky and ne'er-do-wells of nomadic life they did not make haste at preparations to leave until the last." He and two police officers walked down the gangplank to the floating saloon and grocery store operated by Louis Seibt. In the saloon was Anna Massey, "a big freckle-faced Irish girl, 30 years old . . . Fairly good looking . . . [and] something of a coquette with the men of the community." Rose Mosenthein, the highly celebrated women's sculling champion, was also there. Wearing a blue gingham dress and sailor hat, she cracked jokes, laughed, and mingled with others. She no longer lived in the settlement but owned a new houseboat that she kept there, where her brother and one of her sisters lived. Rose was in Little Oklahoma on eviction day to supervise her houseboat's removal upriver to Mosenthein Island. Also in the saloon was Mattie Eden, who clutched a basket of potatoes and half-rotted fruit she picked out of a garbage barrel at the dumping grounds. When the reporter reminded her that large pipes would soon flood the lowland west of the tracks with water and sand from the river, she was unimpressed. "Nursing a glorious jag in her scarred anatomy," she "swore by the gods" that she would not leave her boiler iron shanty "until the water filled it, and then she would crawl out on a ladder and paddle away in a canoe."[5]

Those with seaworthy houseboats moved to a nearby location on the wharf, but for Eden and the poorest who resisted eviction, things were about to turn ugly. Three days later, the police unleashed a waterfront gang of young hoodlums as shock troops against Eden and others who did not comply with the notice. Most if not all who occupied the forty remaining shanties were women. The hoodlums taunted and terrorized the evictees and tore down their homes. A stunned eyewitness reporter described the scene:

> Friday afternoon the Levee arabs swooped down upon the defenseless people of the little hamlet and began their work of destruction. Matilda Eaton [sic], a poor drunken old woman, known as one-eyed Matt, was found in her shanty and evicted.
>
> She refused to go and was dragged out by the heels. One of the crowd hurled a bag of flour at her, which broke and covered her clothing from head to foot. The woman screamed murder, but no one came to her assistance. After dragging her around by the feet until it ceased to be sport, her tormentors began the work of tearing down her shack.

As soon as the poor soul was released she seized a full-grown cur dog, the only thing she ever really loved, and folding it in her arms, started out in the world again to seek a home and fortune wherever Providence might direct her. The crowd jeered and yelled, but she shambled on with her canine burden until she was lost to view in the maze of picturesque shanties and floating house-boats that line the river's edge. Then the young hoodlums began on her curious little house, and within half an hour its remnants were scattered over the wharf.

Other women who refused to go because they had no place else on earth to go were driven out by the same ruthless band. . . . Fifteen shanties were leveled during the day and most of the owners left without a place to lay their heads.[6]

After the gang did the police's dirty work, about twenty-five shanties remained. The police promised to return the next night to arrest anyone still there. An anonymous letter to the editor dated June 14 appeared in the *Post-Dispatch*, criticizing the way newspapers and city officials treated the squatters. "How was it," the letter complained, "that the press of the city chose to make such fun of the people who are independent enough to live in houseboats on the river, instead of paying rents to landlords?" The letter added, "Our Single Tax friends vow we cannot live without land, but in my opinion the reason most of us pay rent all the time is because we are not plucky and independent enough to get or build us a houseboat and live at anchor on the river. There's lots of room there." In solidarity with the shantyboat dwellers, the author of the letter, signed VOX, cheered: "Hurrah for Little Oklahoma!"[7]

Later that summer, the Merchants' Bridge Terminal Railway Company pursued five evictions near the Dock Street section. Four of the settlers agreed to move, but Catherine White, an elderly Black woman in Little Oklahoma for fifteen years, balked when a constable appeared with a notice. She reminded him that she lived there long before there was a Merchants' Bridge Terminal Railway Company or a community known as Little Oklahoma. "The Lord has told me that this house and lot is mine, and I am going to stay right here till I die," she warned. "And if you don't want to be struck dead by lightning or something or other, you had better go on away and leave me alone."[8] In late September, the *Post-Dispatch* reported on the status of the hollow, now cleared of squatters.

At the time that the pumping of sand and water to fill the hollow began, the ground level near the tracks was about seven feet lower. As a result of the project, the level was nearly even with the tracks, but in the middle of the hollow the ground was ten feet lower than the ground along the shore. The newspaper expressed skepticism that the project, which had been delayed, would succeed.[9]

Little Oklahoma thrived despite evictions, but in early 1898 Justin E. Joy, a real estate and lumber businessman (Joy Brothers and Company) who in 1891 leased city wharf space at the foot of Dock Street, took aggressive action against squatters, most of whom were Black, and their church and minister. Some had lived in the Dock Street Addition for more than twelve years in dilapidated houseboats. At one time, they paid Joy small sums of rent, but when the depression of 1893 struck, they stopped. In early February 1898, Joy notified inhabitants to move within three days, claiming they impeded wharf access to his lumberyard. They asked for compensation, but when he offered none, they vowed to resist. Then began a campaign of harassment by Joy and city officials. For weeks, wagonloads of city trash were dumped up against thirty-five shantyboats and Little Oklahoma's Mt. Pleasant Baptist Church. Joy also filed an unlawful detainer suit against Rev. Paul Kates, Black pastor of the congregation of about twenty-five members, to keep him from conducting services in the church. Each day the garbage and filth piled higher and higher, so high that it obscured view of the church, shantyboats, and "miserable huts." On March 5, a reporter noted that "a few more loads of dirt will suffice to bury them."[10]

Residents recognized Seibt as the "King" of Little Oklahoma, but it was Kates who stepped forward as their protector in the conflict with Joy. Kates was a conscientious spiritual leader and longtime preacher who lived with his wife and children in a shantyboat in the settlement. His daughter worked as a stemmer in a local tobacco factory. For many, Kates also acted as a counselor and arbiter of business and personal disputes. He led the resistance against Joy's harassment campaign. Henry R. Watson, a white attorney employed as "citizen's counsel," filed a suit on behalf of the church and eighteen plaintiffs, nearly a third of whom were white, to challenge Joy's assertion of ownership of the property. Among the plaintiffs was John Ramsey, whom Seibt had kicked off his strip of land a couple of months earlier in a rent dispute. Watson argued that the property in dispute with Joy was below street level, that it was a river sinkhole caused by changes in the river channel, and therefore did not belong to Joy, but to the squatters. Residents of the Dock Street Addition triumphed a month later when Joy dropped his suit. He did not possess undisputed legal rights to the strip because the city had not established clear title to the property at the time he leased it. A year and a half later, a judge ruled that Joy owed the city of St. Louis $2,700 for unpaid rent on the Dock Street lease.[11]

In 1899, the harbor and wharf commissioner pushed a renewed war against shantyboat settlements on the south wharf. On September 2, the city marshal served eviction notices from Mayor Henry Ziegenhein's office to angry boat dwellers from Marine Avenue to Cahokia Street on the north end of Chickentown. The mayor invoked an ordinance that authorized removal of persons who encroach upon streets and alleys. In the name of public improvements, he gave residents thirty days to move or face eviction. A newspaper expressed sympathy toward the residents, characterizing them as victims of "the ruthless advance of civilization." The homogenous settlement was more than fifteen years old, and many of its children were born and raised there. Nearby quarries employed many of its men. The settlement contained about three hundred residents who enjoyed its secluded location and freedom from the noisy street sounds of the city. "But now after 15 years of this freedom from the cares and responsibilities of civilization," observed the *Post-Dispatch*, "the city extends its ruthless hand to sweep them from their happy homes."[12]

Squatters regarded the land as their own, based on continuous possession. According to a resident, most would comply with the eviction notices and leave peacefully on their own, but any attempted eviction by a city officer would require an armed guard. The city marshal expressed willingness to be flexible with residents, but they had neither a place to go nor enough money to pay for the expense of removal. Women were especially incensed by the sudden, aggressive intrusion into their homes. "The women will be out with pokers when the officer comes," warned a resident. "They are very angry and can't be made to see that they have no legal right to live here. They have been here many years and have come to regard the land as their own, and any attempt to evict them will provoke violence from some."[13]

A delegation of Chickentown residents paid a visit to Mayor Ziegenhein's office and prevailed upon him to halt the evictions, but a year later he sent out a new round of notices to residents in the Gasconade neighborhood. He did so at the behest of a delegation representing the wealthy Henry Kayser estate. Trustees Daniel Catlin, George B. Leighton, and Julius Pitzman persuaded the mayor to revoke the permit he had previously granted the squatters. The delegation argued that squatters impeded proposed improvements on nearby properties owned by the Kayser estate. "About a year ago," Ziegenhein noted, "I ordered the city marshal to make those people move, but they came to my office in a body and presented a pitiful plea to be allowed to remain until next spring or summer. So I issued a permit to them, but at the time I told them that they ought to be looking for homes elsewhere, as they were in the way of the property owners there, and if another complaint was made about them I should be compelled to make them move. Some of them took my advice and moved away as soon as the cold weather was over, but others have continued to live there."[14]

Trustees of the Kayser estate, along with Augustus Busch, of the Anheuser-Busch Brewery Association, William J. Lemp, of the Lemp Brewery, and Prentiss Batchelor petitioned the Board of Public Improvements for a re-designated harbor line beyond which structures would not be allowed to protrude in south St. Louis. The proposed harbor line in 1901 threatened residents of Squatters' Town and Chickentown, where the petitioners had vast real estate and other business interests in the wharf area. The Board of Public Improvements referred the petition to the Harbor and Wharf Committee for further consideration.[15] Expansion plans by the Anheuser-Busch Brewery brought conflict with residents at the foot of Utah Street in Squatters' Town in July 1903. Busch sought to fill in the land on a piece of property near the wharf in order to construct a new building. He filled part of the land in question, but hit a snag with Iron Mountain Railroad engineer Louis C. Gamache and his wife, Nora, who lived between the levee and the Iron Mountain tracks in a houseboat with their two children. They refused to vacate until Busch showed clear title to the property on which their houseboat sat. The Gamaches examined deed records but found no evidence to support Busch's claim of ownership. They insisted that the land was a riparian accretion and therefore belonged to the federal government, not to Busch. "It must be shown to me in the courts that this is not government land, as I believe it is," Nora insisted.[16]

Busch visited the "tidy four-room houseboat" but got nowhere with the Gamaches. He then took up the matter with Hiram Phillips, president of the Board of Public Improvements, which initiated eviction procedures. Nora, skilled in the use of firearms, kept guns loaded at all times. When the city marshal arrived to serve the eviction notice, she barricaded herself inside the houseboat with guns ready. The marshal slid the papers under her door and left.[17] Louis, who was quite ill, turned matters over to Nora in the conflict. Brandishing a revolver and a shotgun, she forced brewery employees to stop their work nearby. When a brewery official asked what she would do if someone came to drag her houseboat into the river, she did not hesitate: "I will use a revolver or an ax."[18] When Nora had to go into the city on business, she left Robert E. Fox, a houseboat neighbor in Squatters' Town, in charge of guarding her home. Fox, who had lost an arm in the Civil War, took his responsibility seriously. "No one will move the boat while I'm in charge," he warned. "If need be, I have weapons in reach . . . when she leaves me in charge I am not going to let anybody do anything to this house. I haven't been in the regulars for nothing, either."[19]

The Gamaches indicated a willingness to move if brewery officials compensated them in the amount of $150. The brewery refused, but according to Nora, Busch gave other squatters $100 to vacate. Rumors reached the Gamaches that city marshal James Scullin intended to drag their houseboat into the river. "This is my home and I intend to defend it," Nora told a reporter. "All that it contains is the toil of years. If anyone attempts to pull my houseboat off without due process of law, I'll kill the one who attempts it."[20] The matter was put into the hands of the street department, where adjudication by the city was expected. According to Nora, when she visited the street commissioner, he did not order her to move. The Gamaches were angry that a corporation could throw its weight around to evict them whenever it saw fit. They were especially upset that Busch waited until the water was low to force them from their home. As a result, to move their houseboat would mean considerable expense. "I'm an American woman and have just as much right to government land as any rich company with millions of dollars to back it. My husband is a sick man and for the protection of myself and the children, I had no other course but to stand up for my rights. . . . We ask favors of no one. It is a hard struggle, and often I work from 5 in the morning until 10 at night, just to earn enough to keep us from being on the city."[21]

The city's relentless battle against houseboat squatters near Carondolet intensified in 1903 as a result of a project to convert Kingshighway into the "Champs Elysee" of St. Louis. The blueprints included a call for expansion of

Grand Avenue from Carondolet Park to Caldwell Street to the bluffs overlooking the Mississippi. The plan spelled trouble for approximately thirty houseboats and shanties at the foot of Caldwell Street, south of Chickentown.[22] The city served eviction notices on the squatters, some of whom hinted at violence if deputies arrived to evict them. Many were well aware of what had happened recently to a number of waterfront squatters to the north who ignored eviction notices. A harbor boat attached a chain to their shantyboats and dragged them into the river at the behest of police. Tan Marshall, a sixty-year-old squatter, was the Caldwell Street colony's chosen spokesman. According to him, a city authority warned that if they did not move by the fifteenth of October, a harbor boat would drag their homes into the river. A few residents favored hiring an attorney, but most began to scour the shoreline for a new place to live. Marshall hinted that a few might balk at moving, especially women, who were often the fiercest to defend their homes against evictions. Marshall warned, "Some of our women, and men, too, can shoot straight, and we may not move."[23]

Next, the city trained its sights on Chickentown itself. An article, "Chickentown Must Give Way to the March of Municipal Progress," in the *St. Louis Republic* on July 28, 1904, reported that the city was forcing twenty-four shantyboats at the foot of Marine Avenue to move. Authorities ordered the evictions because of plans to build a new street to run along the riverbank north of the intersection of Marine Avenue and the Iron Mountain Railroad tracks. All residents except Mrs. George Eckard agreed to relocate. It took six deputies to evict the eighty-year-old woman who had lived in Chickentown for seventeen years. She claimed that she and her husband, a fisherman, settled there in 1887 and paid a small sum of money for the property on which their houseboat rested. She insisted to no avail that she had a right to live there. Mayor Rolla Wells issued the first eviction notice via Marshal Scullin in June. The squatters' agreement to relocate came only after a confrontation when deputies showed up to enforce the evictions. Louis Christmann, "mayor" of Chickentown, was angry when he returned home to find deputies there to evict residents. For a while it appeared there might be a violent confrontation, but in the end the evicted resigned themselves to their fate and averted trouble. They agreed to move within thirty days. In October the city continued its war on Chickentown, but when officers tried to serve eviction notices at the foot of Osage Street, a confrontation occurred. Squatters who had occupied the area for twenty-five years drove away two deputy marshals on November 16, but Scullin returned with the same two marshals and a police detachment the next morning to tear down the shanties of those who refused to comply with the notices. Herman Meyers, a quarry worker, was among the squatters who insisted that years ago they bought the strip of land on which their homes sat. Meyers said he paid $150 to a man named Rapp, now deceased, but he could not produce a deed of sale.[24]

Once the city surveyor gave the command to tear down the houseboats and shanties, the families removed their clothing, bedding, and furniture. They packed their possessions up to the railroad embankment, where they piled their household effects. Scullin took pity on a few of the more helpless families and, in exchange for a promise to vacate, gave them an additional day to move. Nine heartbroken families sat in despair with their belongings on the terrace of the railroad and watched as the police detachment began their work of destruction in the name of public improvements. A larger crew of forced labor supplied by the nearby Workhouse joined police the next day to finish tearing down twenty-five shanties and many sheds. A *Post-Dispatch* reporter on the scene who described the entire affair as a "pitiable spectacle" wrote: "Some of the families have lived there a long time, and many of the children had been born there. To these, it was hard to leave, and when the destruction of the little houses began it was nothing short of heart-rending."[25] Those who wrote Chickentown's obituary were a bit hasty. Nearly nine months later, Christmann still served as mayor of the settlement at the foot of Osage Street. The community simply resettled and reconstituted itself among other houseboat squatters a couple of streets to the south. The *Post-Dispatch* observed that Christmann's mayoral realm consisted of "shantyboat people who come and go like the wind that rocks their boats on the Mississippi."[26]

Despite attempts to get rid of squatters, the colony persisted. In 1911, however, a family of millionaires went after a Swedish immigrant family of shantyboaters on the wharf. Daniel Catlin, Theron Ephron Catlin, E. C. Lackland, and Emily Kayser, trustees of the Kayser estate, filed a suit to remove them from a lot whose annual rental value was an estimated $5, the equivalent of approximately $150 in today's currency. The lot was a rather desolate sandbar of "made land" near the foot of Gasconade Street. Peter Johnson, a seventy-year-old night watchman at the US Army Corps of Engineers facility, occupied the sandbar for more than three years in the face of opposition from powerful claimants. His widowed daughter, Inkey Dagen, and granddaughter lived in the houseboat with him. The suit also named Johnson's son, a "riverman" who made his home on the sandbar. Chickentown residents, many of whom were fishermen or boat owners engaged in skiff rentals, feared that the suit against the Johnsons represented the opening salvo in a renewed campaign to get rid of them. They complained that when they tried to beautify new "made lands" that appeared around their shantyboats, nearby property holders objected. The property owners feared that cultivation of gardens on the land would lead to soil erosion and increase the likelihood that floods would threaten their hold-ings. Two years after the suit, Dagen still lived in the houseboat at the foot of Gasconade Street.[27]

As the Chickentown cases indicate, St. Louis officials were repeatedly sty-mied in their efforts to evict squatters. For nearly a year in 1906–1907, plans to extend Angelrodt Street from the Burlington railroad tracks to the wharf hit a snag when two squatters in Little Oklahoma refused to move their houseboats from a mud hole on which they sat. The boats were bounded by a lumberyard on the north and a saw mill on the south. Promising a fight, Millard Vail and J. P. Forsman invoked squatters' rights and insisted that their adjoining houseboats were not on city property. They had lived there for four years. On one occasion, Forsman was arrested and fined, but authorities released him from jail without payment of a fine after he threatened to file a damages lawsuit against the city. A deputy in the city marshal's office scoffed at the notion that the squatters would be hard to dislodge. "It will be easier to evict them than it would persons farther away from the river," he remarked to a reporter, "because we only have [to] give those houseboats a swift push and, presto, Angelrodt street is clear."[28] Eviction deadlines came and went, but Vail and Forsman refused to vacate the property. At first, deputies threatened to shove their homes into the river, but after Street Department engineers surveyed the area, they discovered that half of Forsman's houseboat was on property that did not belong to the city. At the time, Vail's boat was uninhabitable due to past flood damages, so he moved into Forsman's houseboat with him. City attorneys urged caution to avoid litigation, but exasperated engineers instructed the city marshal's deputies to arrest Fors-man if he resisted, and to saw his houseboat in half if necessary and remove the half on city property if he still refused to move.[29]

The most sensational conflict with squatters occurred in 1905 on the Illinois side of the river. According to adverse possession laws in Illinois, a squatter who occupied unused, neglected property for twenty continuous years and made improvements on it was entitled to claim ownership. In the East St. Louis shantyboat settlement of Sandy Hook, the struggle by squatters to hang onto their longtime community pitted them against city officials and an unpopular monopolistic ferry company and its parent railroad corporation. The Wiggins Ferry Company, which was under the thumb of the Terminal Railroad Association that formed in 1889 with encouragement from railroad tycoon Jay Gould, held vast interests in St. Louis and East St. Louis. With warehouses, rail yards, elevators, and other holdings, the ferry company enjoyed monopolistic control over other avenues of transit across the river as well as ferrying services. The company asserted riparian rights to the levee in East St. Louis as the city's waterfront moved west because of "made land," or accretions from changes in the Mississippi River channel. In effect, the company claimed ownership of virtually the entire riverfront. When the Chicago, Rock Island & Pacific Railway Company bought Wiggins Ferry in 1902, the Terminal Railroad Association took complete control over the ferry company and the East St. Louis levee.[30]

The war against squatters on the Illinois shore brewed for more than a decade. In 1893, operators of the grain elevator in East St. Louis complained about a small cluster of houseboat squatters on the sandbar south of the Eads Bridge. According to the complaints, squatters stole sacks of wheat and other grains from freight cars that were left loaded overnight near the elevator. Grain elevator officials, insisting that freight cars could not be guarded adequately overnight, asked authorities to remove squatters from the area.[31] The war deepened when the Illinois legislature passed a shantyboat law, effective July 1, 1897. The statute required shantyboat owners to purchase a yearly license from the county clerk. The license, which cost $5 and required payment of the county clerk's fee of $1, imposed a fine of not less than $25 or more than $100, or jail time of between five and twenty-five days for nonpayment. The law required that the license be displayed on the houseboats. The new statute, which exempted ferry boats and steamers, went a step further, requiring applicants to offer proof of good character and intentions to the county clerk. The *Alton Evening Telegraph* cheered the new law: "If the proper enforcement of the law is secured it will do away entirely with the shanty boat evil, which has for a long time been the dwelling place of ignorant and criminal persons, who are anything but desirable citizens, as it is safe to say that not one in ten of such people could raise the $6 to secure the license."[32]

Owners of approximately twenty houseboats in East St. Louis expressed resentment at the new law's application to them. According to them, their houseboats had not been on the water in years except during times when they floated atop floodwaters. They insisted that they paid ground rent to the Wiggins Ferry Company and did not fall within the law's parameters. They expressed a willingness to spend whatever it took in legal costs to fight the statute. If they lost, they said, they would move rather than pay the fee. It was a matter of principle to them.[33] The Wiggins Ferry Company's strategy was to persuade squatters to pay ground rent. Payment of rent indicated tacit recognition of the company's ownership of riverfront property. For those who refused, a company tugboat from time to time dragged their houseboats into the river in order to prevent them from establishing a legal squatter's claim. Such a claim required continuous possession of property for twenty years. Many residents lived there for a dozen years or more. Whenever the company removed their houseboats without legal authorization, squatters took their cases to a justice of the peace and often recovered damages.[34]

The high-handed manner in which the company treated squatters grew out of its monopolistic control over the riverfront. The mayor and East St. Louis city council were in the hip pocket of the company, which was determined to bar public access to the river. Over a number of years, city officials acquiesced as the ferry company asserted dictatorial rights over the riverfront. After the Terminal Railroad Association assumed complete control over Wiggins in 1902, the monopoly tightened its grip on the riverfront even more. Railroads that made up its parent company used Wiggins to prevent competition from steamboats, which avoided East St. Louis because of discriminatory financial charges assessed by Wiggins and those who did its bidding. Railroad tracks paralleled the river, but there was little paved wharf to accommodate steamboat landings. The dictatorship by Wiggins and the Terminal Railroad Association was so absolute that when no delegate from East St. Louis answered the roll call to provide a report on riverfront conditions at the 1911 convention of the Upper Mississippi River Improvement Association in Alton, a convention attendee quipped that East St. Louis was not on the river but was bounded by the Terminal Railroad Association, Wiggins Ferry Company, and Cahokia Creek.

In effect, East St. Louis was a river city without public access to its own river-front. Spearheaded by the city's Commercial Club and a growing anti-Wiggins city council, however, a state investigative committee in 1911 called attention to the longstanding monopoly of the ferry company and its parent railroad association. The committee urged "the most aggressive action in order to preserve to the people of this growing municipality, their right of access to the river front. It is wholly beyond reason that any private individual, company, corporation or association should have the right to wholly control the river front of this city."[35]

In late 1903, the Wiggins Ferry Company decided that residents of Sandy Hook were unwelcome on its riverfront. Stuyvesant Fish, president of the Illinois Central Railroad, filed suits of forcible detainer against Owen J. Curley, Eugene Neighbors, Robert Thompson, William Heinz, John O'Neill, Tom Howell, and Louisa Schwartz. The targeted residents were to move by December 5, but Wiggins extended the eviction deadline for Howell and Schwartz due to their extenuating personal considerations.[36] A few weeks later, the *Post-Dispatch's* Sunday magazine featured a story, "The Passing of Sandy Hook." Describing the "gypsy municipality on keels" as "perhaps the most picturesque community in the Mississippi valley," the article called attention to the Wiggins Ferry Company's campaign to drive squatters from the East St. Louis riverfront. The squatters "did what they could, in their own languid, malarial way to thwart" the evictions, but most had cleared out at the time of the article. The newspaper article pointed to the colony's inevitable fate: "Relentless civilization has wrought its will with the Sandy Hookers. They are no more—and Sandy Hook will soon be but a vacant stretch of bay-indented river front between the East St. Louis grain elevator and the Pittsburg 'dump.'"[37]

The conflict was far from over. Most residents were on their annual river migration south for the winter. The ferry company's campaign to execute the evictions as swiftly as possible while the colony was missing a core of its long-term residents soon hit a bump in the road. Attempts to evict squatters Jane Campbell and Edward Stites ended up in court when they resisted and claimed homestead rights. Stites operated a blacksmith shop on his land and had lived in his houseboat at the corner of Trendley Avenue and Main Street since 1881. For more than twenty years he watched East St. Louis grow in his direction to the west due to land accretions that reshaped the riverfront. Claiming adverse possession, Stites and Campbell fought the attempted evictions in the circuit court in Belleville. Just before the case was to go to the jury in April 1904, they struck a deal with the Illinois Central Railroad. The company compensated them an unspecified amount of money in exchange for agreeing to vacate the disputed property.[38]

The main confrontation between squatters and the subsidiary of the Terminal Railroad Association did not take place until the summer of 1905. On June 9, Judge John J. Driscoll, justice of the peace in East St. Louis, at the behest of the Wiggins Ferry Company, issued a five-day eviction notice to about one hundred houseboats on a ten-mile stretch of shoreline between Brooklyn and Cahokia. The notice targeted "The Sand Bar" and a number of settlements, but the largest, most developed was that of Sandy Hook, which contained nearly fifty houseboats on four hundred acres. The settlement was separated from shore by a marshy slough most of the year. During high water, the only way to access it was by boat. After squatters refused to leave, Judge Driscoll on the 16th issued another order to vacate within five days. The squatters dug in for the upcoming conflict, angry in particular that the eviction orders came after they planted their gardens. Most of them viewed the land as their own, having lived there for such a long time. They raised children and chickens and built sheds, workshops, and outbuildings on the island. They settled their own disputes, either by arbitration or by fists, and asked for nothing in terms of law enforcement protection. The Wiggins Ferry Company contacted St. Clair County Sheriff George W. Thompson, urging him to evict the squatters at once. The company promised to help by providing a steamer and crew to drag the squatters' homes into the river. At first, Sheriff Thompson refused unless the company put up an indemnity bond to protect him from squatters' lawsuits. The company then searched for a constable to serve new eviction notices, promising to furnish Thompson with the requested indemnity bond if force became necessary to remove the squatters.[39]

Sandy Hook squatters chose George Warren as their leader in the confrontation with the ferry company and the sheriff's office. A longtime resident with his wife, Annie, and six children, Warren expressed anger at the company's high-handed muscle flexing: "I always considered an island a body of land surrounded by water and that islands were Government property, but the Wiggins Ferry Co. seems to think that an island is a body of land covered by fordable water and that they are entitled to the land as far out in the river as they are able to ford. The Government has not sold the river to the Ferry Company, and we own this place." Warren made clear he respected federal authority but not local sheriffs when it came to evictions from their homes. "I do not recognize a Sheriff and will not allow him to touch this property," he warned. "If a United States Marshal comes with a warrant, we will take off our hats to him, and when a United States Judge says we must move, we will obey his order, but allow a common, ordinary Sheriff to take our homes—never." Annie shared her husband's views. She, too, expressed contempt for the sheriff's authority. "Land along the river where there is no improved levee is mine if I take it," she insisted. "The river is our native country. We live on the river. We are not going to leave it." She scoffed at the notion that a sheriff might evict their family. "As long as I have a shotgun and a 38-caliber revolver around," she warned, "you can say for me that the Warrens will be living right here on Sandy Hook, Sheriff or no Sheriff. When I heard he was coming I got my revolver and shotgun and kept watch, and it's a good thing for him he did not come, for we had worked too hard to build our house and garden and make our home pleasant to be just put out on the river to swim back and strike shore somewhere else."[40]

Charles Beiser, a longtime resident fisherman who with his wife and children lived next to the Warrens, also resented the way Wiggins trampled on the lives of Sandy Hook residents. His "fish flag," which he ran up a forty-foot pole outside his houseboat when he had fish for sale, was one of the most popular on the river. When a reporter asked Beiser how he felt about the upcoming evictions, he replied:

When I dropped in here 12 years ago, this was a sandbar with not a green spot on it. During the high water of several years I floated above my property when the river was raging, but I held possession of my land and came down all right when the river fell and my possession has never been disputed until now. I was commissioned as a deputy sheriff for Sandy Hook for a couple of years and have seen the island settled and the cottonwood trees grow from the seed. After holding possession so long I am not going to give up now, and if that Sheriff wants a battle we will be ready when he comes and he will get the warmest time he ever had.[41]

Perhaps the most prosperous resident was James E. Neely, a boat builder and painter who lived with his family in a new houseboat set upon stilts near the Warrens on "the most modernly equipped farm on Sandy Hook."[42] On a high bank he built a workshop where he plied his carpentry trade, as well as a freshly painted two-room bathhouse on a piling foundation near the water. He also erected chicken sheds and dug a well. With the most to lose, he denounced efforts to evict residents: "I have lived here for ten years, and my family have lived in the houseboat when it floated 12 feet above the island and dropped back after the water had gone down, and I still have possession, and I own this place as much as anyone on earth, and I will still be here after the Sheriff has gone."[43]

On July 28, 1905, Chief Deputy Sheriff Charles Cashell set out for Sandy Hook from East St. Louis City Hall with six deputies, two private guards of the Wiggins Ferry Company, and W. L. Ward, a US marshal. "As the only entrance to the Hook is by boat through a shallow slough, or else by wading through muddy ditches and swamps," observed a reporter, "it appears to an onlooker as if it will not be a 'bed of roses' for the official or officials who attempt to displace these residents of this almost inaccessible territory."[44] With eviction notices that gave squatters until Tuesday to vacate, officers knocked first on the door of William Franklin, a billing clerk for the Chicago & Peoria Railroad Company. Franklin and his wife insisted they would not move but later agreed to cooperate if someone would tow their houseboat to a new location. "If you don't move," retorted Cashell, "we'll pull your houseboat out into the river and sink it."[45]

Standing inside the screen door of his houseboat with a shotgun, J. E. Neely confronted Cashell and the deputies. "The first man who attempts to get on this houseboat will be killed," he threatened. Cashell assured Neely he did not want to enter the boat, but made clear he had eviction papers to serve. The deputy sheriff warned that if Neely did not leave by Tuesday, he and his deputies would use force, if necessary. Neely stepped out onto his porch and accepted the eviction papers, but made clear he did not intend to move. Suggesting that Cashell and his deputies might as well get started if they intend to evict him, he dared them to step foot on his boat. When a deputy accepted the dare and tried to climb up on the boat, Neely raised the shotgun to his shoulder and pointed it at him. The officers quickly spread out and drew their revolvers. "Now Neely, I'll tell you this," Cashell warned. "We've got enough guns in this bunch to make your house look like a sieve. We don't want to kill your wife and children, but if you don't put down that gun you and your family will have to take the consequences."[46]

Neely half-lowered the shotgun but then raised it again. At that moment, the US deputy marshal spoke up. When Neely found out the marshal represented federal authority, he set his gun inside the door and stooped down from the porch to talk to him. For a moment, it seemed that the marshal had defused the confrontation, but Cashell and a deputy rushed Neely and dragged him to the ground. The other deputies stormed inside to wrest the shotgun from his wife, Minnie. When she and her children screamed, three dogs attacked the officers in a back room where they went searching for weapons. The officers intended to shoot the dogs, but Minnie threw herself between them and yelled that they would have to shoot her first. One of the officers took her husband in handcuffs to the East St. Louis police station, and the others left to serve eviction notices to other houseboats. Before they left, Minnie made clear she intended to defend their property against eviction on Tuesday.[47]

Warren stood inside his screen door with a shotgun hanging on hooks near him when the deputies served papers on him. He, too, explicitly warned that he and his wife did not intend to move. Annie piped up that they would gladly move if the ferry company would buy their houseboat, but Cashell warned that he would sink it if they didn't leave. Similar scenarios were played out as deputies served notices to seven angry residents that morning. Some of the squatters already had received notices. William Franklin, to no avail, offered to pay rent as high as $2 or $3 a month if they allowed him and his wife to stay on the Hook. Frank Hudson assured deputies that for $10 in compensation for his home, they could "blow the whole shebang up with dynamite" if they chose.[48]

On Tuesday, Cashell and six deputies rowed to the island. The ferry company's steamboat *The McClellan* was anchored nearby with a wrecking crew of about twenty-five. George Warren greeted the deputies to minimize trouble. He told them that residents were prepared to leave. Now resigned to their fate, the evicted busily rounded up their chickens. Using rope and tackle, *The McClellan* tore down sheds and chicken houses and dragged them to the river to become driftwood. The steamboat pulled houseboats into the river "with chickens in coops on the roofs and dogs and children playing on decks and roofs."[49] The deputies were treated to a meal on the steamboat before resuming execution of their orders to rid Sandy Hook of squatters and their buildings. After two days of work, the steamboat crew and deputies cleared the island. They had to pull Louisa Schwartz's boat away from the island twice. When they showed up on the second morning, they found that she had repositioned it close to its previous island location. Minnie Neely, whose husband was in jail, did not put up resistance. Powerless, she could only watch as three of their boats sank to the bottom of the slough. As sheds and chicken houses were destroyed and hauled into the river, some of the squatters took to their skiffs to taunt the authorities and crew. The only satisfaction they got from the evictions came when George Merrill, mate of *The McClellan*, slipped and fell into the river. A reporter observed that when sheriff's deputies had to pull Merrill out, "The Hookites got almost enough satisfaction out of it to compensate them for their eviction."[50]

There was little squatters could do against the overwhelming display of power by the Terminal Railroad Association and the ferry company. The only squatter spared was Pete Bramlin, who had inhabited the island for thirty-five years and had saved many lives in the area, including two Wiggins employees. The ferry company, in an expression of benevolent paternalism to offset its ruthlessness, made clear he could live on the "Hook" for the rest of his life. In a carnival-like finale to the evictions, William Franklin wound up his phonograph and treated officers to the tunes of "Sailing, Sailing Over the Bounding Main," and "Home, Sweet Home" as he and his wife drifted downstream in their houseboat in search of a new place to call home. The company's assertion of complete control over the East St. Louis riverfront generated public resentments. With J. E. Neely languishing in jail on charges of resisting arrest and attempted murder of Deputy Sheriff Cashell, his wife was left to find a new home and a way to feed her children. A sympathetic grand jury in October refused to indict her husband.[51]

Heavy-handed evictions of waterfront squatters and the growing political power of railroad corporations on riverfronts were not unique to East St. Louis. In Hannibal, vigilantes and agents of the Chicago, Burlington & Quincy Railroad stormed onto the south-side levee between Bear Creek and the Hannibal Saw Mill with steel bars and axes in January 1901. They shoved unseaworthy boats into the icy waters of the Mississippi and taunted levee dwellers, smashing shanties and scattering possessions on the shoreline. Later that year, efforts to force shantyboat residents from another section of the levee hit a snag when George W. Snell sued the city of Hannibal after he was locked up without being charged with a crime when he refused to vacate the levee. The flexing of muscles by the CB&Q was an indication of its spreading tentacles into city hall, which apparently lacked money or political will to improve its own wharf to attract greater steamboat business. The CB&Q already had access to tracks to the Union Depot along First Street, but sought more. On December 3, 1906, the council passed ordinances that gave city lots to the railroad and granted the right to build double tracks at a much higher grade down the middle of the public levee and to build a spur track to the Union Depot in exchange for a payment of $10,000 and a commitment to pave and upgrade the public landing. The wharf between North, Hill, Center, Bird, and Broadway streets extended west to First Street during times of high water, but with built-up railroad tracks running down the center of it, steamboats would be unable to load and unload during high water. James D. Roland, a Hannibal general contractor, sought to block the deal in the public interest. According to a deed by Stephen Glascock, owner of the land when he platted the city of Hannibal in 1830, part of the waterfront was to be designated for a public landing, or levee. The city council's 1906 action threatened the public interest and the steamboat industry in bitter competition with railroads. Missouri Attorney General Herbert Hadley enjoined the railroad corporation from going forward with its plans for the levee, but the case dragged on for more than three years and ended up in the Missouri Supreme Court.[52]

On June 21, 1910, the high court upheld the Hannibal city council's deal with the CB&Q. Justice Henry Lamm agreed with fellow justices that the court had no jurisdiction to issue an injunction or writ of mandamus in the case, but he disagreed with the majority's decision to go ahead and set a precedent by ruling on the matter anyway in favor of the railroad company. "What we cannot do in a straight line as the bee flies, we ought not to do in a roundabout way as the fox runs," he objected. "The vital question here is that the municipal scheme evidenced by the ordinances *sells* for a price to a railroad company, engaged in a line of transportation inherently antagonistic to river traffic, at least at Hannibal, the right to build such tracks at such grades as amounts to an utter destruction to that portion of the wharf west of the tracks and to a permanent whittling away of the area of wharfage originally dedicated by shoving the real wharf for all time east of the proposed grade and tracks." Justice Lamm insisted that the court had no right to question the wisdom of Glascock's grant, no mat-

ter how little the city government had done to improve the wharf or how badly
the wharf needed improvements. In effect, the Hannibal city government abdi-
cated its responsibility to upgrade the levee. Lamm warned of the shortsighted
trend toward privatization of the public wharf and relying on a railroad company to take care of public improvements: "It is a painful lesson in the history
of American cities that public rights to wharfs and breathing places have been
lost by yielding to-day to the hunger of commercial pressure, only to be too late
and ruefully regretted in the new light of to-morrow."[53]

In 1912, the Memphis fire and police commissioner ordered the levee cleared
of houseboats. For years Memphis was the headquarters of a large squatter
colony. The order came after a visit to the levee by Mayor E. H. Crump, who
was determined to remove the unsightly boats from the riverfront. After the
Keokuk Sand Company lodged a complaint that shantyboats posed an obstruc-
tion to its landing in Quincy, Illinois, and inquired as to who held jurisdiction
over eviction matters in 1915, Major G. M. Hoffman, of the US Army Corps
of Engineers district office in Rock Island, replied that where an established
harbor line existed, municipal governments and riparian owners held jurisdiction. The federal government had the power to evict in matters outside the
established boundary.[54]

Davenport's Levee Improvement Commission led a campaign in 1916 to
evict three hundred families and their shantyboats from Willow Island, Maple
Island, and City Island, an area sometimes facetiously dubbed the "Seventh
Ward." Previous attempts to evict squatters from "Shantyboat Town" failed,
and the legal procedures in this attempt did not produce the desired results.
Attorneys, assured of cooperation by the nearby railroad company, drew up
the eviction papers and gave squatters an April 1 deadline, which was soon extended. Squatters still refused to budge. To test their legal rights as squatters,
the city attorney filed suit in the Scott County district court against a squatter
who defied multiple eviction notices. The Levee Improvement Commission's
lawyer despaired of seeking legal remedies in the form of judgments, which he
dismissed as useless against squatters. In the end, his position prevailed. Both
attorneys endorsed the use of force, urging the mayor to send a large squad of
police to tear down the homes and rid the island of all "undesirable" squatters.[55]

No matter the river town, such was the fate of countless waterfront squatters in the Mississippi valley as they collided with commercial interests. The

threat of violence, whether by lawful authorities or by gangs and vigilantes with more than a wink and a nod from police, was the tool of powerful interests who wished to clear the levee of blight and so-called riffraff. Violence, including destruction of squatters' homes, meager belongings, and gardens, was part of the political process of eviction. Likewise, the threat of violence was part of the strategy of those who resisted. Unlike the evicted, however, the evictors enjoyed the full weight of the state behind their efforts to drive squatters from the levee in the name of waterfront development, public morality, and civic progress.

II

Gone Are the Old River Days

FLOATING PALACES, STEEL BARGES, AND
VANISHING ROUSTABOUTS

Time was when "houseboater" was a name of reproach. It connoted
shiftless and impoverished vagabonds, throngs of curs, squalid and
repulsive quarters. But the word has obtained a new meaning
from wealthy owners of floating residences which are
equipped with every comfort and luxury.

—*St. Louis Post-Dispatch*, 1914

~~~~~~

Instead of the droll chants of the indolent negro roustabouts, as they toil
with the freight, we should hear the creak of machinery and the rattle
of chains as the loads are hoisted from boat to warehouse.

—CAPTAIN J. H. BERNHARD, *Transactions*, 1915

T hanks in part to industrial expansion and technological innova-
tions spurred by the First World War and financed by the federal
government, the early twentieth century brought transformational
changes to the St. Louis levee and the Mississippi valley waterways. The development of modern barges drove a stake in the heart of the crumbling steamboat packet system, which with few exceptions disappeared by 1930. As steamboats vanished, so, too, did roustabouts, representative cultural symbols of the
steamboat era. There remained little demand for roustabouts other than in the
nation's insatiable appetite for cultural expressions of sentimentalized, racist
nostalgia. In the summer of 1915, the *Ottumwa Belle* towed the last raft of logs
down the river from Hudson to Fort Madison as the pine boom went bust.
The chickens came home to roost for the unsustainable lumber industry that

~~~~

ravaged white pine forests in Minnesota and Wisconsin and inflicted serious damage on the ecosystem. St. Louis's elites turned to the river as a recreational outlet for the expression of class status. Shantyboats competed for space on a riverfront that was giving way to greater industrialization and the pursuit of leisure by owners of palatial houseboats, yachts, and cabin cruisers. Middle- and upper-class sportsmen embarked on hunting and fishing trips in comfortable houseboats, and more canoeists paddled the river for sport and adventure. Excursionists on the Upper Mississippi, in particular, enjoyed leisure trips enhanced by the beauty of autumn colors.[1]

In 1895, the *Waterways Journal* promoted houseboats on the Mississippi as retirement homes for the middle class and wealthy, calling attention to the history of elaborate boats on the River Thames in England. Writer Dorothy Richardson in 1901 pointed further to traditions of the English aristocracy, touting the nobility's palatial houseboats with retinues of servants, lavish dinner parties, and stately music-filled drawing rooms. Although she noted that American square-cornered houseboats generally were not beautiful to behold, she highlighted spacious, luxurious houseboats on the Indian River in Florida that ranged in cost from $500 to a few thousand dollars. She endorsed gasoline-powered houseboats and encouraged the wealthy to imitate their English aristocratic counterparts. "Considering the unrivaled opportunities which America offers . . . for this form of pleasure," she wrote, "it seems remarkable that there should not yet be one single houseboat to compare with the palatial floating structures with which the shores of the Upper Thames are literally lined during Henley [Royal Regatta] Week."[2]

Mississippi valley lumber barons, bankers, and businessmen did imitate the English aristocracy, just as the Vanderbilts and other eastern elites did at the time. An occasional palatial houseboat on the Mississippi River awed those on its banks as a symbol of its owner's wealth, power, and prerogative. The lords of lumber and other owners of floating palaces towed by steamers appropriated the seasonal migration patterns of shantyboaters on winter vacations in New Orleans. Lafayette Lamb, a banker and lumber manufacturer from a family in Clinton, Iowa, with nationwide business interests, sank $17,000 into the *Idler* and built a steamer, the *Wanderer*, to tow it up and down the river. On a trip to New Orleans in November 1901, Lamb docked in St. Louis, where he and his wife hosted parties and entertained friends aboard the palatial houseboat, described as "the most elaborate creature of its kind in the west."[3] The *Idler*, one hundred feet long and twenty-five feet in the beam, featured white and gold colors on the exterior, one hundred electric lights, steam heat, and a hardwood interior finish. The boat boasted an elegant drawing room, three bathrooms, a large dining room, private rooms, an Aeolian harp, and a roof deck with swings and a hammock. A number of servants worked on the *Idler*, and a crew of nine served the boat and the *Wanderer*, without which the former would have no lighting or heat. "To the shanty man it will pass on the way down," noted a reporter, "it will doubtless appear in such startling contrast to his little 'John boat' of one little room and leaky hull, a stub mast for a dirty sail, and a coon skin nailed to the single door, that he must be of good courage or else scuttle his own ship and bolt for the brush."[4]

A few days later, Lucian Frederick Easton, of La Crosse, docked at the St. Louis wharf in an extravagant houseboat towed by a steamer. He was from a prominent lumbering, railroad, and banking family. His houseboat, about forty feet long, was smaller than Lamb's, but it featured on the boiler deck an automobile that Easton drove off the boat onto the levee. The jaws of roustabouts, deckhands, and stevedores dropped at the sight of an automobile rolling off a houseboat onto the cobblestone wharf for the first time. In St. Louis, Easton and his wife and friends used the car for sightseeing, shopping, dining, and attending theatrical performances. They, too, were en route to New Orleans for the winter. The men aboard planned to stop in Arkansas for a hunting expedition. "We have taken it leisurely on the way down from Lacrosse and have been charmed by houseboating," wrote Easton. "It is certainly a capital way to travel. You can see we can have here all the charms of home, and we may entertain our friends here without the least trouble." Mockingly, he cast himself in the tradition of shantyboat nomads on the river:

> I am just a johnny-boat man with a john boat on an extensive plan. We are an army, us john-boaters, and we migrate with the birds, going where it is warm in winter and coming back in the spring. It is a delightful life. I am just beginning it, this being my first trip, but I think I shall make such a trip every fall. When I reach the lower river I'm going to satisfy myself on a point that has bothered me a good deal. I'm going to find out what becomes of all the houseboats that go down in the fall. The john-boaters always say

they sell them. If they do the market must be hard to glut, for there must be a fleet of many hundreds of houseboats on the lower river in the winter.[5]

To attend the St. Louis World Fair in 1904, another member of the millionaire family of C. Lamb and Sons from Clinton traveled in a patrician houseboat, *The Summer Girl*, a "veritable floating palace" towed by a steamer, *The Chaperone*. Garrett E. Lamb, president of the People's Trust and Savings Bank, arrived on the wharf in grand style in the boat, which was even larger than his uncle Lafayette's. Garrett brought two automobiles with him down the river for a two-week stay in St. Louis. Before the sizeable Lamb party docked at the wharf, a brass canon on the bow of *The Summer Girl's* upper deck fired a celebratory salute to the city to announce its arrival with great fanfare.[6] The boat was 120 feet long with a twenty-four-foot beam. Electric and steam heating plants installed in the steamer provided four hundred incandescent lights and heat in the houseboat. In the living room stood an upright piano in a corner, and exquisite Persian rugs with Oriental colorings were spread upon the floors. On the walls hung Dutch tapestries, and the windows were adorned with draperies and lace curtains. With six well-appointed staterooms, the houseboat had both hot and cold water, a refrigerator, and toilet rooms, and it included a gentlemen's smoking den and elaborate dining room. The interior cabins featured hand-carved wood designs.[7]

The new manufacturing class was also represented in grand style on the river. In 1904, C. H. Deere, president of Deere and Company in Moline, built a pleasure houseboat of similar style and grandeur for lavish excursions. Constructed in Clinton, the *Markatana* was 110 feet long with twenty-eight-foot beams, fancy staterooms, polished wood floors, a spacious dining room, a stately staircase and observatory deck, and servants' quarters. Deere bought the *C. W. Cowles* steamer (later rechristened the *Kalitan*) to tow the luxurious pleasure boat. The plow company president, who died in 1907, used the *Markatana* mainly on the Upper Mississippi, but William Butterworth, his son-in-law who ran the company after his death, took the pleasure boat on its first trip to New Orleans with two Packard automobiles aboard in 1911. Among its passengers were Mr. and Mrs. C. W. Mansur, secretary of the John Deere Company in St. Louis and a member of the city's Merchants' Exchange.[8] Russell E. Gardner, a St. Louis buggy manufacturer, philanthropist, and yachtsman, set out down the river in November 1901 for a winter in New Orleans on his newly outfitted pleasure steam yacht, the *Alice Edna*. Originally from Union City, Tennessee, Gardner planned to see friends along the way and to enjoy the Mississippi River and several of its tributaries on the trip south. His father, the mayor of Union City, joined him on the excursion, and so did his sisters. Gardner hired a trio of Black musicians in St. Louis to provide music for dancing and entertainment. The steamer yacht, about 115 feet long, cost $32,000 to build plus thousands more for added luxury features and furnishings in the cabins. Replete with electrical lighting, a water-filtering system, gentlemen's smoking room, library, gun racks, and a women's drawing room, the boat required a crew of six. In the hold of the boat was a refrigerator large enough to contain a deer and smaller game.[9]

In 1905, a St. Louis writer advocated greater use of the river by the middle and upper classes for recreation and entertainment. Pointing to the recent organization of the St. Louis Motor Boat Club, he named many owners of large gas-powered boats that cost in the hundreds and even thousands of dollars. He cheered wealthy city residents who were returning to the river instead of running away from it to the west in automobiles. To see the riverfront from the river itself would give residents a new perspective, he stressed. Then, poking fun at shantyboat communities, he wrote: "In contrast to the incessant industry he will see the happiest, idlest people on earth—the shanty boat men of 'Little Oklahoma' and 'Chicken Town.' They pay no rent, and the river brings them about all they want—food and driftwood for fuel."[10]

By the First World War, the number of St. Louis residents with yachts and expensive houseboats on the riverfront had grown sharply. Their boats featured Black servants, telephones, electric lights, bathrooms, gas for cooking, and many other luxuries. Dr. Max C. Starkloff, the city health commissioner, kept a home on South Broadway, but from May to November he and his family lived on their stylish houseboat, *Elsa*, near the shantyboat colony at the foot of Krauss Street in Carondolet. From an upper deck with a beautiful view of the river, he and his family especially enjoyed eating dinner prepared by their maid and listening to a phonograph as their boat drifted lazily with the current from the Eads Bridge to the foot of Krauss Street, where *Elsa* was moored. Starkloff, who won several silver cups for boating, was vice-admiral of the Century Boat Club. In his capacity as city health commissioner, he endorsed houseboat life on the riverfront as a healthier, more satisfying lifestyle. He employed a butler and kept two garages, one of them on land for the family's automobile, and the other on water to house *Irma*, the launch that propelled their houseboat on the river. Many other prominent residents owned summer homes on fancy pleasure craft on the levee, including Hans Toensfeldt, a former commissioner of school buildings, whose boat was in Carondolet, and Dr. George M. Phillips, whose boat was on the north wharf.[11]

At first, St. Louis was slow to respond to the national fad of speedboat racing, but the races grew quickly in popularity. Russell E. Gardner, who formerly owned the *Alice Edna*, converted to a deluxe gasoline-powered cabin cruiser, the *Santa Claus*. Sixty-five feet long with a beam of twelve feet, the craft featured electrical lighting, elegant mahogany furnishings, a pilot's house, galley, and crew's quarters as well as a sun parlor, bathrooms, and spacious quarters for the Gardner family and friends. Its one hundred-horsepower engines sent the cruiser downstream at about twenty miles per hour. The *Santa Claus* and Starkloff's *Irma* were among the luxury cruisers that competed in regattas. In 1911, the Carondolet Motor Boat Club held its first annual regatta on the Mississippi, attracting some of the fastest boats in the Mississippi valley. On September 28, 1912, the club held a two-day regatta that began near Krauss Street. In a ten-mile race in the cabin cruiser competition, Gardner, Starkloff, and others competed for a handsome silver trophy donated by the St. Louis Yacht Club. In 1914, Mississippi valley speedboat races were incorporated into a St. Louis river festival, the crowning event in a week-long Veiled Prophet celebration.[12]

The pleasure craft of the elites gave the waterfront a class facelift. By 1915 there were an estimated three hundred pleasure boats on the St. Louis riverfront. Many were summer homes with all modern amenities, including cooking ranges, electric lights, hot and cold running water, elegant rooms, and spacious berths. One of the newest yachts belonged to the St. Louis Yacht and Boat Company. *The Pegasus*, a forty-foot cruiser built in Alton, resembled a US naval scout cruiser adaptable to the Great Lakes or ocean cruising. With room for twelve passengers and a sleeping capacity of eight, it reached a speed of twenty-five miles per hour. In 1914 a reporter called attention to the brighter look of the levee, noting the changing class images of houseboats: "Time was when 'houseboater' was a name of reproach. It connoted shiftless and impoverished vagabonds, throngs of curs, squalid and repulsive quarters. But the word has obtained a new meaning from wealthy owners of floating residences which are equipped with every comfort and luxury."[13]

Similar forces prevailed in other river towns as boat clubs and local commercial clubs pushed to clean up unsightly waterfronts. The cleanup included evictions of shantyboats to make way for regional regattas and riverfront events to be attended by visitors from other cities and states. In Quincy, boat clubs and a businessmen's river committee lobbied the mayor in 1915 to get rid of shantyboats as a nuisance, disgrace to the community, and an insult to boat club members. In Davenport, the Levee Improvement Commission spearheaded efforts to beautify the riverfront by evicting residents of "Squattertown" in 1916. Alton's chief of police ordered squatters to vacate the city's riverfront in early 1914. After considerable delay and ejectment suits, court-ordered evictions led to the destruction of a settlement in September 1916. The Burlington Northern Railroad and the Illinois Terminal Association planned to build docks and freight yards on the property. About seventy-five squatters, many of them long-term, elderly residents, watched helplessly as work crews tore down and burned their shanties on the Alton riverfront.[14]

Major changes on St. Louis's north wharf in the 1910s signaled greater industrial development and improvement of port facilities. Included in plans for the wharf was the construction of cold storage warehouses, terminals, service tracks, and future industrial sites. In 1911, the municipal assembly granted a ten-year lease to the Meramec Portland Cement Company for storage, shipping, and railway facilities on waterfront property near the foot of Dock and Branch streets. The Upper Mississippi River Improvement Association, formed in 1901, continued to lobby the federal government for a permanent deep-river channel. In late October 1909, the St. Louis Business Men's League chartered the *Alton* to New Orleans with a number of political dignitaries from other towns and states to lobby for a deep waterway. The league and the association, anticipating the opening of the Panama Canal, were eager to take advantage of shipping outlets and markets for Mississippi valley agricultural and industrial products.[15]

Thanks in part to lobbying efforts by the Upper Mississippi River Improvement Association, President Woodrow Wilson's administration provided $3 million for steel barges and boats for the upper river. Businessmen counted on the federal government to appropriate further large sums to build towboats and barges for transportation of freight and crops to feed American soldiers in the war overseas. In December 1917, a major real estate deal by a syndicate of capitalists in Boston, New York, St. Louis, and Louisiana changed the face of St. Louis's north wharf on the site of the C. F. Liebke Lumber Company at Second and Buchanan streets. The central figure in putting the million-dollar deal together was Harry H. Wiggin, president of the Terminal Wharf and Railroad Warehouse Company of Boston. The fifteen-acre site, which included the Liebke lumberyards and the contiguous private holdings of J. F. and F. J. Liebke, extended from Second Street to the river and from Angelrodt south to Dock Street. The acquisition came in anticipation of wartime restoration of traffic from New Orleans to St. Paul.[16]

Although squeezed by north wharf projects, Little Oklahoma maintained its viability through the 1920s. So did waterfront settlements in south St. Louis. In the fall of 1921, a reporter called attention to a settlement of shanties, houseboats, and working-class houses on stilts near what once was known as Chickentown. Railroad tracks ran through the village dubbed "Main Street" at 4100 South. The villagers, who relied on fishing, boat building and repairs, and employment in nearby industrial plants, paid nominal ground rent. "Slim" Peter Williams, a well-known character on the river, was in the "Village on Stilts" at the time of the reporter's visit. Williams and others still made the annual trip south for the winter. "Came in a week ago from Hannibal," he said. "Going south with the ducks as usual."[17] Waterfront authorities, developers, and railroad giants now mostly ignored shantyboat settlements rather than initiate costly eviction lawsuits. Railroads, as long as squatters paid them a nominal sum of rent, generally left them alone. As a result, settlements persisted in evermore crowded levee spaces but drew less publicity. Snapshots of the urban waterfront landscape in south St. Louis revealed a rapidly modernizing city with reminders of its past. Women collecting driftwood, men with soot- and oil-blackened faces returning to shantyboats with empty lunch pails, men and women weaving and mending fishing nets, lonely roustabouts waiting for a distant steamer—scenes that dramatized the persistence of the river poor on the margins of an industrial city. "For even as the Father of Waters scatters logs, branches, rubbish—and now and then a pearl—over the miles of gray beachland," the reporter wrote, "so does the thing called life scatter hundreds of humans along the water's edge."[18]

In an age in which efficiency experts and engineers urged application of the principles of scientific management to industry, American civil engineers blasted the inefficiency of steamboat packets. Much of the criticism was aimed at roustabouts' demands for higher wages. Critics complained that packets were built on an antiquated system dating back to antebellum days. Outdated, inefficient river terminals and "drowsy negro roustabouts" who drew "the preposterous wages of from $80 to $100 per month" were at the root of the problem, according to Captain J. H. Bernhard, a civil engineer and president of the Inland Navigation Company who brought an experimental steel barge up the river from New Orleans to St. Paul in 1914. "We on the Mississippi," he complained in 1915, "are still content with mud levees, slippery and cumbersome, and feel fully compensated for economical inefficiency by the great smokestacks of our steamers belching forth clouds of smoke, in their large whistles which can be heard for miles, and in the wheels that beat the water up in waves higher than a man—steamboats having daily expenses which surpass the weekly expenses of more modern craft of larger capacity."[19]

In 1913, a new line of boats and municipal wharf in Kansas City did not require the use of roustabouts. New machinery loaded and unloaded freight instead. The St. Louis wharf came under fire for its limited access and terminals. To restore traffic on the Mississippi, Bernhard endorsed modern river terminals and construction of concrete walls against which river craft would moor, eliminating the use of gangplanks. Huge cranes, not roustabouts, would then load and unload modern barges. He made no attempt to hide his contempt for roustabouts, whose livelihoods would be threatened by such changes: "Instead of the droll chants of the indolent negro roustabouts, as they toil with the freight, we should hear the creak of machinery and the rattle of chains as the loads are hoisted from boat to warehouse."[20]

Droughts and low water chronically plagued the movement of freight and passengers on the Mississippi in the first half of the 1910s. Frustrated steamboat interests and supporters argued that a revival of traffic would take place if only the federal government would guarantee a fourteen-foot-deep river channel. In 1914, the *Globe-Democrat* devoted a large space in its classified ads section to urge the US Army Corps of Engineers to undertake a deep channel project. The newspaper framed its appeal around a poem, "The Old Darky's Dream," written for the occasion and steeped in racist nostalgia. The opening verse of the cheery poem linked the happiness of roustabouts to the revival of river traffic:

Floating down the Mississip,
With a channel 14 feet deep;
The good old days have come again,
On the cotton bales we'll sleep.

At the end of the poem, the newspaper called on "Uncle Sam" to help out: "We'd like to have good old steamboat days back again. Freight high piled on a hundred landings—waiting for the musical whistle of the boat as she heads for the bank."[21]

The trend toward steel boats and modern cranes to load and unload them was underway before the war. In 1909, the *Waterways Journal* editor complained about "roustabout despotism," blaming roustabouts for holding up river traffic. Citing a Memphis newspaper, Arste acknowledged that mechanical equipment might resolve the "despotism" in cities like St. Louis, Memphis, and New Orleans, but pointed out that roustabouts were still indispensable in other river towns. In January 1911, Henry Leyhe, general manager of the Eagle Packet Company, announced plans to construct a new steel boat to replace a wooden one that had wrecked several months earlier. For use in the St. Louis trade, the new boat, which reportedly cost $10,000, was to feature large cranes that would eliminate the need for roustabouts. The *Globe-Democrat* cheered that steamboat owners, after years of labor shortages, strikes, and militant labor demands, might be on the verge of resolving the "roustabout labor problem" if they followed the Eagle Packet Company's lead.[22] On June 18, 1911, a steel barge docked in St. Louis for the first time in the history of the wharf. The Mississippi Valley Transportation Company's *Edward E. Green* carried a cargo of 1,400 tons of granulated sugar from the American Sugar Refining Company of New Orleans. Built with six waterproof compartments, the "unsinkable" and "fireproof" boat featured a capacity of 1,600 tons and paid cheaper marine insurance premiums. Its arrival turned the wharf into a busy place at once. W. K. Kavanaugh, head of the transportation company, promised a revival of the wharf if only St. Louis shippers would use the river. Fifty stevedores, at 25 cents an hour, hurried to unload 5,500 barrels and 2,000 sacks of sugar, valued at $120,000. They did most of the unloading, but to get the remaining cargo unloaded the company used a crane and an auxiliary "donkey engine." "Not since the olden days when the levee was at its best," observed the *St. Louis Star and Times*, "has such a busy time been seen on the river front."[23]

Temporary derricks and booms were set up on board to help load cargo onto the boat for its return trip to New Orleans A steel drop was used for the first time in St. Louis to facilitate the sliding of boxes into the barge's hold. The company planned to install a new permanent derrick for use on the next trip from New Orleans. The introduction of labor-saving mechanical equipment, a harbinger of things to come, spelled trouble for waterfront laborers in the years ahead. The Mississippi Valley Transportation Company, backed by Harbor and Wharf Commissioner Joseph P. Whyte, secured legislation to build a privately owned warehouse on the public wharf between Walnut and Market streets. The company paid the city $1,200 annually in return. Plans included construction of two railway tracks from the warehouse to the water's edge. Small cars would transport freight from barges to the warehouse. As Whyte explained, "The warehouse proposed is to enable the transportation company to do away with deckhands and roustabouts, which are now used in loading and unloading river steamers."[24] At its 1911 annual convention, the Upper Mississippi River Improvement Association came out strongly in favor of mechanical contrivances to replace roustabouts and stevedores in the loading and unloading of boats. The secretary criticized the archaic packet system and blasted the disgraceful condition of neglected wharves.[25]

According to the *Waterways Journal*, the Streckfus Line planned to install loading and unloading devices, inclines, and a track running from its warehouse at the top of the levee to the wharf's low water stage at all of its main ports. Inside the warehouse, laborers would load and unload freight from a moving conveyor belt. The system was designed to speed up the movement of cargo and eliminate roustabouts. "We are more than anxious to see Capt. Steckfus succeed in solving the roustabout question," noted the *Waterways Journal*, "because this has been one of the principal causes in the decline of steamboating." In 1912, the Lee Line used a small automatic freight handler on the St. Louis wharf to load cotton bales from the levee onto a wagon at a reported rate of fifteen bales in seventeen minutes. At that rate, the crane, which required use of a twenty-horsepower gasoline engine, did the work of an estimated six roustabouts.[26]

Captain Walter A. Blair, of the *Helen Blair* of Davenport, warned against the stampede to blame roustabouts for the slump in river traffic. He pointed instead to conditions under which many roustabouts worked. He emphasized that if packets provided abundant food, decent wages, and mates that were not overly abusive, they would attract adequate crews. In his opinion, the revival of river traffic required major improvements in shore facilities. Pointing out that the public often confused roustabouts with stevedores, he stressed that in cities with modern wharves and facilities, stevedores were in plentiful supply and there were no problems in securing a labor force to load and unload the packets. Problems at times came with hiring roustabouts on the round-trip packets on account of prevailing conditions at small landings. Steep, slippery embankments, ungraded roadways to the landings, and frequent cave-ins at water's edge made the work more arduous and life-threatening as roustabouts loaded heavy cargo that included squealing hogs and uncooperative livestock in all kinds of inclement weather.[27]

As roustabouts pressed for higher wages and better working conditions, they bore the brunt of criticism of the packet system. When Memphis roustabouts refused to work on the cotton boats in the late fall of 1910, although reportedly offered high wages, police backed up the steamboat operators by threatening to arrest roustabouts on the wharf for vagrancy and to send them to the rock pile. The *Globe-Democrat* reported that inadequate sleep and the heaviness of the loads were at the root of the nonunion strike by roustabouts, who avoided the wharf and picked cotton instead. Six months later, the same newspaper urged application of the Sherman Anti-Trust Act of 1890 to prosecute roustabouts for organizing a strike. The statute was aimed at monopolistic corporations, but the *Globe-Democrat* endorsed its use to cripple efforts by roustabouts to gain a few extra dollars each month. The newspaper accused them of "extortion," "combination," and shaking down steamboat owners by preventing steamboats from operating freely. At the time, roustabouts on the short *Cape Girardeau* packet who made between $50 and $60 a month went on strike, demanding $75 a month. Captain Henry Leyhe, caught unable to secure a crew at the last minute, conceded to the demand.[28]

The militancy of Black roustabouts prompted a Tennessee River steamboat captain to fire all of them in the middle of a packet run and to replace them with a crew of "husky white farmhands picked up at way landings." In response to the firings and reported complaints about the unreliability of Black roustabouts, Louisville's *Courier-Journal* emphasized that "few of them can resist the allurements of the barrel houses and the crap games, and when in reach of either or both they are serenely indifferent to steamer schedules." The newspaper conceded, however, that the work was difficult, and that roustabouts understandably sometimes deserted a boat: "It is to be doubted if a crew of white farmhands will prove any more constant or efficient. The particular sort of discipline that prevails on the lower deck is likely to strike a Tennessee farmhand as somewhat too drastic for long continued endurance."[29]

In November 1912 a strike broke out on the St. Louis wharf, targeting the Illinois River steamers *Bald Eagle* and *Keystone State.* The strikers pushed for a ten-hour workday and $120 per month in wages plus an extra penny per barrel of apples loaded and unloaded. The steamers acquiesced on November 6, but still had difficulty hiring a full crew. Labor shortages on the St. Louis wharf during the First World War gave roustabouts added bargaining leverage. In early July 1916, a crew refused to work the *Belle of Calhoun* when the captain rejected their demand for $90 a month in wages. Captain Henry Leyhe also had trouble finding a crew for the *Cape Girardeau* in 1918. "The Negro race is a shiftless care free one," the *Waterways Journal* blasted, "and when he has a little money pleasure and indolence as a general rule is indulged in until his money is gone. He cannot be depended upon for steady work."[30]

The United States' entry into the war in 1917 brought further changes in shipping and transportation. After disarray and chaos in the railroad industry led to federal running of the railroads to ensure that shipping problems did not impede the war effort, the Mississippi River assumed greater strategic importance as an artery of commerce to move soldiers, food, and war materials. In 1918, after coal shortages and a bitterly cold winter paralyzed river freight, businessmen in the Mississippi valley lobbied the federal government for help. President Wilson's administration created the Federal Barge Line to revive shipping on the nation's inland rivers. The Mississippi-Warrior River Service operated under the United States Railroad Administration between 1918 and 1920. After complaints and continued lobbying by businessmen, the government took additional steps. In 1920, the Inland and Coastwise Waterways Service took over the service, which was transferred to the War Department. The aim was to foster a public-private partnership, boost profitability of river carriers, and encourage cooperation and coordination of rates with railroads. By 1922, the Mississippi River Service operated profitably with new terminals under construction in St. Louis, Cairo, Memphis, and New Orleans. Thanks to the federal initiative, too, six modern towboats and forty-five steel barges carried freight on the Mississippi at the time. In 1924, federal support expanded with the Inland Waterways Corporation, successor to the Inland and Coastwise Waterways Service. The new corporation, housed in the War Department, was capitalized at $5 million. Although the initial focus was on the Lower Mississippi, river service between Minneapolis-St. Paul and St. Louis was restored by 1927. The government subsidies of steel barges, gantry cranes, clamshell buckets, and other labor-saving machinery meant shrinking demand for roustabouts and wooden steamboats. New barge lines appeared, spurred by federal initiatives to encourage St. Louis businessman to build towboats, barges, and terminals to boost waterways transportation. Smaller, more compact tow fleets that hauled greater tonnage meant efficiency but threatened steamboats. Not even a city ordinance that eliminated wharf charges for steamboats in 1904 could halt the steady decline of packets. By the late 1920s, river traffic was revitalized through federal initiatives, but the freight carriers were not wooden steamboats.[31]

The cultural fabric of the St. Louis wharf changed markedly. Creaking pulleys and clanking machinery—music to the ears of civil engineers—steadily replaced the sounds of roustabouts singing and "coonjinin'" on the gangplank. The wharf lost its cultural appeal. Fewer citizens dashed to the levee in their finest clothing to greet steamboats when they docked, or to watch lines of roustabouts and stevedores load and unload them. Wharf activity picked up at special times, such as apple harvest in Calhoun County, Illinois, when barrels of apples arrived in great quantities on the *Belle of Calhoun*, but such times were far less common by the early 1920s. In 1922, the secretary-treasurer of the St. Louis & Memphis Transportation Company noted that the Cape Girardeau and Tennessee River boats were the only packets operating out of St. Louis on the Lower Mississippi. Clumsy steamboats appeared clumsier yet on a river with fleets of modern barges. In 1921, a *Kansas City Star* reporter on assignment for an article on the St. Louis wharf aptly titled his piece "Gone Are the Old River Days."[32]

Like steamboats, showboats were wrapped in nostalgia by the time Pulitzer Prize-winning author Edna Ferber's 1926 novel *Showboat* was adapted as a Broadway musical in 1927. Fewer than half of showboats on the waterways in 1910 brought theatrical performances to river towns in 1930. The Great Depression and competition from motion pictures added to the woes of the few steamboat owners who struggled to keep afloat in the face of river mishaps, repairs, and heavy capital requirements. To travel day after day to small rural landings for a single show at each stop became less financially viable than to dock in an urban harbor for a lengthy run of performances. In 1937, when Captain Billy Menke brought his *Goldenrod* to St. Louis, it marked the first time in three years that a calliope was heard on the levee. The showboat, looking worn, shabby, and in need of a fresh coat of paint, was rebuffed by city officials. At first, the director of public safety denied Menke a license, pending proof that the twenty-eight-year-old boat was seaworthy. Menke triumphed when a federal judge issued an injunction against the city, insisting that federal navigation laws took precedence in the case.[33]

Menke found a warm audience for nostalgia in the *Goldenrod*'s presentation of old-time melodramas. Initially, older attendees resented younger audience members, who were loud and raucous-like in their laughter and heckling of stage performers at times. Among older ticket buyers was a greater reverence for the melodramas that reminded them of days when showboats were held in higher regard as cultural institutions of the waterways. When the pianist played "There'll be a Hot Time in the Old Town Tonight" before the curtain went up for the stage production of *Lena Rivers*, the overture recalled the levee days of the 1890s when Mama Lou sang the song at the Castle Club. By the fall of 1937, Menke chose St. Louis as the *Goldenrod*'s permanent home. Although he was often feted in later decades, his showboat became yet another visual relic of the heavily industrialized city's river past. Over time, the persistent peeling of the boat's exterior paint due to industrial pollution symbolized the cultural primacy of factories and railroads over steamboats in the battle to shape St. Louis's waterfront after 1875.[34]

Travel accounts continued to provide occasional snapshots of waterfront squatter communities and a dwindling number of roustabouts at work in the late 1920s. In August 1926, writer Harold Speakman and his wife, Frances Lindsay Speakman, an artist and illustrator, set out in a canoe from Itasca Park en route to New Orleans. When they reached St. Paul, they bought an old houseboat in a squatter settlement near the Robert Street bridge. With help from the shantyboat community, they fixed it up, added an outboard motor, and headed south. Upon reaching St. Louis in November, they docked north of the Eads Bridge and went searching for a skiff to replace one they lost when blustery winds snapped it loose on the river. The search took Speakman to the "large squalid-looking houseboat colonies"[35] on the north wharf. He came away empty handed and unimpressed, noting that Little Oklahoma "seemed to contain a very high percentage of sullen people and bad tempered dogs." He also expressed disappointment in the sorry state of the city's waterfront, concluding that "the city has more or less turned its back on the river."[36]

In 1926, *National Geographic Magazine* commissioned Lewis R. Freeman, a writer and adventurer, to travel down the Mississippi from its headwaters in a skiff. Freeman, a former war correspondent and author of travel books and a novel, was scheduled to speak at the Missouri Historical Society in St. Louis on November 5. On his way downriver, he spent a night in a shantyboat colony of seasoned storytellers in the Missouri town of Louisiana. "Queer people they are when you first meet them," he noted. "They're terrible shy at first, but as soon as you prove to them that you're not a prohibition agent their friendship becomes almost overwhelming and they demand that you seal it with corn liquor, the most terrible stuff I've ever tasted."[37]

In 1928, the simple shantyboat lifestyle attracted Kent and Margaret Emmerling Lighty, graduates of the University of Wisconsin, where Kent's father was a professor and Emmerling as a student edited the *Wisconsin Literary Magazine*. They married in 1924 and moved to Milwaukee, but four years later they left behind a comfortable apartment and jobs in advertising to embark on a houseboat journey down the Mississippi. Kent's appetite for river life was whetted in 1922 when he and a fellow student took a motorboat down the river from La Crosse, writing a few newspaper articles along the way. Eager for a break from the urban bourgeois world of bright lights, advertising, and mass consumption, the Lightys drove to St. Paul and found a suitable houseboat for sale at Clarkson's Minnesota River Canoe Livery at Mendota. They bought it for $300 and dubbed it *The Ark*. It was about ten feet wide and thirty feet long with a screened-in porch, kitchenette, double hardwood floors, and insulated walls. They spent $300 more in added furnishings, and they bracketed twin sixteen-horsepower outboard motors to the back for $200. They also obtained a small speedboat, *The Salamander*, for use on short trips. In total, they invested nearly $1,000 in the river adventure. The Lightys were thrilled to emancipate themselves from clocks, schedules, and the homogenized culture of consumption promoted by Madison Avenue ad executives. "We weren't and aren't rich,"

Margaret later wrote. "But we had given up two nice jobs, an admirable apartment, an automobile, and with them, security. And what for? To loaf without plans down through the middle of America and see what we could see."[38]

With plenty of books, a portable phonograph, a wood- and coal-burning stove, and a shotgun to duck hunt on the islands, the aspiring "river rats" set out. They noticed a marked increase in the tempo and dynamic of levee life once they reached Hannibal, where Black roustabouts were loading the *Belle of Calhoun,* one of the few remaining packets. When they reached Clarksville on election day, 1928, they felt for the first time they were entering into a distinctive "southern" world.[39] St. Louis sneaked up on them quickly after the yellowish-brown flow from the Big Muddy created swirling eddies and darkened the waters of the Mississippi. As the couple negotiated the dangerous Chain of Rocks, they noted that "a thick pall of coal smoke smothered the valley below . . . we were almost under Eads bridge before we realized that we had arrived at the very heart of the St. Louis wharf. Hastily we tied the shanty-boat to an iron ring at the bottom of the levee."[40]

In St. Louis, the Lightys dined, attended the theater, and danced the night away after many quiet nights in villages and isolated nooks, coves, and crannies on the river. They were impressed by the city where Kent was born in 1899, but they were dismayed by the decline of its riverfront, described by canoeist Major Rowland Haven-Hart ten years later as "hideous." At last, the Lightys came upon a few roustabouts poking and prodding mules and pigs up the gangplank of the Eagle Packet Company's *Cape Girardeau,* a side-wheeler that still made a weekly run between St. Louis and Cape Girardeau. The wharf, hidden in the coal smoke and industrial pollution, seemed a lonesome place. "For a moment we stood still, looking up and down," the Lightys wrote. "The place was virtually deserted. This, of course, was the very same wharf where once there had been so much doing that waiting packet-boats sometimes had to moor three deep out into the channel."[41]

As the result of river disasters, financial problems, poor business decisions, old age, and railroad competition, most steamboat packets were out of business. The life expectancy of a steamboat was no higher than the average number of years a roustabout worked on the packets. Without a consistent, coherent national transportation policy, the industry died a slow but certain death after the Civil War. By 1935, the Eagle Packet Company in St. Louis sold the *Cape Gi-*

rardeau and converted the *Golden Eagle* into a tourist boat. The era of steamboat packets on the Mississippi was nearly over. In late September 1929, a *St. Louis Star* reporter noted that the levee seemed a relic from a bygone era. He was struck by the litter, debris, and decayed look of the wharf, a casualty of the decline and death of steamboats and a city's seeming willingness to turn its back on its own history. Grimy, run-down buildings that once were boardinghouses, hotels, and countless small businesses were now warehouses or sat empty. Amid the deafening roar of trains on elevated tracks, an occasional steamboat still docked, and a shrinking number of roustabouts signed on to work the packets, but in many cases the boats arrived simply to transport the men south to pick cotton. Nearly all the old haunts of roustabouts on the waterfront had disappeared. Gone were the saloons, hotels, stores, and hopping dance halls. Prohibition killed the saloons, and most Black-owned small enterprises near the wharf went out of business. As the reporter observed, "The deafening noise of heavy coaches rolling over steel rails seemed like the mocking and deliberate laughter of the machine age in the face of the slower moving age of yesterday."[42]

When the stock market crashed a month later, little remained of steamboat life but memories for a few roustabouts like "Shanty Boat" and "Mule." The municipal wharf was a nearly deserted place to hang out with hoboes and a few other packet old-timers and wharf dwellers—Black and white—who somehow eked out a living by doing odd jobs and picking through commercial refuse heaps. The few surviving small businesses provided a place for the shrinking pool of roustabouts to while away the time as they waited for a rare steamboat to dock. A "boatman" who stopped to talk to the *Star* reporter on the levee offered a story of how the city's waterfront communities originated. According to his account, a white man and a Black man once built a lean-to against a bulkhead on the riverbank. They shared it as a home, and the arrangement worked so well that other squatters were drawn there. In time, they became a nuisance and were evicted by police.[43]

The "origin" story was an expression of the levee's shared class identity across racial lines. Rooted partly in folklore and partly in history, it reflected pride in efforts by the river poor to forge a heritage on the levee that set it apart from the rest of the city. From the vantage point of the river veteran who shared the story with the *Star* journalist, it was the unrelenting police evictions of squatters at the behest of city officials and developers that meant the end of waterfront settlements and their unsophisticated living arrangements. At the end of a decade in which the Ku Klux Klan controlled politics in a number of states and terrorized and lynched Black Americans with impunity, interracial social arrangements among the river poor of St. Louis for the past fifty years offered at least a rudimentary alternative to the hardened segregation of the conventional urban industrial model adopted by the city.

Epilogue

IN SOME FAR-OFF VALHALLA

Lotta blues happenin' out there along the river back then, right there
in them tents and shacks. . . . Oh yea, see they'd have a honky-tonk right
out there with the hobos and po' peoples . . . have moonshine and maybe
some folks be gamblin'. . . . Always be blues musicians out there driftin' in
and out, . . . they'd always be hangin' around playin' in them honky-tonks.
Big crowds, too. Wasn't no work, nothin' to do but hunt for food and
firewood. So lots a peoples be out there in those barrel-houses
singin' and dancin' and carryin' on—rough joints too—
be fights and cuttin' going on.

—BIG JOE WILLIAMS, Looking Up at Down, 1989

W hen the curtain fell on the steamboat era, St. Louis's run-down
levee attracted critics and city planners determined to rid the
riverfront of blight. For architects, planners, and municipal
authorities, a fresh flood of homeless refugees to the riverfront in the Great
Depression created a political nightmare. Racially integrated waterfront settlements swelled with unemployed, dispossessed victims of the world economic
crisis. In the longstanding tradition of shantyboat settlements, a mayor presided
over the affairs of the riverfront's "Hooverville." Tiny, dilapidated churches appeared, a community center was built, charitable groups and private donors
provided food and other items, and a crude building housed "city hall." Big Joe
Williams, J. D. Sharp, and other blues musicians entertained the down-and-out.
The levee drew unwanted national attention to its decrepit shacks and hungry,
poorly clad inhabitants, including large numbers of children. Hooverville was
the largest of the houseboat colonies (others being Hoover Heights, Tin Town,
Merryland, Happyland, and North Hooverville) that stretched from the central

wharf to the south about twenty-five blocks. Squatters also squeezed onto the north wharf near Madison Street and elsewhere. By the end of 1931, Hooverville contained between four hundred and five hundred inhabitants, but the numbers soon exploded. With the city's unemployment rate higher than 30 percent—70 percent in its Black population—more than three thousand Black and white squatters flocked to the levee in numbers not seen since the 1890s. Joining shantyboats in settlements once known as Squatters' Town, Chickentown, and Little Oklahoma, they built ramshackle huts from orange crates, scrap metal, and other salvaged materials amid the deepening economic and social crisis.[1]

Hard times breathed new life into frontier traditions among river folks, especially in rural areas where adaptive river living never was a thing of the past. In light of urban waterfront Hoovervilles, some critics were not as quick to ridicule the alternative lifestyle of simplicity, self-sufficiency, and sustainability led by shantyboat forbears of frontier heritage. For at least sixty years, shantyboat communities with chickens, gardens, and flowers were a thorn in the side of city officials and developers. Now the administration of newly elected Bernard Dickmann, a real estate developer and the first Democratic mayor of St. Louis in twenty-four years, grappled with a large influx of the disinherited to shantyboats, hovels, and huts on the levee. Against a city political backdrop of strikes, police violence and repression, and militant food protests organized by the Unemployed Council of the Communist Party, the reemergence of interracial working-class solidarity reminiscent of 1877 once again concerned city authorities. Much of the ferment came from the levee and nearby Black working-class neighborhoods and factories adjacent to the river. Little Bohemia, a small nightclub on the levee, attracted a group of writers, artists, and political radicals that included playwright Thomas L. "Tennessee" Williams and Jack Conroy, whose proletarian novel The Disinherited appeared in 1933. They hung out together and reinforced each other's commitment to economic and social justice. Joe Jones, a painter with working-class roots who joined the Communist Party in 1933, took up shantyboat living on the levee and offered art classes to the unemployed at the Old Courthouse until he was evicted due to accusations he was using art for propaganda purposes. His paintings often featured riverfront scenes, among them a 1934 painting of Black roustabouts and New Deal murals.[2]

For Mayor Dickmann, the crisis provided an opportunity to implement an aggressive revitalization plan for the levee. At the end of 1933, the formation of the Jefferson National Expansion Memorial Association spelled trouble for those on the central wharf. The association lobbied for federal support for a national memorial in St. Louis to celebrate Thomas Jefferson's role in promoting America's westward imperial expansion in the early republic. A tentative design by architect Louis LaBeaume called for demolition of what once was the vibrant center of the city's history—a section of forty blocks south of the Eads Bridge where the French created a fur-trading outpost in 1764. Dickmann's administration, lacking money to flatten buildings in the targeted district of the old Creole village, asked voters in 1935 to approve a $7.5 million bond issue for what he pitched as a revitalization scheme. With real estate developers in the wings, Dickmann sought federal dollars, but he had no firm commitment, merely an understanding, at the time of the controversial bond election. In a heavy-handed campaign marred by reports of widespread fraudulent voting, the bond issue passed overwhelmingly. Taxpayers afterward filed a legal challenge, but the courts upheld the election. On December 21, 1935, President Franklin D. Roosevelt signed an executive order to create the Jefferson National Expansion Memorial under the purview of the National Park Service, and he authorized federal expenditures for the project via the Public Works Administration and the Works Progress Administration.[3]

With federal job creation funds, the city wharf master sent WPA workers to tear down the huts and shacks on the central levee. To justify the destruction, he emphasized that there was too much drinking in some of the homes. City officials stepped up their attacks on the levee settlements as a public health menace, too. The campaign prompted a letter from Alma Rice, a Hooverville resident, to the *St. Louis Star and Times*:

Have just read where Hooverville is doomed as a health menace. Am glad to say I have lived in Hooverville nearly three years and have had better health than ever before. I have never seen a rat or a roach down here. . . . Mayor Dickmann had better see that some of the places uptown are cleaned up. . . . We don't need pity down here. All we ask is to keep our homes where we are happy and can look out at the beautiful Mississippi. There is something about the river we never tire of. We don't ask people for alms. We work for our daily bread, the same as other folks.[4]

By the end of December 1936, all of the levee shacks were torn down, and in October 1939 wrecking crews began demolition of a condemned forty-block tract of the historic riverfront. Only the Old Courthouse, the Old Cathedral, and the Old Rock House were spared. No matter what a newly designed waterfront of the future might look like, it would hold no place for roustabouts or shantyboat squatter settlements. Included in the demolition were several hundred apartment buildings and homes with Black and white tenants, cafes, nightclubs, and factories that employed several thousand workers, although many industries were at idled capacity. At a time of national concern that uprooted, out-of-work Americans were losing a sense of community and their faith in democratic political institutions, bulldozers and tons of fill dirt buried the district as the city laid waste to its own history in a dramatic, if not shocking, expression of contempt for the people who formed the riverfront neighborhoods. Hard hit were struggling Black-owned businesses and saloons that once were filled with roustabouts, ragtime, blues, and jazz. Due to lack of funding, the intervening world war, and other delays, the Gateway Arch did not become a reality until 1965. For twenty-five years, the flattened district remained little more than a gigantic parking lot. To borrow an analogy from the Vietnam War era, planners, realtors, and city officials rationalized that in order to save the waterfront district, they had to destroy it.[5]

Roustabouts, often blamed for the financial demise of packets, were chewed up and spit out on wharfs from St. Paul to New Orleans in steamboat America. Their singing and great strength and endurance in shouldering burdensome loads up and down the gangplank drew praise, but when they demanded higher wages and better working conditions, they were excoriated for laziness, shiftlessness, and gambling habits. Black organizations and newspapers such as the St. Louis Palladium and the Argus ignored their plight on account of their degraded, lower-class status and lifestyle. When roustabouts fought back on the docks and in the courts against inhumane treatment and exploitation of their labor by those perched comfortably on the Texas deck, they endured blistering criticism. They had few places to turn for protection after the AFL turned its back on them in the strike of 1892, but they contributed to a tradition of waterfront labor militancy that resurfaced in the 1930s. On April 26, 1939, a river strike against the Federal Barge Line drew 3,500 members (1,000 boatmen and 2,500 dockworkers) of the Congress of Industrial Organizations (CIO) and the AFL.

Coordinated by the General Council of River Workers, the strike in St. Louis included 150 members of the CIO's Inland Boatmen's Union (IBU), a National Maritime Union affiliate, as well as 150 white and 200 Black dockworkers of the AFL's International Longshoremen's Association (ILA). An additional 300 Black dockworkers at the East St. Louis terminal also joined the strike. In Memphis, Thomas Watkins, a Black dockworker and powerful union figure on the city's waterfront, spearheaded a coalition of Black and white members of the ILA and the IBU and helped to steer the bitter strike to a successful conclusion. Subsequent reprisals and threats of violence against strike leaders in Memphis, New Orleans, and other ports, however, quickly reduced the leverage Black dockworkers gained in the strike's settlement. Watkins fled Memphis for St. Louis after a nearly successful assassination attempt on his life, but George Holloway, a Memphis unionist and civil rights activist, recalled that the waterfront militancy of the Maritime Union's local affiliate in the strike inspired Black industrial workers in the city to stand up for their rights.[6]

Between 1875 and 1930, shantyboats and roustabouts, though roundly despised, ridiculed, and condemned, figured prominently in St. Louis's riverfront life as well as the cultural history of the Mississippi River valley. As representative symbols of the waterways, they inspired dime novelists, songwriters, and filmmakers in the late 1920s and 1930s. Popular depictions of the river poor reflected to varying degrees the harsh class and racist assumptions of the era. The caricatured representations were not new, but with the spread of sophisticated mass advertising, an expanded literary market, and technology that revolutionized commercial music and motion pictures in the 1920s, images of the levee poor packed added punch and reached larger audiences. The sentimentalized, racist nostalgia in Ben Lucien Burman's writings and Hollywood's adaptations demeaned, infantilized, and robbed both groups of their identity. Louis Armstrong's recording sessions in 1933 included sentimentalized representations of the levee from the perspective of Black songwriters. "Dusky Stevedore," written by Jay Cee (J. C.) Johnson and Andy Razaf, was a high-octane, if not frenetic, tribute to roustabouts and stevedores. The lyrics acknowledge the crushing nature of work on the docks, but they paint a picture of happy Black roustabouts and their "ragtime shuffling gait." In "Mississippi Basin," recorded by Armstrong and written by Razaf and Reginald Charles Foresythe, a dockworker sings longingly for the levee: "Even though the weight was heavy, I was happy on the levee. Want to take my rightful place on the levee in the Mississippi Basin back home. Everybody was for me there, all the folks will be there, used to like to wash my face in the Mississippi Basin back home."[7]

Nostalgic, too, was Armstrong's 1939 recording of "Shanty Boat on the Mississippi." Because of his troubled, impoverished roots, he was well-familiar with shantyboats and roustabouts on the New Orleans *batture* as well as the levee in St. Louis and other ports where he played on the Streckfus excursion boats. Written by white songwriters Terry Shand and Jimmy Eaton, the song expressed the longing of a harried, worn-out worker to flee hard times and bill collectors by returning to a shantyboat "splashing on the shore" with "better times in store." With a "gal" to "sweep my rug" and "fetch my jug," Armstrong sang, "I'm never gonna work no more." His recording staked a Black male claim to the heritage of shantyboat dwellers on the New Orleans levee, reminding fans that the settlements included Black families and a shared culture with white shantyboat families. As a cultural symbol that evoked common stereotypes at the time, shantyboats represented more than a sexist, escapist retreat from civilization. They offered an alternative lifestyle to many desperately poor, unemployed, and homeless people in hard times. "Shanty Boat on the Mississippi" and other river recordings by Armstrong painted nostalgic images of river life at a time when settlements swelled again with economic refugees and millions of Americans were uprooted by the crisis in global capitalism.[8]

Poems written in the late 1950s by W. J. Devine are expressive of a creative dialectic that preserved roustabouts and shantyboat migrants as romanticized cultural figures on the waterways. Devine, the Siebler Tailoring Company's vice president of sales in Cincinnati, was designated as an honorary riverboat captain because of his love for, and collection of, steamboat photographs and memorabilia. From his scrapbook of photographs and prints, he sent Christmas and greeting cards to friends and fellow river enthusiasts. In "Roustabout Man," which appeared in the *Waterways Journal,* he paid tribute to the role of roustabouts in the steamboat industry:

You can dream about old steamboats from the dim and distant past—
Tall stacks and 'scapes and gingerbread—a deep-toned whistle blast;
You can reminisce of packets graceful, gleaming and all white
That have faded with time's passing like the Arabs in the night.

You can spin your yarns of masters and of pilots at the wheel
And the men who manned the steamers—men who knew the river's
    "feel"—
You can talk of clerks and shipments and of mates famed for their shouts
But in this, my humble verse, I toast the lowly roustabouts.

For the rouster too was "steamboat man" with river in his blood
And a heart as full of singing as the mighty streams in flood—
As he bore his heavy burdens he would chant his rhythmic song,
While his fellow rousters answered and the loading moved along.
Hi Ho! Heave ho, Cincinnati man;
What you do in Bucktown?
Sees you, levee man . . .
Sees you down by River Joe's, wid
tall gal Susie Ann.

Sometimes his song was Memphis, Baton Rouge or New Orleans
But he worked and sang the harder loading up the river queens.
And his stout frame never quavered nor his spirit shirked a task,
For it kept him on the boats he loved—and what more could he ask?

'Neath searing sun and misty moon he labored as he sang,
Delighted when, at leaving time, the packet's roof bell rang;
And as the stage was hauled aboard, he danced in childish glee—
While the husky-throated whistle brought him simple ecstasy.

Alas all life is transient and roustabouts are gone,
Like the packets they once loaded, but the picture lingers on;
And in some far-off Valhalla which all river men will share
You'll likely find the rousters waiting on the levee there.[9]

Unlike roustabouts, shantyboat migrants on the waterways were spared the outpouring of racist venom in the steamboat era, but like roustabouts, they endured class-based cultural depictions as lazy, degraded chicken thieves prone to lying, feuding, and childlike superstitions. Marginalized and often dispossessed by cyclical depressions, they were hounded and evicted by local authorities and waterfront developers. They were ridiculed and scorned as backward hold-outs against "civilization," yet at times they were admired and romanticized for the simple way they lived on the water's edge of modern consumer society. As in the case of roustabouts, Burman's affection for shantyboat migrants was wrapped in paternalism. In 1930s Hollywood musical comedy adaptations, they became relics of a premodern world, lovable foot-stomping moonshiners and river trash to entertain moviegoers seeking to escape the harsh realities of the Great Depression.[10]

In 1954, when Lois Lenski, an artist and author of children's literature, set out to write a novel about shantyboats from the perspective of a young white girl, she sought the advice of Anna and Harlan Hubbard. In 1944, the Hubbards built a shantyboat near Cincinnati in Brent, Kentucky, as well as a home of rocks, driftwood, and barn timbers in Payne Hollow, Trimble County. Harlan was a Kentucky-born, New York-educated writer, artist, and musician influenced by the writings of Henry David Thoreau. His wife, Anna Eikenhout, was an honors graduate of Ohio State University, former college teacher, librarian, and pianist. They set out down the Ohio on a five-year river adventure to New Orleans in search of a lifestyle that provided deeper meaning than the culture of consumption from which they fled. With their help and introductions, Lenski located the shantyboat family of Henry and Lou Story, still on the river at O'Donnell Bend near Luxora, Arkansas. For six weeks, Lenski saw them and their children on a daily basis and immersed herself in their life of johnboats, trotlines, and hoop-net fishing to gain material for her novel, Houseboat Girl, published in 1957. "Not the least of my pleasure in this family," she wrote, "was learning and sharing their river philosophy and sensing their happiness and satisfaction in the river as a way of life. By contrast with the increasing commercialization, conventionalism and standardization of our average American way of living, theirs seemed to offer a singularly fresh and wholesome approach, a nearness to the world of nature, and a sense of true freedom and independence of spirit not quite possible on land. I learned not only to know the Story family, but to love and admire them as well."[11]

Shantyboats have never disappeared from our nation's waterways or its culture. They have inspired songs from country artist Jimmy Murphy's "Shanty Boat Blues" (1951), Hal Blair and Louis Duhig's "Shanty Boat" (1957), recorded by Bonnie Guitar and by Glenell and Jonell, and Dickey Lee's "Patches" (1962), by Barry Mann and Larry Kolber, to "Shanty Boat" (2013) by The Tillers, a folk-oriented string band from Cincinnati. When The Tillers shot a video for their song, they paid tribute to the Hubbards by filming it in Payne Hollow. In 1948, seventeen-year-old Tambrey "Tammy" Tyree, who lived in a shantyboat colony near Natchez with her grandfather, a self-styled preacher and moonshiner, appeared as the central character in Mississippi writer Cid Ricketts Sumner's novel *Tammy Out of Time*. Universal-International Pictures latched onto Tammy and in 1957 produced a romantic comedy, *Tammy and the Bachelor*. Three additional *Tammy* movies and a television series followed. In 2017, Lisa Wingate's best-selling novel, *Before We Were Yours*, revived literary interest in lost shantyboat communities by featuring children stolen from a Memphis riverfront family and forced into the corrupt orphanage of the Tennessee Children's Home operated by Georgia Tann.

In the early 1970s, the vast Atchafalaya River Basin Swamp south of Baton Rouge drew childhood friends Gwen Carpenter Roland and Calvin Voisin back to the simpler lifestyle of their grandparents on a houseboat in Bayou Chene. For nearly a decade, the two young adventurers pursued a more ecologically sustainable lifestyle together on their houseboat. Novelist Cormac McCarthy, in a 1979 semiautobiographical account, introduced readers to the fictional character of Cornelius Suttree, who fled from wealth and privilege to take up shantyboat living on the Tennessee River in Knoxville. Writer Macon Fry, fleeing suburban life after graduate school in 1981, moved into a stilt house on the New Orleans *batture*, where he lives in one of twelve remaining riparian camps at Carrollton Bend. In 2014, Wes Modes, a graduate student, artist, and community organizer at the University of California, Santa Cruz, set out down the Upper Mississippi in a shantyboat he built mostly from reclaimed materials. The purpose was to create a digital archive of interviews with contemporary river dwellers to preserve lost histories of marginalized peoples on the waterways. In subsequent summers, he conducted research voyages on the Tennessee, Ohio, and other rivers in a creative, multidimensional interactive project to resurrect "invisibles" whose lives have been shaped by the river. His ongoing interdisciplinary arts project, "The Secret History of River People," illustrates that a meaningful, minimalist, and ecologically sustainable lifestyle on the waterways outside the nation's wasteful economic and cultural parameters has not lost its appeal.[12]

A similar dialectic that inspired "Roustabout Man" prompted W. J. Devine to write a romanticized poem for shantyboaters in June 1957. In heavily industrialized America, the elusive lure of simpler times on the river resonated with the poetic side of Devine as he looked back on a half-century punctuated by the rise of fascism, two catastrophic world wars, the Great Depression, and the Holocaust. Although he was a company sales executive, his love of river lore exerted a strong sentimental tug on his creative heartstrings. He was "captain" of the fictitious National Association of Shantyboaters, described as "a nonprofit, nonexistent organization of harried business and professional men seeking fanciful flight from the frustrations and frantic philosophies of a frenzied, crisis-ridden century in the pleasant contemplation of life on a shantyboat." His poem "Shanty Boat Man" helped to preserve shantyboats as sentimentalized cultural symbols of American waterways:

> Oh! for the life of a shanty boat man
> Who lives for each day without purpose or plan.
> For him not the worries, the trials and the cares—
> The pressure of business, the pitfalls and snares—
> No problem of profits, no quotas to meet—
> No meetings, no speeches, no deadlines to beat;
> Tied up to a tree at the edge of a stream,
> His is the carefree life most of us dream.
>
> Oh! for the life of a shanty boat man—
> Just doing the least that he possibly can—
> He floats down the current—the river's his life—
> A dog, and old stove, yeah! and maybe a wife
> Some canned goods, some books—a philosopher he—
> Content to live simply, just letting things be;
> Aspiring to nothing within his short span—
> Oh! for the life of a shanty boat man.[13]

Notes

Introduction

1. DeVoto, *Mark Twain's America*, 106. On the interrelationship of river culture and Twain's images of the river, see Smith, *Deep Water*.

2. *St. Louis Republican*, August 5, 1875, 8.

3. *The Whole Story Told*, 4. A copy of the pamphlet is in the St. Louis Mercantile Library.

4. Curtis, "On the Upper Mississippi," 28; Scharf, *History of St. Louis City and County*, vol. 2, 1039, 1041.

5. Bishop, *Four Months in a Sneak-Box*, 66; Burman, *Big River to Cross*, 66; Sweeney, "Burman," 135. Between 1929 and 1938, Burman published three novels on Mississippi River life—*Mississippi*, *Steamboat Round the Bend*, and *Blow for a Landing*—and the nonfiction *Big River to Cross*. He was the leading interpreter of shantyboat communities and roustabouts for American literary and film audiences. Marred by deep racism, his writings created sentimentalized, infantilized caricatures of both groups. Hollywood released two film adaptations of his novels.

6. *St. Joseph News-Press* (Missouri), May 14, 1896, 2.

7. *Republic*, June 2, 1903, 9; Burman, *Big River to Cross*, 75.

8. Quoted in *Post-Dispatch*, October 27, 1895, part four, 25. The quotes and information on Berry are in this article.

9. *Post-Dispatch*, October 27, 1895, part four, 25; Twain, *Life on the Mississippi*, 27. At the heart of Burman's novel, *Steamboat Round the Bend*, is the dream to obtain a pilot's license and own a steamboat.

10. Quoted in *Post-Dispatch*, October 27, 1895, 25.

11. *Post-Dispatch*, October 27, 1895, 25.

12. *Post-Dispatch*, April 14, 1889, 21.

13. Ibid.

14. Quoted in ibid.

15. *Globe-Democrat*, May 3, 1897, 10.

16. Hughes, *The Big Sea*, 55; Smith, *Deep Water*, 259. The poem appeared in *The Crisis* in June 1921.

17. Harris, *Mississippi Solo*, 1.

18. Brown, *Narrative of William W. Brown*. See Buchanan, *Black Life on the Mississippi*, for a study of antebellum Black life on the Mississippi.

19. Gibson, "The Old Route to New Orleans," 24. On roustabouts in popular culture, see Smith, *Deep Water*, 157–199.

20. Fishkin, *Lighting Out for the Territory*, 42–48; 1880 US Federal Census, Ward 2, District 0009, Hannibal, Marion County, Missouri. See also Jim's Journey: The Huck Finn Freedom Center, https://jimsjourney.org/hannibals-african-american-notables. The 1909 Hannibal city directory even listed Douglas as "Indian Jo."

21. Quoted in *Indianapolis Star* (Indiana), January 16, 1927, 72.

22. Burman, *Big River to Cross*, 76.

23. *Post-Dispatch*, May 31, 1896, 17.

24. Ibid.

25. Dreiser, *A Book About Myself*, 101.

26. *Alton Evening Telegraph*, July 20, 1897, 3. On New Orleans, see Fry, *They Called Us River Rats*, and Houck, *Down on the Batture*.

27. For a best-selling novel based on the corrupt Memphis adoption agency, see Wingate, *Before We Were Yours*.

1. A Tranquil and Unhurried Life

1. *St. Joseph News-Press* (Missouri), May 14, 1896, 2, and *Post-Dispatch*, April 14, 1889, 21.

2. Howells, *Literature and Life*, 317; Burman, *Big River to Cross*, 68–69; Johnson, *Highways and Byways*, 251; *Post-Dispatch*, December 14, 1902, 79; Illinois Board of Charities, *Annual Report*, vol. 21, 1911, 563–564.

3. Twain, *Life on the Mississippi*, 64–65.

4. Marshall, "The River People," 102.

5. Percy, *Lanterns on the Levee*, 16–17; Burman, *Big River to Cross*, 70.

6. Street, "Meridian, Vicksburg, and the River," 12.

7. Marshall, "The River People," 102.

8. Howells, *Literature and Life*, 317; Burman, *Big River to Cross*, 70.

9. Marshall, "The River People," 102.

10. Aylward, "Steamboating Through Dixie," 521.

11. Meacham, "Sketch Number 10," 83, Meacham Collection.

12. Thwaites, *Afloat on the Ohio*, 52–53.

13. Shaw quoted in *Post-Dispatch*, November 25, 1900, 1; Spears, "The Mississippi 'Tripper,'" 31; Burman, "Music on the Mississippi," 5.

14. Quoted in Hal C. Green, "Adventures of 'Tammany Hall' in a Raging Ohio River Flood," *Times-Democrat* (New Orleans), March 1, 1908, 33.

15. Quoted in *Times-Picayune* (New Orleans, Louisiana), May 3, 1895, 9.

16. Quoted in Johnson, *Highways and Byways*, 262.

17. Quoted in *Star and Times*, November 20, 1929, 1; Andrews, *My Daddy's Blues*, 28–29, 32.

18. Quoted in *Star and Times*, November 20, 1929, 1.

19. *Courier-Journal* (Louisville, Kentucky), January 9, 1888, 5.

20. Quoted in *Muscatine News-Tribune* (Iowa), January 13, 1905, 3.

21. *Clark v. People*, 1906; Andrews, *City of Dust*, 244–245. The legal case information refers to Pryor as Holland.

22. *Times-Democrat* (New Orleans, Louisiana), October 18, 1908, 34. Newspapers in New Orleans, Pittsburgh, and other river towns published articles Green wrote from his diary.

23. Quotes are in ibid.

24. *Times-Democrat* (New Orleans, Louisiana), July 5, 1908, 30.

25. *Times-Democrat* (New Orleans, Louisiana), June 7, 1908, 31, and May 31, 1908, 38; Wetherington, "Shantyboat Life," 77–84; Scott, "Shanty Boats on the Ohio."

26. Quoted by Green in *Times-Democrat* (New Orleans, Louisiana), July 5, 1908, 30.

27. Quoted by Green in ibid.

28. *Times-Democrat* (New Orleans, Louisiana), July 12, 1908, 30

29. Quoted in Wood, "The River Home," 6.

30. Burman, *Big River to Cross*, 75.

31. Quoted in Johnson, *Highways and Byways*, 257. Burman, *Big River to Cross*, 66–67, emphasizes that shantyboaters avoided census takers and disliked the federal government, but his conclusions were drawn from the Prohibition era.

32. Quoted in *Globe-Democrat*, April 27, 1901, 4.

33. *Chattanooga Daily Times* (Tennessee), September 30, 1898, 4; Burman, *Big River to Cross*, 79–80; Tait, "Shanty-boat Folks," 476; *Times-Democrat* (New Orleans, Louisiana), June 18, 1912, 4.

34. Percy, *Lanterns on the Levee*, 17; Savage, "The Romantic Fresh-Water Mussel Industry," 889–891; *Muscatine News-Tribune* (Iowa), September 10, 1902, 7; *The Dispatch* (Moline, Illinois), July 24, 1903, 2; Savage, "The Romantic Fresh-Water Mussel Industry," 889–891; Johnson, "Pearl Rush," 2–15; Claassen, "Washboards, Pigtoes, and Muckets," 1–150.

35. *Muscatine Journal* (Iowa), May 30, 1904, 5.

36. *Daily Times* (Davenport, Iowa), June 28, 1904, 6; *Davenport Morning Star* (Iowa), June 29, 1904, 8, and October 8, 1904, 1; *Quad-City Times* (Davenport, Iowa), July 7, 1904, 6; Iowa, Consecutive Register of Convicts, 1867–1970, Book No. 1, Men's Penitentiary, Fort Madison.

37. Quoted in *Daily Morning Journal and Courier* (New Haven, Connecticut), April 29, 1903, 6.

38. Quoted in ibid.

39. Mathews, *The Log of the Easy Way*, 139–140, 159–163.

40. "Wannigans on the Mississippi River, Minnesota," Anoka County Historical Society, accessed March 6, 2021, https://collection.mndigital.org/catalog/ach:50; *New York Sun*, October 11, 1896, 10. On the life and labor of swampers in the Louisiana logging industry, see also *Times-Picayune* (New Orleans, Louisiana), February 28, 1892, 19.

41. Ibid.

42. *Globe-Democrat*, November 13, 1900, 5; *Courier-Journal* (Louisville, Kentucky), January 9, 1888, 5; Thwaites, *Afloat on the Ohio*, 55.

43. Spears, "'Beating' Prohibition on the Mississippi," 27.

44. Ibid.; *Jackson Daily News* (Mississippi), November 22, 1909, 8; *Grenada Sentinel* (Mississippi), March 13, 1897, 3.

45. Mathews, *Log of the Easy Way*, 155, 188; *Republic*, April 28, 1901, 43; McCoyer, "'Rough Mens' in 'the Toughest Places I Ever Seen,'" 57–80.

46. *Republic*, April 28, 1901, 43; *McComb City Enterprise* (Mississippi), December 27, 1900, 2; *Vicksburg Evening Post* (Mississippi), December 22, 1900, 4; *Westville News* (Mississippi), January 10, 1901, 6; *Vicksburg Evening Post* (Mississippi), December 22, 1900, 4; Mathews, *Log of the Easy Way*, 189.

47. Going, "The Shanty Boat People," 233; *Courier-Journal* (Louisville, Kentucky), September 22, 1900, 9; Black Diamond Coal Company, *The Black Diamond*, October 12, 1901, 524.

48. Quoted in *Times-Democrat* (New Orleans, Louisiana), March 1, 1908, 33; Burman, *Mississippi*.

49. Quoted in *Daily State Ledger* (Jackson, Mississippi), August 22, 1892, 3.

50. *Edwardsville Intelligencer*, April 12, 1893, 8.

51. *Times-Picayune* (New Orleans, Louisiana), August 4, 1895, 24. In 1938, the Federal Writers' Project's *Guide to New Orleans*, referred to the settlement as the "Depression Colony" (280).

52. I have relied on the following 1896 New Orleans newspapers for accounts of the double murder: *Times-Democrat* (New Orleans, Louisiana), January 13, 1; January 14, 4; January 16, 3; and *Times Picayune*, January 13, 8; January 14, 1; January 16, 1, 3; January 17, 12. See also Fry, *They Called Us River Rats*, 68–70.

53. *Times-Picayune* (New Orleans, Louisiana), January 13, 1896, 8.

54. *Times-Picayune* (New Orleans, Louisiana), April 26, 1896, 9.

55. *Times-Democrat* (New Orleans, Louisiana), April 26, 1896, 3, and August 17, 1896, 3. On LaFrance's reputation, career, and death, see *Times-Picayune* (New Orleans, Louisiana), December 28, 1894, 8; *Plaquemines Protector* (Pointe de la Hache, Louisiana), March 2, 1895, 2, and June 11, 1898, 3.

56. Quoted in Illinois Board of Charities, Biennial Report, 1911, 564.

57. Quoted in *Times-Democrat* (New Orleans, Louisiana), November 8, 1900, 9.

58. Ibid.

59. Ibid.

2. Wealth Is Not His God

1. *Globe-Democrat*, May 19, 1907, 73; "Annual Report of the Harbor and Wharf Commissioner," 1880, 271; Municipal Code of St. Louis, 291; *Report of the Commissioner of Corporations*, 215.

2. *Des Moines Register* (Iowa), December 6, 1908, 36; "Annual Report of the Harbor and Wharf Commissioner," 1897, 649.

3. King, *Southern States*, 221.

4. *Republican*, August 5, 1875, 8.

5. Twain, *Life on the Mississippi*, 136.

6. Ibid., 137.

7. Civic League of St. Louis, "Housing Conditions," 20.

8. *Report of the Commissioner of Corporations*, 216.

9. "Annual Report of the Harbor and Wharf Commissioner," 1882, 261. On the city lawsuits, see "Annual Report of the Harbor and Wharf Commissioner," 1886, 367.

10. *Globe-Democrat*, August 23, 1884, 10.

11. *Post-Dispatch*, November 14, 1885, 12.

12. Quoted in ibid; Death of Christian Anderson, October 31, 1898, St. Louis, Missouri, Death Records, 1850–1902.

13. *Swearingen v. The City of St. Louis, et al.*, transcript record, 8, 11–13.

14. Ibid., 10, 11.

15. Ibid., 97.

16. Ibid., 117–119; *Post-Dispatch*, May 10, 1896, 25; "Annual Report of the Harbor and Wharf Commissioner," 706.

17. *Globe-Democrat*, May 30, 1887, 8; *Post-Dispatch*, April 15, 1894, 31.

18. *Post-Dispatch*, September 15, 1901, 43.

19. Ibid.; *Post-Dispatch* January 12, 1896, 23.

20. *Post-Dispatch*, April 15, 1894, 31, and June 12, 1895, 1.

21. *Post-Dispatch*, April 15, 1894, 31.

22. Ibid.

23. *Post-Dispatch*, February 3, 1898, 15.

24. Quoted in *Post-Dispatch*, April 15, 1894, 31.

25. *Post-Dispatch*, June 21, 1896, 25; Johnson, *The Broken Heart of America*, 252–253.

26. Quoted in *Post-Dispatch*, October 30, 1887, 5.

27. *Post-Dispatch*, October 30, 1887, 5.

28. Quoted in ibid.; *Report of the Commissioner of Corporations*, 217.

29. *Globe-Democrat*, May 19, 1882, 8, and *Post-Dispatch*, May 30, 1882, 1.

30. *Globe-Democrat*, April 3, 1892, 27.

31. *Post-Dispatch*, September 3, 1899, 12

32. *Post-Dispatch*, March 31, 1876, 4; *Globe-Democrat*, May 13, 1888, 28.

33. *Post-Dispatch*, May 2, 1891, 6.

34. "Annual Report of the Health Commissioner," 1897, 128.

35. *Post-Dispatch*, July 21, 1898, 5.

36. Online Missouri Coroner's Inquest Database, City of St. Louis, Office of the Coroner Inquests, 1845–1900, case number 346, James Clark, July 21, 1898; *Post-Dispatch*, July 25, 1898, 2.

37. *Post-Dispatch*, March 26, 1905, 62.

38. *Post-Dispatch*, November 2, 1887, 2, and March 19, 1902, 7; *Globe-Democrat*, September 30, 1884, 8; *Biennial Report of the Attorney General of the State of Illinois*, 988–990.

39. Quoted in *Post-Dispatch*, March 7, 1888, 4.

40. 1900 US Federal Census, District 0069, Venice, Madison County, Illinois; *Republic*, December 1, 1903, 7; *Post-Dispatch*, December 27, 1903, 42, and July 27, 1905, 11.

41. *Post-Dispatch*, December 27, 1903, 42; October 27, 1895, 25; July 27, 1905, 11.

42. *Globe-Democrat*, May 19, 1907, 73. For a regional study of violence in the era, see Hutton, *Bloody Breathitt*, and "Eureka!: Law and Order for Sale in Gilded Age Appalachia," in Forret and Baker, eds., *Southern Scoundrels*, 220–234.

43. *Post-Dispatch*, December 30, 1894, 1, January 7, 1895, 1, and November 18, 1895, 1; *Cincinnati Enquirer* (Ohio), January 23, 1895, 5; *Alton Evening Telegraph*, January 3, 1895, 10; Marriage of Lizzie Pack and John Lakey, August 17, 1886, Madison County, Illinois, U.S., Marriage Index, 1860–1920; *Globe-Democrat*, January 1, 1895, 7, and January 23, 1895, 8.

44. *Globe-Democrat*, January 1, 1895, 7; *Post-Dispatch*, December 30, 1894, 2, and November 18, 1895, 1.

45. *Post-Dispatch*, January 3, 1895, 1; January 7, 1895, 1; and November 21, 1895, 14; *Globe-Democrat*, December 29, 1894, 6.

46. *Post-Dispatch*, January 6, 1895, 9; November 27, 1895, 7; June 25, 1896, 12; October 2, 1924, 3; October 24, 1924, 3.

47. *Post-Dispatch*, November 25, 1900, 1.

3. The Roughest Life There Is

1. Like *Big River to Cross*, 41–63, Burman's novels and nonfiction writings are filled with racist stereotypes of roustabouts. On roustabouts in popular culture, see Smith, *Deep Water*, 161–224. Photographs of roustabouts ducking for coins in a pan of white flour aboard the *Golden Eagle* in 1935 are in box 1, folder 3, Ferris Research Notes Collection.

2. Twain, "Old Times on the Mississippi, VI," 721.

3. Way, *Log of the Betsy Ann*, 24.

4. Peter Corn Interview, 7–8; *Post-Dispatch*, December 4, 1895, 1.

5. *Post-Dispatch*, August 3, 1878, 4, and November 17, 1901, 48; *Compendium of the Tenth Census*, 1284; Merrick, *Old Times on the Upper Mississippi*, 250; Stepenoff, *Working the Mississippi*, 53–54; Smith, "Report on the River-Boatmen of the Lower Mississippi," 145; Wyman, "Hygiene of the Steamboats on the Ohio Rivers," 265–266; *Globe-Democrat*, July 28, 1887, 12; Cooley, "The Mississippi Roustabout," 290.

6. Quoted in *Post-Dispatch*, October 225, 1887, 3; Smith, "Report on the River-Boatmen," 144.

7. *Republican*, August 5, 1875, 8; *Post-Dispatch*, April 12, 1882, 8.

8. See *Post-Dispatch*, December 9, 1878, 2; August 30, 1882, 5; October 25, 1887, 3.

9. Quoted in *Post-Dispatch*, August 21, 1904, 47. See also *Post-Dispatch*, November 17, 1901, 48, and Kenney, *Jazz on the River*, 96.

10. Handy, *Father of the Blues*, 27, 28.

11. *Post-Dispatch*, October 20, 1907, 27.

12. Curtis, "On the Upper Mississippi," 27.

13. Gardener quoted in *Post-Dispatch*, August 30, 1882, 5; *Republican*, August 5, 1875, 8; *Post-Dispatch*, August 3, 1878, 4; Smith, "Report on the River-Boatmen," 144.

14. Ben Lawson interview, 176–177; "Rousters Pay," box 1, folder 3, April 1, 1922, Ferris Research Collection Notes.

15. Kenney, *Jazz on the River*, 96; *Post-Dispatch*, April 30, 1908, 24.

16. Zang, "Steaming on the Mississippi," 46; *Post-Dispatch*, November 17, 1901, 48, and April 30, 1908, 24.

17. White interview and memoir, 7–8; Knoepfle, "Some Notes on the Men of the Inland Rivers," 57; Wyman, "Hygiene of the Steamboats," 273; Cooley, *The Captain of the Amaryllis*, 61–62; *Post-Dispatch*, August 3, 1878, 4; *Republican*, August 5, 1875, 8; *Times-Democrat* (New Orleans, Louisiana), October 24, 1901, 3.

18. Burman, *Big River to Cross*, 43; Cooley, "The Mississippi Roustabout," 293–294; Stepenoff, *Working the Mississippi*, 59.

19. Wyman, "Hygiene of Steamboats," 274; Smith, "Report on the River-Boatmen," 144.

20. White interview and memoir, 8, and Coomer, interview and memoir, 4–5; *Moline Dispatch*, January 19, 1911, 6.

21. Heckman's recollection appeared in the *Waterways Journal*, August 30, 1952. A clipping is in box 1, folder 3, Ferris Research Collection Notes.

22. *Republican*, August 5, 1875, 8. On roustabouts in New Orleans, see Arnesen, *Waterfront Workers of New Orleans*, 103–106.

23. Roberts, *Adrift in America*, 216. On the role of a "sailor man," see Zang, "Steaming on the Mississippi," 47.

24. "The Steamboat Rouster," Notes from the *Waterways Journal*, May 20, 1893, 9, f. 6, Waterways Journal Collection.

25. Quoted in *Post-Dispatch*, October 27, 1887, 3.

26. Curtis, "On the Upper Mississippi," 26.

27. Wyman, "Hygiene of the Steamboats on the Ohio River," 268. See also "Cruelty Aboard Ship," 3.

28. Wyman, "Hygiene of the Steamboats," 269; *Courier-Journal* (Louisville, Kentucky), November 19, 1881, 12; *Daily Register* (Wheeling, West Virginia), April 18, 1882, 4.

29. *Globe-Democrat*, June 7, 1895, 12.

30. Gibson, "The Old Route to New Orleans," 25.

31. Arnold, *Under Southern Skies*, 73–74; *Public Ledger* (Memphis, Tennessee), August 26, 1887, 3, and *Memphis Commercial* (Tennessee), November 21, 1892, 5.

32. Arnold, *Under Southern Skies*, 85.

33. Quoted in *Post-Dispatch*, August 24, 1904, 47.

34. *Riley v. Allen and others*; *Memphis Daily Appeal*, February 22, 1885,4; *Jenkins v. "The Elenore,"* 447–448; "The T.P. Leathers," 20–23; Wyman, "Hygiene of the Steamboats," 268–269; Buchanan, *Black Life on the Mississippi*, 161. For an application of the "assumed risk" doctrine, see "Red River Line v. Smith et al.," 520–525.

35. *Post-Dispatch*, March 28, 1890, 8; *Jones v. The St. Louis, Naples and Peoria Packet Company*.

36. Wyman, "Hygiene of the Steamboats," 270; 1890 Veterans Schedules of the U.S. Federal Census, Hannibal, Marion County, Missouri.

37. Quoted in Wyman., "Hygiene of the Steamboats," 271.

38. Quoted in ibid., 271.

39. Quoted in *Post-Dispatch*, November 17, 1901, 48.

40. Arnold interview.

41. Knoepfle, "Some Notes on the Men of the Inland Rivers," 58.

42. *Post-Dispatch*, November 17, 1901, 48; Smith, "Report on the River-Boatmen," 145; *Globe-Democrat*, December 3, 1886, 8.

43. *Post-Dispatch*, November 17, 1901, 48.; *Globe-Democrat*, August 9, 1892, 3; Stepenoff, *Working the Mississippi*, 51–61.

44. Coomer, interview and memoir, 8. The other quote is in Knoepfle, "Some Notes on the Men of the Inland Rivers," 59.

45. *Post-Dispatch*, July 16, 1881, 5; July 28, 1881, 8, and December 17, 1883, 7; *Globe-Democrat*, July 17, 1881, 8, and November 19, 1881, 10; Emmett Jones, register no. 4055, Missouri State Penitentiary Database.

46. *Post-Dispatch*, August 13, 1895, 1; *Globe-Democrat*, August 14, 1895, 12, and August 21, 1895, 9.

47. *Post-Dispatch*, August 13, 1895, 1; *Globe-Democrat*, August 21, 1895, 9.

48. *Vicksburg Herald,* September 14, 1905, 2; Snook, "Echoes on the River," 71–72.

49. Cooley, "The Mississippi Roustabout," 293; *Davenport Morning Star,* March 13, 1904, 5; Mack Davis interview and memoir. On the Leyhe brothers and the Eagle Packet Company, see Stepenoff, *Working the Mississippi,* 13–20.

50. *Globe-Democrat,* July 17, 1907, 1; Stepenoff, *Working the Mississippi,* 16.

51. *Globe-Democrat,* July 16, 1907, 1; Stepenoff, *Working the Mississippi,* 16; *Post-Dispatch,* July 17, 1907, 4.

52. Quoted in Kruger, *The St. Louis Commune of 1877,* 208.

53. *Globe-Democrat,* July 27, 1877, 5; *Post-Dispatch,* July 26, 1877, 1, and November 17, 1901, 48; Roediger, "'Not Only the Ruling Classes to Overcome, but Also the So-Called Mob,'" 213–2 39. The best treatment of the strike and the role of international communist influences is Kruger, *The St. Louis Commune of 1877.*

54. Foner, *History of the Labor Movement in the United States,* 2:197; Mandel, "Samuel Gompers and the Negro Workers," 43–44.

55. *Post-Dispatch,* March 31, 1892, 4; and May 1, 1892, 8; Missouri Bureau of Labor Statistics, "Fourteenth Annual Report," 22; Samuel Gompers to William P. Newell, Sec., Marine Engineers Pro. Union No. 5622, March 28, 1892, vol. 7, reel 6, Gompers Letterbooks.

56. *Post-Dispatch,* March 31, 1892, 4; Missouri Bureau of Labor Statistics, "Fourteenth Annual Report," 25.

57. *Post-Dispatch,* March 31, 1892, 4.

58. Ibid.

59. *Post-Dispatch,* April 7, 1892, 12; *Globe-Democrat,* April 7, 1892, 12. On Mason, see Scharf, *History of St. Louis City and County,* 1:718–719; and Hyde and Conard, eds., *Encyclopedia of the History of St. Louis,* 1375–1376.

60. *Post-Dispatch,* April 7, 1892, 12; *Globe-Democrat,* April 7, 1892, 12.

61. *Post-Dispatch,* April 8, 1892, 4, and May 21, 1892, 8; *Globe-Democrat,* June 15, 1892, 12.

62. Gompers to Norton, April 28, and May 3, 16, 17, 1892, vol. 7, reel 6, Gompers Letterbooks. Only recently had Gompers commissioned John M. Callaghan, a white cotton screwman, as a general organizer in New Orleans. Gompers urged Norton to meet with Callaghan and to limit his own organizing efforts to workers in the marine services, respectful of biracial unionism. On New Orleans roustabouts and the Inland Seamen's Union in the 1892 strike, see Arnesen, *Waterfront Workers of New Orleans,* 103–106.

63. Engineer quoted in *Post-Dispatch,* June 3, 1892, 2; Missouri Bureau of Labor Statistics, "Fourteenth Annual Report," 23; Gompers to Norton, April 28, May 3, 16, 17, and June 3, 1892, vol. 7, reel 6, Gompers Letterbooks. To reassure Norton that the AFL valued his efforts, Gompers extended his commission as an organizer until June 1, 1893.

64. *Globe-Democrat,* July 2, 1892, 8, and August 11, 1892, 9.

65. *Post-Dispatch,* July 31, 1892, 12; *Globe-Democrat,* July 28, 1892, 9; Gompers to Norton, September 7, 1892, vol. 7, reel 6, Gompers Letterbooks.

66. Quoted in *Macon Republican* (Missouri), April 3, 1909, 1.

67. *Post-Dispatch,* April 30, 1908, 24; *People's Weekly Tribune* (Birmingham, Alabama), March 17, 1900, 2; *Times-Democrat* (New Orleans, Louisiana), April 30, 1900, 3; and *Courier-Journal* (Louisville, Kentucky), October 20, 1906, 4.

68. Thompson, "Time, Work-Discipline, and Industrial Capitalism," 56–97; Knoepfle, "Some Notes on the Men of the Inland Rivers," 58. Genovese, *Roll, Jordan, Roll,* applied Thompson's pioneering conceptual framework to the study of American slavery.

69. Quoted in *Post-Dispatch,* November 17, 1901, 48. See also *Post-Dispatch,* October 25, 1887, 3, and July 17, 1907, 4; Smith, "Report on the River-Boatmen," 144.

4. The River Gives Up Its Dead Slowly

1. Quoted in Mathews, *Log of the Easy Way,* 158.

2. Julian Street, "Meridian, Vicksburg, and the River," *Collier's,* August 18, 1917, 12.

3. Kritzler and Neely quoted in *Post-Dispatch,* November 25, 1900, 1; Hendrick, "Following Wild Fowl in a Shantyboat," 482–486.

4. Quoted in *Post-Dispatch,* November 25, 1900, 1.

5. King, *Southern States,* 232.

6. *Republic,* February 6, 1903, 1; *Globe-Democrat,* February 28, 1905, 1.

7. *Nebraska State Journal* (Lincoln), January 1, 1910, 1; *Globe-Democrat,* January 1, 1910, 1, and January 14, 1910, 1; *Star and Times,* January 14, 1910, 9; *Post-Dispatch,* January 13, 1910, 4.

8. Quoted in *Indianapolis Star,* January 16, 1927, 72.

9. *Globe-Democrat,* December 30, 1879, 6.

10. *Post-Dispatch,* January 13, 1903, 1.

11. *St. Joseph Gazette* (Missouri), December 10, 1909, 4.

12. *Post-Dispatch,* January 6, 1924, 1.

13. *Post-Dispatch,* January 27, 1898, 9.

14. Quoted in *Post-Dispatch,* December 12, 1904, 5.

15. *Post-Dispatch,* December 19, 1900, 1.

16. *Paducah Sun* (Kentucky), February 2, 1902, 1.

17. *Post-Dispatch,* May 15, 1892, 10.

18. *Post-Dispatch,* December 20, 1895, 7.

19. *Globe-Democrat,* December 21, 1895, 8; *Post-Dispatch,* December 20, 1895, 7.

20. *Globe-Democrat,* January 5, 1897, 7.

21. *Globe-Democrat,* April 5, 1897, 5.

22. Quoted in ibid.

23. *Globe-Democrat,* April 5, 1897, 5.

24. *Globe-Democrat,* May 3, 1897, 10.

25. *Globe-Democrat,* May 16, 1892, 2.

26. *Globe-Democrat,* March 29, 1898, 16.

27. *Post-Dispatch,* July 4, 1902, 5.

28. Quoted in *Republic,* June 2, 1903, 9.

29. *Globe-Democrat,* June 6, 1903, 2; *Laclede County Sentinel* (Lebanon, Missouri), June 12, 1903, 3.

30. *Post-Dispatch,* August 20, 1904, 2.

31. *Post-Dispatch,* July 12, 1904, 3; Hugh Arthur Preller, Certificate of Birth, November 28,

1910, Augusta, Woodruff County, Arkansas, Birth Certificates, 1914–1917; Hugo Arthur Preller, Certificate of Death, July 20, 1950, Augusta, Woodruff County, Arkansas, Death Certificates, 1914–1969.

32. Dains, "The St. Louis Tornado of 1896," 431–450; Ciampoli, "The St. Louis Tornado of 1896," 24–31; "Annual Report of the Harbor and Wharf Commissioner," 1897, 643.

33. *Kansas City Star* (Missouri), June 3, 1896, 3; *Post-Dispatch*, June 2, 1896, 10.

34. Curzon, comp. and ed., *The Great Cyclone at St. Louis*, 377–379.

35. *Globe-Democrat*, July 28, 1892, 9; *Post-Dispatch*, June 21, 1896, 25.

36. Quoted in *Post-Dispatch*, July 11, 1897, 22.

37. *Weekly Democrat* (Natchez, Mississippi), January 30, 1895, 4.

38. *Post-Dispatch*, August 31, 1906, 1–2.

39. *Globe-Democrat*, September 2, 1909, 4.

40. Percy, *Lanterns on the Levee*, 251–252.

41. Burman, *Big River to Cross*, 88–91.

5. The Pride of St. Louis

1. *Post-Dispatch*, December 25, 1897, 7; Andrews, "'Little Oklahoma,'" 17–25.

2. Quoted in *Post-Dispatch*, December 25, 1897, 7.

3. *Post-Dispatch*, December 25, 1897, 7.

4. 1880 US Federal Census, City of St. Louis, District 0030, St. Louis, Missouri; Marriage of Louis Seybt and Maria Wender, July 2, 1882, St. Clair County, Illinois, U.S., Marriage Index, 1860–1920.

5. Hall, *The Great Strike on the "Q,"* 26.

6. *Post-Dispatch*, February 4, 1888; February 9, 1888, 4; March 23, 1887, 4.

7. *Post-Dispatch*, April 15, 1894, 31; November 5, 1893, 3; November 7, 1893, 7; November 20, 1893, 2; November 24, 1893, 10.

8. Quoted in *Post-Dispatch*, February 13, 1898, 15. On the rejection of Seibt's license renewal, see *Post-Dispatch*, April 15, 1894, 31.

9. *Post-Dispatch*, June 10, 1894, 25; June 11, 1894, 2; June 13, 1894, 1; August 5, 1894, 19; February 13, 1898, 15.

10. Quoted in *Post-Dispatch*, February 13, 1898, 15.

11. *Post-Dispatch*, June 12, 1895, 1; September 27, 1895, 3; October 27, 1895, 25; December 6, 1896, 24; *Republic*, September 19, 1903, 14.

12. *Post-Dispatch*, February 13, 1898, 15.

13. *Post-Dispatch*, November 16, 1897, 2, and November 30, 1897, 4.

14. *Post-Dispatch*, September 24, 1897, 3, and February 13, 1898, 15.

15. *Post-Dispatch*, November 30, 1897, 4.

16. Seibt quoted in *Post-Dispatch*, December 18, 1897, 3; February 1, 1898, 2.

17. *Waterways Journal*, April 16, 1898, 10.

18. *Post-Dispatch*, November 17, 1897, 7, and November 16, 1897, 2.

19. Quoted in *Post-Dispatch*, November 17, 1897, 7.

20. Ibid.

21. Ibid.

22. Quoted in *Post-Dispatch*, February 13, 1898, 15.

23. *Post-Dispatch*, February 19, 1898, 3; *Globe-Democrat*, February 19, 1898, 7, and February 20, 1898, 2.

24. *Post-Dispatch*, December 27, 1897, 8. Quote is in *Post-Dispatch*, February 1, 1898, 2.

25. Seibt quoted in *Post-Dispatch*, February 23, 1898, 7; *Waterways Journal*, April 16, 1898, 10.

26. *Post-Dispatch*, November 17, 1897, 7, and January 1, 1905, 20; *Republic*, August 3, 1900, 5.

27. *Waterways Journal*, July 23, 1898, 7.

28. *Waterways Journal*, October 15, 1898, 10; October 22, 1898, 10, March 4, 1899, 5; April 29, 1899, 7; *Globe-Democrat*, March 26, 1899, 14; May 10, 1899, 14; May 11, 1899, 1; May 13, 1899, 4.

29. *Globe-Democrat*, June 29, 1900, 9; *Republic*, June 29, 1900, 4.

30. *Republic*, August 3, 1900, 5, and August 8, 1900, 5; *Post-Dispatch*, August 7, 7, and December 7, 1900, 5.

31. *Post-Dispatch*, December 7, 1900, 5; Death Certificate of Louis Seibt, August 6, 1926, Missouri Death Certificates, 1910−1967; Emma Schreiner, October 26, 1906, Missouri Death Records, City of St. Louis, 1850−1931.

32. *Post-Dispatch*, August 20, 1900, 2.

33. *Post-Dispatch*, August 9, 1900, 4.

34. 1870 US Federal Census, Emporia, Ward 3, Lyon County, Kansas; 1880 US Federal Census, City of St. Louis, Missouri; *Globe-Democrat*, August 7, 1897, 16, and January 9, 1928, 26; *Republic*, December 22, 1900, 9; *Burlington Patriot* (Kansas), October 16, 1873, 4; Marriage of Gustave Steimel and Ora Doyle, December 21, 1912, St. Charles County, Missouri, U.S., Marriage Records, 1805−2002; 1920 US Federal Census, City of St. Louis, Ward 2, District 0033, St. Louis, Missouri; Ora Viola Steimel, Certificate of Death, St. Louis, May 14, 1919, and Gustave Steimel, Certificate of Death, St. Louis, January 7, 1928, Missouri Death Certificates, 1910−1970.

35. 1900 US Federal Census, City of St. Louis, Ward 2, District 0025, St. Louis, Missouri; *Republic*, December 22, 1900, 9.

36. Quoted in *Post-Dispatch*, December 28, 1900, 2.

37. *Republic*, August 3, 1901, 6.

38. *Post-Dispatch*, October 18, 1906, 13.

39. Quoted in ibid.

40. *Post-Dispatch*, February 13, 1907, 1.

41. Quoted in ibid.

42. *Post-Dispatch*, February 14, 1907, 13; *Globe-Democrat*, February 14, 1907, 5.

43. *Post-Dispatch*, December 14, 1902, 79.

6. Ain't Got No Place to Lay My Haid

1. Kenney, *Jazz on the River*, 10, 51−52; *Post-Dispatch*, August 21, 1904, 47; White memoir and interview by John Knoepfle, 8; "The Jolly Roustabout," August 26, 1899, 12, Notes from the *Waterways Journal*. On coonjine, roustabouts' work songs, and folklore, see Eskew, Coonjine in

Manhattan and "Folklore Anecdotes Draft 2," United States Works Progress Administration of Louisiana, Ouachita Parish Public Library.

2. *Republican,* August 5, 1875, 8.

3. Curtis, "On the Upper Mississippi," 27.

4. The song's origins remain unclear. See Paul Oliver, "Looking for 'The Bully': An Enquiry into a Song and Its Story," in Springer, ed., *Nobody Knows Where the Blues Come From,* 108–125; Smith, *Deep Water,* 218–221; Handy, *Father of the Blues,* 118–119; Kenney, *Jazz on the River,* 97; lyrics in Ammen, *May Irwin,* 94–95.

5. Quoted in *Spokane Chronicle,* July 22, 1899, 6; Kenney, *Jazz on the River,* 97.

6. *Globe-Democrat,* December 26, 1895, 7; *Post-Dispatch,* December 27, 1895, 3.

7. Odum, "Folk-Song and Folk-Poetry," 288–289.

8. McHenry, "The Baddest Man in Town"; Eberhart, "Stack Lee," 1–70; Polenberg, *Hear My Sad Story,* 28–37; Levine, *Black Culture and Black Consciousness,* 413; Mack, *Fictional Blues,* 25–66; Brown, *Stagolee Shot Billy.* Memphis also claimed birthrights to the song, based on the hard-living, notorious womanizing exploits of riverboat captain Samuel Stack Lee, son of James Lee, founder of the Lee Line of steamers. The Memphis connection remains mere speculation perpetuated by John and Alan Lomax and by McIlwaine, *Memphis,* 199–200. On Memphis's Samuel Stack Lee, see Stepenoff, *Working the Mississippi,* 118–119.

9. *Palladium,* January 16, 1904, 8; Kenney, *Jazz on the River,* 98.

10. Dowden-White, *Groping toward Democracy,* 29–30.

11. Lyrics in *Post-Dispatch,* August 3, 1878, 4; Burman, *Big River to Cross,* 53–55.

12. King, *Southern States,* 258; Buchanan, *Black Life on the Mississippi,* 77.

13. *Post-Dispatch,* August 21, 1904, 47; Hetherington, "Lost Channels," 447–458; *Macon Chronicle-Herald* (Missouri), August 10, 1943, 6.

14. Bronner, ed., *Lafcadio Hearn's America,* 37–53.

15. Ibid., 41–42.

16. Handy, *Father of the Blues,* 27.

17. Ibid., 28.

18. Ibid., 142.

19. Ibid., 121; Polenberg, *Hear My Sad Story,* 9–17.

20. Pennell, "The Trip of the 'Mark Twain,'" 400.

21. The song is from a set of *Roustabout Songs* collected by Mary Wheeler, a Kentucky music educator who interviewed former roustabouts in Paducah, where she was born and raised. In 1946, singer Conrad Thibault and Decca Records released "Roustabout Songs: A Collection of Ohio River Valley Songs," using words and melodies collected by Wheeler, arranged by William J. Reddick, and with an introduction by Irvin S. Cobb. It was published in New York by the Remick Music Corporation. Wheeler also published *Kentucky Mountain Folksongs* (1937) and *Steamboatin' Days.* See Bradley, "Mary Wheeler," 53–67.

22. Snook, "Echoes on the River," 72; Caffery, *The 1934 Lomax Recordings,* 223–224. "Stavin' Chain" was among the songs sung by river roustabouts interviewed by Mary Wheeler in the 1930s. On the elusive search for "Stavin' Chain" in the history of the blues, see Richard A. Noblett's four-part series, "Stavin' Chain: A Study of a Folk Hero," in *Blues Unlimited* 130 (May–August 1978): 31–33; 134 (March–June 1979): 14–17; 139 (autumn 1980): 31–33; and 142 (summer 1982): 24–26.

23. "Notes by Alan Lomax," Alan Lomax Collection, Roustabout Songs, 1946.

24. Burman, "Music on the Mississippi," 4.

25. Kenney, *Jazz on the River*, 16–21; Chevan, "Riverboat Music," 153–154, 159.

26. Kenney, *Jazz on the River*, 44–50; *Globe-Democrat*, July 22, 1945, 31; Chevan, "Riverboat Music," 159–160.

27. Chevan, "Riverboat Music," 165; Kenney, *Jazz on the River*, chapter 2. Marable fired Armstrong for failing to show up at morning classes. Dodds recalled that he and Armstrong handed in letters of resignation at the same time in September 1921. See "Baby Dodds' Story: As Told to Larry Gara," 156.

28. Kenney, *Jazz on the River*, 30.

29. "Baby Dodds' Story," 144. See also Chevan, "Riverboat Music," 157–158.

30. Danny Barker quoted in Shapiro and Hentoff, eds., *Hear Me Talkin' to Ya*, 75. New Orleans pianist and singer Jelly Roll Morton also worked on the city's docks, where he heard the singing and rhythmic shuffling of roustabouts on the gangplanks. See Rosenberg, *New Orleans Dockworkers*, 48.

31. *Ralls County Record* (New London, Missouri), October 9, 1925, 4.

32. "Baby Dodds' Story," 152. See also Kenney, *Jazz on the River*, 29–30.

33. *Post-Dispatch*, November 17, 1897, 7, and January 1, 1905, 20; *Republic*, August 3, 1900, 5; Henry Beeman, July 16, 1836, New York, Index to Petitions for Naturalization filed in New York City, 1792–1989; 1850 US Federal Census, Ashford, Cattaraugus County, New York; 1870 US Federal Census, Richfield, Adams County, Wisconsin; 1880 US Federal Census, City of St. Louis, District 0131, St. Louis County, Missouri; 1880 US Federal Census, Dyersburg, District 4, Dyer County, Tennessee; Hannah Beeman, January 3, 1889, City of St. Louis, Missouri Death Records, 1850–1931; 1880 US Federal Census, Dyersburg, District 4, Dyer County, Tennessee; *Des Moines Register*, December 6, 1908, 36.

34. 1900 US Federal Census, Venice, District 0069, Madison County, Illinois.

35. *Post-Dispatch*, April 15, 1894, 31.

36. *Post-Dispatch*, January 1, 1905, 20.

37. Quoted in Ibid.

38. *Edwardsville Intelligencer*, June 23, 1908, 1; *Perry County Advocate* (Pinckneyville, Illinois), July 10, 1908, 2. John F. Beeman, death record, November 20, 1908, Missouri Death Records, City of St. Louis, 1850–1931; St. Louis City Directory, 1908, U.S. City Directories, 1822–1995.

39. *Post-Dispatch*, December 24, 1901, 1; and December 25, 1901, 1.

40. William B. Worthen, https://encyclopediaofarkansas.net/entries/arkansas-traveler-505/.

41. Burman, "Music on the Mississippi," 5; *Post-Dispatch*, March 4, 1956, 34.

42. Burman, *Mississippi*, 94; *Democrat-Argus* (Caruthersville), June 26, 1903, 5; *Post-Dispatch*, February 6, 1888, 8.

43. *Globe-Democrat*, April 3, 1892, 27.

44. Lyrics in *Alton Evening Telegraph*, February 22, 1916, 2; Pearson, "The Philosophy and Art of Dancing," 611–616. On traditional fiddle music in Missouri, see Marshall, *Play Me Something Quick and Devilish*. Jamison, *Hoedowns, Reels, and Frolics*, examines the interconnected European, African American, and Native American roots of Appalachian dance.

45. *Post-Dispatch*, July 31, 1898, 23.

46. Quoted in ibid.

47. *Post-Dispatch,* July 31, 1898, 23.

48. Quoted in ibid.

49. Quoted in ibid.

50. Quoted in ibid.

51. Quoted in *Post-Dispatch,* September 4, 1898, 21.

52. Quoted in *Post-Dispatch,* August 7, 1898, 22.

53. Quoted in ibid.

54. *Republic,* August 8, 1898, 5; *Post-Dispatch,* August 8, 1898, 8; *Globe-Democrat,* August 8, 1898, 5.

55. *Post-Dispatch,* August 21, 1898, 16.

56. *Post-Dispatch,* August 21, 1898, 16; Baldwin, "The Cakewalk," 205–218; Brown, *Babylon Girls,* 128–155; Papanikolas, *An American Cakewalk,* 47–78; Jamison, *Hoedowns, Reels, and Frolics,* 122–128.

57. *Post-Dispatch,* September 4, 1898, 21.

58. Quoted in *Post-Dispatch,* September 25, 1898, 21. Melroy's ad is in the Classified Advertisement section of the *Post-Dispatch,* September 22, 1898, 10.

59. *Post-Dispatch,* October 5, 1898, 7. On the Veiled Prophet celebration as an elite cultural tool to reinforce class control in the face of working-class unrest and other challenges, see Spencer, *The St. Louis Veiled Prophet Organization.*

60. *Post-Dispatch,* June 8, 1899, 6; lyrics to "Petie Quinn's Pettie" in *Post-Dispatch,* March 18, 1899, 45.

61. *Post-Dispatch,* September 11, 1898, 27, and October 26, 1898, 7.

62. *Globe-Democrat,* December 3, 1898, 5. By 1899, Spider Meyers replaced Oliver as the King of Raggerdom. By then, Oliver no longer worked in Seibt's saloon. *Post-Dispatch,* January 2, 1899, 11, and May 25, 1899, 15.

63. Quoted in *Post-Dispatch,* September 4, 1898, 21.

64. *Post-Dispatch,* September 16, 1902, 10.

65. *Globe-Democrat,* October 3, 1901, 4; March 1, 1902, 4; and June 27, 1905, 1.

66. Franklin Fyles, "Arizona Camp in Saint Louis," *Buffalo Morning Express and Illustrated Buffalo Express* (Buffalo, New York), August 14, 1904, 29.

67. *Globe-Democrat,* May 19, 1907, 73.

7. The American Fondness for Humbug

1. Adams, *The Great American Fraud,* 1; Cassedy, "Muckraking and Medicine," 85–99; Young, *The Toadstool Millionaires;* Holbrook, *The Golden Age of Quackery.*

2. *The British Medical Journal,* December 21, 1907, 1800; *Treasury Decisions,* 107; Cassedy, "Muckraking and Medicine," 87–88; *Journal of the American Medical Association* 74, no. 22 (May 29, 1920): 1534–1535; *Post-Dispatch,* May 23, 1922, 2.

3. Burman, *Steamboat 'Round the Bend;* McNamara, *Step Right Up,* 56; *Pittsburgh Press,* August 6, 1911, 28; *The Tribune* (Union, Missouri), November 23, 1888, 2; *Post-Dispatch,* May 16, 1908, 1.

4. *Muscatine News-Tribune,* October 9, 1900, 1; McNamara, "The Indian Medicine Show," 431–445; Young, *The Toadstool Millionaires,* 190–202.

5. *Post-Dispatch,* October 3, 1902, 14; *Helena Weekly World* (Arkansas), December 24, 1902, 4.

6. Advertisement in *Bloomfield Vindicator* (Bloomfield, Missouri), October 13, 1883, 3. See also *Tipton Times* (Tipton, Missouri), May 1, 1884, 2; *National Druggist,* 1888, 19; *Republican-Journal* (Darlington, Wisconsin), June 4, 1886, 2; 1880 US Federal Census, City of St. Louis, St. Louis County, Missouri.

7. Mathews, *The Log of the Easy Way,* 155; *Waterloo Times* (Waterloo, Illinois), September 6, 1894, 3, and July 25, 1895, 2. Wilson L. Blake was a salesman and traveling agent for the *Waterways Journal.*

8. Spears, "Floating Down the Mississippi," 390–391.

9. *Bland Courier* (Bland, Missouri), February 12, 1909, 12; *Saint Paul Globe* (Minnesota), May 2, 1890, 5; 1880 US Federal Census, Sigourney, Keokuk County, Iowa; 1870 US Federal Census, Goshen, Ward 2, Elkhart County, Indiana; John D. Seba, M.D., Bland, Missouri, to Editor, in *Sanborn Pioneer* (Iowa), September 6, 1907, reprinted in *Milford Mail* (Iowa), September 18, 1907, 1; 1900 US Federal Census, Benton, District 0001, Crawford County, Missouri; Mathews, *The Log of the Easy Way,* 158; *Quad-City Times* (Davenport, Iowa), April 6, 1895, 4. *Banner-Democrat* (Lake Providence, Louisiana), March 14, 1896.

10. Mathews, *The Log of the Easy Way,* 158, 235.

11. Quoted in ibid., 236.

12. Quoted in ibid., 236; *Courier* (Waterloo, Iowa), November 10, 1908, 6.

13. Mathews, *The Log of the Easy Way,* 235–236.

14. Quoted in ibid., 236–237. For the advertisement, see *Banner-Democrat* (Lake Providence, Louisiana), March 3, 1899, 3.

15. Quoted in Mathews, *The Log of the Easy Way,* 237.

16. *Banner-Democrat* (Lake Providence, Louisiana), March 18, 1899, 3.

17. Quoted in *Republic,* September 16, 1902, 1; *Bland Courier* (Missouri), February 12, 1909, 12.

18. *Republic,* September 16, 1902, 1.

19. Quoted in Mathews, *The Log of the Easy Way,* 238.

20. *Courier* (Waterloo, Iowa), May 27, 1905, 8; *Crawford Mirror* (Steelville, Missouri), July 6, 1905, 1.

21. *Courier* (Waterloo, Iowa), February 13, 1905, 2.

22. *Globe-Democrat,* December 3, 1906, 6.

23. *Bland Courier* (Missouri), February 12, 1909, 12; *Spirit Lake Beacon* (Iowa) September 20, 1907, 5, and September 27, 1907, 5. Seba's letters are in *Milford Mail* (Iowa), September 18, 1907, 1.

24. *Post-Dispatch,* January 22, 1909, 16, and July 27, 1909, 14; *St. Joseph Gazette* (Missouri), January 25, 1908, 7; Marriage of W.M. Netterfield and Scotty Rutherford, September 14, 1909, Bowie County, Texas, U.S., County Marriage Records, 1817–1965.

25. St. Louis City Directory, 1913; *The Miami News* (Florida), June 7, 1917, 2; *Fort Lauderdale News* (Florida), July 26, 1930, 4, and May 9, 1954, 32. When Judge Shippey died on March 16, 1930, his obituary omitted mention of Anna. See *Fort Lauderdale News* (Florida), March 17, 1930, 15.

26. *Sunday Evening Star* (Washington, D.C.), September 29, 1935, F-4, image 76, Chronicling America; *Binghamton Press and Sun Bulletin* (New York), May 24, 1935, 10, and S. R. Winters,

"Frauds That Flourish—Until Uncle Sam Takes a Hand," *Hygeia, the Health Magazine* 14 (May 1936), 420; 1930 US Federal Census, Volusia, Lake Helen (Cassadaga Spiritualist Camp), Florida; Marriage of William Netterfield and Elsie Selecman, November 13, 1924, Volusia, Florida, U.S., County Marriage Records, 1823–1992; *Quad-City Times* (Davenport, Iowa), July 26, 1931, 14, and August 23, 1931, 34.

27. *Vicksburg American* (Mississippi), June 16, 1906, 1; *Public Ledger* (Memphis, Tennessee), August 6, 1887, 2; *Clarksdale Banner* (Tennessee), December 5, 1902, 8; *Greenwood Commonwealth* (Mississippi), March 25, 1905, 4.

28. *Nashville Journal* (Tennessee), November 28, 1884, 5; 1880 US Federal Census, St. Mary Parish, Ward 4, New Orleans, Louisiana; *Daily Press* (Newport News, Virginia), October 21, 1906, 9.

29. *Greenwood Commonwealth* (Mississippi), March 25, 1905, 4; *Weekly Iberian* (New Iberia, Louisiana), February 23, 1895, 2; *Public Ledger*, August 6, 1887, 2; Foster, "The Rocky Road to a 'Drug Free Tennessee,'" 547–564.

30. *Vicksburg American*, June 16, 1906, 1, and July 26, 1906, 1; 1900 US Federal Census, Civil District 15, Shelby County, Tennessee; 1900 US Federal Census, Natchez, Ward 3, District 0009, Adams County, Mississippi; 1910 US Federal Census, City of Memphis, Ward 27, District 0281, Shelby County, Tennessee; Memphis City Directory, Miss Ada Patti, 1899, U.S., City Directories, 1822–1895, 720; Mary McQuinn, Death Certificate, July 27, 1955, Memphis, Shelby County, Tennessee, U.S., Death Records, 1908–1965.

31. *State of Tennessee v. William Patti; Public Ledger*, October 24, 1891, 1; U.S. City Directories, 1822–1995, City of Memphis, 1892, 1894; *Vicksburg American*, June 16, 1906, 1; *Vicksburg Herald*, June 16, 1906, 5, and June 19, 1906, 6. Patti appeared twice in court during his stay in Vicksburg, charged with practicing medicine without a license.

32. *Vicksburg Herald*, June 23, 1906, 5.

33. *Vicksburg American*, July 24, 1906, 1; *Port Gibson Reveille*, August 2, 1906, 1.

34. Spears, "The Mississippi Boat Theatres," 13; *Daily Press* (Newport News, Virginia), October 21, 1906, 9; *New-York Tribune*, December 18, 1910, 19.

35. Spears, "The Mississippi Boat Theatres," 13; Holliday, "American Showboats," 246.

36. Quoted in *Post-Dispatch*, September 26, 1889, 6.

37. *Post-Dispatch*, July 12, 1905, 3, and its Sunday Magazine, July 23, 1905, 40; Wesley W. Stout, "Tonight at the River Landing," *Saturday Evening Post*, October 31, 1925, 16–17, 39–40, 42; Graham, *Showboats*; Graham, "Showboats in the South," 174–185; Bryant, *Here Comes the Showboat*.

38. Menke interview and memoir.

39. Percy, *Lanterns on the Levee*, 41. In 1917, Holliday described showboat players as "the most mysterious" and "the most happy-go-lucky" of all the nation's actors and musical entertainers ("American Showboats," 246).

40. Graham, *Showboats*, 105–106; Julia A. Henderson and Ellsworth Eugene Eisenbarth, February 28, 1886, West Virginia, U.S., Marriages Index, 1785–1971.

41. Graham, *Showboats*, 106–107.

42. Ibid., 107–114; Spears, "The Mississippi Boat Theatres," 13; *Daily Gate City* (Keokuk, Iowa), June 23, 1910, 8.

43. *Star and Times*, June 18, 1949, 8; Bryant, *Here Comes the Showboat*.

8. In the High Waters of Sin

1. Burman, *Big River to Cross*, 50–51.

2. *Post-Dispatch*, July 15, 1900, 29.

3. Smith, "Looking for the New Jerusalem," 74.

4. *Globe-Democrat*, October 25, 1890, 8; *Post-Dispatch*, November 30, 1890, 22. On Wilson, see *Globe-Democrat*, February 15, 1895, 12. See the essays in Pasquier, ed., *Gods of the Mississippi*, for fresh, diverse approaches to the study of religion and culture on the river.

5. *Cape Girardeau Democrat* (Missouri), September 12, 1891, 3; *Post-Dispatch*, November 30, 1890, 22, December 10, 1891, 11, and December 13, 1890, 4; M. A. Shepard to Frank W. Havill, February 2, 1891, letter printed in *Mount Carmel Register* (Illinois), February 5, 1891, 8.

6. *Post-Dispatch*, March 29, 1896, 29; Arnold, *Under Southern Skies*, 11, 23, 25, 26, 60, 73, 87, 88.

7. *Post-Dispatch*, March 29, 1896, 29. Quote is in *The Times* (Philadelphia, Pennsylvania), May 19, 1895, 26.

8. *Pittsburgh Daily Post* (Pennsylvania) May 20, 1889, 2; *Western Methodist* (Wichita, Kansas), February 22, 1894, 4; *Record of Christian Work*, 336.

9. Quoted in *Boston Post* (Massachusetts), May 9, 1895, 4; *Fremont Tribune* (Nebraska), September 18, 1883, 3; *Clyde Herald* (Kansas), August 13, 1885, 4; *Burr Oak Herald* (Kansas), July 30, 1885, 4; *DeKalb Chronicle* (Illinois), May 19, 1888, 5; Arnold, *Under Southern Skies*, 19.

10. *Quincy Daily Herald* (Illinois), December 17, 1901, 1, December 21, 1901, 8, December 30, 1901, 6, and March 25, 1902, 7; *Globe-Democrat*, December 18, 1901, 9; *Post-Dispatch*, March 29, 1896, 29; *Boston Post*, May 9, 1895, 4.

11. Arnold, *Under Southern Skies*, 41, 150. On the divorce suit, see *Cincinnati Inquirer*, April 24, 1906, 6; *Washington Times* (District of Columbia), May 7, 1906, 3; and *Belvidere Daily Republican* (Illinois), April 28, 1906, 9; and Turley, *A Wheel Within a Wheel*, 136–137; *Pittsburgh Daily Post*, September 23, 1908, 4.

12. Quoted in *Post-Dispatch*, September 12, 1907, 8; *Globe-Democrat*, January 23, 1907, 8, and January 26, 1908, 11.

13. Burman, *Big River to Cross*, 76.

14. Quoted in *Times-Democrat* (New Orleans, Louisiana), April 12, 1908, 39. See also *Cincinnati Enquirer* (Ohio), March 23, 1907, 8, and *Times-Democrat* (New Orleans, Louisiana), March 22, 1908, 35.

15. Quoted in Johnson, *Highways and Byways*, 259. The mission of the Seventh-Day Adventists on the *Morning Star* in 1894 was to convert and uplift Black freedmen, particularly in the Mississippi delta. See Graybill, *Mission to Black America*. On Durbin, see the *Des Moines Register* (Iowa), May 2, 1909, 42. The *Megiddo* launched in Clinton, Iowa, on October 24, 1901. See Patzwald, *Waiting for Elijah*. In 1904, Nichols and his followers sold their boat and relocated to Rochester, New York. On "Brother Isaiah," see Fletcher, "The Miracle Man of New Orleans," 113–120, and Fry, *They Called Us River Rats*, 93–100.

16. Quoted in Wood, "The River Home," 6.

17. Orne quoted in *Indianapolis Journal* (Indiana), January 20, 1893, 4; *Morning Courier-Journal* (New Haven, Connecticut), January 24, 1893, 1; 1860 US Federal Census, Wolfborough, Carroll

County, New Hampshire; *Vermont Chronicle* (Bellows Falls), March 16, 1888, 5; *Times and Democrat* (Orangeburg, South Carolina), February 5, 1890, 1; *Pittsburgh Dispatch*, July 3, 1890, 11; Ida B. Orne, date of death, January 17, 1893, Haverhill, Massachusetts Death Records, 1841–1915; and *Boston Globe*, February 4, 1893, 4.

18. For Simpson's teachings and theology, see his writings, *A Larger Christian Life* and *The Gospel of Healing*. On Orne in Brooklyn, see *Times Union* (Brooklyn), April 13, 1895, 7; *Brooklyn Citizen*, November 26, 1894, 1; December 3, 1894, 6; and April 5, 1895, 6. Reports of the Ornes's early gospel wagon travels in Vermont are in *Brandon Union*, July 3, 1896, 5; *Rutland Daily Herald*, July 28, 1896, 3; *Bristol Herald*, July 30, 1896, 8. See also *Sioux City Journal*, July 14, 1898, 7.

19. *Chicago Tribune*, October 2, 1897, 7; *Post-Dispatch*, November 2, 1897, 5. Wilson quoted in *Post-Dispatch*, November 5, 1897, 3.

20. *Post-Dispatch*, November 5, 1897, 3, and January 17, 1903, 10; *Republic*, January 8, 1903, 8; *Globe-Democrat*, January 9, 1903, 14; Stepenoff, *The Dead-End Kids of St. Louis*, 55–67.

21. Orne quoted in *Evening Times-Republican* (Marshalltown, Iowa), September 1, 1906, 2; *Quincy Daily Herald* (Illinois), September 14, 1906, 6. See also *Omaha Daily Bee*, October 4, 1903, 15; *Quincy Daily Herald* (Illinois), September 17, 1903, 8; *Pittsburgh Weekly Gazette* (Pennsylvania), May 31, 1904, 11; *Natchez Democrat* (Mississippi), May 8, 1904, 6; *Chattanooga Daily Times* (Tennessee), April 22, 23, 25, 1905, 6, 10, and 8; *Nashville Banner* (Tennessee), May 24, 1905, 10, and June 6, 1905, 9; *Muscatine News-Tribune* (Iowa), August 31, 1906, 7; *Bismarck Daily Tribune* (North Dakota), July 27, 1911, 5; *Evening Star*, (Washington, D.C.), March 19, 1912, 5.

22. *Chattanooga Daily Times* (Tennessee), April 22, 1905, 6; April 23, 1905, 10; April 25, 1905, 8; *Nashville Banner* (Tennessee), June 6, 1905, 9.

23. Quoted in *Post-Dispatch*, October 29, 1908, 4; *Globe-Democrat*, October 30, 1908, 10; *Star and Times*, October 2, 1911, 3.

24. *Jackson Daily News* (Mississippi), May 27, 1916, 12, and *Natchez Democrat* (Mississippi), June 9, 1916, 3; *Cape County Herald* (Cape Girardeau, Missouri), October 13, 1911, 1; Death Certificate of Clara B. Orne, April 2, 1920, El Paso, Texas, Death Certificates, 1903–1982. On the "Betsy Ann," see Way, *The Log of the Betsy Ann*.

25. Quoted in *Post-Dispatch*, August 21, 1924, 21. See also *Sioux City Journal* (Iowa), October 8, 1922, 6, and June 6, 1923, 7; *Democrat-Argus* (Caruthersville, Missouri), November 27, 1923, 7; *Nebraska Daily Press* (Nebraska City, Nebraska), August 4, 1923, 2; *St. Joseph Gazette* (Missouri), August 19, 1923, 3.

26. Lighty and Lighty, *Shanty-Boat*, 162–164.

27. Ibid., 165

28. Ibid., 194.

29. Quoted in *Oklahoma State Register* (Guthrie, Oklahoma), April 20, 1905, 2; James Sharp, Certificate of Death, March 8, 1946, Jasper County, Missouri, Missouri Digital Heritage Death Certificates, 1910–1970.

30. Quoted in *Weekly Times-Journal* (Oklahoma City), January 26, 1906, 4; *Daily Times-Journal* (Oklahoma City), April 18, 1905, 1; *Oklahoma State Register* (Guthrie), April 20, 1905, 2; Marriage of James Sharp and M. F. Roper, November 12, 1887, Lawrence County, Arkansas, U.S., County Marriages Index, 1837–1957; *Sulphur Post* (Oklahoma), April 20, 1905, 6. On fraudulent preachers

in the antebellum South, see John Lindbeck, "Preachers and Peddlers: Credit and Belief in the Flush Times," in Forret and Baker, eds., *Southern Scoundrels*, 12–36.

31. Quoted in *Oklahoma State Register*, April 20, 1905, 2.

32. Quoted in *Weekly Times-Journal* (Oklahoma City), July 20, 1906, 2.

33. Quoted in ibid.

34. Quoted in *Weekly Times-Journal* (Oklahoma City), July 20, 1906, 2; *Oklahoma State Register*, April 20, 1905, 2.

35. *San Francisco Examiner*, February 17, 1907, 70.

36. *Weekly Times-Journal* (Oklahoma City), July 20, 1906, 2; *Post-Dispatch*, July 22, 1906, 8; *Shawnee Herald* (Shawnee, Oklahoma), July 15, 1906, 1; *Shawnee News-Herald*, (Shawnee, Oklahoma), August 9, 1906, 1; *Tulsa Daily World*, August 4, 1906, 3, and August 11, 1906, 3; *Oklahoma City Times*, August 20, 1906, 8.

37. Pratt quoted in *Kansas City Times*, November 3, 1906, 14; *Wyandott Herald* (Kansas City, Kansas), November 8, 1906, 3.

38. Quoted in *Bowbells Tribune* (North Dakota), December 18, 1908, 1; *Calgary Herald* (Calgary, Alberta, Canada), July 30, 1907, 10; *Evening Statesman* (Walla Walla, Washington), August 28, 1906, 5; *Spokesman-Review* (Spokane, Washington), October 4, 1907, 6.

39. *Kansas City Times*, December 9, 1808, 1.

40. Ibid. On the shootout and Sharp's trial, I relied mainly on newspaper coverage in the *Kansas City Times* and *Kansas City Star*. See also https://www.kcpolicememorial.com/pages/1908 _dolbow_mullane/.

41. *Kansas City Times*, May 27, 1909, 14.

42. *Kansas City Times*, December 12, 1908, 1, and December 17, 1908, 1; James Sharp, alias Adam God, register 10890, Missouri State Penitentiary Database, Missouri Digital Heritage; *Fort Worth Record and Register* (Texas), May 11, 1909, 7; *Houston Post* (Texas), May 14, 1909, 14.

43. Quoted in *Springfield Leader and Press* (Missouri), December 6, 1926, 5. See also the *Messenger-Inquirer* (Owensboro, Kentucky), August 26, 1925, 10.

44. Quoted in *Kansas City Star*, March 8, 1931, 12.

45. *Joplin Globe* (Missouri), March 9, 1946, 3, and March 12, 1946, 7. Melissa died at ninety-five in Joplin's Grandview Nursing Home on June 28, 1966. Pratt, age ninety, died in the Maddox Nursing Home on November 24, 1967. Their death certificates are in Missouri Death Certificates, 1910–1969, Missouri Digital Heritage.

9. Neither Pumpkin nor Paw-paw

1. On women in early rowing, see Schweinbenz, *Against Hegemonic Currents*, and Huntington, "Women on the Water," 105–136.

2. *Chicago Tribune*, December 6, 1865, 4; *St. Joseph Weekly Gazette* (Missouri), December 24, 1868, 2; *Leavenworth Times* (Kansas), November 2, 1869, 2; *Weekly News-Democrat* (Emporia, Kansas), December 29, 1869, 4, January 4, 1871, 3, and August 9, 1872, 3; 1870 US Federal Census, Emporia, Ward 3, Lyon County, Kansas. On the divorce, see *Burlington Patriot* (Kansas), October

16, 1873, 4. Rose Buckley, Certificate of Death, St. Louis, December 26, 1913, Missouri Death Certificates, 1910–1970; Ferdinand C. Steimel, Registers, U.S. National Homes for Disabled Volunteer Soldiers, 1866–1938, Sawtelle, 1893; *Le Roy Reporter* (Kansas), September 28, 1894, 3; 1900 US Federal Census, City of St. Louis, Ward 2, District 0032, St. Louis, Missouri.

3. *Globe-Democrat,* April 18, 1876, 8, and July 8, 1883, 16; 1880 US Federal Census, City of St. Louis, District 0260, St. Louis County, Missouri; 1900 US Federal Census, City of St. Louis, Ward 5, District 0069, St. Louis County, Missouri; *Post-Dispatch,* November 14, 1885, 12. See interview with Otto Mosenthein in the *Star and Times,* July 23, 1949, 8.

4. Quoted in *St. Louis Republic,* reprinted in *Harrisburg Telegraph* (Harrisburg, Pennsylvania), September 15, 1894, 3.

5. *Star and Times,* July 23, 1949, 8; *Edwardsville Intelligencer,* June 24, 1898, 1.

6. *Post-Dispatch,* June 17, 1891, 3; October 15, 1893, 7; April 30, 1894, 2; *Globe-Democrat,* March 11, 1893, 8.

7. *Globe-Democrat,* October 15, 1894, 9.

8. Ashley quoted in *Kenosha News* (Wisconsin), August 1, 1903, 2.

9. Quoted in ibid.

10. *Boston Globe* (Massachusetts), August 11, 1894, 1; *Globe-Democrat,* October 4, 1894, 4, and October 15, 1894, 9; *Hartford Courant* (Connecticut), August 24, 1894, 3.

11. *Globe-Democrat,* October 15, 1894, 9. Quote from Ashley in *Fall River Daily Evening News* (Massachusetts), August 9, 1894, 8.

12. In a female sculling regatta on the north bank of the Monongahela River in Pittsburgh, Lottie McAlice, a sixteen-year-old orphan who lived near the waterfront, defeated Maggie Lew in a one-mile race on July 16, 1870. *Pittsburgh Daily Commercial* (Pennsylvania), July 23, 1870, 1.

13. *Globe-Democrat,* September 24, 1894, and October 4, 1894, 4.

14. *Globe-Democrat,* October 8, 1894, 9; *Post-Dispatch,* October 7, 1894, 15. Loughlin and Anderson, *Forest Park,* 38, mistakenly claims that Ashley won the race, and fails to mention Mosenthein.

15. *Globe-Democrat,* October 15, 1894, 9. See also *Butte Daily Post* (Montana), October 8, 1894, 3.

16. *Globe-Democrat,* October 15, 1894, 9; *Waterways Journal,* October 20, 1894, 3–4.

17. *Globe-Democrat,* October 15, 1894, 9; *Austin American-Statesman* (Texas), November 5, 1895, 5. On the famous 1870 steamboat race and its impact on racing between New Orleans and St. Louis, see Klinkenberg, "Chasing the Robert E. Lee," 18–35.

18. *Waterways Journal,* October 20, 1894, 3.

19. Ibid., 3.

20. Ibid., 4.

21. *Hartford Courant* (Connecticut), October 17, 1894, 6; *Waterways Journal,* October 20, 1894, 4.

22. *Hartford Courant,* October 27, 1894, 3. Koenig won a gold medal for the amateur single sculls at the 1893 Austin regatta. See *Austin Weekly Statesman,* June 15, 1893, 7.

23. *Butte Daily Post* (Montana), December 11, 1894, 3; *Globe-Democrat,* August 19, 1895, 9; *Waterways Journal,* April 13, 1895, 9.

24. *Post-Dispatch,* June 12, 1895, 1.

25. Quoted in *Galveston Daily News* (Texas), November 6, 1895, 6.

26. *Hartford Telegram* quoted in *Austin American-Statesman,* April 2, 1895, 4.

27. *Galveston Daily News,* November 6, 1895, 6; *Austin Weekly Statesman,* November 7, 1895, 4.

28. *The Journal* (Meriden, Connecticut), August 11, 1898, 6.

29. Quoted in *Baltimore Sun,* May 24, 1903, 12.

30. *Post-Dispatch,* July 5, 1903, 10.

31. Quoted in *Post-Dispatch,* July 12, 1903, 21.

32. Quoted in ibid.

33. Quoted in ibid.

34. Quoted in ibid.

35. *Oregon Daily Journal* (Portland), August 13, 1903, 8.

36. *Post-Dispatch,* September 13, 1895, 3.

37. Quoted in ibid.; *Edwardsville Intelligencer,* June 24, 1898, 1.

38. Quoted in *Post-Dispatch,* September 13, 1895, 3.

39. *Globe-Democrat,* May 16, 1899, 9.

40. *Edwardsville Intelligencer,* June 24, 1898, 4; *Bellefontaine Improvement Company et al. v. Niedringhaus et al.,* 184–189. In 1871, the Report of the Chief of Engineers pointed out a long, irregular island between Gabaret Island and the Missouri shore. The island, which was covered with willows, did not have a name and was not shown on maps before 1843. Between it and Gabaret Island was Pocket Chute (later known sometimes as Mosenthein Chute). See *Report of the Secretary of War,* 316–317.

41. Quoted in *Star and Times,* July 23, 1949, 8.

42. *Post-Dispatch,* October 19, 1899, 7.

43. Quoted in *Star and Times,* August 6, 1949, 8.

44. *Globe-Democrat,* December 24, 1907, 10; Rose Buckley, Certificate of Death, December 26, 1913, Missouri Death Certificates, 1910–1969; *Post-Dispatch,* December 28, 1913, 27; 1910 US Federal Census, City of St. Louis, Ward 2, District 0030, St. Louis County, Missouri.

10. The Ruthless Advance of Civilization

1. Quoted in *Republic,* January 13, 1903, 9.

2. Burman, "Music on the Mississippi."

3. Schnell, "Lawyers, Squatters, and the Transformation of the Public Domain," 237–263; Pisani, "The Squatter and Natural Law," 443–463; Peñalver and Katyal, *Property Outlaws,* 55–63.

4. *Post-Dispatch,* June 12, 1895, 1; September 27, 1895, 3; October 27, 1895, 25.

5. *Post-Dispatch,* June 12, 1895, 1.

6. *Post-Dispatch,* June 15, 1895, 2.

7. Reproduced in ibid., 4.

8. Quoted in *Globe-Democrat,* August 18, 1895, 24.

9. *Post-Dispatch,* September 27, 1895, 3.

10. *Post-Dispatch,* March 5, 1898, 1.

11. 1900 US Federal Census, City of St. Louis, Ward 2, District 0025, St. Louis County, Missouri; *Post-Dispatch,* April 3, 1898, 13, and September 2, 1899, 3; *Globe-Democrat,* October 26, 1899, 9. On September 1, 1899, Justin's son, Wilford P. Joy, failed to eject the city of St. Louis from a strip in dispute at the foot of Dock Street, claiming rightful ownership as the result of convey-

ances dating back to the estate of Louis LaBeaume. See "Annual Report of the Harbor and Wharf Commissioner," 1901, 706. On April 2, 1906, the US Supreme Court ruled against Wilford P. Joy in a similar ejectment suit. See *Joy v. City of St. Louis and Hafner-Lothman Manufacturing Company, Supreme Court Reporter: Cases Argued and Determined in the United States Supreme Court, December, 1905-July 1906* (St. Paul: West Publishing Company, 1906), 478–481.

12. *Post-Dispatch*, September 3, 1899, 12.

13. Quoted in ibid.

14. Quoted in *Post-Dispatch*, November 16, 1900, 7.

15. *Republic*, March 2, 1901, 11.

16. Quoted in *Post-Dispatch*, July 10, 1903, 1. See also *Republic*, July 10, 1903, 2.

17. *Post-Dispatch*, July 19, 1903, 1; *Republic*, July 10, 1903, 2.

18. Quoted in *Post-Dispatch*, July 10, 1903, 1.

19. Quoted in *Republic*, July 10, 1903, 2.

20. Quoted in *Post-Dispatch*, July 10, 1903, 1.

21. Quoted in ibid.

22. *Globe-Democrat*, March 29, 1903, 56.

23. Quoted in *Post-Dispatch*, October 1, 1903, 24.

24. *Republic*, July 28, 1904, 3; *Globe-Democrat*, November 18, 1904, 2; *Post-Dispatch*, November 17, 1904, 1.

25. *Post-Dispatch*, November 17, 1904, 1.

26. *Post-Dispatch*, March 26, 1905, 62.

27. *Star and Times*, March 11, 1911, 12; 1910 US Federal Census, City of St. Louis, Ward 11, District 0181, St. Louis County, Missouri;1900 US Federal Census, City of St. Louis, Ward 10, District 0148, St. Louis County, Missouri; St. Louis City Directory, 1913, 579, U.S., City Directories, 1822–1995. Daniel Catlin owned millions of dollars in downtown St. Louis real estate. See *Post-Dispatch*, December 6, 1914, 56.

28. Quoted in *Post-Dispatch*, September 3, 1907, 19. See also *Globe-Democrat*, September 4, 1907, 11.

29. *Post-Dispatch*, September 3, 1907, 19; September 4, 1907, 2; and September 5, 1907, 8.

30. Wallace, "The Wiggins Ferry Monopoly," 1–19. See also Jackson, *Rails Across the Mississippi*.

31. *Post-Dispatch*, July 16, 1893, 19.

32. *Alton Evening Telegraph*, July 20, 1897, 3. Hurd, comp. and ed., *The Revised Statutes of the State of Illinois*, 628–629. The Illinois statute was similar to one passed in 1895 in Kentucky, where an appeals court upheld the licensing law as constitutional. See *Robertson v. Commonwealth of Kentucky*, 920.

33. *Globe-Democrat*, September 21, 1897, 14.

34. *Republic*, April 24, 1904, 8, and July 25, 1905, 10.

35. *Report of the Commissioner of Corporations*, 224; *Globe-Democrat*, October 27, 1911, 1; *Report of the Submerged and Shore Lands Legislative Investigating Committee*, 128.

36. *Republic*, December 1, 1903, 7; *Post-Dispatch*, April 15, 1904, 2.

37. *Post-Dispatch*, December 27, 1903, 42.

38. *Post-Dispatch*, April 15, 1904, 2.

39. *Post-Dispatch*, July 24, 1905, 1, and July 27, 1905, 11.

40. Warrens quoted in *Post-Dispatch*, July 27, 1905, 11.

41. Quoted in ibid.

42. *Post-Dispatch*, July 27, 1905, 11.

43. Quoted in ibid.

44. *Post-Dispatch*, July 27, 1905, 11.

45. Quoted in *Post-Dispatch*, July 28, 1905, 1.

46. Neely and Cashell quoted in ibid.

47. *Post-Dispatch*, July 28, 1905, 1.

48. Quoted in ibid.

49. *Post-Dispatch*, August 1, 1905, 15; *Globe-Democrat*, August 2, 1905, 10.

50. *Post-Dispatch*, August 2, 1905, 12.

51. *Post-Dispatch*, August 1, 1905, 15; August 2, 1905, 12; and October 7, 1905, 5.

52. Andrews, *City of Dust*, 28–29; *Quincy Daily Herald* (Illinois), August 19, 1901, 8; *The State of Missouri, ex rel. James D. Roland v. John D. Dreyer, Mayor et al.*, June 21, 1910, 201–246.

53. *State of Missouri v. Dreyer, Reports of Cases*, 245–246.

54. *Nashville Banner*, February 9, 1912, 1; *Waterways Journal*, October 23, 1915, 6.

55. *Quincy Daily-Journal* (Illinois), September 24, 1912, 10; *Quad-City Times* (Davenport, Iowa), February 16, 1916, 12, and May 7, 1916, 3; *Daily Times* (Davenport, Iowa), August 1, 1916, 7, and October 3, 1916, 5.

11. Gone Are the Old River Days

1. *Quad-City Times* (Davenport, Iowa), August 13, 1915, 6; *LaCrosse Tribune* (Wisconsin), April 15, 1916, 7; *Star Tribune* (Minneapolis), September 4, 1898, 19.

2. Richardson, "A Houseboat," 236; *Waterways Journal*, March 23, 1895, 5; Mayo, "Ideal Summer Homes Afloat," 351–356.

3. Quoted in *Cedar Rapids Republican* (Iowa), November 24, 1901, 6.

4. Quoted in ibid.

5. Easton's article in *Post-Dispatch*, December 1, 1901, 48. See also *Post-Dispatch*, November 24, 1901, 9.

6. *Daily Times* (Davenport, Iowa), November 13, 1903; *Post-Dispatch*, May 19, 1904, 3.

7. *Post-Dispatch*, May 19, 1904, 3; *American Lumbermen*, 25–28.

8. *Dispatch* (Moline, Illinois), July 12, 1904, 2; *Daily Times* (Davenport, Iowa), September 8, 1904, 11; *Rock Island Argus* (Illinois), June 24, 1908, 2; *Vicksburg Evening Post*, October 31, 1911, 1; *Natchez Democrat*, November 2, 1911, 10.

9. *Post-Dispatch*, November 3, 1901, 48; *Helena Weekly World* (Arkansas), November 13, 1901, 1.

10. *Post-Dispatch*, June 4, 1905, 57.

11. *Post-Dispatch*, May 24, 1914, 75; *Globe-Democrat*, May 30, 1909, 50; *Post-Dispatch*, July 5, 1914, 54.

12. *Post-Dispatch*, September 25, 1911, 12, and April 27, 1913, 64; *Globe-Democrat*, September 28, 1912, 10; *News-Times* (Webster Groves, Missouri), October 2, 1914, 6; *Star and Times*, September 16, 1914, 8.

13. *Post-Dispatch*, May 24, 1914, 75, and July 11, 1915, 67.

14. *Quincy Daily-Journal* (Illinois) September 24, 1912, 10; *Quad-City Times* (Davenport, Iowa), February 16, 1916, 12; *Post-Dispatch*, January 16, 1914, 11; *Globe-Democrat*, July 9, 1914, 7, and September 24, 1914, 7; *Star and Times*, September 20, 1916, 3.

15. *Star and Times*, February 4, 1911, 7; Scarpino, *Great River*, 37–39; Andrews, *City of Dust*, 117–118; Stevens, *The Log of the Alton*.

16. *Post-Dispatch*, December 16, 1917, 45, and December 23, 1917, 27; *Globe-Democrat*, December 23, 1917, 1.

17. *Star and Times*, October 23, 1921, 37.

18. *Star and Times*, October 23, 1921, 37; *Post-Dispatch*, April 5, 1925, 109.

19. St. Paul Dispatch, *Almanac and Year Book*, 612; *Engineering News-Record*, September 30, 1915, 668–669, and January 8, 1920, 85–87. Captain J. H. Bernhard in American Society of Civil Engineers, *Transactions*, 961.

20. Captain J. H. Bernhard in American Society of Civil Engineers, *Transactions*, 961; Kohr, "Not a Rouster Aboard," 886–889.

21. *Globe-Democrat*, October 9, 1914, 12.

22. *Globe-Democrat*, January 11, 1911, 16; *Waterways Journal*, December 4, 1909, 4.

23. *Star and Times*, June 20, 1911, 5; *Globe-Democrat*, June 16, 1911, 10; *Post-Dispatch*, June 21, 1911, 10. Kavanaugh was president of the Missouri Waterways Commission and the Wiggins Ferry Company, which controlled the East St. Louis riverfront.

24. Quoted in *Globe-Democrat*, March 31, 1911, 6. See also *Globe-Democrat*, March 18, 1911, 13; April 4, 1911, 7; and June 20, 1911, 9.

25. *Globe-Democrat*, October 27, 1911, 1.

26. *Waterways Journal*, August 12, 1911, 8, and November 2, 1912, 8.

27. *Moline Dispatch*, (Illinois), January 19, 1911, 6; *Waterways Journal*, January 28, 1911, 7.

28. *Globe-Democrat*, November 3, 1910, 2, and May 31, 1911, 8.

29. *Courier-Journal* (Louisville, Kentucky), November 24, 1911, 4.

30. *Waterways Journal*, November 2, 1912, 8; *Globe-Democrat*, November 7, 1912, 16, and July 23, 1916, 16; *Star and Times*, July 16, 1913, 4; *Post-Dispatch*, July 7, 1916, 10, and July 17, 1918, 16.

31. Citizens Committee, *Waterways*, 24–25; "Barges for Grain Transportation," *The Price Current-Grain Reporter*, March 1, 1922, 12–13; Sumner, "An Analysis of Mississippi River Traffic," 355–366; *Preliminary Report of the Inland Waterways Commission*, 143–145; *Post-Dispatch*, July 17, 1918, 16, and December 7, 1919, 71; Hubbell, "Federal Barge Lines"; Secretary of War, *Inland Waterways Corporation*, 1. In 1953, Herman T. Pott, founder of the St. Louis Shipbuilding and Steel Company, bought the corporation and renamed it Federal Barge Lines, Inc. Its records are in the Pott Library. See his obituary in *Post-Dispatch*, March 28, 1982, 28.

32. *Kansas City Star*, October 23, 1921, 51; C. M. Berkley, "The Good Old Days on the River," *Post-Dispatch*, January 15, 1922, 85, and August 8, 1926, 51; *Star and Times*, October 27, 1922, 3, and October 29, 1927, 9.

33. *Post-Dispatch*, August 2, 1937, 29; *Star and Times*, October 5, 1937, 1; October 20, 1937, 5; and October 27, 1937, 26; Stepenoff, *Working the Mississippi*, 133.

34. *Star and Times*, October 27, 1937, 26; National Park Service, "Goldenrod Showboat"; Stepenoff, *Working the Mississippi*, 133–13; *Post-Dispatch*, October 23, 2017, A07.

35. Speakman and Speakman, *Mostly Mississippi*, 199.

36. Ibid., 201, 204, 273; *Post-Dispatch*, November 18, 1926, 21. Speakman and Speakman estimated that the largest shantyboat colony at the time was in Vicksburg, where it stretched for a mile on the narrow Yazoo River.

37. Quoted in *Globe-Democrat*, November 3, 1926, 7; *Post-Dispatch*, November 2, 1926, 3.

38. Margaret Emmerling Lighty, "Shanty Boat Cruise on Mississippi," in *Capital Times* (Madison, Wisconsin), December 29, 1929, 18; Lighty and Lighty, *Shanty-Boat*, 3–14; *LaCrosse Tribune* (Wisconsin), August 31, 1922, 6. Kent later headed his own medical advertising firm in New York, and Margaret worked as an editor. See Kent's obituary in *Capital Times* (Madison, Wisconsin), January 11, 1943, 4.

39. *Globe-Democrat*, March 29, 1930, 5; Lighty and Lighty, *Shanty-Boat*, 120, 125–126.

40. Lighty and Lighty, *Shanty-Boat*, 135–136.

41. Ibid., 136. Raven-Hart quoted in *Post-Dispatch*, September 12, 1938, 27. On the *Cape Girardeau*, see Stepenoff, *Working the Mississippi*, 17–18.

42. *Star and Times*, September 24, 1929, 9; Stepenoff, *Working the Mississippi*, 18.

43. *Star and Times*, September 24, 1929, 9.

Epilogue

1. *Globe-Democrat*, September 27, 1931, 50. and December 28, 1931, 2; *Star and Times*, November 24, 1931, 1; Barlow, *Looking Up at Down*, 267; Lang, *Grassroots at the Gateway*, 23; Towey, "Hooverville," 4–11; Primm, *Lion of the Valley*, 452–457; Wanko, *Great River City*, 230–235.

2. Johnson, *The Broken Heart of America*, 264–282; Ervin, *Gateway to Equality*, chapter 1; Conroy, *The Disinherited*; Marling, "Joe Jones," 46–59; Iarocci, "The Changing American Landscape," 68–71; *Post-Dispatch*, January 21, 1934, 8; and October 9, 1935, 21.

3. Johnson, *The Broken Heart of America*, 294–295.

4. Rice's letter in *Star and Times*, June 20, 1936, 10.

5. *Star and Times*, December 26, 1936, 10; Grady, *The Lost St. Louis Riverfront*. On the racial impact of the demolition, as well as future bond issues and the continued war by city planners on Black neighborhoods torn down in the name of urban renewal after 1945, see Johnson, *The Broken Heart of America*, 291–336, and Gibson, *The Last Children of Mill Creek*.

6. *Star and Times*, April 27, 1939, 14; Honey, *Southern Labor and Black Civil Rights*, 93–116; *Post-Dispatch*, September 19, 1939, 10; Honey, *Black Workers Remember*, 86–87. The *St. Louis American*, founded in 1928, originated in large part due to the *Argus*'s conservative bent and opposition to organized labor, especially A. Phillip Randolph's Brotherhood of Sleeping Car Porters. See interview with Judge Nathan B. Young Jr., transcript, 2–4.

7. Lyrics in Kenney, *Jazz on the River*, 84. On Burman's writings, see his novels, *Mississippi*, *Steamboat Round the Bend*, and *Blow for a Landing*, as well as his nonfiction *Big River to Cross*. Hollywood adapted two comedies from his novels: *Heaven on Earth* (1931), directed by Russell Mack, and *Steamboat 'Round the Bend* (1933), directed by John Ford.

8. Among Armstrong's other river-themed recordings with his orchestra in the 1930s are W. C. Handy's "Saint Louis Blues" (Vic 24320), Billy Baskette's "Mighty River" (Vic 24351), and "Lazy

'Sippi Steamer Going Home" (Decca 3283), which Armstrong and Luis Russell composed and released in 1940 with words by Victor Selsman. See Kenney, *Jazz on the River*, 84–86.

9. The poem is in box 1, folder 5, Ferris Research Notes Collection. See Devine's obituary in the *Cincinnati Enquirer* (Ohio), December 14, 1996, 10.

10. See *Heaven on Earth* (1931), *Steamboat 'Round the Bend* (1933), and *Banjo on My Knee* (1936), directed by John Cromwell, produced by Darryl F. Zanuck, and based on Harry Hamilton's novel, *Banjo on My Knee*. For other shantyboat novels, see Randolph Parrish, *Don McGrath*; Spears, *Driftwood*; Cowan, *The Jo-Boat Boys*; Adams, *The Houseboat Boys*; Gillham, *The Adventures of William Tucker*; Lenski, *Houseboat Girl*; Hamilton, *River Song*; Sumner, *Tammy Out of Time*; and Butler, *The Jack-Knife Man*. In 1920, King Vidor produced a silent movie, *The Jack-Knife Man*, that is arguably the most realistic, sympathetic film treatment of shantyboat settlements.

11. Lenski, *Houseboat Girl*, xvi–xvii; Hubbard, *Shantyboat*. Hubbard kept a journal of the trip, published as *Shantyboat Journal*. See, too, his *Shantyboat on the Bayous* and *Payne Hollow Journal*; Berry, *Harlan Hubbard*; and Cunningham, *Anna Hubbard*. In 1933, Clarence Jonk set out from St. Paul on a shantyboat, but inexperience, bad timing, ice floes, and mishaps plagued him. He never made it south of La Crosse, but he left behind snapshots of Depression-era life on the Upper Mississippi. See his *River Journey*.

12. McCarthy, *Suttree*. Roland, who later left the swamp, wrote a memoir, *Atchafalaya Houseboat*. About twenty years ago, Fry began to record the histories of his fellow *batture* dwellers. *They Called Us River Rats* tells their stories and his own. On Modes, see the project's website: https://peoplesriverhistory.us/project/history/.

13. The poem, published in the *Waterways Journal* and reproduced as the frontispiece in Bogardus, *Shantyboat*, 21, and a membership certificate of the National Association of Shantyboaters are in "Shanty Boats, 1955–1959," Waterways Journal Collection.

Bibliography

Archives and Libraries

Herman T. Pott National Inland Waterways Library, University of Missouri-St. Louis
  Dorothy Heckmann Shrader Collection.
  John Hartford Collection.
  Ruth Ferris Research Collection Notes.
  Captain William F. and Betty Streckfus Carroll Collection Photographs.
  Waterways Journal Collection.

Inland Rivers Library, The Public Library of Cincinnati and Hamilton County, Ohio
  Digital Services Department and Photograph Collection.

Library of Congress, Manuscript Division, Washington, D.C.
  Samuel Gompers Letterbooks, *American Federation of Labor Records, 1883–1925.*
  Decca Records, Notes by Alan Lomax. Lyrics copyright by Remick Music Corporation, 1939. Alan Lomax Collection, Manuscripts, Roustabout Songs. 1946. Manuscript/Mixed Material. https://www.loc.gov/item/afc2004004.ms300136/.
  Eskew, Garnett L. *Coonjine in Manhattan.* Chicago, Illinois, 1939. Manuscript/Mixed Material, Library of Congress, https://www.loc.gov/item/wpalh000067/.
  Ben Lawson Interview, November 5, 1937, Oklahoma Writers' Project, Ex-Slaves, *Slave Narratives, Oklahoma: A Folk History of Slavery in the United States from Interviews with Former Slaves,* The Project Gutenberg EBook of Slave Narratives, Oklahoma, 2007.
  George W. Arnold Interview, Evansville, Federal Writers' Project: Slave Narrative Project, vol. 5, Indiana, 1936. Manuscript/Mixed Material, https://www.loc.gov/item/mesn050/.
  Peter Corn Interview, Federal Writers' Project: Slave Narrative Project, vol. 10, Missouri, 1936. Manuscript/Mixed Material, https://www.loc.gov/item/mesn100/.

Louisiana Digital Library, https://louisianadigitallibrary.org
    Federal Writers' Project. United States. Works Progress Administration of Louisiana.
        Fifth District Works Progress Administration, Ouachita Parish Public Library.
        George Francois Mugnier Collection, 1880–1920, Louisiana State Museum, New
        Orleans.

McCracken County Public Library, Paducah, Kentucky
    Mary Wheeler Collection.

Memphis Public Library and Information Center, Memphis and Shelby County Room,
Memphis, Tennessee
    Emma K. Meacham Collection.

Minnesota Digital Library
    "Wannigans on the Mississippi River, Minnesota," circa 1880. Anoka County Histor-
        ical Society. Accessed March 6, 2021. https://collection.mndigital.org/catalog
        /ach:50.

Missouri Historical Society, St. Louis, Missouri
    Grossman Disaster Album: 1903 Flood.
    Steamboats and River History Collection, 1802–1986.

Missouri State Archives, Jefferson City, Missouri
    Missouri Bureau of Labor Statistics. "Fourteenth Annual Report of the Bureau of
        Labor Statistics," 1892.
    Missouri Death Certificates, 1910–1970, Missouri Digital Heritage, https://s1.sos
        .mo.gov/records/Archives/ArchivesMvc/DeathCertificates/.
    Missouri State Penitentiary Database.

St. Louis Public Library
    Dr. Glen Holt and Tom Pearson. St. Louis Public Library. "St. Louis Streets Index,"
        1994. http://rbsc.slpl.org/STL_STREETS_(A-Z).pdf.

State Historical Society of Missouri, Columbia
    Digital Photograph Collection, https://digital.shsmo.org/digital/collection/imc.
    Missouri Historical Review Archive.
    Oral History Collection (S0829).
        Transcript T-020, Interview with Judge Nathan B. Young, Jr. Interviewed by
            Dr. Richard Resh, July 15, 1970.

Transcript T-316, Interview with E.A. McKinney. Interviewed by Patricia Ann Immekus and Irene Cortinovis, Jazzman Project, March 15, 1974.
Transcript T-124, Interview with Leah Trattner and Sylvia Ehrlich. Interviewed by Steve Webb, Depression Era Project, July 5, 1972.

Tennessee State Library and Archives, Nashville, Tennessee
Tennessee Supreme Court Records.
State of Tennessee v. William Patti, 1892.
Tennessee Virtual Archive, https://teva.contentdm.oclc.org.

University of Illinois at Springfield, Norris L. Brookens Library, Archives/Special Collections, Springfield, Illinois
Oral History Collection.
J. Harvey Coomer Interview and Memoir, Interview by John Knoepfle, 1958.
Mack Davis Interview and Memoir, Interview by John Knoepfle, 1957.
John W. Menke, Interview and Memoir, Interviewed by John Knoepfle, 1957.
Captain Volney White Interview and Memoir, Interview by John Knoepfle, 1957.

University of Louisville, Louisville, Kentucky
Standard Oil (New Jersey) Collection, Photographic Archives.

University of Wisconsin, La Crosse
Historic Steamboat Photographs.

Upper Mississippi Valley Digital Image Photo Archive, www.umvphotoarchive.org

Court Cases

Riley v. Allen and others, 23 F. 46 (1885), United States District Court for the Western District of Tennessee. Accessed at https://cite.case.law/f/23/46/.
Bellefontaine Improvement Company et al. v. Niedringhaus et al., October 16, 1899, Supreme Court of Illinois. *Northeastern Reporter*, vol. 55. St. Paul, Minn.: West Publishing, 1900.
Clark, Ida, et al. v. The People of the State of Illinois, December 22, 1906, 224 Ill. 554 (1906) Illinois Supreme Court. Accessed at https://cite.case.law/ill/224/554/#p563.
James Edward Jones, Respondent, v. The St. Louis, Naples and Peoria Packet Company, Appellant, 43 Mo. App. 398 (1891), St. Louis Court of Appeals. Accessed at https://cite.case.law/mo-app/43/398/.

Joy, Wilford v. City of St. Louis and Hafner-Lothman Manufacturing Company, Supreme Court Reporter: Cases Argued and Determined in the United States Supreme Court, December, 1905–July 1906. St. Paul, Minn.: West Publishing, 1906.

Pim, Celestine v. City of St. Louis et al., June 12, 1894, Supreme Court of Missouri, Division 2. Southwestern Reporter, vol. 27. St. Paul, Minn.: West Publishing, 1894.

Red River Line v. Smith et al., Appeal from the District Court of the United States for the Eastern District of Louisiana, Fifth Circuit, February 13, 1900. *The Federal Reporter: Cases Argued and Determined in the Circuit Courts of Appeals and Circuit and District Courts of the United States, March–April 1900.* St. Paul, Minn.: West Publishing, 1900.

Robertson v. Commonwealth of Kentucky, Court of Appeals, May 15, 1897, *The Southwestern Reporter,* vol. 40, 1897.

State of Missouri, ex rel. James D. Roland v. John D. Dreyer, Mayor et al., June 21, 1910, *Reports of Cases Determined in the Supreme Court of the State of Missouri Between June 14, and July 2, 1910,* vol. 229. Columbia, Mo.: E. W. Stephens, Publisher, 1910.

State of Tennessee v. William Patti, 1892, Box Number 352, West Division, Tennessee Supreme Court. Tennessee State Library and Archives, Nashville, Tennessee.

Swearingen, Martha J. v. The City of St. Louis, et al., Supreme Court of the United States, October term, 1900. Washington, D.C., Judd and Detweiler, Printers, 1901.

Tom Jenkins v. "The Elenore," Circuit Court of Appeals, Sixth Circuit, November 4, 1914. Appeal from the District Court of the United States for the Western District of Tennessee, *United States Circuit Courts of Appeals Reports with Annotations.* St. Paul, Minn.: West Publishing, 1915.

The T. P. Leathers, Appeal from the District Court of the United States for the Eastern District of Louisiana, Fifth Circuit, February 17, 1896. *United States Courts of Appeal Reports.* New York and Albany: Banks and Brothers, Law Publishers, 1898.

Whyte, Victoria D. v. City of St. Louis, Supreme Court of Missouri, December 5, 1899. Southwestern Reporter, vol. 54. St. Paul, Minn.: West Publishing, 1900.

Reports and Transactions

American Society of Civil Engineers. *Transactions of the American Society of Civil Engineers.* New York: American Society of Civil Engineers, 1915.

"Annual Report of the Health Commissioner." *The Mayor's Message with Accompanying Documents to the Municipal Assembly of the City of St. Louis,* 1897.

Annual Report of the Supervising Surgeon-General of the Marine-Hospital Service of the United States for the Fiscal Year 1882. Washington, D.C.: Government Printing Office, 1882.

"Annual Reports of the Harbor and Wharf Commissioner." *The Mayor's Message with Accompanying Documents to the Municipal Assembly of the City of St. Louis,* 1880–1911.

Biennial Report of the Attorney General of the State of Illinois. Springfield, Ill.: Illinois State Journal Company, State Printers, 1913.

Citizens Committee on City Plan of Pittsburgh. *Waterways: A Part of the Pittsburgh Plan.* Report No. 6, October 1923.

Civic Improvement League of St. Louis. "A City Plan for St. Louis." St. Louis, 1907.

Civic League. Report on the St. Louis Workhouse. [St. Louis, 1911]. https://www.loc.gov /item/ca15001498/.

Civic League of St. Louis. "Housing Conditions in St. Louis: Report of the Housing Committee." St. Louis, 1908.

Illinois Board of Public Charities. *Biennial Report,* 1911.

National Park Service. "Goldenrod Showboat." National Register of Historic Places Inventory—Nomination Form, Historic Sites Survey, United States Department of the Interior, 1967. https://mostateparks.com/sites/mostateparks/files/Goldenrod %20Showboat.pdf.

Preliminary Report of the Inland Waterways Commission. Washington, D.C.: Government Printing Office, 1908.

Report of the Commissioner of Corporations on Transportation by Water in the United States, Part III: Water Terminals. Washington, D.C.: Government Printing Office, 1910.

Report of the Secretary of War Being Part of the Message and Documents Communicated to the Two Houses of Congress at the Beginning of the Second Session of the Forty-Second Congress, vol. 2. Washington, D.C.: Government Printing Office, 1871.

Report of the Submerged and Shore Lands Legislative Investigating Committee, Made in Pursuance of the Statute to the Governor of the State of Illinois and the Forty-Seventh General Assembly of Illinois, vol. I. Springfield, Ill.: Illinois State Journal Company, State Printers, 1911.

Smith, Orasmus, M.D., Surgeon United States Marine Hospital Service, New Orleans, La. "Report on the River-Boatmen of the Lower Mississippi." *Annual Report of the Supervising Surgeon of the Marine-Hospital Service of the United States for the Fiscal Year Ending 1873.* Washington, D.C.: Government Printing Office, 1873.

Treasury Decisions Under Internal Revenue Laws of the United States, vol. 9, January– December 1906. Washington, D.C.: Government Printing Office, 1907.

Wyman, Surgeon Walter. "Hygiene of the Steamboats on the Ohio River," 265–278. *Annual Report of the Supervising Surgeon-General of the Marine-Hospital Service of the United States for the Fiscal Year 1882.* Washington, D.C.: Government Printing Office, 1882.

Newspaper Archives

Chronicling America: Historic American Newspapers. Library of Congress.
NewspaperArchive.com.
Newspapers.com.
Quincy Public Library Newspaper Archive, Quincy, Illinois.

St. Louis Area Newspapers

Alton (Ill.) Evening Telegraph.
Edwardsville (Ill.) Intelligencer.
Argus.
Post-Dispatch.
Globe-Democrat.
Palladium.
Republic.
Republican.
Star and Times.
Waterways Journal.

Websites

https://www.afloatontheohio.com/who-we-are.
https://www.ancestry.com.
https://mississippivalleytraveler.com.
https://peoplesriverhistory.us/.
https://www.rivermuseum.com/

Books and Articles

Adams, Samuel Hopkins. *The Great American Fraud.* New York, N.Y.: P. F. Collier and
    Son, 1906.
Allen, Michael. *Western Rivermen, 1763–1861: Ohio and Mississippi Boatmen and the Myth
    of the Alligator Horse.* Baton Rouge: Louisiana State Univ. Press, 1990.
American Lumberman. Chicago: American Lumberman, 1906.

Ammen, Sharon. *May Irwin: Singing, Shouting, and the Shadow of Minstrelsy.* Urbana: Univ. of Illinois Press, 2017.

Andrews, Clarence A. "The Mississippi and the Missouri: A Bibliography." *The Great Lakes Review* 9/10 (fall 1983–spring 1984): 52–75.

Andrews, Gregg. "Black Working-Class Political Activism and Biracial Unionism: Galveston Longshoremen in Jim Crow Texas, 1919–1921." *Journal of Southern History* 74 (August 2008): 627–668.

———. *City of Dust: A Cement Company Town in the Land of Tom Sawyer.* 1996. Columbia: Univ. of Missouri Press, pap. ed., 2002.

———. "'Little Oklahoma': St. Louis's Shanty-Boat Kingdom." *Gateway* 41 (spring 2021): 17–25.

———. *My Daddy's Blues: A Childhood Memoir from the Land of Huck and Jim.* San Marcos, Tex.: Mudcat Press, 2019.

———. "Rose Mosenthein: From Shanty Boat to Sculling Champion." *Gateway* 42 (spring 2022): 17–25.

———. "River Roustabouts of St. Louis." *Missouri Historical Review* 116 (January 2022): 87–122.

———. *Thyra J. Edwards: Black Activist in the Global Freedom Struggle.* Columbia: Univ. of Missouri Press, 2011.

Arnesen, Eric. *Waterfront Workers of New Orleans: Race, Class, and Politcs, 1863–1923.* New York: Oxford Univ. Press, 1991.

Arnold, Helen. *Under Southern Skies: Reminiscences in the Life of Mrs. Adelia Arnold.* Atlanta: Repairer Publishing Company, 1924.

Aylward, William J. "Steamboating Through Dixie." *Harper's Magazine,* September 1915, 512–522.

"Baby Dodds' Story: As Told to Larry Gara." *Evergreen Review* 1, no. 1 (1957): 118–156.

Baldwin, Brooke. "The Cakewalk: A Study in Stereotype and Reality." *Journal of Social History* 15 (winter 1981): 205–218.

Barlow, William. *Looking Up at Down: The Emergence of Blues Culture.* Philadelphia: Temple Univ. Press, 1989.

Barry, John M. *Rising Tide: The Great Mississippi River Flood of 1927 and How It Changed America.* New York: Simon and Schuster, 1997.

Bartholomew, Harland. "Zoning for St. Louis: A Fundamental Part of the City Plan." St. Louis: Nixon-Jones Printing, 1918.

Berlin, Edward A. *King of Ragtime: Scott Joplin and His Era,* 2nd ed. New York: Oxford Univ. Press, 2016.

Berry, Wendell. *Harlan Hubbard: Life and Work.* Lexington: Univ. Press of Kentucky, 1990.

Bishop, Nathaniel H. *Four Months in a Sneak-Box: A Boat Voyage of 2600 Miles Down the Ohio and Mississippi Rivers, and Along the Gulf of Mexico.* New York: Charles T. Dillingham, 1879.

Bissell, Richard. *Good-Bye, Ava.* Boston: Little, Brown, 1960.

Black Diamond Coal Company. *The Black Diamond.* October 12, 1901, 524.

Bogardus, Carl. *Shantyboat.* Austin, Ind.: Muscatatuck Press, 1959.

Botkin, B. A., ed. *A Treasury of Mississippi Folklore: Stories, Ballads, Traditions and Folkways of Mid-America River Country.* New York: Crown, 1955.

Bradley, Bonnie Cave. "Mary Wheeler: Collector of Kentucky Folksongs." *Kentucky Review* 3, no. 3 (1982): 53–67.

Braude, Ann. *Radical Spirits: Spiritualism and Women's Rights in Nineteenth-Century America.* Bloomington: Indiana Univ. Press, 1989.

Bronner, Simon J., ed. *Lafcadio Hearn's America: Ethnographic Sketches and Editorials.* Lexington: Univ. Press of Kentucky. 2002.

Brown, Cecil. *Stagolee Shot Billy.* Cambridge, Mass.: Harvard Univ. Press, 2003.

Brown, Jayna. *Babylon Girls: Black Women Performers and the Shaping of the Modern.* Durham, N.C.: Duke Univ. Press, 2008.

Brown, Sterling. "Negro Folk Expression: Spirituals, Seculars, Ballads and Work Songs." *Phylon* 14, no. 1 (1953): 45–61.

Brown, William Wells. *My Southern Home: or, The South and Its People.* Boston: A. G. Brown, 1880.

———. *Narrative of William W. Brown, a Fugitive Slave. Written by Himself.* Boston: Anti-Slavery Office, 1847.

Bryant, Betty. *Here Comes the Showboat.* Lexington: Univ. Press of Kentucky, 1994.

Buchanan, Thomas C. *Black Life on the Mississippi: Slaves, Free Blacks, and the Western Steamboat World.* Chapel Hill: Univ. of North Carolina Press, 2004.

———. "Rascals on the Antebellum Mississippi: African American Steamboat Workers and the St. Louis Hanging of 1841." *Journal of Social History* 34 (summer 2001): 797–816.

Burman, Ben Lucien. *Big River to Cross: Mississippi Life Today.* New York: Day, 1940.

———. *Blow for a Landing.* 1938. Reprint, New York: Dutton, 1946.

———. *Mississippi.* New York: Cosmopolitan, 1929.

——— "Music on the Mississippi," Liner notes, included in *Steamboat 'Round the Bend: Songs and Stories of the Mississippi.* Washington, D.C.: Smithsonian Folkways Recordings, 2007. Originally produced in 1956.

———. *Steamboat 'Round the Bend.* New York: Farrar and Rinehart, 1933.

Butler, Ellis Parker. *The Jack-Knife Man.* New York: Century, 1913.

Caffery, Joshua Clegg. *The 1934 Lomax Recordings: Traditional Music in Coastal Louisiana.* Baton Rouge: Louisiana State Univ. Press, 2013.

Cassedy, James H. "Muckraking and Medicine: Samuel Hopkins Adams." *American Quarterly* 16 (spring 1964): 85–99.

Chevan, David. "Riverboat Music from St. Louis and the Streckfus Steamboat Line." *Black Music Research Journal: Papers of the 1989 National Conference on Black Music Research* 9 (autumn 1989): 153–180.

Ciampoli, Judith. "The St. Louis Tornado of 1896: Mad Pranks of the Storm King." *Gateway: The Magazine of the Missouri Historical Society* 2 , no. 4 (1982): 24–31.

Claassen, Cheryl. "Washboards, Pigtoes, and Muckets: Historic Musseling in the Mississippi Watershed." *Historical Archaeology* 28, no. 2 (1994): 1–150.

Compendium of the Tenth Census (June 1, 1880), Part Two (Washington, D.C.: Government Printing Office, 1883).

Conroy, Jack. *The Disinherited: A Novel of the 1930s.* 1933. Reprint, Columbia: Univ. of Missouri Press, 1991.

Cooley, Stoughton. *The Captain of the Amaryllis.* Boston: Clark, 1910.

———. "The Mississippi Roustabout." *New England Magazine* 11 (November 1894): 290–301.

Cowan, John Franklin. *The Jo-Boat Boys.* New York: Crowell, 1891.

Cox, Karen L. *Dreaming of Dixie: How the South Was Created in American Popular Culture.* Chapel Hill: Univ. of North Carolina Press, 2011.

"Cruelty Aboard Ship—Suffering on Western Waters." *Sailor's Magazine and Seamen's Friend* 55 (January 1883): 1–5.

Cunningham, Mia. *Anna Hubbard: Out of the Shadows.* Lexington: Univ. Press of Kentucky, 2009.

Curtis, W. A. "On the Upper Mississippi." *Magazine of History* 20 (January 1915): 25–30.

Curzon, Julian, comp. and ed. *The Great Cyclone at St. Louis and East St. Louis.* St. Louis: Cyclone Publishing, 1896.

Dains, Mary K. "The St. Louis Tornado of 1896." *Missouri Historical Review* 66 (April 1972): 431–450.

DeVoto, Bernard. *Mark Twain's America.* 1932. Reprint, Lincoln: Univ. of Nebraska Press, 1997.

Dickson, Harris. "The Way of the Reformer." *Saturday Evening Post,* January 12, 1907, 6–7, 22.

Dodson, Heidi. "'The River Is Part of Our Life': African Americans and Water Landscapes in the Missouri Bootheel." *Missouri Historical Review* 114 (October 2019): 16–39.

Dowden-White, Priscilla A. *Groping toward Democracy: African American Social Reform in St. Louis, 1910–1949.* Columbia: Univ. of Missouri Press, 2011.

Dreiser, Theodore. *A Book About Myself.* New York: Boni and Liveright, 1922.

Early, Gerald, ed. *Black Heartland: African American Life, the Middle West, and the Meaning of American Regionalism.* St. Louis: Washington University, 1997.

Eberhart, George M. "Stack Lee: The Man, the Music, and the Myth." *Popular Music and Society* 20 (1996): 1–70.

Ervin, Keona K. *Gateway to Equality: Black Women and the Struggle for Economic Justice in St. Louis.* Lexington: Univ. Press of Kentucky, 2017.

Eskew, Garnett Laidlaw. *The Pageant of the Packet.* New York: Holt, 1929.

Federal Writers' Project. *Guide to New Orleans.* Boston: Houghton Mifflin, 1938.

Ferber, Edna. *Showboat.* 1926. Reprint, New York: Vintage Music Classics, 2014.

Fishkin, Shelley Fisher. *Lighting Out for the Territory: Reflections on Mark Twain and American Culture.* Oxford: Oxford Univ. Press, 1996.

Fletcher, John M. "The Miracle Man of New Orleans." *American Journal of Psychology* 33 (January 1922): 113–120.

Foner, Philip S. *History of the Labor Movement in the United States.* Vol. 2: *From the Founding of the A. F. of L. to the Emergence of American Imperialism.* New York: International Publishers, 1975.

Ford, John. "Steamboat Round the Bend." Hollywood, Calif.: Fox Film Corporation, 1935.

Forret, Jeff, and Bruce E. Baker, eds. *Southern Scoundrels: Grifters and Graft in the Nineteenth Century.* Baton Rouge: Louisiana State Univ. Press, 2021.

Foster, B. Brian. *I Don't Like the Blues: Race, Place, and the Backbeat of Black Life.* Chapel Hill: Univ. of North Carolina Press, 2020.

Foster, Jeffrey Clayton. "The Rocky Road to a 'Drug Free Tennessee': A History of the Early Regulation of Cocaine and the Opiates, 1897–1913." *Journal of Social History* 29 (spring 1996): 547–564.

Fraiser, Jim. *Mississippi River Country Tales: A Celebration of 500 Years of Deep South History.* Gretna, La.: Pelican Publishing, 2001.

Freeman, Lewis R. *Waterways of Westward Wandering: Small Boat Voyages Down the Ohio, Missouri and Mississippi Rivers.* New York: Mead, 1927.

Fry, Macon. *They Called Us River Rats: The Last Batture Settlement of New Orleans.* Jackson: Univ. Press of Mississippi, 2021.

Genovese, Eugene. *Roll, Jordan, Roll: The World the Slaves Made.* New York: Pantheon, 1974.

Gibson, Vivian. *The Last Children of Mill Creek.* Cleveland, Ohio: Belt Publishing, 2020.

Gibson, Willis. "The Old Route to New Orleans: The Mississippi." *Scribner's Magazine* 33 (January 1903): 3–26.

Gillette, William. "Houseboat in America." *Outlook* 65 (August 2, 1900), 266.

Gillham, George Halsey. *The Adventures of William Tucker in a Shanty Boat on the Mississippi.* Boston: Houghton Mifflin, 1927.

Glazier, Captain Willard W. *Down the Great River: Embracing An Account of the Discovery of the True Source of the Mississippi.* Philadelphia: Hubbard Brothers, 1892.

Goff, Lisa. *Shantytown, USA: Forgotten Landscapes of the Working Poor.* Cambridge, Mass.: Harvard Univ. Press, 2016.

Going, Charles Buxton. "The River-Front of a Western City." *Harper's Weekly,* December 12, 1896, 1227–1228.

———. "The Shanty Boat People." *Harper's Weekly,* March 9, 1895, 231–233.

Gordon, Colin. *Mapping Decline: St. Louis and the Fate of the American City.* Philadelphia: Univ. of Pennsylvania Press, 2008.

Grady, Thomas C. *The Lost St. Louis Riverfront, 1930–1943.* St. Louis: St. Louis Public Mercantile Library, 2019.

Graham, Philip. "Showboats in the South." *Georgia Review* 12 (summer 1958): 174–185.

———. *Showboats: The History of an American Institution.* Austin: Univ. of Texas Press, 1951.

Graybill, Ronald D. *Mission to Black America: The True Story of James Edson White and the Riverboat Morning Star.* Westlake Village, Calif.: Oak and Acorn Publishing, 2013.

Gudmestad, Robert. *Steamboats and the Rise of the Cotton Kingdom.* Baton Rouge: Louisiana State Univ. Press, 2011.

Guthrie, John J., Jr., Phillip Charles Lucas, and Gary Monroe, eds. *Cassadaga: The South's Oldest Spiritualist Community.* Gainesville: Univ. Press of Florida, 2000.

Hall, John A. *The Great Strike on the "Q," with a History of the Organization and Growth of the Brotherhood of Locomotive Engineers, Brotherhood of Locomotive Firemen, and Switchmen's Mutual Aid Society of North America.* Chicago: Elliott and Beezley, 1889.

Hamilton, Harry. *Banjo on My Knee.* Indianapolis: Bobbs-Merrill, 1936.

———. *River Song.* Indianapolis: Bobbs-Merrill, 1945.

Handy, W. C. *Father of the Blues: An Autobiography.* 1941. Reprint, New York: De Capo, 1969.

Harris, Eddy L. *Mississippi Solo: A River Quest.* New York: Henry Holt, 1988.

Havighurst, Walter. *Voices on the River: The Story of the Mississippi Waterways.* Minneapolis: Univ. of Minnesota Press, 2003.

Heathcott, Joseph. "Black Archipelago: Politics and Civic Life in the Jim Crow City." *Journal of Social History* 38 (spring 2005): 705–736.

Heckman, Captain William L. *Steamboating: Sixty-Five Years on Missouri's Rivers.* Kansas City, Mo.: Burton, 1950.

Hendrick, Emil. "Following Wild Fowl in a Shantyboat." *Outing* 41 (January 1903): 482–486.

Hetherington, Sue. "Lost Channels." *Missouri Historical Review* 36 (July 1942): 447–458.

Hiller, Ernest Theodore. *Houseboat and River Bottoms People: A Study of 683 Households in Sample Locations Adjacent to the Ohio and Mississippi Rivers.* Urbana: Univ. of Illinois Press, 1939.

Holbrook, Stewart H. *The Golden Age of Quackery.* New York: Macmillan, 1959.

Holliday, Carl. "American Showboats." *Theatre Magazine* 25 (May 1917): 246.

Honey, Michael Keith. *Black Workers Remember: An Oral History of Segregation, Unionism, and the Freedom Struggle.* Berkeley: Univ. of California Press, 1999.

———. *Southern Labor and Black Civil Rights: Organizing Memphis Workers.* Urbana: Univ. of Illinois Press, 1993.

Houck, Oliver A. *Down on the Batture.* Jackson: Univ. Press of Mississippi, 2010.

Howells, William Dean. *Literature and Life.* New York: Harper and Brothers, 1902.

Hubbard, Harlan. *Payne Hollow Journal.* Lexington: Univ. Press of Kentucky, 2009.

———. *Shantyboat: A River Way of Life.* 1953. Reprint, Lexington: Univ. Press of Kentucky, 1977.

———. *Shantyboat Journal.* Edited by Don Wallis. Lexington: Univ. Press of Kentucky, 1994.

———. *Shantyboat on the Bayous.* Lexington: Univ. Press of Kentucky, 1990.

Hubbell, Daniel. "Federal Barge Lines Helped Spawn Modern River Industry." *Waterways Journal*, December 14, 2018. https://www.waterwaysjournal.net/2018/12/14/federal-barge-lines-helped-spawn-modern-river-industry/.

Hughes, Langston. *The Big Sea: An Autobiography.* New York: Hill and Wang, 1940.

Huntington, Anna Seaton. "Women on the Water." In *Nike Is a Goddess: The History of Women in Sports*, edited by Lissa Smith, 105–136. New York: Atlantic Monthly Press, 1998.

Hurd, Harvey B., comp. and ed., *The Revised Statutes of the State of Illinois, 1903.* Chicago: Chicago Legal News Company, 1904.

Hurley, Andrew. "Narrating the Urban Waterfront: The Role of Public History in Community Revitalization." *Public Historian* 28 (fall 2006): 19–50.

Hutton, T.R.C. *Bloody Breathitt: Politics and Violence in the Appalachian South.* Lexington: Univ. Press of Kentucky, 2015.

Hyde, William, and Howard L. Conard, eds., *Encyclopedia of the History of St. Louis: A Compendium of History and Biography for Ready Reference*, vol. 3. New York, Louisville, St. Louis: Southern History Company, 1899.

Iarocci, Louisa, "The Changing American Landscape: The Art and Politics of Joe Jones." *Gateway Heritage* 12 (fall 1991): 68–71.

Jackson, Robert Wendell. *Rails Across the Mississippi: A History of the St. Louis Bridge.* Urbana: Univ. of Illinois Press, 2001.

Jamison, Phil. *Hoedowns, Reels, and Frolics: Roots and Branches of Southern Appalachian Dance.* Urbana: Univ. of Illinois Press, 2015.

Johnson, Clifton. *Highways and Byways of the Mississippi Valley.* New York: Macmillan, 1906.

———. "Houseboat Life on the Mississippi." *Outing* 46 (April 1905), 81–91.

Johnson, George. "Pearl Rush: Its Wisconsin Beginnings." *Wisconsin Magazine of History* 95 (spring 2012): 2–15.

Johnson, Walter. *The Broken Heart of America: St. Louis and the Violent History of the United States.* New York: Basic, 2020.

———. *River of Dark Dreams: Slavery and Empire in the Cotton Kingdom.* Cambridge, Mass.: Belknap Press of Harvard Univ. Press, 2013.

Jonk, Clarence. *River Journey.* 1964. Reprint, St. Paul, Minn.: Borealis, 2003.

Junkin, C. M. *The Cruise of the Morning Star: The Log of a Journey on the Mississippi River from St. Paul to New Orleans.* Fairfield, Iowa: Ledger Printing House, 1911.

Kenney, William Howland. *Jazz on the River.* Chicago: Univ. of Chicago Press, 2005.

King, Edward. *Southern States of North America: A Record of Journeys in Louisiana, Texas, the Indian Territory, Missouri, Arkansas, Mississippi, Alabama, Georgia, Florida, South Carolina, North Carolina, Kentucky, Tennessee, Virginia, West Virginia, and Maryland.* Profusely Illustrated from Original Sketches by J. Wells Champney. London and Edinburgh: Blackie and Son, Paternoster Buildings, E.C, 1875.

Klinkenberg, Dean. "Chasing the Robert E. Lee: Boat Races on the Mississippi River." *Confluence* (spring/summer 2020): 18–35.

Knoepfle, John. "Some Notes on the Men of the Inland Rivers." *Midcontinent American Studies Journal* 4 (spring 1963): 56–59.

Kohr, Harry F. "Not a Rouster Aboard." *Technical World Magazine,* August 19, 1913, 886–889.

Kruger, Mark. *The St. Louis Commune of 1877: Communism in the Heartland.* Lincoln: Univ. of Nebraska Press, 2021.

Laim, Roman. "The State of Riverbank." *Scribner's Magazine* 83 (March 1928): 291–303.

Lang, Clarence. *Grassroots at the Gateway: Class Politics and Black Freedom Struggle in St. Louis, 1936–1975.* Ann Arbor: Univ. of Michigan Press, 2009.

Larson, Agnes M. *The White Pine Industry in Minnesota: A History.* Minneapolis: Univ. of Minnesota Press, 2007.

Lass, William E. *A History of Steamboating on the Upper Missouri River.* Lincoln: Univ. of Nebraska Press, 1962.

Lenski, Lois. *Houseboat Girl.* Philadelphia: Lippincott, 1957.

Levine, Lawrence. *Black Culture and Black Consciousness: Afro-American Folk Thought from Slavery to Freedom.* New York: Oxford Univ. Press, 1977.

Lighty, Kent, and Margaret Lighty. *Shanty-Boat.* New York: Century, 1930.

Lott, Eric. *Love and Theft: Blackface Minstrelsy and the American Working Class.* New York: Oxford Univ. Press, 1993.

Loughlin, Caroline, and Catherine Anderson. *Forest Park.* Columbia: Junior League of St. Louis and Univ. of Missouri Press, 1986.

Lund, Jens. *Flatheads and Spooneys: Fishing for a Living in the Ohio River Valley.* Lexington: Univ. Press of Kentucky, 1995.

Mack, Kimberly R. *Fictional Blues: Narrative Self-Invention from Bessie Smith to Jack White.* Amherst: Univ. of Massachusetts Press, 2020.

Mandel, Bernard. "Samuel Gompers and the Negro Workers, 1886–1914." *Journal of Negro History* 40 (January 1955): 43–44.

Marling, Karal Ann. "Joe Jones: Regionalist, Communist, Capitalist." *Journal of Decorative and Propaganda Arts* 4 (spring 1987): 46–59.

Marshall, Dexter. "The River People." *Scribner's Magazine* 28 (July 1900): 101–111.

Marshall, Howard Wight. *Play Me Something Quick and Devilish: Old-Time Fiddlers in Missouri.* Columbia: Univ. of Missouri Press, 2013.

Mathews, John Lathrop. *The Log of the Easy Way.* Boston: Small, Maynard, 1911.

Mayo, Earl. "Ideal Summer Homes Afloat." *New Broadway Magazine* 20 (April 1908): 351–356.

McCarthy, Cormac. *Suttree.* New York: Random House, 1979.

McCoyer, Michael. "'Rough Mens' in 'the Toughest Places I Ever Seen': The Construction and Ramifications of Black Masculine Identity in the Mississippi Delta's Levee Camps, 1900–1935." *International Labor and Working-Class History* 69 (March 2006): 57–80.

McHenry, Eric. "The Baddest Man in Town: On the Trail of a Historical Figure Immortalized in African-American Folklore." *American Scholar,* March 21, 2021. https://theamericanscholar.org/the-baddest-man-in-town/.

McIlwaine, Shields. *Memphis: Down in Dixie.* New York: Dutton, 1948.

McNamara, Brooks. "The Indian Medicine Show." *Educational Theatre Journal* 23 (December 1971): 431–445.

———. *Step Right Up,* rev. ed. Jackson: Univ. Press of Mississippi, 1996.

Merrick, George Byron. *Old Times on the Upper Mississippi: The Recollections of a Steamboat Pilot from 1854 to 1863.* Cleveland: Clark, 1909.

Mizelle, Richard, Jr. "Black Levee Camp Workers, the NAACP, and the Mississippi Flood Control Project, 1927–1933." *Journal of African American History* 98, no. 4 (2013): 511–530.

Moore, Neal, and Cindy Lovell. *Down the Mississippi: A Modern-Day Huck on America's River Road.* Hannibal, Mo.: Mark Twain Museum Press, 2012.

Morris, Ann. "A Guide to the Research Collection of the *Waterways Journal.*" St. Louis: Herman T. Pott National Inland Waterways Library and the St. Louis Mercantile Library Association, 1989.

The Municipal Code of St. Louis, Approved April 3, 1900. St. Louis, Missouri: Woodward and Tiernan Printers, 1901.

Norman, W. P. "Houseboat Life in the United States." *Harper's Weekly* 45 (August 17, 1901), 820.

Odum, Howard W. "Folk-Song and Folk-Poetry As Found in the Secular Songs of the Southern Negroes." *Journal of American Folklore* 24 (July–September 1911): 255–294.

Oklahoma Writers' Project, Ex-Slaves. *Slave Narratives, Oklahoma: A Folk History of Slavery in the United States from Interviews with Former Slaves.* The Project Gutenberg EBook of Slave Narratives, Oklahoma, 2007.

Owsley, Dennis. *City of Gabriels: The History of Jazz in St. Louis, 1895–1973.* St. Louis, Mo.: Reedy Press, 2006.

Papanikolas, Zeese. *An American Cakewalk: Ten Syncopators of the Modern World.* Redwood City, Calif.: Stanford Univ. Press, 2015.

Parrish, Randall. *Don McGrath: A Tale of the River.* Chicago: McClurg, 1910.

Pasquier, Michael, ed. *Gods of the Mississippi.* Bloomington: Indiana Univ. Press, 2013.

Patzwald, Gari-Anne. *Waiting for Elijah: A History of the Megiddo Mission.* Knoxville: Univ. of Tennessee Press, 2002.

Pearson, Norman. "The Philosophy and Art of Dancing." *Lippincott's Magazine* (December 1884), 611–616.

Peñalver, Eduardo Moisés, and Sonia K. Katyal. *Property Outlaws: How Squatters, Pirates, and Protesters Improve the Law of Ownership.* New Haven, Conn.: Yale Univ. Press, 2010.

Pennell, Joseph. "The Trip of the 'Mark Twain.'" *Century Magazine* 25 (January 1883): 399–403.

Percy, William Alexander. *Lanterns on the Levee: Recollections of a Planter's Son.* 1941. Reprint, Baton Rouge: Louisiana State Univ. Press, 2006.

Pisani, Donald J. "The Squatter and Natural Law in Nineteenth-Century America." *Agricultural History* 81 (fall 2007): 443–463.

Polenberg, Richard. *Hear My Sad Story: The True Tales That Inspired "Stagolee," "John Henry," and Other Traditional American Folk Songs.* Ithaca, N.Y.: Cornell Univ. Press, 2015.

Primm, James Neal. *Lion of the Valley: St. Louis, Missouri, 1764–1980.* St. Louis: Missouri Historical Society Press, 1981.

Quick, Herbert, and Edward Quick. *Mississippi Steamboatin': A History of Steamboating on the Mississippi and Its Tributaries.* New York: Holt, 1926.

Ralph, Julian. *Dixie or Southern Scenes and Sketches.* New York: Harper and Brothers, 1896.

Rankin, Tom, ed. *"Deaf Maggie Lee Sayre": Photographs of a River Life.* University, Miss.: Center for Southern Culture and the Univ. Press of Mississippi, 1995.

———. "The Photographs of Maggie Lee Sayre: A Personal Vision of Houseboat Life." *Folklife Annual,* vol. 90. Washington, D.C.: Library of Congress, American Folklife Center, 1991). 100–131.

Rathborne, St. George. *The Houseboat Boys; or, Drifting Down to the Sunny South.* Chicago: M. A. Donohue, 1912.

Raven-Hart, Rowland. *Down the Mississippi.* Boston: Houghton Mifflin, 1938.

Record of Christian Work. New York: Revell, 1892.

Richardson, Dorothy. "A Houseboat—The Modern Palace." *Cosmopolitan* 31 (July 1901): 235–240.

Roberts, Cecil. *Adrift in America, or Work and Adventure in the States.* London: Lawrence and Bullen, 1891.

Roediger, David. "'Not Only the Ruling Classes to Overcome, but Also the So-Called Mob': Class, Skill and Community in the St. Louis General Strike of 1877." *Journal of Social History* 19 (winter 1985): 213–239.

———. *The Wages of Whiteness: Race and the Making of the American Working Class.* London: Verso, 1999.

Rosenberg, Daniel. *New Orleans Dockworkers: Race, Labor, and Unionism, 1892–1923.* Albany: State Univ. of New York Press, 1988.

Roland, Gwen. *Atchafalaya Houseboat: My Years in the Louisiana Swamp.* Baton Rouge: Louisiana State Univ. Press, 2006.

Savage, Courtenay. "The Romantic Fresh-Water Mussel Industry." *The Outlook,* May 16, 1923, 889–891.

Scarpino, Philip V. *Great River: An Environmental History of the Upper Mississippi, 1890–1950.* Columbia: Univ. of Missouri Press, 1985.

Scharf, J. Thomas. *History of St. Louis City and County, From the Earliest Periods to the Present Day: Including Biographical Sketches of Representative Men.* 2 vols. Philadelphia: Everts, 1883.

Schnell, Christopher A. "Lawyers, Squatters, and the Transformation of the Public Domain in Early-Statehood Illinois." *Journal of the Illinois State Historical Society* 110 (fall/winter 2017): 237–263.

Schweinbenz, Amanda. *Against Hegemonic Currents: Women's Rowing in the First Half of the Twentieth Century.* New York: Routledge, 2014.

Scott, Roxanne. "Shanty Boats on the Ohio: Louisville's Lost Neighborhood." August 9, 2016, https://wfpl.org/shanty-boats-ohio-louisvilles-lost-neighborhood/.

Secretary of War, Brigadier-General Thomas Q. Ashburn, U.S. Army, Chairman and Executive, *Inland Waterways Corporation.* Washington, D.C.: Government Printing Office, 1924.

Shapiro, Nat, and Nat Hentoff, eds. *Hear Me Talkin' to Ya: The Story of Jazz as Told by the Men Who Made It.* New York: Dover, 1955.

Simpson, Albert Benjamin. *A Larger Christian Life.* New York: Christian Alliance Publishing Co., 1890.

Smith, Thomas Ruys. *Blacklegs, Card Sharps, and Confidence Men: Nineteenth-Century Mississippi River Gambling Stories.* Baton Rouge: Louisiana State Univ. Press, 2010.

——. *Deep Water: The Mississippi River in the Age of Mark Twain*. Baton Rouge: Louisiana State Univ. Press, 2019.

——. "Looking for the New Jerusalem: Antebellum New Religious Movements and the Mississippi River." In *Gods of the Mississippi*, edited by Michael Pasquier, 74–94. Bloomington: Indiana Univ. Press, 2013.

——. "'The Mississippi Was a Virgin Field': Reconstructing the River Before Mark Twain, 1865–1875." *Mark Twain Journal* 53 (fall 2015): 24–66.

——. *River of Dreams: Imagining the Mississippi Before Mark Twain*. Baton Rouge: Louisiana State Univ. Press, 2007.

——. "Roustabouts, Steamboats, and the Old Way to Dixie: The Mississippi River and the Southern Imaginary in the Early Twentieth Century." *Southern Quarterly: A Journal of the Arts in the South* 52 (spring 2015): 10–29.

Smyth, J. E., and Thomas Schatz. *Edna Ferber's Hollywood*. Austin: Univ. of Texas Press, 2010.

Snook, Sidney. "Echoes on the River." *Midwest Folklore* 10 (summer 1960): 70–78.

Speakman, Harold, and Frances Lindsay Speakman. *Mostly Mississippi: A Very Damp Adventure*. New York: Dodd, Mead, 1927.

Spears, Raymond. "'Beating' Prohibition on the Mississippi." *Harper's Weekly*, May 29, 1909, 27.

——. *Driftwood*. New York: Century, 1921.

——. "Floating Down the Mississippi." *Forest and Stream*, May 20, 1905, 390–391.

——. "The Mississippi Boat Theatres." *Harper's Weekly*, September 4, 1909, 13.

——. "Mississippi Tripper." *Harper's Weekly*, April 16, 1910, 31.

——. *The River Prophet*. Garden City, N.Y.: Doubleday, Page, 1920.

——. "The Romance of the American Pearl." *Harper's Weekly*, July 17, 1909, 32.

Spencer. Thomas M. *The St. Louis Veiled Prophet Organization: Power on Parade, 1887–1995*. Columbia: Univ. of Missouri Press, 2000.

Springer, Robert, ed. *Nobody Knows Where the Blues Come From: Lyrics and History*. Jackson: Univ. Press of Mississippi, 2006.

Stepenoff, Bonnie. *The Dead End Kids of St. Louis: Homeless Boys and the People Who Tried to Save Them*. Columbia: Univ. of Missouri Press, 2010.

——. *Working the Mississippi: Two Centuries of Life on the River*. Columbia: Univ. of Missouri Press, 2015.

Stevens, Walter B. *The Log of the Alton: Being a Narrative of the Voyage of the Business Men's League to New Orleans October 25 to 30, 1909*. St. Louis, 1909.

——. *St. Louis: The Fourth City, 1764–1909*. 2 vols. St. Louis: Clarke, 1911.

St. Paul Dispatch and St. Paul Pioneer Press. *Almanac and Year Book*. St. Paul, Minn.: Dispatch Printing Company, 1916.

Street, Julian. "Meridian, Vicksburg, and the River." *Collier's*, August 18, 1917, 11–13, 28, 30, 32, 34, 39.

Sumner, Cid Ricketts. *Tammy Out of Time*. Indianapolis: Bobbs-Merrill, 1948.

Sumner, John D. "An Analysis of Mississippi River Traffic: 1918–1930." *Journal of Land and Public Utility Economics* 7 (November 1931): 355–366.

Sweeney, Michael. "Burman, Ben Lucien." In *The Encyclopedia of Northern Kentucky*, edited by Paul A. Tenkotte and James C. Claypool. Lexington: Univ. Press of Kentucky, 2009.

Tait, John Leisk. "Shanty-boat Folks." *The World Today* 12 (May 1907): 473–478.

The Whole Story Told: The Mysterious and Dark Places of St. Louis. St. Louis: Olive, 1885.

Thompson, E. P. "Time, Work-Discipline, and Industrial Capitalism." *Past and Present* 38 (December 1967): 56–97.

Thwaites, Reuben Gold. *Afloat on the Ohio: An Historical Pilgrimage of a Thousand Miles in a Skiff, From Redstone to Cairo*. Chicago: Way and Williams, 1897.

Thwaites, Reuben Gold, Robert L. Reid, and Dan Hughes Fuller. *Pilgrims on the Ohio: The River Journey and Photographs of Reuben Gold Thwaites, 1894*. Indianapolis: Indiana Historical Society, 1997.

Towey, Martin G. "Hooverville: St. Louis Had the Largest." *Gateway Heritage* 1 (1980): 4–11.

Tranel, Mark, ed. *St. Louis Plans: The Ideal and the Real St. Louis*. St. Louis: Missouri Historical Society Press, 2007.

Turley, Brian K. *A Wheel Within a Wheel: Southern Methodism and the Georgia Holiness Association*. Macon, Ga.: Mercer Univ. Press, 1999.

Twain, Mark. *Adventures of Huckleberry Finn*. 1885. Reprint, New York: Modern Library, 2001.

———. *The Adventures of Tom Sawyer*. 1876. Reprint, New York: Modern Library, 2001.

———. *Life on the Mississippi*. New York: 1883. Reprint, Modern Library, 2007.

———. "Old Times on the Mississippi: VI." *Atlantic Monthly* (June 1875): 721–730.

———. *Pudd'nhead Wilson*. 1894. Reprint, New York: Modern Library, 2002.

Twain, Mark, and Charles Dudley Warner. *The Gilded Age: A Tale of Today*. Hartford, Conn.: American Publishing Company, 1873.

Wallace, Agnes. "The Wiggins Ferry Monopoly." *Missouri Historical Review* 42 (October 1947): 1–19.

Wanko, Andrew. *Great River City: How the Mississippi Shaped St. Louis*. St. Louis: Missouri Historical Society Press, 2019.

Waugh, William F. *The Houseboat Book: The Log of a Cruise from Chicago to New Orleans*. Chicago: Clinic Publishing Company, 1904.

Way, Frederick, Jr. *The Log of the Betsy Ann*. New York: McBride, 1933.

————, comp. *Way's Packet Directory, 1848–1994: Passenger Steamboats of the Mississippi River System since the Advent of Photography in Mid-Continent America*, rev. ed. With Joseph W. Rutter, contributor. 1944. Reprint, Athens: Ohio Univ. Press, 1995.

Wetherington, Mark V. "Shantyboat Life." *Ohio Valley History* 19 (spring 2019): 77–84.

————. "Shantyboat Louisville: Documenting a Lost Neighborhood." *The Filson* 16 (winter 2016): 12–15.

Wheeler, Mary. *Roustabout Songs: A Collection of Ohio River Valley Songs* (New York: Remick Music Corporation, 1939).

————. *Steamboatin' Days: Folk Songs of the River Packet Era*. Baton Rouge: Louisiana State Univ. Press, 1944.

Wilkins, Roy. "Mississippi Slavery in 1933." *The Crisis* 40 (April 1933): 81–82.

Wingate, Lisa. *Before We Were Yours: A Novel*. New York: Ballantine, 2017.

Winters, S. R. "Frauds That Flourish—Until Uncle Sam Takes a Hand." *Hygeia, the Health Magazine* 14 (May 1936), 420.

Wood, Henry S. "The River Home." *Hunter Trader Trapper* 1 (May 1925): 6.

Young, James Harvey. *The Toadstool Millionaires: A Social History of Patent Medicines in America before Federal Regulation*. Princeton, N.J.: Princeton Univ. Press, 1961.

Zang, Robert. "Steaming on the Mississippi: As Told to Teresa Maddux." *Bittersweet* 5 (winter 1977): 46–52.

Index

CPSIA information can be obtained
at www.ICGtesting.com
Printed in the USA
LVHW101827061222
734408LV00029B/86